AMKinaha

W9-AJT-476

THE POLITICAL ECONOMY
OF COMMUNICATION

The Media, Culture & Society Series

Editors: John Corner, Nicholas Garnham, Paddy Scannell,
Philip Schlesinger, Colin Sparks, Nancy Wood

Capitalism and Communication
Global Culture and the Economics of Information
Nicholas Garnham, edited by Fred Inglis

Media, State and Nation
Political Violence and Collective Identities
Philip Schlesinger

Broadcast Talk
edited by
Paddy Scannell

Journalism and Popular Culture
edited by
Peter Dahlgren and Colin Sparks

Media, Crisis and Democracy
edited by
Marc Raboy and Bernard Dagenais

Culture and Power
A Media, Culture & Society Reader
edited by
Paddy Scannell, Philip Schlesinger and Colin Sparks

Interpreting Audiences
The Ethnography of Media Consumption
Shaun Moores

Feminist Media Studies
Liesbet van Zoonen

Television and the Public Sphere
Citizenship, Democracy and the Media
Peter Dahlgren

Popular Cultures
Rock Music, Sport and the Politics of Pleasure
David Rowe

Dynamics of Modern Communication
The Shaping and Impact of New Communication Technologies
Patrice Flichy, translated by Liz Libbrecht

THE POLITICAL ECONOMY OF COMMUNICATION

Rethinking and Renewal

Vincent Mosco

SAGE Publications
London • Thousand Oaks • New Delhi

© Vincent Mosco 1996

First published 1996

All rights reserved. No part of this publication may be
reproduced, stored in a retrieval system, transmitted or utilized
in any form or by any means, electronic, mechanical,
photocopying, recording or otherwise, without permission in
writing from the Publishers.

SAGE Publications Ltd
6 Bonhill Street
London EC2A 4PU

SAGE Publications Inc
2455 Teller Road
Thousand Oaks, California 91320

SAGE Publications India Pvt Ltd
32, M-Block Market
Greater Kailash - I
New Delhi 110 048

British Library Cataloguing in Publication data

A catalogue record for this book is available
from the British Library.

ISBN 0 8039 8560 6
ISBN 0 8039 8561 4 (pbk)

Library of Congress catalog card number 96–69120

Typeset by Photoprint, Torquay
Printed in Great Britain by The Cromwell Press Ltd,
Broughton Gifford, Melksham, Wiltshire

To my students

Contents

Acknowledgements

It is appropriate that a book about a changing political economy should have begun in what was once Yugoslavia, now Slovenia. The project originated in a set of informal discussions with Colin Sparks of Westminster University and Stephen Barr of Sage during the August 1990 conference of the International Association for Mass Communication Research at Lake Bled. I appreciate the support they provided at the time and their patience throughout the project.

This book would not be possible without the help of many people who gave me their time, advice, and criticism. I want to thank first of all a group of people who generously spoke into my microphone in a series of formal interviews on the development and prospects for a political economy of communication. These include, in chronological order, the late Dallas Smythe, who inspired three subsequent generations of communication scholars; Janet Wasko, University of Oregon; Herbert Schiller, professor emeritus of the University of California, San Diego; James Halloran, former director of the Center for Mass Communication Research, University of Leicester, and former President of the International Association for Mass Communication Research; Peter Golding and Graham Murdock, Loughborough University; Thomas Guback, Institute for Communication Research, University of Illinois; and Nicholas Garnham, Westminster University. Thank you all for your time, for the openness with which you spoke of your careers and your lives, and for your candor about the state of communication research.

In addition to the above, many people also contributed with helpful suggestions, ideas, and critique at various stages in the preparation of this book. These include Jeanne Allen, Robert Babe, Jack Banks, Ronald Bettig, Oliver Boyd-Barrett, Peter Bruck, William Buxton, Andrew Calabrese, Levon Chorbajian, Andrew Clement, Wallace Clement, Thomas Cooper, Arthur Cordell, Gerald Coulter, James Curran, Susan Davis, Marjorie Ferguson, Oscar Gandy, George Gerbner, Jill Hills, Sue Curry Jansen, John Lent, Eileen Mahoney, Michèle Martin, Robert McChesney, Stephen McDowell, Catherine McKercher, Eileen Meehan, James Miller, Anthony Oettinger, Manjunath Pendakur, Colleen Roach, Eileen Saunders, Dan Schiller, Sid Shniad, Fred Sperounis, Gerald Sussman, and Dwane Winseck.

Several research assistants and graduate students from Carleton University provided outstanding assistance and advice. These include Carla

Brown, Anthony Ferrare, Lewis Kaye, Patricia Mazepa, Roger Perritt, Andrew Reddick, Vanda Rideout, Aurora Wallace, and Wendy Zatylny. Along with them, Nancy Peden of the Carleton University Library tracked down sources and sent along many she thought would help. It has been a real pleasure to work with people who not only locate the material you request, but also anticipate and find the material you need.

I would also like to thank my students, particularly those whose theses in political economy I have supervised and who have participated in my seminar in political economy. Your thoughts, criticism, and support have been very helpful.

This book was completed with grants from the Canadian Social Sciences and Humanities Research Council, which provided the funding for research assistance, travel, research materials, and a year's leave to complete the project. I appreciate the help of the Carleton University Office of Graduate Research, particularly Anne Burgess, whose advice and support was essential for securing the grants, and Gail Mutton, my grant administrator. Carleton University also provided an additional year's leave in the form of a research award. I want to thank Janice Yalden, then Dean of the Faculty of Arts, her successor G. Stuart Adam, and Peter Johansen, Director of the School of Journalism and Communication, all of whom supported this project.

Several institutions kindly gave me an opportunity to test ideas and research strategies. These include the University of Toronto, whose School of Library and Information Science annual Sharpe Lecture offered me the first opportunity to reflect on how the founding figures in political economy contribute to contemporary thinking in communication and information research, and Harvard University, whose Program on Information Resources Policy generously provided me with a position as a resident scholar. In addition, several organizations hosted lectures and seminars on the subject: the Canadian Association for Information Studies, the Canadian Library Association, the City University of London, George Washington University, Harvard University, the University of Illinois, the University of Massachusetts at Lowell, Muehlenberg College, Northwestern University, Ottawa University, Queen's College of the City of New York, the University of California at San Diego, and Westminster University.

Special thanks to the International Association for Mass Communication Research, which has provided a welcome home for a wide range of communication scholars, including those with a commitment to political economy. I have been privileged to serve as the head of the IAMCR section on Political Economy and this book has benefited from intense discussions at several IAMCR conferences.

I acknowledge an enormous debt to many people, but I also fully accept responsibility for the final result.

1

Introduction

What can be contributed is not resolution but perhaps, at times, just that extra edge of consciousness.

(Williams, 1976: 21)

Political economy is a major perspective in communication research. Over the past fifty years the approach has guided the work of scholars in several centers around the world. Numerous article-length works have provided important overviews and maps of the field.[1] *The Political Economy of Communication* aims to fill a gap by providing a book-length overview of the discipline, its accomplishments, debates, and relationships to other approaches in communication research. It starts with an historical, descriptive, and critical overview of political economy as a general approach to social analysis and proceeds with an analysis of the political economy approach to communication which assesses accomplishments, proposes new departures, and examines the relationship of political economy to policy studies and cultural studies.

Although a synthesis of major contributions to political economy is central to the book's purpose, it aspires to do more than map the field. In addition to examining major contributions, it aims to rethink and renew central elements in the political economy of communication. A few such undertakings have appeared in recent communication research (e.g. Curran, 1990; Hardt, 1992; Mattelart and Mattelart, 1992). My approach to this rethinking and renewal starts from a recognition, addressed chiefly in Chapters 2 and 3, of political economy's accomplishments across a range of subject areas, but particularly in communication studies. This process leads to what Merton (1968) and Bell (1973) referred to as the codification of knowledge or mapping the discipline. However, it departs from their meaning by recognizing that codes of knowledge are situated within social and historical contexts, thereby reflecting Williams' (1976: 21–22) admonition:

Not a tradition to be learned, nor a consensus to be accepted, nor a set of meanings which, because it is 'our language,' has a natural authority, but as a shaping and reshaping, in real circumstances and profoundly different points of view: a vocabulary to use, to find our ways in, to change as we find it necessary to change it, as we go on making our own language and history.

1. Recent examples include Gandy (1992), Golding and Murdock (1991), and Wasko (1989). See also 'Colloquy' (1995).

Bearing in mind this view, Chapters 4 to 6 approach the political economy of communication from the perspective that social change is ubiquitous and can be understood from three dynamic processes that serve as entry or starting points to the social field: commodification, spatialization, and structuration. Finally, rethinking and renewal means examining the relationship of a political economy approach to approaches on its borders, in this case policy studies and cultural studies (Chapter 7).

A Theory of Theory: A Realist, Inclusive, and Critical Epistemology

This analysis of political economy is built on a realist, inclusive, and critical theory of theory, providing what Shimony (1993) calls an *integral episte-mology*.[2] *Realism* starts from the view that reality is made up of more than a set of subjectively determined nominal categories or of material embodi-ments of ideal categories (Garnham, 1990: 3). Not satisfied with nominalist or idealist views, a realist sees existence as mutually constituted by *both* sensory observation and explanatory practices. According to this view, reality is made up of both what we see and how we explain what we see. This view derives from the constitutive linguistics of Bakhtin (1981) and the socio-historical approach to literary theory developed in Williams (1977). In practice, as Murdock (1989b: 226–227) has noted, the realist is careful to avoid exclusive reliance on abstract theorizing or on empirical and inter-pretive description by giving equal weight to theoretical and empirical considerations.

Kuhn (1970) popularized the view that concepts, their arrangement in conceptual schemes, and theoretical paradigms are real in the sense that they have a formative influence in explanation. Theory is more than an arrange-ment of categories that summarize empirical material. It helps to constitute descriptive and interpretive material by pointing to connections among elements of the material and between these and the processes and practices that provide the context for empirical description and interpretation (Resnick and Wolff, 1987). Reference to 'the facts,' those singular essences that positivists present as purified from conceptual contamination, can never simply settle disputes over theory, because those facts, as such, do not exist. Conception or thought extends beyond execution or empirical fact. On the other hand, theory is lifeless, what common sense calls 'idle speculation,' without an empirical and interpretive grounding. In that sense, fact can extend beyond theory, to present itself as what the pragmatic philosopher William James called the 'coercive fact,' jolting the conceptual pattern into self-reflection, thereby pressing one to justify a particular conception or to change it. But there is no pure theory or pure fact – each presents itself as mutually contaminated. Theoretical and empirical/interpretive practices

---

2. Shimony bases part of his approach on Donald Campbell's 'descriptive, contingent, and synthetic epistemology', whose influence can be found in the approach taken here.

influence and are influenced by one another *and* by the wider environment of social practices in which they reside. Consequently, the book refers to the relationship between theory and empirical/interpretive practices as *multiply determined* and *mutually constitutive.*[3]

Acknowledging the wide range of approaches taken by political economists and communication scholars, the book adopts an *inclusive*, open, and non-reductionist perspective. Above all, this means two things. First, there is the general sense that all of social life cannot be subsumed under theory. Analysis is marked by the conflict between knowing what social life is and the awareness that social life contains within it something that makes complete knowledge impossible. This view insists on our ability to comprehend social experience, even as it maintains that complete knowledge is beyond our grasp. Recognizing this contradiction, Marx pushed beyond theory to praxis, Freud beyond the psychoanalysis of explanation to therapeutic provocation, and so on. Second, it means that there is no single correct approach that, by itself, constitutes a definitive political economy of communication. Political economy and communication studies are considered entry points to examine the broad scope of social life. The political economy approach to communication is one starting point or gateway among a range of others, such as cultural studies and policy studies, major approaches that reside on the borders of political economy.

This inclusive position is central to two important dimensions of the book's structure. First, it is neither merely a map of different perspectives nor just an argument in defense of specific ones, but rather an attempt to acknowledge the value of both. It seeks to convey a broad sense of major perspectives in political economy and of how political economists have approached communication, even as it recognizes the limitations of such an encyclopedic or 'textbook' approach, particularly the tendency to present elements of a map without a sense of structure, process, relationship, or outcome. The book responds by balancing the value of breadth with a set of themes or arguments about the field which suggests different ways of comparing and contrasting the various pieces. Second, this approach is neither just a restatement of what political economy has accomplished nor one attempt to transform it. Again, guided by a commitment to inclusiveness, the book aims to do both. The first part addresses the research tradition that has guided political economy in general and its use in communication research. Although the aim is to map achievements, it is carried out from a comparative and critical viewpoint. The second part of the book foregrounds

---

3. Ahmad (1992: 287) makes the case for theory by arguing that for theory to correct itself, it must refer '*simultaneously*, to the history of the facts as well as to its own prehistory and present composition.' The result of trying to correct theory simply with fact results in 'mere repression, which then keeps returning to haunt and disrupt the present both of theory and of history itself.' The same must be said, however, for efforts to correct fact with theory. For centuries, rather than rethink a theory that sent the heavens spinning in perfect orbits about the earth, the intellectual descendants of Ptolemy tried to 'correct' the facts that their observations forced on them with mathematical legerdemain.

specific ways to rethink and renew the political economy of communication by reflecting on a range of entry points and by addressing challenges to political economy posed by the boundary disciplines of policy studies and cultural studies.

There are certainly risks in taking an inclusive position. Fundamental among these is the tendency to encompass more than one book treatment can sustain. This risk alone guarantees a steady flow of books that limit themselves to either mapping the field in textbook form or proposing new approaches to remap it. Notwithstanding the value of such well-defined limits, there are good reasons for aiming to challenge them. The textual approach presumes an agreed upon position, set of positions, or at least a set of debates that can be recounted. Most disciplines, particularly those located in the humanities, but the social, biological, and physical sciences as well, are in ferment over their respective disciplinary warrants. More than ever, the maps are up for grabs. Limiting oneself to reproducing one is not unlike trying to defend the value of a map of the former Soviet Union or of Newton's map of how the universe works. In times of disciplinary ferment, there is greater value in reflecting more deeply on the basic epistemological and theoretical positions that propel the process of constituting a discipline. This involves critical reflection both on what has been accomplished and on how it might be reconstituted, i.e., on restating, resynthesizing, rethinking, and thereby renewing.

The risk is worth taking for more than what can be accomplished for the political economy of communication. Self-conscious reflection on epistemology, theory, disciplinarity, and political practice lifts the discussion out of the narrow band of defining a 'field within a field' and encourages articulation with a broader stream of debate about the state of communication studies and, more importantly, the state of intellectual life today. The book therefore attempts to be inclusive by reflecting inwardly on the state of a discipline and outwardly on the wider concerns that occupy people who work within it.

Combined with a realist approach to epistemology, inclusiveness provides a means of overcoming understandable but not particularly fruitful dualisms. In this respect, the approach taken here follows from the feminist critique of traditional epistemology (Harding and Hintikka, 1983; Massey, 1992). According to this view, dualistic thinking is 'related to the radical distinction between genders in our society, to the characteristics assigned to each of them, and to the power relations maintained between them' (Massey, 1992: 72). Although dichotomies are typically presented to suggest a formal equality based on difference, or on the relationship between objects, the reality suggests a preference that borders on the distinction between presence and absence or between 'A and non-A.' Moreover, dualisms are not only conducive to such thinking, they disincline reflection on third possibilities or alternatives that would take one outside the boundary formed by the dualism. As a result, the only alternative to the dual, in practice closer to the singular, is chaos.[4] Among the numerous examples of common dualisms are the distinctions between subject and object, concrete and abstract, base and superstructure, empirical and theoretical, and political and economic. Much is also made of distinctions in the work of specific political economists such as the familiar distinction between the early and later Marx and the less well known, but similarly relevant, distinction between the Adam Smith of *The Wealth of Nations* and the Smith of *The Theory of Moral Sentiments*. The approach taken here is inclusionary. Rather than press for a specific, 'truer' reading of a particular theorist or line of thought, the aim is to incorporate differences by emphasizing the diversity of thought in political economic analysis. Of course, choices have to be made, but they are made within an epistemological framework that is open, inclusive, and non-reductionist.

Specifically, the book takes an explicitly non-reductionist and over-determined or multiply determined[5] approach to research. Drawing on recent critical work in epistemology (Outhwaite, 1987; Resnick and Wolff, 1987; Shimony, 1993), it declines to reduce any apparent complexity in a person, relationship, or historical occurrence to a core essentiality or simplicity, e.g. that the economic or the cultural provides the essential causal impetus for historical change and that others are non-essential. Moreover, following on the work of Gramsci, Lukács, Althusser, and Williams, it holds that definitions of theory and society are overdetermined or multiply determined. This means that the existence of individuals, social institutions, and ideas is determined by each and every other constitutive process. Following particu-larly the interpretation of Williams, determination means setting limits and exerting pressures. In the words of Ahmad (1992: 6), determination refers not to 'entrapment' but rather 'to the givenness of the circumstance within which individuals *make* their choices, their lives, their histories.' An approach based on overdetermination, or, as I prefer, multiple determination, more easily avoids the tendency to isolate practices in autonomous categor-ies and permits emphasis on both relatively autonomous and interactive practices. By overcoming traditional divisions, we are in a better position to examine how, as O'Connor (1987: 11) puts it, 'modern economic, social, political, and cultural crises interpenetrate one another in ways which transform them into different dimensions of the same historical process – the disintegration and reintegration of the modern world.' The analysis based on mutual constitution remains open to specifying the nature, strength, direc-tion, and duration of a relationship between processes. Mutuality does not

4. Following Massey (1992: 75), this is not to suggest the introduction of a feminist essentialism to replace others. As she puts it:

> Rather, the argument is that the dichotomous characterization of space and time, along with a whole range of other dualisms that have been briefly referred to, and with their connotative interrelations, may both reflect and be part of the constitution of, among other things, the masculinity and femininity of the sexist society in which we live.

5. In addition to generally observed weaknesses with the concept of overdetermination, I add a concern that the prefix 'over' suggests excessive. Consequently, I tend to use the term multiply determined, which, if more awkward, is, nonetheless, more precise.

mean equal influence. The specification of mutual constitution grows out of the relationship between one's theoretical formulation and empirical investigation.

Multiple determination is connected to a particular view of causality. Drawing on the work of Althusser and others, Slack (1984) has replaced the notion of linear causality with structural causality in order, among other things, to address overdetermination and properly understand the social context of technology. I take this view one additional step. The term 'causality' needs to be rethought because, even when expanded from linear or expressive causality to structural causality, it retains the mechanistic quality characteristic of Newtonian physical models. These models are responsible for substantial analytical and practical achievements. Furthermore, there is considerable evidence for the view that the so-called reductionist program, of which Newtonian physics is a part, but which started in Greece about 2,500 years ago, is reaching a culmination with efforts to unify what are believed to be the fundamental forces of gravity, electromagnetism, and the strong and weak nuclear forces (Weinberg, 1993).[6] Nevertheless, numerous commentators, across a range of disciplines, have identified shortcomings (Gleick, 1987; Kuhn, 1970). One of the principal difficulties, with unfortunate consequences for many disciplines, including economics and political science, is that classical physics gave primacy to objects which, it maintained, exist prior to their relationships. The observer is positioned outside the field of objects capable of taking in both objects and their subsequent relationships *in toto*. Contemporary physics tends to argue that *the reality or identity of things is constituted out of their relationships and that the observer is part of this relational field*. Indeed, the fundamental units of space and time which were once considered to be comprised of discrete dimensions are now thought to exist in the four interrelated dimensions that occupy space–time. The point is not that classical physical models are useless. In fact, they are perfectly fine for practical tasks like determining how to navigate a Boeing 747 from Los Angeles to Toronto. Nevertheless, even as the classical models of objects and unmediated observation continue to undergird practical activity, they are challenged by a fundamental shift that foregrounds relationships, processes, and the inclusion of the observer in the observational field.

Drawing on this critical literature and current work on non-linear models, e.g. chaos theory (Gleick, 1987), this book approaches the relationship among variables from the perspective of *mutual constitution*. Causality means that the essence of a thing, summarized in its conceptual label, influences some other similarly summarized essence. Mutual constitution

6. Yet, even supporters of this effort recognize that the so-called final theory would not mean an explanation for everything and therefore does not signal the end of science. According to mathematical physicist Paul Davies (1993: 11), 'Nobody supposes that such a theory, formulated in the context of subatomic processes, would be much help in explaining, say, the turbulence of fluids or the patterns of snowflakes, still less in illuminating the mysteries of life and consciousness.'

removes the implication that things, defined typically as fully formed structures, act on other fully formed structures. Rather, the chief units of analysis are processes, e.g. commodification, which serve as starting or entry points that frame an analysis and relate dialectically to other processes, such as creating a public sphere, that would change it. These processes act on one another's various parts, in some detectable, if often not clearly definable manner. The emphasis is therefore on rethinking the sociological and political economic tendencies which start from invariant social structures and to examine how these structures are reproduced by suggesting the alternative of foregrounding the constitution of social processes.

One of the difficulties in definition is that mutual constitution takes place in non-linear as well as linear fashion. Linear relationships are easy to think about; they can be depicted with a straight line on a graph; they can be taken apart and reconstructed; most importantly, as any student of elementary physics knows, they are solvable. On the other hand, by definition, non-linear systems cannot be solved. Consequently, scientists tend to remove what they believe creates non-linearity, e.g. friction, before proceeding to create a system of differential equations that accounts for and explains what they observe. This has been successful where non-linearity is trivial and where prediction is required in the short term, e.g. the non-linear element of explaining the tides is insignificant for most weather conditions (except big storms) and when we need only rough approximations of tides (high/low) for the short run (tomorrow or next month). As frustrated meteorologists have discovered, even the power of a state-of-the-art computer system is inadequate to the task of predicting the weather for your area one month from now. Such systems are subject to what is only half-jokingly referred to as the Butterfly Effect: that a butterfly stirring the air today in Beijing can transform weather systems next month in New York. Specifically, sensitive dependence on initial conditions, a central position in what is generally known as chaos or complexity theory, makes outcomes unpredictable.

Since the 1960s, chaos theory has so challenged the foundations of science that it is now compared with the theory of relativity and quantum physics. According to one physicist:

> Relativity eliminated the Newtonian illusion of absolute space and time; quantum theory eliminated the Newtonian dream of a controllable measurement process; and chaos eliminates the Laplacian fantasy of deterministic predictability. (Cited in Gleick, 1987: 6)[7]

The mathematician and meteorologist Konrad Lorenz dramatically demonstrated the significance of sensitive dependence on initial conditions in 1961

7. Quantum theory brought us the Heisenberg Principle, which, in essence, says that it is impossible to predict the precise state of a system because the very process of examination alters it. This is another way of saying that science is multiply determined and mutually constitutive: science is constituted by and constitutes the object of its examination. Laplace was an eighteenth-century mathematician who, inspired by Newton and the accomplishments of the Enlightenment, believed that science would create a system of equations to embrace all processes and thereby open the door to complete knowledge across time and space.

when he developed a simple computer model for long-range weather forecasting. He ran the same basic weather model twice from the same starting point. The only difference was that, unknown to him at the time, one contained data rounded to the nearest thousandth decimal place, a seemingly inconsequential difference. This difference, like a small puff of wind, was enough to make the two models move in radically different directions after a short time. He suddenly understood why long-range forecasting had been and likely would always be out of the question without a fundamental reorientation in thinking. It would not be sufficient to establish a new subdiscipline, e.g. non-linear analysis. According to the mathematician Stanislaw Ulam, this would be like calling zoology 'the study of non-elephant animals' (Gleick, 1987: 68). Or, one might add, like calling sociology the study of two-person relationships or political economy the study of rational, optimizing behavior, or communication the analysis of signal to noise ratios. Any attempt to map a discipline and suggest how we might rethink and renew it needs to take into account the transformation in twentieth-century scientific thought, something that the social sciences have only just begun. As Chapter 5 suggests, social scientists have attempted to address changes in our concept of space and time. Moreover, the Hawthorne and Pygmalion effects, familiar to students of sociology and psychology, acknowledge an equivalent of the Heisenberg Principle, i.e., the need to account for the impact of the researcher on what is examined. However limited these efforts have been, even less has been done to examine how the growth of chaos and complexity theory changes our conception of social science. It is not just ironic that social scientists continue to call for building theory around causal, determinist models long after much of the scientific establishment has questioned this goal. Political economists are not alone in continuing to debate determination (full, partial, first instance, last instance) with a remarkable confidence in the capacity to establish either determination or even precisely what, in this context, full, partial, first, and last actually mean.[8]

This book takes into account developments in non-linear science principally by recognizing the limitations they raise for traditional methods of thinking about political economy. One way to accomplish this is to examine the work of those who have advanced fundamental, paradigmatic questions about traditional approaches. In addition to acknowledging limitations, it is useful to draw on approaches inspired by non-linear thinking in both the epistemological and substantive analysis. The emphasis on the ubiquity of social change, multiple determination, mutual constitution, and non-reductionism is in keeping with the former. The latter is exemplified in the set of entry points used to think about political economy and in how we conceptualize communication. Specifying non-linear paths is difficult, but

8. Coletti (1979), for example, has argued that Marxian analysis has a tendency to mistake *first in time* or the historical starting point of analysis with *first in analysis* or its actual foundation.

recognizing the need to do so is an improvement over falling back on linear models which, though easier to comprehend, more often obscure relationships than describe or explain them. This is therefore an early effort to take on board notions that are beginning to comprise a new bridge between the physical world and social science.[9] Mattelart and Mattelart offer one of the few published accounts of the need to approach the political economy of communication from a non-linear perspective (though Smythe referred to this need in his unpublished work). According to them (1992: 191), we need to take into account new paradigms that

> call for transversality. These upset the unilateral relations that linear thought had established between cause and effect, source and receiver, center and periphery. They challenge the exclusive determinism that had marked a certain conception of history and progress.

Additionally, Wallerstein (1991: 14) offers an example of how to look at the world economy in the non-linear fashion of chaos theory:

> the capitalist world-economy constitutes an historical system, which thereby has an historical life: it had a genesis; it has a set of cyclical rhythms and secular trends that characterize it; it has internal contradictions which will lead to its eventual demise. The argument is that the short-run contradictions lead to middle-run solutions which translate into long-run linear curves approaching asymptotes. As they approach these asymptotes, the pressures to return to equilibria diminish, leading to ever greater oscillations and a bifurcation. Instead of large random fluctuations resulting in small changes in the curve, small fluctuations will result in large changes. (See also Peters, 1991)

The approach taken here is also *critical*. In this context, critical refers to a set of relationships: between the standards set by practitioners of the political economy of communication and the research record; between the political economy of communication and the wider discipline of political economy; between both of these and a set of standards developed out of rethinking and renewing political economy, central to which is a process of setting limits defining what the political economy approach can fruitfully address and what is more usefully left to other approaches; and between both approaches and a conception of practice that sees intellectual work as a form of social intervention, i.e., praxis. Fundamental to the latter is a broad conception of professional activity that envisions a wider public than scholars tend to accept. Such a view places an additional demand on the text: make it accessible beyond one's profession.[10]

---

9. Note that I refer to a *bridge* between the two worlds. This is not a plea to simply incorporate uncritically and with no mutual dialogue current thinking in the physical sciences.

10. Cutting against a current grain of highly technical critical scholarship, it follows advice the critic Alfred Kazin (in Sutherland, 1993: 23) once offered: 'Criticism should never be so professional that only professionals can read it.' Or, as J.L. Austin (cited in Phillips, 1993: vii) put it: 'It is not enough to show how clever we are by showing how obscure everything is.'

A Political Economy of Communication: Three Starting Points

In addition to this particular epistemological orientation, which specifies an approach to knowing, the book takes an *ontological* position that describes an approach to being which places in the foreground social change and social process. In doing so, it aims to overcome the understandable tendency to examine social life by describing the characteristics and relationships among definable social essences such as institutions, values, or people. Social change, according to the traditional view, is typically described as a series of snapshots in time that take us from one set of essences to the next, or, using the familiar billiard ball image commonly applied to describe classical physics, as a changing set of relationships determined by the impact of singular essences on one another. Starting from the view that *social change is ubiquitous*, the book emphasizes characteristics of the change process, including the mutual constitution of uneven development within and across the range of processes and actors in the social field. No social actor, social relationship, or social institution is essential. Each is involved in manifold, ubiquitous, and multiply determined processes of mutual constitution. The aim is to understand those processes that embody the political economy of communication, itself one entry point to the communication processes that make up the social field.

The book approaches this task with a substantive focus organized around three specific entry points or processes: *commodification*, *spatialization*, and *structuration*. Entry points are insertions into the social field that provide a substantive focus for thinking about characteristic social practices without suggesting that they provide the essential definition that captures the totality of the field. They fall somewhere between Heidegger's suggestion that concepts are weapons and Wittgenstein's view that they are simply tools. More specifically, this approach argues for the mutual constitution of knowledge arising from the relationship between what Ahmad (1992: 122) calls 'the problematic of final determination' and 'the utter historicity of multiple, interpenetrating determinations.' It argues for a creative tension between these two dimensions of the Marxian dialectic, between the view that material labor determines ideational content and the view that history arises from the multiplicity of time–space-specific forces and agents.

The decision to enter and frame a political economy of communication with these substantive concepts is a choice about what to emphasize. However, from the vantage point of an open, inclusive, and non-reductionist epistemology, these are simply starting or gateway points that reflect a particularly useful strategy for approaching society, not essentials to which all political economy can be reduced. They constitute a theoretical framework for examining the global political economy which acknowledges that their operation takes specific forms which depend on the particular time–space or historical/locational factors at work in concrete social formations. Just as political economy is one entry point to understand communication, commodification is a starting point for examining the political economy of communication. Moreover, these are process terms which, rather than defining a state of being, suggest how we might think about a socially contested process. Finally, these terms are multiply determined, i.e., their character is constituted by one another and by every other process at work in society.

The book is also constructed out of a dialogue with two approaches or disciplines on its borders: *cultural studies* and *policy studies*. The former draws on a range of disciplines, particularly literary criticism, hermeneutic social science, and various strands of structuralism and post-structuralism, which offer alternative approaches centered on textual and discourse analysis. Cultural studies has levelled a strong and sustained critique of traditional science and its underlying epistemological, linguistic, and sociological foundations. In turn, it has been criticized for its relativism, idealism, and obscurantism. Policy studies is built on research traditions in political science, economics, and institutional political economy. It aims to evaluate alternative courses of actions, particularly, though not limited to, government or state actions, in communication. A leading wing of the policy studies approach, public choice theory, is an explicit attempt to apply neoclassical economic models to political science with the aim of creating a policy science. In contrast to cultural studies, public choice theory draws heavily from rational-actor models of society. This approach has influenced communication research chiefly in spirit (conservative) and in some of its less rigorous applications. The dialogue between the political economy of communication and these two perspectives is reflected throughout the book (e.g. in the concern over epistemology and praxis) but is given particular focus in the final chapter, which concentrates on the challenges which cultural studies and policy studies pose to political economy and how a renewed political economy of communication responds.

A Changing Global Political Economy

In addition to the intellectual and academic reasons for writing a book about the political economy of communication, such a study is warranted by the significant changes that have shaken the global political economy over the last few years. These include the defeat of communism, stagnation and transformation in capitalism, deepening divisions in what was once called the Third World, and the rise of social movements that cut across traditional class divisions.

Political economy originated in the eighteenth century partly to explain, justify, and support the acceleration of capitalism. It rejected as inefficient and unproductive mercantilist policies that required strong state support. The critique of political economy rested on a range of movements (e.g. Owenite Utopian communities) and intellectual currents, mainly founded on the work of Marx, but also including a wide range of democratic, communal, and socialist thinking.

The rise of the media industries in the twentieth century led business to take a close look at the economics of communication. The result was research on everything from how to produce and market radio and television receivers to how to sell products to mass audiences. The growth of a critical political economy was built in part on an effort to understand this process critically, i.e., to connect mass marketing to wider economic and social processes and to criticize them from a range of humanistic values. Much of this work was built on a Marxian framework which served as the intellectual wellspring for most communist and socialist movements. All but a few of these movements are now dead, as in the case of the former Soviet Union and Eastern Europe. Of those that remain, some are in serious trouble, e.g. Cuba. Others uphold both authoritarian and market principles (a type of Market Stalinism), i.e. China, or, as in the case of many Western social democratic parties, have accommodated, however uneasily, the mainstream political structure. Certainly, the work of Gramsci, Lukács, Brecht, Baran and Sweezy, and the Frankfurt School of critical theory offer strong evidence of the relentless capacity for self-reflection and renewal in Marxian political economy. Nevertheless, the demise of much of actually existing socialism is an unprecedented challenge to this theoretical framework.

This is no less true of a critical political economy of communication which drew from the socialist world the models, evidence, and inspiration for alternatives to market-based systems of communication. These include the pre-Stalinist Soviet Union, where artistic and cultural movements, such as the Russian avant-garde of the 1920s, promised a cultural as well as a political revolution (Lunn, 1982). Later on, the political economy of communication drew from the dissident and samizdat media of Russia and Eastern Europe (Downing, 1984). Revolutionary and Maoist China also served as an important source (Smythe, 1981). However, it was the prospect of democratic socialism in the underdeveloped world of post-colonial Africa, Asia, and Latin America that inspired much of the research (Mattelart and Siegelaub, 1983; Schiller, 1976). Considerable commitment and energy went to build a New World Information and Communication Order that promised development, democracy, equality, and access in the media and information systems of the less developed world (Preston et al., 1989; UNESCO, 1979). Today that hope has been almost entirely vanquished.

Although much has been made of the social and intellectual consequences of communism's fall, there is little room to rejoice in the developed capitalist societies where stagnation and transformation in the wealthiest regions of the world make a sustained political economic analysis all the more timely. Starting in the early 1970s, the richest of the world's nations have been experiencing an economic crisis that challenges traditional explanations and remedies on offer from economists and policy-makers. Declining rates of productivity and economic growth, stagnant real wages, and growing inequality of wealth and income befuddle policy analysts and deeply worry those at the highest levels of decision-making (Bartlett and

Steele, 1992; Bowles et al., 1990; Harvey, 1989).[11] The inability of the U.S., Canada and Western Europe to meet their economic performance of the 1960s (matched in the early 1990s by Japan's plunge into its most severe recession of the post-war era) has left many analysts puzzled and set off a range of critical assessments of economics, some of which are taken up in the next chapter (Block, 1990; Bowles et al., 1990; Lane, 1991).

Equally profound have been the structural and spatial transformations, particularly in business and government. Although the process by which nationally and locally owned firms have become international enterprises has been a central force in modern capitalism, business has typically retained more than a symbolic national base. Today, that base is less significant. Conglomerate companies like the giant media firms Time Warner, Matsushita, News Corp. , Sony, Hachette, Fininvest, and Bertelsmann operate from numerous sites throughout the world. Moreover, general economic restructuring has blurred traditional industrial divisions, including those in the media industry. It is increasingly difficult to distinguish among publishing, broadcasting, telecommunication, and information services. Taking advantage of diminished government regulation and the growth of a common digital code, companies like AT&T operate across the former industry boundaries. These divisions are all the more difficult to sustain as traditionally non-media firms like banks, insurance firms, and retailers enter the communication and information business. Furthermore, the range of business structures has expanded markedly, again partly as a result of advances in communication and information technology.

There is considerable debate about the significance of these developments and widespread differences about precisely what to make of a new form of organization which, as Harvey (1989: 147) puts it, 'rests on flexibility with respect to labor process, labor markets, products and patterns of consumption' and which result in 'entirely new sectors of production, new ways of providing financial services, new markets and, above all, greatly intensified rates of commercial, technological and organizational innovation.' This line of analysis poses several challenging questions for a political economy of communication. What is the significance of transformative notions such as 'time–space compression' (Harvey) or 'time–space distanciation' (Giddens, 1990: 10–21) which characterize the shrinking time horizons for decision-makers and mark their ability to take advantage of declining transportation and communication costs to spread decisions over a wider and more diverse

---

11. It is no longer shocking to hear the head of the U.S. Federal Reserve, the chief of the U.S. government banking system and the architect of U.S. monetary policy, speak out publicly (in this instance at a 1992 Tokyo meeting with senior Japanese economic officials) to say that standard economic analyses and monetary tools no longer seem to work. According to Alan Greenspan, 'No models can explain the types of patterns we are having' (cited in Sterngold, 1992). Echoing Greenspan, this is how Lawrence King, an economist from Harvard, responds to the question of how to address the lagging productivity growth that has held hourly earnings constant for the last quarter century: 'We're fairly clueless about what to do about it' (cited in Passell, 1992).

space? Does this reflect, as some argue, a fundamental transformation, a remapping of capitalism, brought about by fundamental shifts in the space of flows of fundamental labor and capital resources (Castells, 1989)? Or is this just the latest way of thinking about patterns put in place in the earliest days of commercial capitalism?

Along with stagnation and transformation in capitalism, we are daily confronted with massive upheavals in what a relatively more stable time referred to, even then inadequately, as the Third World. Though likely the case then, it is certainly true now that the Third World is breaking up into many worlds. One segment of it has achieved significant overall growth rates, surpassing the West and Japan. Combining the newest technologies with the oldest means of authoritarian control, several South Asian nations have put substantial economic distance between themselves and the rest of the underdeveloped world. These Newly Industrialized Countries (NICs) are looked on as development models for the rest of the world. However, much of this talk glosses over the price that South Korea, Singapore, Taiwan, Thailand, Malaysia, the Philippines, and Indonesia have exacted from their workers. There is extensive evidence that contemporary versions of Blake's 'dark Satanic mills' and worse have hatched this development success story. Moreover, aggression has not been limited to building the domestic economy. With the support and weaponry of the United States and other Western powers, Indonesia responded to a mild nationalist surge in neighboring East Timor by attacking the Timorese so viciously that many observers conclude that genocide is the only accurate way to describe it. It is also the case that rising production costs, including militant labor-induced wage increases, have taken the bloom off the rose of some of the economic success (Bello and Rosenfeld, 1992). Nevertheless, even as analysts slowly come to recognize that the NICs bear some resemblance to the industrialization of the West in both the success and the horror, it is also important to acknowledge that their overall economic performance puts them in a different class from much of the underdeveloped world.

At the other extreme, many of the world's underdeveloped nations, in effect, have dropped off the map of the global political economy. The school of thought known as the dependency approach could once claim, with reasonable support, that most of the poorer nations were kept in a state of dependent underdevelopment whose terms were set by the leading Western powers. As one of the leading figures in the dependency approach now argues, this perspective needs to be modified for the world's poorest peoples (Cardoso, 1993). The reason for this is that the poorest nations have grown so irrelevant to the global economy that it is no longer fitting to call them dependent on the developed nations. Their irrelevance makes it more appropriate to see them as excluded nations, simply cut off from all but a trickle of global flows of goods, services, and people. The gap between the NICS and the excluded nations is widening. The economic chasm separating, for example, South Korea and Somalia is so wide that it makes less sense than ever to refer to a class of societies as the Third World.[12] The upheavals that brought about the defeat of communism, stagnation and transformation in capitalism, and deepening divisions in the less developed regions of the world fundamentally challenge and make all the more pressing a political economic analysis. Furthermore, since communication is playing a central role in the economic, social, political, and cultural dimensions of these upheavals, we need to apply that analysis in a sustained and systematic fashion to the political economy of communication.

Widespread social change has also given rise to and been accelerated by global social movements. It is difficult to overestimate the impact of the women's movement on the global political economy because we are in the middle of what is arguably history's most significant challenge to worldwide patriarchy. The movement has shaken social practices and beliefs encrusted with centuries of taken-for-granted male dominance. It has also brought about a fierce backlash in defense of privilege. As an organic discipline, mutually constituted with its social environment, political economy has felt the impact of feminism. Classical political economy was taken with the idea of applying the models of Newtonian physics to the problems of economic production, distribution, and exchange in order to advance material wealth. As Joan Robinson (1962) has noted, although economics claimed to be a general science, it tended to identify with the nation state. The response of critical political economy, in its Marxian and utopian socialist varieties, was to unmask the class nature of classical analysis and the stark inequities it justified. Although critical analysis made reference to patriarchy, there was little sustained analysis. Contemporary feminism has uncovered this gaping blindspot in analysis and has begun to remedy it by building a feminist economic analysis that thinks about the world, in Waring's (1988) words, as 'if women counted.' Such an approach faces enormous challenges, for despite all the upheavals, we still live in a world in which, as Connell (1987) puts it, 'the state arms men and disarms women.' The challenge for a renewed political economy of communication is to address that reality even as it maintains a commitment to understanding and overcoming social class divisions.

Major worldwide social movements committed to the environment and to peace have also grown out of the increasing recognition that the global political economy is destroying life on the planet. Like most social movements, these contain a wide range of practices and beliefs ranging from acceptance to outright rejection of capitalism. The politics are complex and

---

12. The fall of the Soviet Union appears to strengthen the case for a world systems approach which has consistently maintained that the communist world did little to challenge the idea that the world contained one economy (capitalist) organized around a single division of labor (Wallerstein, 1991). Nevertheless, Cardoso argues that the growing number of excluded nations can hardly be said to participate in that single economy. For him, it is not simply a case of sustaining global inequalities through a system of unequal exchange and dependencies. Rather, whole nations have been removed from the system, no longer needed, even as dependencies.

outcomes are never certain. However, these movements challenge political economists to rethink the view that land is first and foremost a factor of production and that weapons are products like cardboard boxes whose central significance is in their marginal productivity. They challenge critical political economy which understood class exploitation, but tended to defend the exploitation of material resources as the primary means of overcoming it. The challenge for political economy is to address these issues without falling into the trap of a neo-Malthusian response that uses environmentalism as a defense of privilege. Chapter 2 begins to address these issues that create widespread ferment in the global political economy by taking up the fundamental question: what is political economy?

PART I

Mapping the Political Economy of Communication

The main purpose of this book is to offer a guide to the political economy approach, to how it has been used in communication studies, and to the debates surrounding its relationship to a range of disciplines in social science and in cultural studies.

The first part of the book starts by taking up the wide variety of approaches that comprise the richly textured field of political economy. It begins by assessing contrasting definitions of political economy, from the very concrete concern with the production, distribution, and consumption of resources to the more general interest in the processes of control and survival in social life. These alternative ways of identifying the field are symptomatic of a wider debate over the nature of political economy. Is it to be a narrow discipline whose fundamental concepts are chosen because they are relatively simple to use in empirical research? Or should political economy provide the disciplinary foundation for all other approaches to knowledge about social life? The latter warrants the most general of definitions that can be applied to fundamental processes of human, if not of all organic, activity.

Moving beyond debates about how to define political economy, we address those major characteristics that have preoccupied political economists from the time of the discipline's modern foundation in the work of eighteenth-century Scottish and English moral philosophers. From that time forward, through to the work of contemporary political economists of communication, we can observe a strong commitment to historical analysis, to understanding the broad social totality, to moral philosophy or the study of social value and of the good social order, and, finally, to social intervention or praxis. These four characteristics broaden the meaning of political economy and serve as zones of engagement with alternative approaches to social and cultural analysis.

The political economy approach is also distinguished by the many schools of thought that guarantee significant variety of viewpoints and vigorous internal debate. Arguably the most important divide emerged in responses to the classical political economy of Smith and his followers. One set built on the classical emphasis on the individual as the primary unit of analysis and the market as the principal structure, both meeting in the central process, the individual decision to register wants or demands in the marketplace. Over time, this response progressively eliminated the classical concerns for history, the social totality, moral philosophy and praxis in order to transform political economy into the science of economics founded on empirical investigation of marketplace behavior conceptualized in the language of mathematics. This approach, broadly understood as neoclassical economics or simply, in recognition of its hegemonic position as the orthodoxy, economics, reduces labor to one among the factors of production, which, along with land and capital, is valued solely for its productivity, or the ability to enhance the market value of a final product.

A second set of responses opposed this tendency by retaining the classical concern for history, the social whole, moral philosophy, and praxis, even if that meant giving up the goal of creating a positive science. This set constitutes the wide variety of approaches to *political economy*. A first wave was led by conservatives who replaced marketplace individualism with the collective authority of tradition, by Utopian Socialists who accepted the classical faith in social intervention but urged putting community ahead of the market, and by Marxian thought, which returned labor to the center of political economy. According to the latter, *Homo Faber*, or man the maker, defined our species-being, specifically the unique integration of conception and execution that separated, in Marx's example, the thinking architect from the instinctual bee.

Subsequent formulations, which built on conservative, socialist, and Marxian thought, leave us with a wide range of contemporary formulations. Although orthodox economics occupies the center and center-right of the intellectual spectrum, a conservative political economy thrives among those who apply the categories of neoclassical economics to all of social behavior with the aim of expanding individual freedom. Institutional political economy occupies a slightly left-of-center view, arguing, for example, that institutional and technological constraints shape markets to the advantage of those corporations and governments with the power to control them. Among their accomplishments, institutionalists produced economic histories of labor and trade unions that challenged the narrow, individualist conception of the neoclassical economists. Neo-Marxian approaches, including the French Regulation School, world systems theory, and others engaged in the debate over Fordism, continue to place labor at the center of analysis, and are principally responsible for debates on the relationship between monopoly capitalism, deskilling, and the growth of an international division of labor. Finally, social movements have spawned their own schools of political economy, principally feminist political economy, which addresses the persistence of patriarchy and the dearth of attention to household labor, and environmental political economy, which concentrates on the links between social behavior and the wider organic environment.

Following this attempt to answer the question 'what is political economy?', the book proceeds to examine how communication studies has drawn on the various schools of political economic analysis. At this stage in its development, it is useful to map the political economy of communication from the perspective of regional emphases. Although there are important exceptions and cross-currents, North American, European, and Third World approaches differ enough to receive distinctive treatment. Moreover, the political economy approach to communication is not sufficiently developed theoretically to be explained in a single analytical map.

North American research has been extensively influenced by the contributions of two founding figures, Dallas Smythe and Herbert Schiller. Smythe taught the first course in the political economy of communication at the University of Illinois and is the first of four generations of scholars, linked together in this research tradition. Schiller, who worked for a time with Smythe at Illinois, has similarly influenced several generations of subsequent political economists. Their approach to communication studies draws on both the institutional and Marxian traditions. However, they have been less interested than, for example, European scholars, in providing a theoretical account of communication. Rather, their work and, through their influence, a great deal of the research in this region, have been driven more explicitly by a sense of injustice that the communication industry has become an integral part of a wider corporate order which is both exploitative and undemocratic. Although they have been concerned with the impact within their respective national bases, both have led a research program that charts the growth in power and influence of transnational media companies throughout the world. Partly owing to their influence, North American research has produced a large literature on industry- and class-specific manifestations of transnational corporate and state power, distinguished by its concern to participate in ongoing struggles, including those of labor, to change the dominant media and to create alternatives. A major objective of this work is to advance public interest concerns before government regulatory and policy organs. This includes support for those movements that have taken an active role before international fora, such as the United Nations, in defense of a new international economic, information, and communication order.

European research is less clearly linked to specific founding figures and, although it is also connected to movements for social change, particularly the defense of public service media systems, the leading work in this region has been more concerned to integrate communication research within various neo-Marxian theoretical traditions. Of the two principal directions this research has taken, one, most prominent in the work of Garnham and in that of Golding and Murdock, has emphasized *class power*. Building on the Frankfurt School tradition, as well as on the work of Raymond Williams, it documents the integration of communication institutions, mainly business and state policy authorities, within the wider capitalist economy, and the resistance of subaltern classes and movements reflected mainly in opposition to neo-conservative state practices promoting liberalization, commercialization, and privatization of the communication industries. A second stream of research foregrounds *class struggle* and is most prominent in the work of Armand Mattelart, who has drawn from a range of traditions including dependency theory, Western Marxism, and the worldwide experience of national liberation movements to understand communication as one among the principal sources of resistance to power.

Third World research on the political economy of communication has covered a wide area of interests, though a major stream has grown in response to the modernization or developmentalist paradigm that originated in Western, particularly U.S., attempts to incorporate communication into an explanatory paradigm congenial to mainstream intellectual and political interests. The thesis held that the media were resources which, along with urbanization, education, and other social forces, stimulate progressive economic, social, and cultural modernization. As a result, media growth was viewed as an index of development. Drawing on, variously, dependency, world systems, and other streams of international neo-Marxian political economy, Third World political economists challenged the fundamental premises of the model, particularly its technological determinism and the omission of practically any interest in the power relations that shape the terms of economic and social exchange between First and Third World nations and the multilayered class relations between and within them.

The failure of development schemes incorporating media investment sent modernization theorists in search of revised models that have tended to incorporate telecommunication and new computer technologies into the mix. Political economists have responded principally by addressing the power of these new technologies to integrate a global division of labor. A first wave of research saw the division largely in territorial terms: unskilled labor concentrated in the poorest nations, semi-skilled and more complex assembly labor in semi-peripheral societies, and research, development, and strategic planning limited to First World corporate headquarters where the bulk of profit would flow. More recent research acknowledges that class divisions cut across territorial lines and maintains that what is central to the evolving international division of labor is the growth in flexibility for firms that control the range of communication and information technologies which overcome traditional time and space constraints.

In the course of providing this substantive mapping, Part I demonstrates that the political economy of communication covers a wide intellectual expanse including diverse standpoints, emphases, and interests which belie charges of essentialism that, in the extreme, dismiss the approach as economistic. The approach brings together an international collection of scholars who share not so much a singular theoretical perspective or even a sense of community, but an approach to intellectual activity and a conception of the relationship between the scholarly imagination and social intervention. Moreover, it suggests that political economy faces numerous challenges that grow out of global social and cultural transformations as well as from developments on its intellectual borders, particularly from the fields of cultural studies and policy studies. Drawing from these challenges, Part II aims to renew the discipline by rethinking some of its central ideas with the aim of strengthening its intellectual approach and its commitment to both the scholarly imagination and social intervention.

2

What is Political Economy?

> In order to understand the structure of our culture, its production, consumption and reproduction and of the role of the mass media in that process, we need to confront some of the central questions of political economy in general.
>
> (Garnham, 1979: 129)

This chapter provides an overview of some of the central issues in political economy. It starts with a set of definitions that identify different ways of thinking about the boundaries of the field. Recognizing that there are different views about what constitutes the history of political economy, the chapter builds on the range of definitions by offering a brief overview of the discipline's development and major approaches. Beginning with the classical political economy of Adam Smith, David Ricardo, and others, this chapter takes up the conservative and Marxian critiques. By the late nineteenth century, influenced by the drive to create a science of society modelled after developments in physical and biological sciences, William Jevons, Alfred Marshall, among others, established the neoclassical paradigm that continues to provide a model for mainstream economics. Choosing to concentrate on describing, preferably through a set of differential equations, the outcomes of different combinations of productive factors (land, labor, and capital), this school of thought eliminated most of the political from political economy.[1]

In the twentieth century, the neoclassical view earned the warrant to occupy what Kuhn (1970) calls the 'normal science' practice of economics. Not unlike the way Newtonian mechanics came to mean physics, the neoclassical approach came to mean economics. But the process of normalizing economics was one of continuous intellectual and political ferment that itself merits a volume on the political economy of economics (e.g. Slaughter, 1984). The so-called Austrian and Cambridge wings of the neoclassical school debated the centrality of markets and the role of the state. Institutional, Marxian, and corporatist approaches levelled more fundamental criticisms at the paradigm's assumptions, concepts, conclusions, and engagement with political and social life.

This tension between normal science and ferment continues today. On the one hand, neoclassical economics appears to have triumphed in the academy

---

1. This does not mean that the new science of economics lacked a political theory. The explicit choice of eliminating the word *political* reflects an important view of power and government that has carried forward in debates among neoclassical economists and between defenders of the paradigm and its critics.

and in political life. Economics journals chiefly address the puzzles that remain to be solved and the relationships that need to receive mathematical codification within the neoclassical paradigm. The ranks of government and corporate policy analysts and policy-makers are filled with some of the discipline's smartest and shrewdest practitioners. On the other hand, fundamental criticisms mount about the limits of normal economics. Scholars trained in the discipline question its ability to explain even that limited sphere defined as the formal domain of economics (McCloskey, 1985). Policy-makers complain that the traditional medicines do not work or, worse, make the patient sicker (Reich, 1991). Alternatives to neoclassical orthodoxy multiply. Ranging widely over the political spectrum (from heirs to the conservative tradition of Edmund Burke, such as Michael Oakeshott, to the range of institutional and neo-Marxist perspectives) and equally widely over substantive terrain (e.g. feminist, ecological, and moral economics; the 'positive' political economy of the family, sexuality, etc.), there is no shortage of pretenders to the throne. What they all seem to share is a commitment to expand the conceptual, methodological, and substantive parameters of conventional economics. It would take more than this chapter to do justice to the full weight of the debates within contemporary economics and political economy. This chapter is limited to offering a map of the territory and an analysis of the major differences between mainstream economics and the variety of political economies.

One might wonder about the appropriateness of a chapter on general political economy in a book whose focus is communication. There are a few major reasons for this. First, an overview of political economy provides a basis from which to think about the emphases and gaps in the political economy of communication. Nevertheless, one might accomplish this goal by introducing a chapter on the political economy of communication with a brief on the field of political economy. But in addition to setting the stage for an assessment of the political economy of communication, this chapter incorporates the thinking of communication scholars who have reflected on the general field of political economy. It suggests some of the ways communication scholars have thought about the wider field of which they claim a share. Finally, rethinking the political economy of communication also means reflecting on the fundamental assumptions of the wider discipline and this calls for assessing the significance of upheavals in the fields of political economy and economics.

Definitions of Political Economy

Raymond Williams suggests that when taking up a definition, one should start with basic social practices, not fully formed concepts. He (1977: 11) calls for an etymology based on social as well as intellectual history:

> When the most basic concepts ... are suddenly seen to be not concepts but problems, not analytical problems either but historical movements that are still unresolved, there is no sense in listening to their sonorous summons or their

resounding clashes. We have only, if we can, to recover the substance from which their forms were cast.[2]

Offering a conceptual point of view, *The New Palgrave* tells us that 'political economy is the science of wealth' and 'deals with efforts made by man [*sic*] to supply wants and satisfy desires' (Eatwell et al., 1987: 907). But following Williams' social etymology, before political economy became a science, before it served as the intellectual description for a system of production, distribution, and exchange, it meant the social custom, practice, and knowledge about how to manage, first, the household and, later, the community. Specifically, the term 'economics' is rooted in the classical Greek *oikos* for 'house' and *nomos* for 'law', hence, economics initially referred to household management, a view that persisted into the work of founding influences in classical political economy, Scottish Enlightenment figures like Francis Hutcheson and, crucially, Adam Smith.[3] 'Political' derives from the Greek term (*polis*) for the city-state, the fundamental unit of political organization in the classical period. Political economy therefore originated in the management of the family and political households. Writing fifteen years before Smith's *Wealth of Nations*, Steuart (1967, orig. 1761: 1:2) made the connection by noting that 'What oeconomy is in a family, political oeconomy is in a state.'

It is also important to note that from the very beginning political economy combined a sense of the descriptive and the prescriptive. As communication scholar Dallas Smythe describes its driving force or 'meta-political economy,' it is 'the body of practice and theory offered as advice by counsellors to the leaders of social organizations of varying degrees of complexity at various times and places' (letter, December 4, 1991). This is in keeping with the *Dictionary of Economic Terms*, which defined the original intent of political economy as a 'branch of statecraft,' but which is now 'regarded as a study in which moral judgments are made on particular issues' (Gilpin, 1977).

Other definitions concentrate on how the development of economics narrowed what was originally a broadly based discipline. As early as 1913, the original *Palgrave* noted that 'although the name political economy is still preserved, the science, as now understood, is not strictly *political*: i.e., it is not confined to relations between the government and the governed, but deals primarily with the industrial activities of individual men' (Palgrave,

2. Moreover, Williams reminds us in another work that once we remove the naturalized character of meaning, authenticity requires leaving behind claims to simple neutrality. After all:

This is not a neutral review of meanings. It is an exploration of a crucial area of social and cultural discussion, which has been inherited within precise historical and social conditions and has to be made at once conscious and critical – subject to change as well as continuity – if the millions of people in whom it is active are to see it as active. (1976: 21–22)

3. It is hard to pass without comment on the irony that a discipline organized for two thousand years around household management must still be pressed by feminist economists to account for the value of household labor (Waring, 1988).

1913: 741). Similarly, in 1948, the *Dictionary of Modern Economics* defined political economy as 'the theory and practice of economic affairs' and noted that:

> Originally, the term applied to broad problems of real cost, surplus, and distribution. These questions were viewed as matters of social as well as individual concerns. ... With the introduction of utility concepts in the late nineteenth century, the emphasis shifted to changes in market values and questions of equilibrium of the individual firm. Such problems no longer required a broad social outlook and there was no need to stress the political. (Horton, 1948: 110)

This process is not without its own tensions and reactions. This same 1948 volume notes the beginnings of a revival of interest in a more broadly defined political economy. It senses that 'the emphasis is once again returning to political economy' with the 'recent rise of state concern for public welfare.' *The New Palgrave* (Eatwell et al., 1987: 906) also acknowledges this tendency. According to it, the combination of Marxists who 'never abandoned the old terminology of political economy' and 'by the 1960s the radical libertarian right from Chicago and the Center for the Study of Public Choice at Virginia Polytechnic' gave a renewed life to this old discipline.

Drawing on these ways of seeing political economy, the next sections concentrate on definitions and characteristics of the field that have influenced the political economy of communication. One can think about political economy as the study of *the social relations, particularly the power relations, that mutually constitute the production, distribution, and consumption of resources*. From this vantage point the products of communication, such as newspapers, books, videos, films, and audiences, are the primary resources. This formulation has a certain heuristic value for students of communication because it calls attention to fundamental forces and processes at work in the marketplace. It emphasizes the institutional circuit of communication products that links, for example, a chain of primary producers to wholesalers, retailers, and consumers, whose purchases, rentals, and attention are fed back into new processes of production. The definition provides a set of basic categories that distinguish among the functions of, for example, a major film producer like Warner Brothers, a leading distributor like Cineplex-Odeon, and the various types of consumers and consumption patterns, such as cinema attendance and television-viewing. Moreover, political economy tends to concentrate on a specific set of social relations organized around power or the ability to control other people, processes, and things, even in the face of resistance. This would lead the political economist of communication to look at shifting forms of control along the production, distribution, and consumption circuit. For example, Mattelart (1991) documents how international marketing firms have strengthened their power in the media business by becoming primary producers of valuable information about consumers.

The primary difficulty with this definition is that it assumes we can recognize and distinguish among producers, distributors, and consumers with relative ease. But this is not always so and particularly not in some of the more interesting cases. For example, it is useful to separate film producers, those who organize and carry out all steps in creating a finished product, from distributors or wholesalers, who find market outlets. But film-making is not so simple. Distributors are often critical to the production process because they can guarantee the financing and marketing necessary to carry on with production. Does that make our distributor in reality a producer or a producer-distributor? Similarly, notwithstanding the heuristic value in seeing audiences as consumers of media products, there is a sense in which they are also producers. One might argue, in fact as Marx did in the *Grundrisse*, that consumers produce themselves in the process of consumption. Alternatively, one might say that consumers produce the symbolic value (or meaning) of media products (or texts) as they consume them. One could go on – producers consume resources in the process of production. They also distribute by virtue of their reputation as producers. This suggests that while the definition is a useful starting point, it is limited by what we miss when we apply it in what amounts to a too rigidly categorial or mechanistic fashion.

A far more general and ambitious definition of political economy is *the study of control and survival in social life*. Control refers specifically to the internal organization of individual and group members, while survival takes up the means by which they produce what is needed to reproduce themselves. Control processes are broadly political in that they involve the social organization of relationships within a community. Survival processes are fundamentally economic because they concern production and reproduction. The strength of this definition is that it gives political economy the breadth to encompass at least all of human activity and arguably all organic processes. This is in keeping with the pattern of analysis in environmental, ecological, and biodiversity studies, which, among other things, aim to identify processes at work in all forms of life and to assess their differences and interrelationships (Benton, 1989; Lovelock, 1987; E.O. Wilson, 1992). There are not many explicit examples of this view in communication and information research. James Beniger (1986: 107–109) applies information systems theory to determine fundamental processes in living systems: organization, metabolism and growth, responsiveness, adaptability, reproduction, and evolution. Addressing the complexity and social contestation of control and survival, Dallas Smythe (1991) drew on chaos theory to understand the dialectical relationship of communication and information in living systems.

There is a great deal to be said for a definition that raises basic questions about the narrowness of both political economy and communication studies. It is hard to question the claim that these disciplines have been rooted in the study of human behavior (mainly male) in the present. The result is neglect of how humans relate to the rest of life, and a neglect of social, particularly communication, practices in human orders other than contemporary capitalism.[4] The drawback of the approach is that it can lead one to overlook what distinguishes human political economy from general processes of control and survival. These include the power of a goal-oriented consciousness and a reflexive subjectivity literally aware of its own awareness. It can also lead one to underestimate the overwhelming transformation, what amounts to an historical break, forged out of contemporary capitalism. By looking for common processes that transcend natural and historical differences, we can lose sight of how those processes have been transformed in the contemporary world to a point where the one species responsible for the transformation has the power to eliminate both nature and history for all species. Notwithstanding these limitations, the broad reading of political economy reminds us that whatever our specific entry point or focus of analysis may be, it is inextricably bound up with a long history and with a vast organic totality. This point is taken up in the following review of major features of political economy.

Central Characteristics

Another way to describe political economy is to focus on a set of central qualities that characterize the approach. These broaden the meaning of political economy beyond what is typically provided in definitions. Drawing on the work of Golding and Murdock (1991), among other scholars, this section focuses on four ideas at the cornerstone of political economy: social change and history, the social totality, moral philosophy, and praxis.

Political economy has traditionally given priority to understanding *social change and historical transformation*. For classical theorists like Adam Smith, David Ricardo, and John Stuart Mill, this meant comprehending the great capitalist revolution, the upheaval that transformed societies based primarily on agricultural labor into commercial, manufacturing, and, ultimately, industrial societies. For critical political economists like Marx, it meant examining the dynamic forces in capitalism responsible for its growth and change. The object was to identify both cyclical patterns of short-term expansion and contraction and more long-term transformative cycles that signal fundamental change in the system. For example, here is how Ingram (1923: xviii) explains the central role of history in the mind of the political economist:

> It is now universally acknowledged that societies are subject to a process of development, which is itself not arbitrary, but regular; and that no social fact can be really understood apart from its history. Hence the 'pocket formulas' in favour with the older school, which were supposed to suit all cases and solve all

4. Communication studies suffers deeply from the view that history takes place almost exclusively in the West and began with the invention of the telegraph. This bias owes a great deal to the understandable but mistaken tendency to mark the field (broadcasting, telecommunication, publishing) and its history (print, broadcasting, computer communication) with forms of technology.

problems, have lost the esteem they once enjoyed, and Economics has become *historical* in its method, the several stages of social evolution being recognized as having different features, and requiring in practice a modifying intervention which ought to vary from one stage to another.

Looking back over the development of economics, Ingram's optimism about the triumph of history in the discipline was clearly misplaced. History would remain central to political economy but the neoclassical synthesis, which gained the warrant on normal economics, set history aside or at least kept it in the background. This was chiefly because history made all the more difficult the drive to turn economics into a science.[5] Compare Ingram's optimism with the view of Baran and Sweezy (1965: 29), who, after praising the historical sensibility of Adam Smith and his followers, attack contemporary economics:

> Anti-historical to the core, present-day bourgeois economics scorns any effort to investigate the nature of the changes that are taking place or where they are leading.

For Bell (1981: 79), the absence of a sense of time and history is part of the general crisis in economic theory:

> And finally, economic theory has to return to time (in the logical sense) and to history (in the empirical fact) in order to be responsive to the complex new social arrangements that derive from the widening of the scales and new arenas of economic and social actions.

One source of renewed interest in political economy is the drive to determine whether we are in the midst of an epochal transformation similar to the one that occupied the thinking of political economy's founding figures. People experience what appears to be profound social change and wonder whether they are witnessing a fundamental rearrangement of social structures and processes that reflect the turn to one or a combination of post-industrialism, postmodernism, post-Fordism, or, instead, a deepening and extension of fundamental tendencies at work since the earliest days of capitalism. The answer to this question is central to how we think about social change. Moreover, the question itself suggests a turn to the historical

---

5. I am indebted to Dallas Smythe, himself a pioneer in the political economy of communication, for suggesting Ingram's work. Smythe notes (letter, December 4, 1991) that he read Ingram as a doctoral student in 1932 and that it had a significant influence on the development of his thought about the political economy of communication. The field was beginning to move away from the emphasis on history even as Ingram wrote about the triumph of historical thinking. Nevertheless, for a young economics graduate student, this book would occupy the center of a curriculum. Eric Roll's 1942 *A History of Economic Thought* appears to have played a similar part in the development of another central figure in the political economy of communication, Herbert Schiller.

Today, as McCloskey (1985) notes, economic history is a marginalized subdiscipline in a field that pays more attention to building mathematically rigorous models of the present. Parker (1986) offers one of the better recent critiques of economics (mis)treatment of history.

thinking that propelled the development of a political economy approach.[6] This historical orientation is centrally placed in the 'new Canadian political economy,' two of whose leading proponents define the field as the study of the 'process whereby social change is located in the historical interaction of the economic, political, cultural, and ideological moments of social life, with the dynamic rooted in socio-economic conflict' (Clement and Williams, 1989: 7). In both its traditional and renewed support for historical analysis, political economy is well prepared to take on central questions of our time. However, in order to do so effectively, it needs to pay closer attention to the relationship of history to its position on social structure and social reproduction. Political economy has tended to concentrate on the production and reproduction of invariant structures. This is understandable considering the sheer power of structures like Time Warner, Sony, Bertelsmann, Matsushita, the News Corp., AT&T, IBM, etc. However, this has made it difficult to integrate an historical understanding because, as Connell (1987: 44) puts it, 'history enters the theory as something *added on* to the basic cycle of structural reproduction.' One solution is to focus on constituting processes more so than on the reproduction of structures. Again, Connell (1987: 44):

> For history to become organic to theory, social structure must be seen as constantly *constituted* rather than constantly reproduced. And that makes sense only if theory acknowledges the constant possibility that structure will be constituted in a different way. Groups that hold power do try to reproduce the structure that gives them their privilege. But it is always an open question whether, and how, they will succeed.

Political economy, from the time of its founders, has also maintained that the discipline should be firmly rooted in an analysis of the wider *social totality*. This means that political economy spans the range of problems that today tend to be situated in the compartments of several academic disciplines, where those with an interest in social class go to sociology, those interested in government to political science, in the market to economics, and so on. From the time of Adam Smith, whose *Wealth of Nations* knew no disciplinary boundaries, political economy has been taken up with the mutual constitution and multiple determination of social life. Early in the development of political economy, Mill (cited in Stone and Harpham, 1982: 12) described the necessity of a broad approach to social life:

> For practical purposes, Political Economy is inseparably intertwined with many other branches of Social Philosophy. Except on matters of mere detail, there are

---

6. It was not just mainstream economics that jettisoned a concern for history. As Frederic Jameson (1985) notes, Jacques Attali's *Noise*, an interesting, unconventional political economy of music, is important because it is part of the renewed interest in historiography 'after a period in which "historicism" has been universally denounced (Althusser) and history and historical explanation generally stigmatized as the merely "diachronic" (Saussure) or as sheer mythic narrative (Lévi-Strauss), (Attali, 1985: vii).

perhaps no practical questions which admit being decided on economical premises alone.

Like many political economists, Mill is interested in using political economy as one means of understanding the social whole, even while acknowledging that his own approach is interconnected with the other branches of what he calls Social Philosophy. From this perspective, political economy is not just another approach; it is also a guide to understanding the relationships that prevail among numerous approaches. Political economy starts from particular aspects of social life, but it is also a guide to understanding the relationships that prevail among many aspects of social life. As Heilbroner (1986: 15) put it, 'the great economists were no mere intellectual fusspots. They took the whole world as their subject and portrayed that world in a dozen bold attitudes – angry, desperate, hopeful.'

This view held sway for quite some time as the generally accepted goal of political economy. Even as the name was changing to economics, general texts continued to support this broad-based view of the political. Again, Ingram (1923: xvii):

> As to the place of Economics in the general system of the sciences, it holds that the study of wealth cannot be isolated, except temporarily and provisionally, from the other social phenomena; that it is essential to keep in view the connections and interactions of the several sides of human life.[7]

This concern for the social totality is reflected in otherwise fundamentally different approaches to political economy. The perspective variously referred to as public choice theory or, more broadly, positive or constitutional political economy takes its inspiration from the conservative wing of economic theory. Setting aside for the moment the assumptions and ideas that propel this view, this branch of political economy maintains that it can and ought to be applied to all forms of social behavior. According to Brennan and Buchanan (1985: x), constitutional political economy marks a return to the classical tradition that viewed economics as the study of 'how markets work,' with markets understood so broadly as to encompass 'the coordination of individual behavior through the institutional structure.' For those who advance this view, the subject of political economy is the study of the rules governing the connection between individual and institution. Such rules are constituted, they contend, out of the choices made by 'homo economicus, the rational, self-oriented maximizer of contemporary economic theory' (p. 65). Hence, the entire social arena is the field of analysis for political economy. The choices that create rules governing markets in everything from the traditional private markets in goods and services, to the

---

7. It is also interesting that Ingram (1923: xvii) would see economics as simply one part of sociology: 'There is, in fact, properly speaking, but one great Science of Sociology, of which Economics forms a single chapter which must be kept in close relation to the others.' This provides a sobering reminder to those who would see the latest disciplinary status rankings as the last word.

markets for votes, spouses, children, sex, and so on, are its subject matter.[8]

On the other side, there is the political economy inspired by Marxian, socialist, and institutionalist approaches. These differ from the public choice view on almost all points except this one: notwithstanding variations among theorists, they approach political economy with an eye to understanding the social totality. This view is firmly rooted in the work of Marx and carries forward among Fabian Socialists, Western Marxists, theorists of under-development, post-Keynesian Cambridge political economists like Robin-son, and institutionalists who trace their lineage to Commons, Veblen, and Galbraith. These perspectives have clashed over most central points of political economic theory, but recognize and seek to account for, in distinct ways, the relationship between the economic and the political as well as between these and the wider arena of socio-cultural institutions and prac-tices.

First and foremost, a commitment to the social totality means under-standing the connections between the political and the economic. In reaction to what were considered economistic and instrumentalist versions of Marx-ian theory, numerous works appeared in the 1970s and 1980s that aimed to correct this by arguing for the 'relative autonomy' of the state vis à vis the economy (Jessop, 1990). This sparked a lively debate that has revived interest in the growth of the state, its relationship to social class, gender, and race, and called attention to the dynamic relationship of the political to the economic in political economy. The ferment is likely to continue for some time (Wood, 1986).[9] Nevertheless, the debate has always been about *relative* autonomy. Although the term 'relative autonomy' is slippery and can get in the way of an informed exchange of views, none of the parties to the debate seriously called for separating political from economic analysis. Most recognized that the existing division of academic labor tends to reflect numerous influences, including the formal separation of the political from the economic in contemporary capitalism, the pressure to model economics after the physical sciences, and the view that economics can be rendered free from ideological biases by eliminating political content. Though admitting to

8. One is struck by the near messianic zeal of the positive political economists. This is more than building a discipline, it is, in the words of Brennan and Nobel laureate James Buchanan (1985: 150), creating a 'civic religion' that will 'return, in part, to the scepticism of the eighteenth century concerning politics and government.' They intend to 'concentrate our attention on the *rules that constrain government* rather than on innovations that justify ever expanding political intrusions into the lives of citizens. Our normative role, as social philosophers, is to shape this civic religion, surely a challenge sufficient to us all.' The examination of the social whole is a moral imperative in defense of what they call individualism.

9. Wood takes the view that the political and the economic are strongly connected. According to her (1986: 150), the only significant separation is the formal one which, in capitalism, 'makes possible the maximum development of purely juridical and political freedom and equality without fundamentally endangering economic exploitation.'

the formal separation of the political and economic in capitalism, most conclude that economists purchase their warrant on science by avoiding many of the interesting questions, and that the goal of eliminating the political from economics carries its own quite weighty ideological baggage.

Political economists who work in the institutionalist, socialist, and Marxian traditions are also concerned to identify the links between society's political economy and the wider social and cultural field. Drawing on the work of Veblen (1934), institutional economists are interested in the relationship of acquisitiveness and what he called 'conspicuous consumption,' or the drive for power and status which, in their view, is fuelled not by the rationality featured in mainstream economics, but by deeply buried irrational drives.

Inspired by Marxian theory, the writers of the French Regulation School look to identify the relationship between regimes of accumulation and associated modes of social and political regulation which encompass but extend beyond the state (Aglietta, 1979; Boyer, 1986; Lipietz, 1988). Similarly, in *After the Wasteland* (Bowles et al., 1990), scholars prominent in the Union for Radical Political Economics offer an American variation on the regulation approach that centers on their idea of a social structure of accumulation, i.e., the socio-economic institutions and practices that characterize a period by shaping the accumulation process. Additionally, in an effort to explain what they perceive to be transformations in the political economic order brought about by the decline of a mass production/mass consumption economy organized around large national businesses, Piore and Sabel (1984) argue for the need think about a broad social, economic, and cultural shift from a Fordist to a post-Fordist society built on the principle of flexible specialization. Finally, world systems theorists led by Wallerstein (1991) reject the particularity that they argue pervades both subjectivist (idiographic) and empiricist (nomothetic) varieties of social science research and call for reversing the tendencies that have 'pushed us away from holistic and systemic realities toward the individual (or its organizational equivalent: the firm, the family, the state) as the appropriate unit of analysis' (p. 129).

This broadly based effort to examine the wider social totality does not receive complete intellectual support. For example, those aligned with streams of postmodernist and post-structuralist thinking reject, sometimes emphatically, the idea of a social totality. Across the range of differences within these views, one finds agreement that the term *society* is an attempt to apply a unity in discourse to something fundamentally divided, disconnected, and hence undefinable. The general tendency is to argue that there is no social totality, no individual totality, and no discursive totality. According to this view, the implosions of twentieth-century life, set off in part by the power of new communication and information technologies, have broken apart totalities, taking with them measures of time and space that ultimately used to provide some degree of unity (Lyotard, 1984). We are left with the task of understanding the local, the fragmented, the parts, of what used to be thought of as elements of a wider whole, but which are, in reality, unconnected or loosely tied pieces. By removing the ideological glue of social unity, one can comprehend the real value of these pieces and, ultimately, celebrate them in their resistance to all totalizers – including capitalism, the state, and the producers of all metanarratives.

Chapter 7 examines the relationship of this perspective to political economy. For now, it suffices to concentrate on one particular response in political economy that acknowledges the weight of the postmodern view and yet retains an understanding of the social totality. It starts with the understanding of social totality found in the work of Adam Smith and Marx (particularly evident in the early work and in the *Grundrisse*) as opposed to that of classical structuralists like Durkheim or, more recently, of Parsons and Althusser. Smith and Marx differed fundamentally, but agreed on the need to reject the essentialist view that all is reducible to the social whole, all analysis to what Durkheim would later refer to as the 'social fact.' Their historicity, the recognition of the contingent nature of social life, ruled out such essentialist thinking. But making use of the social totality does not require essentialism or reductionism of thought. In fact, as Marx, Gramsci, and Lukács remind us, dialectical thinking leads us to recognize that reality is comprised of both parts and a whole, organized in the *concrete totality* of integration and contradiction that constitutes social life. The relationship among parts varies from loose to tight and the whole itself may contain numerous fissures, eruptions, and distortions. Nevertheless, according to this view, any discussion which addresses solely the parts or the whole is elliptical. It rejects both the idealism of systems thinking and the positivism of conventional science that calls for direct sensory observation of each and every link in the social field. It rejects as equally essentialist any attempts to provide unassailable priority to the global or the local.

David Harvey (1989), a leading proponent of this view, acknowledges the growth of a dispersed, mobile, flexible, and recombinant political economy and culture. Such developments can signal shifting identities and local resistance. But they can also mark a more tightly organized capitalism which uses its control over technologies and expertise to give it the flexibility to tolerate, resist, absorb, commodify, or ignore these resistances. Indeed, it is a sign of the contemporary ferment that intellectual paradigms respond in fundamentally different ways to the critique of classical, analytical science.

The tendency in postmodernism is to respond by concentrating on the local, on 'otherness,' on the parts. The tendency in scientific thought is to respond with a stronger sense of the whole:

> relativity and quantum theory share the notion of unbroken wholeness even though they achieve this in very different ways. As we have already explained in the previous section, we need a new notion of order that will encompass these different kinds of unbroken wholeness, which could open the way for new

physical content that includes relativity and quantum theory, but has the possibility of going beyond both. (Bohm and Hiley, 1993: 353)[10]

Research determines the nature and extent of resistance and control, weakness and strength, etc. Defending the use of totality in the field of literary criticism, Ahmad (1992: 121) nevertheless cautions about the need 'to specify and historicize the determinations which constitute any given field.' Nevertheless, 'with sufficient knowledge of the field, it *is* normally possible to specify the principal ideological formations and narrative forms.'[11] Political economy lays the groundwork for such research with its openness to a contingent, non-essentialist social totality.

social justice

Moral philosophy provides a third characteristic of a political economy approach. We use moral philosophy to refer to social values (wants about wants) and to conceptions of appropriate social practices. The goal of this particular form of analysis is to clarify and make explicit the moral positions of economic and political economic perspectives, particularly because moral viewpoints are often masked in these perspectives.

When Harvard economist Jeffrey Sachs, a leading architect of economic reconstruction in the former communist world, was asked about his work in the region, he began by calling it 'the greatest moral challenge of our time' (cited in Rusk, 1991). When his colleague Benjamin Friedman wrote a book (1988) attacking the excesses of Reaganomics, he introduced each chapter with a biblical citation. In their overview of the political economy of communication, Golding and Murdock (1991: 18–19) maintain that what distinguishes critical political economy is that 'perhaps most importantly of all, it goes beyond technical issues of efficiency to engage with basic moral questions of justice, equity and the public good.' These are examples from across the spectrum of perspectives in economics and political economy that suggest some unease with what has become the customary practice of separating science from morality. Their interest in moral philosophy reflects a central concern of some of the founding figures in political economy.

Adam Smith, professor not of economics but of moral philosophy, offers a vision of how to advance the social good, not through self-interest, as he would later argue in *The Wealth of Nations*, but through systematic social benevolence:

10. Levins and Lewontin (1985: 3) offer a similar view from the vantage point of contemporary biology. According to them, part and whole are inextricably bound. As the parts develop properties from their relationship,

> they impart to the whole new properties, which are reflected in changes in the parts and so on. . . . These are the properties of things that we call dialectical: that one thing cannot exist without the other, that one acquires its properties from its relation to the other, that the properties of both evolve as a consequence of their interpenetration.

11. Ahmad's (1992: 121) defense of what he calls 'Totality' comes in the midst of a longer argument attacking its misuse by those who refer to singular tendencies (e.g. nationalism) within 'Third World Literature' based on analysis of 'the few texts that become available in the metropolitan languages.'

And hence it is that to feel much for others, and little for ourselves, that to restrain our selfish, and to indulge our benevolent affections, constitutes the perfection of human nature; and can alone produce among mankind that harmony of sentiments and passions in which constitutes their whole grace and propriety. (Smith, 1976: Pt. 1, Sec. 1, Chap. 5, p. 71)

Similarly, Thomas Malthus, son of a preacher, warns of the moral consequences of unchecked population and Karl Marx offers a critique of political economy to create a society based not on class power but on satisfying human needs. However one responds to their specific visions and values, it is hard to deny that visions and values were central to their analyses, that the moral sphere was integral to their work. As the noted political economist Joan Robinson (1962) put it, it would be left for later analysts to take 'this branch of ethics' and turn it into a discipline 'that is striving to be a science.'

There are two central points here. First, the moral, cultural, or spiritual domain is itself the central subject of analysis. Adam Smith chose to write *The Theory of Moral Sentiments* before his analysis of the division of labor in the marketplace because it was essential to understand the moral basis of a commercial society on the ascent in Britain in the last half of the eighteenth century. He felt that it was a better work than *The Wealth of Nations* and returned to it near the end of his life because, according to Lux (1990: 98), 'there was a more serious problem with unmoderated commercial motives than he was aware of earlier.' Similarly, Marx began with moral philosophical treatises that are too readily dismissed as the writings of the 'young Marx,' but which form the core of understanding the values of a growing industrial society. These people were moral visionaries in another sense. They felt that an essential element of their responsibility as social philosophers was identifying visions of a morally appropriate way of living. For them, the moral vision became the feature that distinguished reason from rationality. This can be difficult to comprehend because Western culture has tended to separate science from morality. One voice speaks the language of rationality, logic, and positivism; the other, a normative language that is generally permitted to talk back but not with the other. One is customarily permitted to go only so far as Max Weber (1946), who felt that it was acceptable to be motivated by moral concerns, but that the canons of science left no room for them in analysis. The defense of this standpoint is that moral concerns get in the way of scientific achievement and ultimately prevent science from developing the means to address the very problems that moralists raise. The latter respond by pointing to the many problems, from nuclear proliferation to environmental devastation, that an unreflective science has helped to create.

One of the central breaks in the transition from political economy to economics was the acceptance of the Weberian view that value neutrality defined the limits of the relationship between economics and moral philosophy. Economics could study values, though in practice this meant identifying values with preferences registered by marketplace choices. Moral comment would hold little or no explicit place in the economist's explanation or assessment. Some would contend that the separation of moral philosophy from economics meant simply that the form went underground only to insinuate itself into economists' assumptions and choices of ideas, concepts, and variables. For example, the decision to define labor along with land and capital as a factor of production may very well make analytical sense, but it also reflects a certain moral vision, however implicit, that people are interchangeable with capital. The economist argues that such a view is limited to the economic domain and reflects economic practice. Critics respond that visions spill over into other forms of social life so that workers viewed as tools for the economist's purpose come to be seen more widely as such and treated accordingly.[12] By naturalizing specific economic practices that reduce living labor to a factor of production, economics opens the back door to a powerful moral vision.

The debate over the separation of fact and value, analysis and prescription, economics and moral philosophy continues. There are signs of changes in the wind. As noted at the start of this section, today's leading mainstream economists are less adverse to using moral language in their economic discourse; though it is more likely that 'moral challenge' appears in speeches rather than in journal articles. They are also more likely to make use of specific moral philosophical work, particularly Rawls' theory of justice, which offers connections between moral thinking and welfare economics (Amsden, 1992). This has inspired explicit attempts to rethink the mainstream from a moral philosophical perspective (Etzioni, 1988; Lane, 1991). Nevertheless, it is chiefly the heterodox schools of thought, rooted in political economy, that take up the moral concern. The conservative wing of 'positive' or constitutional political economy seeks to extend the tools of economic analysis to moral choice and aims to use economics to establish what Brennan and Buchanan (1985) refer to as a 'civic religion' (see footnote 8). The Marxian and institutional traditions are steeped in debates over the place of moral philosophy. One of the major forms these have taken in recent years is over the challenge that Althusserian structuralism posed to the humanistic versions of Marxian thought. Seeking to apply the logic of *Capital* to general forms of thought and action, Althusser called for eliminating the moral philosophical dimensions from the Marxian tradition. The attack continues today, though protagonists tend to take up the cause of post-structuralism and postmodernism, drawing on a Nietzschean tradition to attack the value of moral philosophy. Nevertheless, the moral dimension remains strong in Marxian political economy because it provides a strong defense of democracy, equality, and the public sphere in the face of powerful private interests. This is one reason why, despite the attacks from analytic and deconstructionist quarters, political economists of communica-

---

12. Rabinach (1990) argues that the identification of people with machinery, the productivist ethos, is one of the defining characteristics of modernism.

tion retain a strong position on the importance of a moral philosophical position (Golding and Murdock, 1991; Schiller, 1993).

The fourth characteristic of a political economy approach is *praxis*, an idea with deep roots in the history of philosophy and one which finds its most direct path to communication studies in the work of the Frankfurt School. Most generally, praxis refers to human activity and specifically to the free and creative activity by which people produce and change the world and themselves. The word originates in the ancient Greek, where it typically referred to the political and business activities of free men (as well as the name of a lesser known goddess of mythology).[13] It reached some prominence in the work of Aristotle, who considered economic, political, and ethical studies forms of practical knowledge to be distinguished from theory and poiesis. Where theory sought truth and poiesis the production of something, the goal of praxis was action. The term played a major role in debates about the division of knowledge in medieval and early modern philosophy.

Praxis came to occupy a central place in the work of Kant, Hegel, and Marx. For Kant, praxis or practical reason takes primacy in the unity with theory that comprises full reason. Indeed morality is defined as the 'absolutely practical.' Hegel also recognized the superiority of praxis to theory, but looked to a higher unity for truth to be found in freedom where the absolute spirit realizes itself in philosophy, the arts, and religion. Marx was concerned with praxis from his earliest work, a doctoral dissertation on Greek philosophy, which insisted that philosophy be made practical. His principal interest in the term was to create an alternative to alienated labor. In Marx's view, capitalism freed labor from the alienation of necessity only to replace it with a new form of alienation – the reduction of labor power to a marketable commodity. The revolutionary goal was to transform alienated labor into praxis or free, universal, self-activity.

Gramsci and Lukács made use of praxis to attack the more deterministic forms of Marxism contained in *Capital* and in Engels' rereading of Marx. The term entered debates in communication theory through the work of the Frankfurt School and particularly that of Marcuse and Habermas, who added weight to praxis by defining it as a general form of action, of which labor was one type. Traditionally, labor occupied a central place in economic thought because human history has been forced to live in the realm of necessity. As the productive forces develop and offer the first historical opportunity to overcome necessity, Frankfurt theorists turned to other forms of praxis to envision what was to constitute the realm of freedom. In his critique of Marx, Habermas (1973) argued for the distinction between work, or purposive rational action, and interaction, or communicative action. Marx was understandably taken by the former because labor was central to the

---

13. This apparently inspired the writer Fay Weldon to build a novel around a woman named Praxis, 'meaning turning point, culmination, action; orgasm.'

transformations brought about by capitalism. For Habermas, however, social praxis was made up of both work and communicative action. The latter, based on consensual norms and constitutive symbols, offered an alternative model of social life provided that it could be freed from the distortions that restrict democratic, open communication.

Praxis is important to both the epistemological and substantive premises of political economy. In brief, praxis guides a theory of knowledge to view knowing as the ongoing product of theory and practice. It rejects as partial those epistemologies which conclude that truth can only result from contemplation. Knowledge requires more than a process of honing and purifying conceptual thought but grows out of the mutual constitution of conception and execution.[14] Praxis has also occupied an important place in the substantive development of political economy. After all, political economy began as household management and control of the *polis*. Aristotle placed it among the practical disciplines whose wisdom would guide the conduct of rulers. There is a notable tension in classical political economy between the desire to understand the sources of wealth and productivity and the need to advise elites on the appropriate labor, trade, and social welfare policies. Those schooled in the Marxian tradition explicitly united the role of political economist and activist in, for example, Gramsci's conception of the organic intellectual. Writing from prison, where he was incarcerated for opposition to Italian fascism, Gramsci offered a model of the intellectual schooled in both the theoretical tools of analysis and the common sense of practical political struggle and resistance. The tension continues in a far different part of the intellectual universe where contemporary mainstream economists struggle over the drives to purify economics with mathematical rigor and to market their advice to businesses and governments. This is not to suggest that the problems posed by praxis are identical for the wide range of thinking that encompasses political economy and economics. More importantly, however hard one might try, it is impossible to escape the problems that praxis poses for the scholar who would work in these fields. Specifically, political economy is inextricably bound to policy studies and the political economy of communication needs to address both the strengths and the pitfalls the relationship creates. Chapter 7 considers these points at greater length. The present chapter now turns to an overview of central perspectives in political economy and concludes with an assessment of the critical distinctions between mainstream economics and political economy and with intimations of a crisis in contemporary economic thought.

---

14. Marxian theory views the separation of conception from execution as a central step in the process of alienation. Braverman (1974) makes use of the distinction in pathbreaking work on the contemporary labor process. Praxis resonates beyond Marxian theory. It is particularly prominent, in substance if not in name, in the work of the pragmatic philosophers, including Peirce, James, and Dewey. In his history of communication research, Hardt (1992) suggests that praxis can provide one bridge between Marxian and pragmatic thought.

The Classical Paradigm

Histories of political economic thought tend to begin with either the period of classical Greece, which allows for a start at the etymological origin of the term, or with the eighteenth-century Scottish Enlightenment moral philosophers, culminating in Adam Smith.[15] Whatever the choice, one cannot review major histories without recognizing that most build on a meta-narrative that sees the discipline rooted firmly within characteristic patterns of Western white male intellectual activity. To cite one example of notable omission, histories neglect the development of social science in the Arab world that anticipated by centuries, particularly in the work of Ibn Khaldun, what we in the West call classical political economy.[16] One of the difficulties of this overview is that, in a brief space, it must balance the need to present the canonical positions, what most people are taught, and the heterodox views that aim to modify and transform them.[17] Keeping these aims in mind, the primary objective is to provide a general grounding in the traditions that inform most political economic analysis so as to prepare for the next chapter, which takes up the development of a political economy of communication.

Classical political economy was founded on two of the pillars of the Enlightenment: Cartesian rationality and Baconian empiricism. In general, it sought to extend the seventeenth-century revolution in the physical sciences by applying the principles of Galilean and Newtonian mechanics to the world of eighteenth- and nineteenth-century capitalism. As Bell (1981) reminds us, central to the scientific project was the shift from studying concrete objects to concentrating on their abstract properties such as mass, acceleration, and velocity. For Adam Smith, an heir of the Scottish Enlightenment, as well as for his English counterparts, David Ricardo, Thomas

15. There is no agreement even among those who start from the modern era. Most contemporary texts begin with the work of Smith, though some start with earlier figures like Sir William Petty, whose 1690 book *Political Arithmetic* discussed the division of labor in the production of timepieces and implied that labor is the source of all wealth.

16. I would like to thank Hamid Mowlana for reminding me of this omission and my first economics professor Ibrahim Oweiss and my professor of intellectual history Hisham Sharabi who struggled to broaden the dominant tradition at Georgetown University. See Gran (1990) for a discussion of the contemporary relationship between Western political economy and Islamic thought.

17. The editors of *The New Palgrave* learned how difficult this balancing act can be when they were soundly criticized in Nobel laureate Robert Solow's review of the book in *The New York Times Book Review*. Objecting to what he perceived to be the book's excessive indulgence of critical views, Solow adopts a fatalistic demeanor, concluding that economics will always be 'contaminated by ideology.' Citing Marxism ('the most persistent') but Austrian, post-Keynesian and neo-Ricardian paradigms as well, Solow attacks *The New Palgrave* because it failed to 'keep the various "paradigms" in proportion.' The editors replied with a count that totalled about 15 percent of entries falling outside the 'current professional consensus' (Amsden, 1992: 795–797).

Malthus, and John Stuart Mill, this meant determining the economic constants that constituted the stable, underlying reality for a world undergoing massive transformation. Arguably the most important of these was anchoring the concept of value in productive labor, a marked departure from the prevailing view, defended by the Physiocrats, that economic wealth was literally rooted in land.

Focusing on variables like value, price, and cost led to abstract laws, codified in a mathematical form, that described their interrelationships. Additionally, by abstracting the specific concept of value from the narrow context of the precious metal so dear to the mercantilists and from land, the alternative offered by the Physiocrats, the classical school of political economy opened the way to its general application to all forms of industry and trade. The classical position was not the first school of economic thought, but it was arguably the first such system, i.e., a set of abstract variables believed to be applicable to all economic activity.[18]

According to Roll (1942), the classical view was rooted in three immediate traditions. From the Lockean tradition of political philosophy, it derived the ideas of self-interest, private property, and the labor theory of value. Mercantilist thought contributed the notion of exchange value, though the classical political economists would modify this in the labor theory of value. Finally, although this also meant a rejection of the view that land was the ultimate source of value, classical theory supported the French physiocratic notion of laissez-faire, an alternative to the interventionist views of mercantilists.

Following the Enlightenment tradition, classical theorists maintained that individuals were capable of using reason to maximize their self-interest and, by extension, the interests of society. The latter was reduced to an aggregation of individuals with no existence *sui generis* and no teleology. Institutions were natural results of human interaction, but were to be watched with a skeptical eye because of their tendency to restrict freedom of individual choice and social intercourse, including the free flow of ideas, commerce, and labor. Only the latter could maximize efficiency and therefore the wealth of nations. The institution of government bore special watchfulness because the tradition of sovereignty, which gave it the power to defend the realm, could easily be used to create special privileges, including combinations that would restrain industry and trade.

Wide variations within the classical approach gave subsequent generations of political economists much to claim and to contest. The dominant view is to be found in Smith's (1937: Book I, Chap. 2, p. 14) resounding defense of self-interest over benevolence:

---

18. For Smith and others, the method of abstraction was a general one, not limited to the analysis of economic activity, a point which led a commentator on Smith's assessment of the market for religion to call him the 'first economic imperialist' (Anderson, 1988).

It is not from the benevolence of the butcher, the brewer or the baker, that we expect our dinner, but from their regard to their own interest.[19]

In the extreme, this view would propel Thomas Malthus to defend the practice of permitting raw sewage to flow freely in the streets as a means of ensuring population control and survival of the fittest. According to this view, governments should not act to control the spread of disease. Such action would only lead to more misery in the long term, because unchecked population and resources diverted to the weakest would undermine the strength of society.[20] Nevertheless, for all his concern about government controls, even Smith rejected the view that the state's role should be limited to national defense. Recognizing the relationship between labor and culture, the man who defended the division of labor in pin making also acknowledged that 'the man whose whole life is spent in performing a few simple operations ... generally becomes as stupid and ignorant as it is possible for a human creature to become unless the government takes some pains to prevent it' (1937: 734–735). Moreover, in *The Theory of Moral Sentiments*, written in 1759, seventeen years before *The Wealth of Nations*, Smith attacked Hobbes' notion of self-interest with a call to benevolence:

And hence it is that to feel much for others, and little for ourselves, that to restrain our selfish, and to indulge our benevolent affections, constitutes the perfection of human nature. (Smith, 1976: 71)

The point is not to argue for one or the other as the real Adam Smith, but to suggest that Smith has been oversimplified by his critics, particularly those who see in his position a defense of the unbridled market.

The work of David Ricardo (1819) and John Stuart Mill (1848) departs further from the image of classical political economy as the unabashed home of free market economics. Their attention to the distributional consequences of the free market raised the specter of inequality and exploitation. Ricardo levelled his strongest criticism at landowning interests who used their control of a vital resource to attract higher rents that hurt both workers and capitalists. Mill, at heart a pragmatist, backed off from a flirtation with socialism, calling instead for expanding education to control population and thereby diminish want. It would be left to the Ricardian and Utopian Socialists, and, of course, to Marx and his followers, to place systematic alternatives to the unrestricted marketplace on the intellectual agenda.

The classical political economists are important for many reasons. For all of their differences, they succeeded in focusing intellectual attention away

19. Smith's butcher, brewer, baker quote is widely repeated. Another, also from *The Wealth of Nations* (Book III, Chap. 4, para. 10) suggests that he was not entirely comfortable with the pre-eminence of self-interest:

All for ourselves, and nothing for other people, seems, in every age of the world, to have been the vile maxim of the masters of mankind.

20. Malthus' consistent attack on government intervention did not extend to the Corn Laws, which permitted the government to protect British landowners with a high tariff. Malthus supported the laws by arguing that political economy, which more greatly resembled 'morals and politics' than mathematics, did not apply in this case (Lux, 1990: 41).

from the prevailing emphasis on bullion and land to productive labor. They understood the power of the division of labor in the marketplace to create wealth. They also realized that the extension of this practice was transforming the world as they knew it and shared the profound ambiguity of many at that time about the overall benefit of the changes they were just beginning to experience.

The classical position attracted substantial criticism from conservative and Marxian socialist positions. Before turning to these criticisms, which lay the groundwork for alternative perspectives, it is useful to consider one fundamental way in which the classical position fell short of its own fundamentals. For all of its attention to freedom and individuality, classical political economy took for granted the goal of economic nationalism. It was, for example, to explain and advance the wealth of *nations* that Smith wrote his major work, and by that he meant primarily the wealth of Britain. Trade would enhance the productivity of one or more *nations*. As Joan Robinson remarked in her *Economic Philosophy* (1962: 125), though their position 'purported to be based on universal benevolence, yet they naturally fell into the habit of talking in terms of National Income. . . . Our nation, our people were quite enough to bother about.' So powerful was the hegemony of nationalism that, although classical political economy successfully demystified many of the ideas entrenched in earlier schools of thought, e.g. land is the source of wealth, the conflict between national and general welfare was simply not entertained.

ie, didn't anticipate NIDL

The Radical Critique

Utopian and Marxian socialists developed a powerful critique of the classical position on a wide range of grounds, from the human devastation brought about by policies enacted in its name to the theoretical shortcomings of its presumed commitment to Enlightenment rationality. Their radical response was supported and sustained by a wide range of social, particularly workers', movements that enlarged the critique beyond its intellectual coordinates to include a wide range of democratic forces erupting in response to the industrial revolution.

Utopian critics built their arguments out of involvement with oppositional social movements such as the Levellers in Britain and the radicals of the French Revolution. People like Godwin and Paine also chronicled the growth of exploitation accompanying the removal of what few government protections stood between the poor and starvation. Moreover, they attacked the classical view for failing to direct the Enlightenment spirit of rationality against a cornerstone of the new economy: private property. What system (and what, in Carlyle's words, 'dismal science') could be more irrational than one that would defend the practice of excluding the masses of people from the fruits of their own sweated labor? Their strong moral voice and political commitment rejected the classical retort that hunger and misery cannot be avoided because population was growing and land was shrinking.

Several of the later utopians, notably Owen, Fourier, and Saint-Simon, aimed to build alternatives to what they called the anarchy of the market with an explicit commitment to planned, communal societies.

Marx built on this critique, accepting its concern to shift the terms of debate to equality and community, but rejected the substitution of moral outrage, however well justified, in defense of an abstract and idealistic notion of humanity for sustained materialist analysis. The power of this analysis has itself attracted a legion of critics but it has also won their grudging and even not so grudging respect.[21] This overview cannot and is not intended to do justice to the contribution of Marxian theory and to the numerous interpretations of its legacy. Rather, the goal is to describe some of the major dimensions of its reading of political economy which grew out of a critical engagement with the classical school of thought.

Marx built on a number of the contributions in classical theory. He accepted their focus on labor as the chief source of value, although he systematically recast it to take into account divergences between the use and exchange value of labor to develop a theory of exploitation. This identified the difference between the value and price of labor or the *surplus value* that accrued to capital as a result of increasing the work day (absolute exploitation) or of intensifying the work process during the work day (relative exploitation).

Marx's response came in his critique of political economy which turned, in part, on a thorough attempt to historicize the perspective and, particularly, its view of labor. The classical school was interested in the historical transition from feudalism to capitalism, but tended to limit application of its historical imagination when it examined capitalism itself, save for specific debates on the question of whether capitalism contained an inherent, natural tendency to immiseration. For Marx, capitalism was a system of unprecedented dynamism, continuously revolutionizing its productive processes with new technologies and new forms of organizing the labor process. Although capitalism faced a continuous maelstrom of conflict and struggle that changed its practices and forms, at the end of the day no custom, ritual, or value would block the development of the market, the production of commodities, including labor, and the growth of surplus value. The capitalist tendency to continuous revolution, what Schumpeter (1942) would later appropriately call the process of 'creative destruction,' could only be undone

21. In 1942, Joseph Schumpeter (p. 3), one of Marx's more towering adversaries, put it quite well, in words that hold particular meaning in a world that celebrates 'post-Marxism' and 'the end of history':

Most of the creations of the intellect or fancy pass away for good after a time that varies between an after-dinner hour and a generation. Some, however, do not. They suffer eclipses, but they come back again, not as unrecognizable elements of a cultural inheritance but in their individual garb and with their personal scars which people may see and touch. These we call the great ones – it is no disadvantage of this definition that it links greatness to vitality. Taken in this sense, this undoubtedly is the word to apply to the message of Marx.

by forces that capitalism alone was able to release. Included among these was the working class, defined as those who are made to sell their labor power and give up control over the means of production. Classical theory identified the forces propelling capitalism but tended to naturalize them.[22] Marx sought to situate capitalism within the dialectical flow of history. Moreover, this was to be a material history, one that would break with established tendencies in historiography, epitomized in the work of Hegel, which above all valued the history of ideas, beliefs, and states.[23] In fact, in addition to building on much of the Hegelian tradition, particularly Hegel's *Logic* and his goal of a practical philosophy (meant to fuse theory and practice), Marx took up the challenge of revolutionizing it. He would do so by showing how people make history and themselves, albeit under conditions that are not of their own making. For Marx, history meant above all how people make themselves through labor.

In addition to this radical view of history, the Marxian critique of political economy developed an equally radical social conception of capitalism. Capitalism is a material system, not because of what it appears to be, i.e., a system of things (of machinery, workplaces, products, etc.), but because it contains an historically unique set of *social relations*. The appearance of naturalism masks the reorganization of social life principally along class lines. For Marx, moreover, capitalism is not a material system because it engages in commodity production. This is important, but it is still literally the stuff of commodities. Granted, Marx makes a great deal of this stuff. Consider that he begins *Capital* (1976a), arguably his most mature work, with a chapter on 'The Commodity.' But as the first sentence makes clear, although the commodity is ubiquitous, it is nevertheless a ubiquity of appearances: 'The wealth of societies in which the capitalist mode of production prevails appears as an immense collection of commodities' (p. 125). Peel back the layers of appearance and we find a set of social relations, specifically 'all commodities are merely definite quantities of *congealed labour-time*' (p. 130).

More generally, the social relations of capitalism embody a mass of producers who do not own the means of production but have to sell their

22. Marx stressed this in his critique of classical political economy. In *Capital* (1976a: 175), he singled out their theoretical formulations in this way:

> These formulas, which bear the unmistakable stamp of belonging to a social formation in which the process of production has mastery over man, instead of the opposite, appears to the political economists' consciousness to be as much a self-evident and nature-imposed necessity as productive labour itself.

23. Marx (1976b: 467) was stinging in his criticism of 'true socialists,' who, he argued, refused to confront the material roots of conflict and change:

> It is difficult to see why these true socialists mention society at all if they believe with the philosophers that all *real* cleavages are caused by *conceptual cleavages*. On the basis of the philosophical belief in the power of concepts to make or destroy the world, they can likewise imagine that some individual 'abolished the cleavage of life' by 'abolishing' concepts in some way or other.

labor power to a class of owners organized in separate firms that compete in various commodity, labor, raw material, and capital markets. Competition drives these different firms to maximize surplus value from producers in order to increase capital accumulation. The Marxian literature is filled with the debate over the precise definition and consequences of the capital–labor relationship. Nevertheless, the tendency in the traditional Marxian view is to argue that the system built on the capital/wage–labor relationship leads to the growing mechanization of labor, the concentration and centralization of capital, and periodic crises, of which the tendency to overproduction is probably the most pronounced (Mandel in Marx, 1976a: 82). One can certainly find the seeds of this view in some of the work of classical political economy, particularly in that of Ricardo and his left of center followers. However, until Marx, no one ventured an analysis of capitalism that so thoroughly sought to strip away the power of its apparent features that define a natural, taken-for-granted world to reveal a set of socially dynamic, but fundamentally contradictory and, therefore, unstable practices.

Among the numerous critiques of the traditional Marxian view, one is particularly important to communication studies: Marx did not carry the social analysis of capitalism far enough. This does not refer to the widespread, but generally mistaken view that Marx missed the rise of managerial capitalism and of a service economy. For sympathetic critics like Williams (1977), Baudrillard (1981), and Dallas Smythe (1981) these are far less consequential than what results from an essentialist and narrow view of labor. The traditional Marxian analysis places a great deal of weight on the concept of labor. In his early work, as well as in the *Grundrisse* (which connects that work to *Capital*), Marx envisions labor as a broad category encompassing the social activity by which people constitute themselves and history. Nevertheless, even here, the emphasis is on the instrumental and productive nature of labor rather than on its expressive and constitutive qualities. *Capital* takes an even more productivist view of labor, largely, according to Marx's defenders, because it is a critique of capitalism, one of whose central features is the narrowing of labor into the instrumental–productivist wage relationship. However, one consequence of a formulation that identifies labor as the essential material activity but narrows it into the wage system is that other material practices which we would identify with communication, culture, language, and social reproduction are rendered nonmaterial, dependent, and, in extreme formulations, superstructural reflections of a material base defined by labor. According to Haraway (1991: 132), although Marx and Engels recognized that labor encompassed the production of human beings themselves, they give greatest weight to the production of the means of existence and thereby offer little more than a starting point for theories of, among other things, the sex/gender division of labor. One of the central tasks of a political economy of communication that aims to build on a critical encounter with traditional Marxian analysis is to demonstrate how communication and culture are material practices, how labor and language are mutually constitutive, and how communication and information are dialectical instances of the same social activity.

The Conservative Critique

Responding to the social and intellectual transformations that were surging across Europe in the last half of the eighteenth century, the British conservative philosopher Edmund Burke (1910, orig. 1790: 73) pronounced: 'But the age of chivalry is gone. That of sophisters, economists, and calculators has succeeded, and the glory of Europe is extinguished forever.' For Burke, the French Revolution not only failed as a political project, it was an intellectual failure as well. For him, as for other conservatives like Thomas Carlyle, the French Revolution demonstrated the utter failure of the Enlightenment view that the universe was a grand rational machine that, much like a clock, could be understood, fixed, and changed for the better. A revolution carried out in the name of reason, democracy, and freedom brought about terror and authoritarianism instead. According to this view, society is not a mechanism that can be taken apart and put back together, but a fragile organism bound together by tradition and wisdom.

This prototypical anti-modernist view held little hope that the proponents of a political economy could improve material or intellectual life. Carlyle, in fact, was the first to dub political economy 'the dismal science,' adding that it was little more than 'pig philosophy.' If the big clock of Galileo and Newton cannot work for society (in fact only adding to the hubris that would inspire failed revolutions), then it cannot work in those economic models inspired by it. Specifically, conservatives opposed the assumption that economic development results from self-interested individuals rationally seeking to maximize their wealth. The self-interest of Smith's butcher, brewer, and baker might also drive them to destroy one another. Rather, wealth grows out of an organic order that produces respect for traditions offering people a clear sense of their social role and a moral grounding that motivates them to carry it out. The alternative might work in the short run (although the French Revolution proved how short that run could be), but in the long term, rational self-interest was a weak basis for social unity.

At one extreme, the conservative view supported all defenses of hierarchy and difference, whether based on gender, race, or class. The natural order would be led by those who were male, white, and wealthy. There was no Mill, Marx, or Wollstonecraft in their ranks to defend the need for equality as the basis for an ordered community. On the other hand, however, there was more support for working people among conservatives than could be found in most classical political economy. For example, Carlyle (1984) proposed giving more power to direct producers in order to create a greater sense of community and harmony in the workplace. He also supported government intervention to regulate health and safety in the workplace and to provide social assistance for those the system rejects. There was no Malthus in their ranks to support free-flowing sewage as a form of population control. But neither would social utopians or Marxians find a welcome. Whatever the surface affinity in their concern for recognizing the needs of working people and of the poor, the conservative and socialist/Marxian paradigms were fundamentally at odds. Conservatives drew the line at social intervention that would ameliorate the worst consequences of social change. They rejected the Enlightenment view, pressed by social democrats and Marx, that one could intervene in social life to fundamentally alter its arrangements and bring about a more rational world. They particularly opposed giving power to the masses to carry out this social transformation.

From Political Economy to Neoclassical Economics

There is no sharp break that permits a precise designation of when classical political economy became economics. However, during roughly about the last half of the nineteenth century, several developments began to coalesce around a formulation that would eventually come to embody the neoclassical approach. One of the critical sources for the shift was the increasing willingness to accept Bentham's utilitarian attack on the classical defense of natural law and rights. In *Utilitarianism* (1890), Bentham argued that pleasure and pain were to be the sole determinants of ethical and moral behavior not some natural code, however well reasoned and well founded. For him, the philosopher's task is to develop the Felicific Calculus made up of precise measures of social welfare based on maximizing pleasure over pain and to recommend the necessary social changes to bring it about. Drawing explicitly from this work in his 1870 book that would rename the discipline, Jevons (1965: 101) defined economics as the study of 'the mechanics of utility and self-interest':

> to satisfy our wants to the utmost with the least effort – to procure the greatest amount of what is desirable at the expense of the least that is undesirable – in other words, to maximize pleasure, is the problem of economics.[24]

Unlike political economy, economics was not concerned with the impossible task of determining human needs or rights, natural or otherwise. Rather, it would be the wants expressed in preferences, the determinable and measurable choices made in the marketplace for capital, labor, and consumer goods and services, that would comprise the substance of the discipline.

24. Though Bentham provided an immediate influence on the development of neoclassical economics, his work is well rooted in that of predecessors who arguably took stronger positions. Consider David Hume's remarks on sorting out the wheat from the chaff in libraries:

> If we take in our hand any volume; of divinity or school metaphysics, for instance, let us ask, *Does it contain any abstract reasoning concerning quantity or number?* No. *Does it contain any experimental reasoning concerning matter of fact and existence?* No. Commit it then to the flames: for it can contain nothing but sophistry and illusion. (Cited in McCloskey, 1985: 8)

Moreover, economics was less interested in the absolute utility of a good than in the utility of the last available item or its *marginal utility*. In 1871, Jevons in Britain, Menger in Austria, and, later on, Clark in the United States hit upon the idea that, all things being equal, the utility of any good or service declines with its increasing availability. It is the utility of the marginal unit, the last and least wanted, that sets the value for all. Furthermore, the concept of marginality could be extended from the demand for a good or service to its supply. Ricardo had demonstrated that continued pressure for agricultural production drove landowners to cultivate at the less arable margins, thereby increasing production costs. Jevons and his contemporaries noted the same tendency in manufacturing: factories incur increasing costs as they press to extract more from machinery and labor. As a result, the supply side faced the same problem of diminishing returns and utility determined at the margin.

These insights would be put together by numerous successors, though Alfred Marshall is most often credited with having achieved the synthesis that makes up the neoclassical system. In simple terms, market price (for goods, services, labor, and capital) is determined at the intersection of a downward sloping demand curve (downward because of the decreasing propensity to consume at the margin) and an upward sloping supply curve (upward because of the rising costs at the margin). In his *Principles of Economics*, Marshall developed this idea into a universe of discourse that John Maynard Keynes, who produced one of the major ruptures in the neoclassical world, called 'a whole Copernican system, in which all the elements of the economic universe are kept in their places by mutual counterpoise and interaction' (cited in Heilbroner, 1986: 208).

Marshall's *Principles*, which was published in 1890 with new editions appearing until 1920, was driven by two notions that continue to characterize economics as a discipline. First, following particularly on the work of Walras, economics was concerned with social order, i.e., with describing forces in equilibrium. Just as astronomers and physicists had identified the essential harmony of the physical world, the economist would locate and describe qualities of economic units and their relationships that maintained balance in the world of goods. To use Walras' term, movement consists largely of *tatonnement*, the groping movements of individuals in response to signals from an external environment. Second, as the book's motto succinctly states: *Natura non facit saltum*, nature makes no sudden changes. The economic universe, just as the Newtonian, was comprised of small, incremental changes and therefore favored an analysis that took for granted wider institutional arrangements. It takes hardly a leap to go from these ideas to the conclusion, stated most clearly by Jevons, that 'economics, if it is to be a science at all, must be a mathematical science' (cited in Galbraith, 1987: 125).

In the drive to become a mathematical and parsimonious science, economics shed most of the fundamental characteristics that characterize political economy. Given the interest in equilibrium states, economics would concentrate on synchronic analysis to the neglect of the traditional interest in history. Concluding that the study of institutional change and structural transformation could not be rendered with mathematical precision, economics would limit its interest in social change to small, incremental adjustments in general equilibrium patterns. The methods of economic analysis would apply across the range of historical periods. However, they were admittedly incapable of addressing the transition from one period to another, particularly when the transition was marked by disjunctions and upheavals.

Furthermore, parsimony demanded that economics give up a systematic concern for understanding the wider social totality. There was no room for the political in this new science of economics because the tools were not available and probably never would be to examine the political system with mathematical certainty.[25] Economics would also best give up the goal of understanding those social institutions, psychological forces, and cultural values that political economy argued was central to a complete analysis. Even Alfred Marshall, whose interests tended to roam as widely as those of his political economic predecessors and counterparts, called for the strict limitation of economics to 'that part of individual and social action which is most closely connected with the attainment and with the use of the material requisites of well-being' (cited in Clark, 1991: 92). Unlike others who saw their work taken up solely with understanding the allocation of scarce material resources to any goal, Marshall was interested in and commented on the distribution of power in the workplace and society. Nevertheless, economic analysis would have to stand the test of mathematical rigor and scientific objectivity. That meant breaking the tie to sociology and political science, as well as to history.

It also meant breaking the connection to moral philosophy. Working in a transition period, the best of the new economists were well versed in what they were setting aside. Marshall, for example, had studied ethics and demonstrated a solid understanding of both Kantian and Hegelian approaches to moral concerns. This contributed to his concern over environmental pollution ('negative externalities') and over the market's ability to provide for universal goods like education. Nevertheless, Marshall and his fellow neoclassicists held firmly to the view that economists should study wants expressed in preferences and not needs determined by a moral philosophy. Of course, they would admit, wants are often formed out of a moral position, but the position is irrelevant to understanding the economic significance of wants. Therefore, although one might take an intellectual or more broadly humanistic interest in moral concerns, one would not get very far by incorporating them in analysis.

25. Jevons spoke for many in the neoclassical camp when he acknowledged that 'About politics, I confess myself in a fog' (cited in Heilbroner, 1986: 184). It is no wonder that he recommended the name 'economics' replace 'political economy', 'the old troublesome double-worded name of our science' (cited in Clark, 1991: 32).

Finally, the paring-down process led economists to set aside an interest in social praxis. Like other disciplines, economics was increasingly institutionalized in universities and subjected to the formal and informal rules governing the academic division of labor. As a consequence, it was more and more likely that academics would be separated from social movements and a public intellectual life. Some, like the institutional economist Thorstein Veblen, resisted this tendency with some measure of success. More typically, academics settled into the relative comfort of a university life that kept away the people and events that might prove disruptive. In sum, the purchase of a warrant on mathematical and scientific legitimacy came with a substantial price tag: set aside political economy and the integration of history, the social totality, moral philosophy, and praxis into the meaning of research and of intellectual life.[26]

Notwithstanding this, it is important to resist the understandable tendency to comment on the early history of a discipline as if it were simply the seed of what we observe today. Today's Samuelson, Tobin, Friedman, and Summers are not the inevitable result of Jevons, Menger, Clark, Walras, and Marshall. The transition from political economy to neoclassical economics took place over widespread disagreement and intellectual conflict. One stream of neoclassical thought was more reluctant to yield the historical and moral ground even as it insisted on an analysis grounded in individual self-interest, rational action, and the efficiency of free markets. This so-called Austrian branch of the neoclassical paradigm was established in the work of Menger and Böhm-Bawerk and later in that of von Mises and Nobel laureate Friedrich Hayek. Sensitive to the long, slow decline of the Habsburg empire and morally repulsed by the more proximate threat of class conflict and socialism, these economists were demanding in their insistence on the virtues of pure capitalism. Their work provides the ringing defense of neoclassical methods and the justification for exacting whatever price to achieve a pure market economy. Only a market economy could provide the discipline of supply and demand essential to guarantee the most efficient allocation of resources, including goods, services, labor, capital and the information required for rational action.

The other principal, or Cambridge, wing of neoclassical thought was less willing to completely accept an individualistic, market-centered approach. Fundamentally committed to these units of analysis, the heirs to Marshall's tradition, notably Pigou, Robinson, and Keynes, were nevertheless concerned about the range of market failures and externalities that justified corrective mechanisms including government intervention. Pigou's work on externalities was used to defend taxation and subsidy policies for firms that

---

26. Heilbroner (1986: 211–212) ruminates on the consequences of what he considers an 'intellectual tragedy of the first order':

> For had the academicians paid attention to the underworld, had Alfred Marshall possessed the disturbing vision of a Hobson, or Edgeworth the sense of social wrong of a Henry George, the great catastrophe of the twentieth century might not have burst upon a world utterly unprepared for radical social change.

created respectively net external costs and benefits. Finding that the market-place fails to guarantee full employment output, Keynes recommended government fiscal intervention. These struggles within the developing neo-classical paradigm suggest difficulties that continue to raise critical questions today.

The triumph of the neoclassical model could not easily be foreseen at the turn of the century. In fact, in the early decades, up to around 1930, neoclassical economics fell out of general favor because it appeared to be too academic, abstract, ahistorical, and incapable of addressing the growth of large, vertically integrated corporations that devoured the competition in practically all major industries. The neoclassical model saved itself by developing new tools and new responses to attacks on the right and left. The growth of statistical analysis and econometric modelling gave the approach strong tools and, of no small import, strong-looking tools with which to represent the state of the economy and to simulate the impact of changes in its major features.[27] In addition, Chamberlin's work on how one could think about monopolistic competition and Keynes' insistence on the inherent tendency to disequilibria and underemployment of resources led some of the neoclassicists to incorporate elements of the left of center critique. Furthermore, the development of a quantity theory of money firmed up the monetarist wing of neoclassical thought. These developments helped provide the groundwork for what Bell has called the 'golden age of economics,' roughly the period from 1947 to 1973. That these years corresponded to those of the great post-war boom suggests that economic growth also gave a shot in the arm to the economic approach that held the warrant on explaining and representing the boom period.

Today, the neoclassical paradigm occupies the center and right of center space in the political spectrum. The center reflects the vestiges of a Keynesian approach which took issue with the view that business cycles were natural products of market activity which would invariably provide the appropriate signals for making business decisions. For Keynes and his followers, the price of this signalling mechanism, i.e., high unemployment and deep income inequalities, was not worth the gain. According to this view, the Great Depression of the 1930s was the inevitable consequence of economic policies that concentrated on the lack of saving, on the assumption that the latter would be *naturally* channelled into productive investment. Keynes (1964) demonstrated that in recessionary periods this was not at all likely, and the consequences of the failure to turn savings into investment would multiply throughout the economy, thereby aggravating the decline. The Keynesian approach called for government fiscal policies, mainly increased spending in recessionary periods, to counter declines in consumer and business spending and eventually stimulate investment. In the short

---

27. The attraction that the sheer formal elegance of these tools provides should not be discounted. As Kenneth Burke (in McCloskey, 1985: 55) once noted: 'A yielding to the form prepares for assent to the matter identified with it.'

term, this would create budget deficits in government accounts, but these would be overcome by the increase in revenues brought about by economic growth and by controlling government spending once the expansion was underway. Numerous forms of Keynesian economics influenced both the discipline and economic policy in the post-World War II period.[28] Sustained economic growth in the 1950s led economists to see Keynesian fiscal policies as the solution to the chronic boom–bust cycles in capitalism (Heller, 1967). By far the dominant textbook, produced by Nobel laureate Paul Samuelson, made Keynesian economics the standard for macroeconomic analysis. But the global recession of the mid-1970s, bringing with it a new wrinkle, economic 'stagflation' or slow growth *and* inflation, reminded people why economics was called the 'dismal science' and sparked a shift in both the direction of neoclassical economics and the economic strategies of governments.[29]

By the late 1970s, right of center economists like Milton Friedman increased their influence over the discipline and government economic policy. Contrary to the Keynesians, these monetarists held that the cornerstone of the explanatory apparatus was the money supply and their policy advice centered on controlling inflation with reduced government spending and high interest rates. Though they admitted that, in the short term, a tight money policy would lead to higher unemployment, this was a price worth paying in order to control what they felt was the more significant damage that inflation was inflicting on the world monetary system. By the 1980s, Western governments adopted monetarist policies and used their control over international organizations like the World Bank and the International Monetary Fund to impose them on much of the rest of the world.[30] Today, versions of Keynesian and monetarist economics continue to contend for the neoclassical mainstream, raising questions about the state of this paradigm and its value in economic policy-making. More fundamental questions come from streams of thought outside the mainstream.

Varieties of Political Economy or Heterodox Economics

Contemporary economics presents this paradox: the neoclassical paradigm, for all its internal disagreements, appears to have triumphed in the pro-

28. These differences were heavily influenced by domestic political considerations. The United States practiced military Keynesianism, a policy that channelled public investment mainly into the defense sector. Western European countries, particularly the nations of Scandinavia, as well as Japan, Canada, and Australia, tended to build fiscal policy around the civilian sector, favoring national companies and domestic social welfare programs such as national health care.

29. Many Keynesians defend their analysis and policy advice by arguing that governments ignored their prescription to cut back on spending during periods of economic growth.

30. There were numerous variations on the monetarist theme, again, greatly influenced by domestic political developments. The United States, under Reagan and Bush, appeared to practice a mixture of stepped-up military Keynesianism and monetarism in the civilian sector.

fession and·in public policy; nevertheless, criticism of the perspective deepens from familiar sources and new voices add to the attack. The next section explores these critical schools of thought, several of which contribute to the foundation of research in the political economy of communication. The following section takes up what some claim to be a general crisis in economics and the fundamental distinctions between modes of thought in economics and in political economy. This discussion lays the groundwork for Chapter 3, which takes up the development of a political economy of communication.

Neo-conservatism

Since mainstream economics occupies the center and right of the political spectrum, there would not appear to be much room for a conservative critique. Much of the anti-modernist critique of liberalism (Oakeshott, 1962, 1975) is contained within the right wing of neoclassical economics. Nevertheless, one can observe important responses from conservatives in two different schools of thought that often compete with one another. One departure characterizes those who argue that mainstream economics has been excessively cautious in concentrating on economic behavior. Variously labelled public choice theory, the rational expectations school, the new or positive political economy, this approach aims to extend the principles of economic analysis to all forms of social, political, and cultural activity (Stigler, 1988). For example, Stigler (1971) and Wilson (1980) laid the groundwork for analyses of government regulatory behavior by arguing that we should view regulation as an organizational market that tends to be captured by rent-seeking civil servants who increase the amount and scope of regulation, even as they restrict access to valuable information, in order to maximize their gains. One solution, popular in the 1980s, is to cut back on regulation and thereby eliminate this form of state restriction on competitive activity. This perspective has taken on a more adventuresome spirit in recent applications of the perspective to the family, gender, and sexuality (Posner, 1992). The same staff capture argument is used to explain the long delays and 'red-tape' that clog child adoption agencies. The remedy is not much different. According to Judge Richard Posner, an economist elevated to the U.S. federal bench by then-President Reagan, efficiency calls for allocating babies by establishing a market in what he calls 'parental-right selling.' According to this view, neoclassical economics is too timid: the fundamental precepts of market behavior and marginal utility can be applied across the range of human behavior. This conserves, in a more systematic fashion, the goal of Adam Smith, whom Anderson (1988) dubbed 'the first economic imperialist,' which envisioned a general science of economics.

Another wing of the conservative critique, the *corporatist* position prominent in the work of Nisbet (1986) and Kristol (1983), takes issue with some of this vision. Although not nearly as coherent a perspective, this view criticizes the neoclassical school for neglecting the *political* in political economy. In essence, the conservative price paid for its scientific warrant is setting free the political for capture by liberal and socialist thought. Public choice theory is one attempt at recapture but, according to this view, it fails because of its excessive commitment to individualism and contractualism. The alternative to individualism is to see society as a collectivity of communities, with organic normative orders of which economic activity is merely one part. Rather than following rational expectations, individuals act with reference to social custom, including customs of deviant practice, often bearing no resemblance to economic logic. This form of conservative thought would build a political economy on the need to identify traditional social practice, determine the civic virtue, and intervene politically to uphold the moral value of that practice. Taking up a conservative variation on corporatism, according to this approach, the best guide to appropriate conduct is the standard established by elites across the range of social institutions. The fondness for 'making markets' in public choice theory is tempered and often resisted by political conservatives, who view it as an intrusion, often a radical one, into the organic, moral order.

These two conservative positions have gotten along to the extent that they have been able to maintain the division between the economic and political worlds. The former is the place where utility reigns, the latter is the home of custom and order. The growth of the new positive political economy signals a dissatisfaction with this division and the likelihood that these positions will clash as much with one another as with mainstream economics. The new 'civic religion' that Nobel laureate James Buchanan and his followers aim to establish may not usher in a peaceable kingdom.

Institutional Economics

The major established heterodox positions on the left draw from the institutional and Marxian perspectives. The former departs from neoclassical economics by maintaining that the organizational structure of the economy, not the market, is the major force in the production, distribution, and exchange of goods and services. The analysis of organizational structure incorporates institutional history, the sociology of bureaucratic activity, the assessment of technological constraint and opportunity, and the influence of social custom, law, and culture on the social construction of value. By demanding an explicitly historical and holistic point of view, the institutional school sought to replace what neoclassical economics gave up to achieve parsimony, mathematical rigor, and scientific legitimacy. In its strongest formulations, the institutional paradigm provided more than the replacement of one set of emphases (markets, value as price) with another (institutional constraint and custom); it offered a different epistemology, one based on a combination of German historicist thinking (e.g. Max Weber) and Anglo-American pragmatism (e.g. John Dewey on social value and pragmatic action).

The early contours of the institutional perspective were laid out principally by Thorstein Veblen, Charles Ayres, John R. Commons, and Wesley Mitchell. Each, but especially Veblen, described a world in which the exceptions to the neoclassical world appeared to rule. This was the late nineteenth and early twentieth centuries when the great trust companies and monopolies seemed to mock the competitive market models at the heart of the neoclassical universe. Veblen's *The Theory of the Leisure Class* (1934, orig. 1899) drove home the point that neither rationality nor common sense informed consumer choice. Rather, consumers decided on the basis of deeply buried irrationalities that found expression in the status emulation practices we know as conspicuous consumption. Veblen was particularly skeptical of both the working class, who would rather imitate than overthrow their bosses, and business leaders, whose 'function was not to help make goods, but to cause breakdowns in the regular flow of output so that values would fluctuate and he could capitalize on the confusion to reap a profit' (cited in Heilbroner, 1986: 236). Following a line of thought dating back to Saint-Simon, he argued that the machine and the engineer would eventually triumph.[31] Commons and his followers tended to disagree with this conclusion, concentrating on understanding the relationship of technology to institutions as instruments of collective action. Nevertheless, they more or less agreed that the neoclassical paradigm missed central features of the contemporary economy: the breakdown of competition and the growth of monopoly, the social construction of wants and of value, and the transformational consequences of technological innovation.

Contemporary institutional theory is represented in the work of John Kenneth Galbraith, Kenneth Gordon, and Walter Strassman, among others. Galbraith is certainly the most widely read, partly because he has written for a wider public and is skilled in peppering his prose with an acerbic wit that Veblen would appreciate.[32] Galbraith has also popularized a continental European variation on institutional theory, best exemplified in the work of Schumpeter.[33] His work extends Veblen's analysis of consumption by attacking the neoclassical assumption that wants registered in the marketplace embody consumer sovereignty. *The Affluent Society* (1958) was one of the early examinations of how the advertising industry influences the social

31. Veblen placed little faith in the ability of higher education to either understand or act on this analysis. He subtitled his book *The Higher Learning in America* 'A Study in Total Depravity.'

32. Consider this comment on the prominence of individual price theory in current textbook economics:

In the future the economist who is too exclusively concerned with what anciently has been called price theory will, indeed, shrink to a public stature not above that of Keynes's dentist. (Galbraith, 1987: 289)

33. Schumpeter's legacy is claimed by numerous schools of thought. He left both a large corpus and sufficient ambiguity to defy easy categorization. Institutionalists lay claim to his view that economic concentration and bureaucratization are logical consequences of capitalist development.

construction of wants. Perhaps more importantly, in *The New Industrial State* (1967), Galbraith returned to the traditional interests of institutional theory in technology and structure to examine what he called the corporate *technostructure*. This defined the bureaucratic combination of technical and organizational strength that enabled companies to leverage size and power to control formally free markets. Other contemporary institutionalists, like Kenneth Boulding, have concentrated on one particularly powerful embodiment of the technostructure – the growth of a military–industrial complex and on structural alternatives to concentrated economic power. However, they all tend to share a characteristic that separates them from both neoclassicists and the range of Marxian perspectives. Institutionalists view the maximization of power within bureaucratic structures as a more potent driving force, for better and for worse, than the maximization of profit.

Marxian Political Economy

There are many Marxian political economies directing criticisms at the neoclassical synthesis. On the understanding that no overview can be exhaustive, this section offers major exemplars that owe their inspiration and influence to different elements of the Marxian legacy. Political economists like Baran and Sweezy, Mandel, and Gunder Frank developed their critique explicitly from the Marx of *Capital*. Following a largely determinist epistemology, their work took up the labor theory of value, class exploitation and struggle, the concentration of economic power, imperialism and crisis. It attacked neoclassical economics for its failure to address social change in anything more than an incremental fashion. According to them, the transition to capitalism and, within it, to monopoly capitalism represents central shifts in the economy that the neoclassicists tend to ignore. It also took the neoclassicists to task for creating a narrow, technical discipline that did not permit the examination of the wider social totality encompassing the state and class struggle. Furthermore, traditional Marxists found a central place for both the technical and the moral analysis of irrationality (a market that 'allocates' more to sales than to education) and exploitation (absolute in the Third World and relative in the industrial world).

The contribution of those advancing Marxian political economy in the 1950s and 1960s is important in itself and all the more remarkable because its practitioners came under constant attack from those who would silence people perceived to be on the wrong side of the Cold War. When Baran died in 1964, he was considered virtually the only Marxian economist in American academia.[34] However, social upheavals brought about by the Viet Nam War, the civil rights movement, feminism, and student activism contributed to a resurgence of many neo-Marxian political economies. Just

---

34. Writing at the time of Baran's death, one friend noted that this 'almost completely closes the door of the professed open society whose establishment apparently cannot find it possible to tolerate in academia or elsewhere any other acknowledged Marxist theoretician' (Miller, 1992: 4).

four years after Baran's death, a group of American graduate students met following the tumultuous Democratic Party convention of 1968 to form the Union for Radical Political Economics (URPE). The Union grew throughout the 1970s and sustained about 1,000 members in the neo-conservative 1980s to become what one member (Miller, 1992: 4) calls 'the oldest and largest disciplinary group of leftists in the academy.'[35]

There is not a clear-cut boundary between those who carried on the tradition of deepening and extending the application of *Capital* to the contemporary political economy and those neo-Marxists who sought to rethink *Capital* and the entire Marxian corpus in fundamental ways. In the United States, the journal *Monthly Review* and its book series tend to reflect the former. Although open, for example, to analyses of patriarchy and the environmental crisis, it tends to concentrate on *class analysis* – the structure and operation of capital, the nature and consequences of class divisions, the labor process, class struggle – and on inquiries into *imperialism and dependency* – the globalization of capital, militarism, class oppression and struggle in the dependent world.

One bridge between this traditional Marxian perspective and neo-Marxian political economy is the work of the *world systems perspective*, a position that combines the materialist historical analysis of the *Annales* school of French historiography pioneered by Fernand Braudel (1975) and the global sociology of the American Immanuel Wallerstein (1979, 1991). Critics and supporters alike acknowledge the central place that materialist history and a comprehensive view of the social totality take in this perspective. These views are tightly interwoven: history is taken up with the development of the world economy comprised of an international class system, a core–periphery hierarchy, an interstate system, and a world market (Chase-Dunn, 1989). World systems theorists tend to accept essential elements of the Marxian analysis of capitalism, including generalized commodity production, private appropriation of the major means of production, and the wage system. Criticized for their early neglect of class analysis, they have come to incorporate and examine a multiplicity of central locations of class contradictions, including the workplace, the state, and in the core–periphery relationship. Although recent work suggests an interest in conceptions of culture, communication, and information technology (Wallerstein, 1991), the perspective gives considerably less attention to these than do other neo-Marxian streams of thought.

Neo-Marxian political economy sustained the critique of neoclassical economics, often in critical encounter with Marxian theory. *Analytical Marxism* (Cohen, 1978), which, in its integration of political philosophy, economics, sociology, and history, is true to the spirit of political economy,

---

35. This popularity has brought with it mainstream media attention which tends to accentuate the compromises radicals make in the face of a changing world. After all, *Business Week* asks: 'What do you do when you're caught on the wrong side of history?' (Mandel, 1991: 78).

attacks the neoclassical defense of capitalism not because it contributes to inequality, but principally because even when capitalism can reduce labor-time, it chooses, obsessively, to opt for growth. The neoclassicists are attacked at the heart of their values: not because their system denies a safety net, which it does, but because it fails to guarantee free time to pursue freedom.

Neo-Marxian political economy has also been influenced by work that accepts the benefits of the marketplace without accepting capitalism. Nove (1983) and Miller (1989) have pursued the vision of *market socialism* as a form of social organization that abolishes the distinction between capital and labor – a class of owners facing workers who give up control over the means of production – and replaces it with a market system based on worker-owned firms (see also Bowles and Gintis, 1986). This work has sparked consider-able debate within Marxian political economy (McNally, 1993). A leading Analytical Marxist (Cohen, 1991) accepts the view that inefficiency and anarchy are critiques of the market that can be adequately handled by neoclassical theorists. Nevertheless, Cohen maintains that it is even more clear that the market has historically been unjust in its results and demeaning in its motivational presuppositions.[36]

Debates have also addressed the significance of corporate structure and the labor process. The neoclassicists tend to view corporate concentration as an addressable aberration. Institutionalists see it as more deeply embedded in capitalism but correctable through state intervention (e.g. anti-trust enforce-ment and independent regulation). In its analysis of monopoly capitalism, Marxian political economy views concentration as a logical consequence of capitalist development and an indicator of crisis. The neo-Marxian literature is less certain about the meaning of economic concentration and debates about 'post-Fordism,' 'flexible specialization,' and modes of regulation reflect considerable ferment.

These debates respond to perceived major changes in the global political economy, including transformations in production technology, industrial organization, and world markets. One response to this perception is an approach, exemplified in the work of Piore and Sabel (1984), which argues that capitalism is undergoing a profound transformation from mass produc-tion to craft production or *flexible specialization*. This involves a transition to a production system based on the manufacture of a shifting and diverse range of products, customized to specific market segments, and produced with sophisticated ('intelligent') machinery and an adaptable, skilled labor force. Christopherson and Storper (1989) have opened a debate on the implications of flexible specialization for the media industries by maintain-

---

36. According to Cohen (1991: 18), the market demeans those of any social position:

The immediate motive to productive activity in a market society is usually some mixture of greed and fear, in proportions that vary with the details of a person's market position. In greed other people are seen as possible sources of enrichment, and in fear they are seen as threats.

ing that this process diminishes the power of the major Hollywood film companies (for a critique, see Aksoy and Robins, 1992).

Variations on the flexible specialization perspective aim to combine its acceptance of contingency while asserting the systemic nature of capitalism, something that tends to disappear in the flexible specialization literature. One of the more prominent is the *regulation* approach (Boyer, 1986; Lipietz, 1988), which examines successive developmental periods in capitalism that are based on combinations of regimes of accumulation and modes of regulation. Regimes of accumulation are stable and reproducible relationships between production and consumption that, though defined for the global economy, contain unique characteristics for each national economy depending on its history and position in the international division of labor. There are four chief regimes identified in the history of modern capitalism: extensive accumulation, Taylorism or intensive accumulation without mass consumption, Fordism or intensive accumulation with mass consumption, and an emerging post-Fordist regime whose definition is unclear. The mode of regulation is made up of the institutional and normative apparatus that secures accommodation at the individual and group level to the dominant regime. According to this view, capitalism is undergoing a transition from monopolistic to flexible regulation.[37]

Systemic alternatives to the regulation approach assert more explicitly a turn to a *post-Fordist* period. This includes work, heavily influenced by radical geography, that aims to integrate post-Fordist with *postmodernist* scholarship to produce an analysis of transformation in the global space of flows: material, informational, and cultural (Castells, 1989; Harvey, 1989; Thrift, 1987). Alternatives also encompass research steeped in the institutional literature of political science that argues for a transition from organized to *disorganized capitalism* (Lash and Urry, 1987). Finally, there is the work of Freeman and his colleagues (1984) which concentrates more explicitly on economic theory, particularly Schumpeter on technology and institutional change and Kondratiev on *long waves of innovation*. According to this work, we are entering a fifth wave of innovation, carried forward on new information and communication technologies, that contains some of the characteristics of post-Fordism (see also Hall and Preston, 1988).

The Marxian tradition continues to inspire a wide variety of positions in political economy. In spite of numerous differences, they are generally alike in their commitment to history, the social totality, moral philosophy, and praxis. The final two perspectives in this overview, feminist and environmental political economy, contain strong affinities to the Marxian tradition, but are sufficiently different from it to merit distinct treatment. Both grow out of arguably the most important social movements of our time. Both provide substantial critical assessments of the neoclassical school.

37. Bowles et al. (1990) provide an American version of regulation theory in their analysis of social structures of accumulation. Block (1990) offers a more explicitly sociological variant.

Feminist Political Economy

In *The Politics of Reproduction* (1981), Mary O'Brien makes the case for scholarship that matches the breadth of the feminist movement. In doing so, she suggests a familiar line of distinction from mainstream analysis:

> Feminist scholarship cannot engage in the disciplinary fragmentation which currently pervades social science, nor can it afford ahistorical indulgences of here and now empiricism. (p. 196)

She presses further, arguing for a 'unified social science, a unification which also transcends the partiality of political economy.' An admirable goal, Waring (1988) responds, but unreachable without the development of a political economy that, after over two thousand years, finally acknowledges the need for the science of 'household management' to address those chiefly responsible for household labor. In essence, the problem with political economy is not that it is economistic, but, on the contrary, that it is not sufficiently economic to account for the work of most of the world's women. Waring's thinking has contributed to the formulation of a distinct feminist economics, but, as she herself points out, this is certainly not a new critique. Towards the end of the nineteenth century, Charlotte Perkins Gilman (1966, orig. 1889: 235–236) attacked the neoclassical view, what she calls 'the infant science of political economy,' as 'naively masculine':

> They assume as unquestionable that 'the economic man' will never do anything unless he has to; will only do it to escape pain or attain pleasure; and will, inevitably, take all he can get and do all he can to outwit, overcome, and, if necessary destroy his antagonist.

Mainstream and, with few exceptions, heterodox economics have generally ignored these arguments.

Feminist economics springs from activism. For example, Marilyn Waring started in social movement work that propelled her into the New Zealand Parliament, where she had the responsibility of evaluating a proposal to adopt the United Nations System of National Accounts (UNSNA).[38] It did not take her long to recognize that since the System is based on market and exchange value principles, it 'supports and formalizes the invisibility of women's labor, environmental values, and the like' (1988: xx). For example, the UNSNA counts institutional childcare, the use of energy fuels purchased in the marketplace, the processing or manufacture of foodstuffs in a factory, tap-delivered water, and a meal taken at a restaurant or laundry. But when a Zambian woman does all of this by herself as housework, it does not count. The UN International Labor Organization counts the work of a man in the eight hour a day workforce as an 'active laborer' but not that of his wife who puts in eleven hours in and around home. She is simply 'helping the head of the household in his occupation' (Waring, 1988: 29–30).

Conceptual and methodological problems are typically cited as principal reasons for ignoring household labor. But, feminist critics point out, more

---

38. For his role in creating this accounting system, Sir Richard Stone won a Nobel Prize in 1974.

energy is spent on solving the conceptual and methodological problems posed by the underground economy of crime, the drug trade, and prostitution than on how to include housework and childrearing. In her 1934 work on household labor, Margaret Reid offered a guiding principle to account for it: any activity that results in a service or product that one can buy or hire someone else to do is an economic activity whether or not a financial transaction takes place. Nevertheless, economic practice and the policies of governments worldwide continue to reflect the view offered in this entry on 'The Labour Force – Definitions and Measurement' provided in the 1968 edition of the *International Encyclopedia of Social Science*:

> Housewives are excluded from what is measured as the working force because such work is outside the characteristic system of work organization or production. Moreover their inclusion in the working force would not help policy makers to solve the significant economic problems of American society.

There are a wide range of sometimes differing views about what constitutes a feminist economics. Feminist economics aims to uncover the ideological dimensions of economics that present a male-controlled system of work as characteristic and natural.[39] One of the central points of attack in recent years is directed against the concept of a 'family wage', which ostensibly accounts for women's labor through the wages of men because this payment ostensibly covers the production and reproduction of the family. Reform would therefore call for expanding the family wage, rather than accounting separately for household labor. Barrett and McIntosh (1980; see also Seccombe, 1974) began to mount the attack by showing that, beyond the fundamental denigration that this view holds for women in general because it accounted for their labor indirectly through that of their husbands, it failed to hold up on economic grounds. Women have always been underpaid members of the labor force in capitalism and men are paid the same whether or not they have families. Today, the notion of a family wage has changed because almost everyone recognizes that the majority of families cannot manage on one income. Nevertheless, the view persists that, although women should earn more than 'pin money,' their wages should be seen in the context of a family income. This is why feminist political economy aims not only to account for the value of formally 'unproductive labor,' but to situate all forms of women's work in a system of power that reduces it to less than the value of men's wage labor. Politically, a feminist perspective would dismantle a system of public policy organized to invest in

---

39. Again, feminist economics argues that although some heterodox positions acknowledge the patriarchal organization of work, little is made of this observation. For example, Engels (1972) examined the relationship of the sexual to the economic division of labor, but set it aside, along with other elements of the social construction of economic relationships, in part because he, along with Marx, chose to pursue a Newtonian quest for the laws of motion of capitalism.

and reward activities that correspond to patriarchal definitions of productive labor.[40]

Environmental Political Economy

Feminist political economy addresses irrationalities in a mode of analysis that literally cannot figure how to count the work of most of the world's women. Environmental political economy identifies the irrationalities in a paradigm that assigns economic growth to a massive oil spill because the clean up increases spending on labor and capital equipment. There is nothing new in the view that ecological matters are important to economic analysis. Classical political economy, particularly the work of Malthus and Ricardo, was especially concerned with the carrying capacity of land in the face of growing human populations.

Today, we are observing renewed interest in a wide variety of viewpoints. Neo-Malthusians have reintroduced population dynamics into economic analysis and warn of approaching the natural limits to growth. Mainstream environmentalists, not unlike mainstream economists, aim to save capitalism from its own self-destructive tendencies either by moderating marketplace excesses or by creating markets that would ostensibly make the value of the environment more transparent. A strong environmentalist position, reflected principally in 'Green economics,' attacks both neoclassical and Marxian traditions because:

> Both are dedicated to industrial growth, to the expansion of the means of production, to a materialist ethic as the best means of meeting people's needs, and to unimpeded technological development. (Porritt, 1984: 52)

Finally, there is socialist ecology, a perspective, more appropriately a loose coalition of perspectives, that aims to reach an accommodation with Marxian and feminist political economy. Given prominence in the journal *Capitalism Nature Socialism* (see also Benton, 1989), this position starts from a commitment to both socialism and environmentalism, claiming that only the collectivist and participatory decision-making characteristic of democratic socialism can produce a healthy ecology. Furthermore, it argues that building an alliance among socialists, feminists, and environmentalists calls for correcting the Marxian tendency to a form of reductionism 'which in arguing the dominance of social over natural factors literally spirits the biological out of existence altogether' (Soper in J. O'Connor, 1991: 10). Sensitive to charges of reinventing social Darwinism, with its own baggage of biological determinism, socialist ecology calls for uniting political economy with a new biology based on ideas prominent in ecology and geography that focus on material location and material exchanges within nature and between it and society. This is a biology of process that introduces structure principally to speak of the structure of processes, or, to use language popular in contemporary geography, the space of flows.

---

40. These would include so-called workfare programs that reward single-parent women who choose to enter the workforce rather than work at home as mothers.

Socialist ecology expands political economy's interest in the idea of the social totality to incorporate the natural totality of organic life. Concomitantly, it broadens political economy's concern for moral philosophy by expanding the moral vision beyond human life to all life processes. Nevertheless, it recognizes that humans are the sole moral actors and the only beings capable of reuniting conception and execution in forms of democratic praxis.

Economics and Political Economy

The wide range of conservative, institutional, Marxian, feminist, and environmentalist critiques of mainstream neoclassical economics describe a discipline in ferment, if not crisis. This contrasts sharply with the triumphant bearing economics brings to the tables of social science and public policy. This chapter concludes by bringing together the various critiques of economics described above and by defining the specific points of difference that help to specify the alternative in political economy.

The overview of perspectives suggests that there has always been intellectual struggle over what constitutes economics and political economy. These struggles have reflected and influenced the state of political economic forces at work in society. One clear example is the growth of Keynesian economics in response to the Great Depression and the impact of its policy proposals on the direction of Western economies in the post-World War II period. A similar case can be made for the growth of monetarism in the aftermath of 1970s stagflation. The overview concentrated on the substantive problems with economics, particularly with inadequacies in its social theory, that call for a political economic alternative.

Economics prefers to describe static models that are resolved in equilibrium. It is limited to taking up incremental change within one given set of institutional relations. Actual economic practice, like the wider social and physical world, is not so easily constrained. Equilibrium is only one outcome; incremental change is only one form; the given set of institutional relations is one among many possible sets.

Economics does not take into account many of the significant socioeconomic determinants of productivity, including corporate structure and ownership, education and training, and family background. It tends to ignore the relationship of power to wealth and thereby neglects the power of structures to control markets. Sounding like followers of Ptolemy rejecting the Copernican insistence that the earth revolves around the sun, economists persist in the view that market competition tames power. They maintain that monopoly and oligopoly are exceptional practices, requiring a few Ptolemaic adjustments to incorporate them within the competitive model. Critics insist that the growth of concentrated economic power has forced the model to the breaking point.

Economics assumes that information flows freely to consumers who register their wants in the marketplace. It contends that the distinction between needs, which are common to everyone, and wants, which are idiosyncratic and psychological, can be eliminated so that all demands can be treated as wants. According to its critics, the discipline provides at best a primitive theory of how wants are created, at worst a useless tautology that defines wants as whatever takes place in the market. Economics excludes the complex interactions among production, marketing, and desire. These structure the flows of information, diverting them into specific directions. It underestimates both the power of marketing to construct wants and the complexity of human desire. The latter is left unexplained (desire is what desire chooses) or, when it is taken up, it is reduced to rational choice. Scarce resources force painful, but rational choices. Bell (1981: 71) puts the critique of this view clearly in concluding that 'this hedonic calculus is itself the most narrowly culturally-bound interpretation of human behavior, ignoring the large areas of traditionalism on the one hand and moral reflection on the other.'[41] This is important because both tradition and morality, bound up with need and desire, create their own calculus which rests uncomfortably on and often simply refuses the constraints of a calculus of wants.

Economics tends to view markets as natural products of individual interaction rather than one among several sites of social activity. It therefore tends to exaggerate what Block (1990) calls the 'marketness' of society, or the extent to which transactions take place in clearly defined market circumstances. The economist's market model, in which people are motivated solely by instrumental considerations of price, best typified in commodity markets, is rarer than we are led to believe. According to Lane (1991: 6), who situates market behavior within a broad psychology of action, 'The market may or may not be a superior device for "the satisfaction of human wants," but for many wants it is not even the theatre of greatest importance.' Moreover, when attempting to explore non-market behavior, economics situates it within the realm of market imperfections or, at best, identifies non-market activity with organizational hierarchies that provide, again, less than optimal results. Such imperfections and sub-optimalities lead orthodox economics to reduce non-market or organizational activity by widening the scope of markets. This conforms to the economist's notion that social welfare is simply the product of individual welfare and that individuals are in the best position to determine their own welfare. As a consequence, economics neglects the fact that markets tend to underproduce public goods and overproduce negative externalities, like polluted rivers.

This view carries over into social relations so that markets are abstracted from class, race, and gender, as well as other forms of social division that provide the vast social system of supports for market activity, such as a flexible supply of low-wage labor, unpaid household labor, and a social

41. According to Bell (1976: 23), the absence of a sociological approach creates numerous problems for economics. Among these is the failure to see that what is called a market economy is more appropriately a 'bourgeois economy' defined as one whose ends of production are individual and not collective and whose motives for the acquisition of goods are wants and not needs.

system of desire that organizes the relationship of want to need in a form amenable to market transactions. Consequently, market success, the smooth operation of a market system, is viewed as social success, even if the consequences deepen class, race, and gender divisions or advance the general commodification of social life. Those who would oppose these consequences are seen to be acting out of irrational motives that are themselves best corrected by the discipline of the marketplace. The failure of the marketplace to do so reflects a reality that economics tends to reverse. As political economy has persistently maintained, it is not the pricing system that shapes behavior and gives direction to the economy, but the wider system of values and of power in which the economy is embedded.

The wide range of heterodox views tend to agree that the substantive weakness of economics can be traced to a fundamentally inadequate understanding of the social. Economics is based on the view that one can eliminate what cannot be rendered scientific without giving up what is fundamental to understanding the economy. Alternatives to the mainstream contend that it is a hollow science indeed that would try to comprehend economic behavior without understanding the complexities of power, social structure, organizational behavior, and cultural practice. Where economics begins with the individual, naturalized across time and space, political economy starts with the socially constituted individual, engaged in socially constituted production.

Some would take this substantive critique to a deeper level; as Bell (1981: 47) puts it, 'in short, there is the question not only of whether there is a crisis *in* economic theory but also a crisis *of* economic theory itself.' According to this view, there is a crisis in economic theory because economics has an inadequate theory of the social which rests on the view that society is the sum of individuals, that human action is predominantly rational, that information tends to flow freely, and that markets best disperse power, signal human wants, and register social needs. But in addition to these short-comings, there is the deeper crisis *of* economic theory that stems from its positivist and modernist roots.

McCloskey provides a detailed critique of economic positivism in *The Rhetoric of Economics* (1985). Trained as a conventional economist, he fears that many economists are 'crippled' by a set of epistemological and methodological demands more appropriate to a religious system:

> The faith consists of scientism, behaviorism, operationalism, positive economics, and other quantifying enthusiasms of the 1930s. In the way of crusading faiths, these doctrines have hardened into ceremony, and now support many nuns, bishops and cathedrals. (p. 4)

The positivist faith system includes numerous commandments: prediction and control is the point of science; only observable implications of a theory matter to its truth; observability is defined by objective, reproducible experiments; a theory is false if and only if an experimental implication proves false, etc. Moreover, positivism treasures objectivity, the separation of fact from value, and the language of mathematics. According to McCloskey, this regimen stultifies the minds of economists, who, as a result, 'are bored by history, disdainful of other social scientists, ignorant of their civilization, thoughtless in ethics and unreflective in method' (p. 7). This methodological approach is in keeping with the modernist view that is both ahistorical and given to seeing science as axiomatic. Furthermore, he contends that in their concern for the substantive shortcomings of mainstream thought, heterodox approaches within (Austrian economics) and outside (institutional and Marxian) the mainstream have neglected fundamental deficiencies in its epistemological and methodological assumptions.

A major consequence of what McCloskey considers the fetishistic commitment to a rule-bound methodology and a slavish devotion to observable fact is that much of the richness of description and explanation is lost. On these grounds Popper closed the door on psychoanalysis and Marxism. Would this view not also give the boot to subatomic physics, whose major constituents are not observable? Would not its enforcement have derailed Keynesian economics, whose 'insights were not formulated as statistical propositions until the early 1950s, fifteen years after the bulk of younger economists had become persuaded they were true.' McCloskey agrees with Dewey that this represents 'the triumph of the quest for certainty over the quest for wisdom' (p. 30), and with Polanyi, who concluded that the rigorous application of this methodology 'if rigorously practised would lead to voluntary imbecility' (p. 17).

Admittedly, McCloskey tends to get carried away with his own rhetoric. More importantly, his interest in derailing economic positivism by uncovering fundamental philosophical shortcomings leads him to neglect the vital connection between the discipline of economics and systems of political and economic power. Conventional economics does not succeed only because economists agree on the rules of research and discourse. Of arguably greater importance is the tendency for mainstream economics to serve power by providing information, advice, and policies to strengthen capitalism. Important as it is to see economic orthodoxy as a system of rhetoric, it is at least equally important to situate it within a system of power.

In addition, McCloskey attempts to replace positivism with a conversational or communicative epistemology. He argues explicitly that 'the rhetoric of conversation, not the logic of inquiry provides the standards of science' (p. 153). Specifically, this means that standards of thought are to be located not in relationship to some external reality but in the overlapping conversations that conform to the rules of civilized discourse. In this respect McCloskey admits to a faith, reminiscent of Kenneth Burke (1969a, 1969b), in the power of rhetoric to lead to conversations about truth. This is predicated on, to reverse Dewey's formulation, elevating the quest for wisdom over the quest for certainty.

The strength of the conversational approach is that it acknowledges the value of social communication in the intellectual process. Truth is constituted out of more than the application of empirical methods to observables.

According to this view, it is also the case that truth results when people speak to one another and thereby produce a conscious, critical social consensus. The principal drawback of the approach is that it tends to give precedence to conversation as a social practice ahead of all others. As a result, it directs attention away from the field of non-conversational social practices to discussions about them. In his understandable eagerness to replace the epistemological essentialism of positivist economics, McCloskey would replace it with a form of rhetorical, conversational, or communicative essentialism. Furthermore, McCloskey follows the pattern of Rorty and others who take a conversational approach by restricting the talk to the world of intellectuals. For them, as Ahmad (1992: 2) puts it, ' "theory" is now seen ... as a "conversation" among academic professionals.' As a result, theory, including Left literary criticism, tends to leave behind those many different voices, including that of labor, for whom and with whom the Left's conversation began.[42]

In fact, one useful way to describe this is through metaphors from the field of communication and information. A conversational approach draws from communication the models for shared, cooperative work. These differ from information seeking and those information processing activities that make up the work of mainstream economics. The chief problem with McCloskey's formulation is that it reacts against the extreme commitment to information processing that occupies much of neoclassical work by turning to an essentialist commitment to communication. Consequently, although he provides a useful critique of economics, McCloskey's epistemological alternative is also partial. Indeed, it is as partial as any approach which would take up only one side of the dialectic comprising communication and information. As Dallas Smythe suggests, communication and information are two sides of the same process, dialectically linked in mutual constitution. A complete epistemology also contains both communicative and informational processes, both conversation and observation. However fruitful the conversation, it cannot replace the experience of rigorous observation. Similarly, information seeking and processing approaches, which focus single-mindedly on gathering and organizing data, tend to ignore the social constitution of reality, including our assessments of it.

---

42. Ahmad (1992: 5) marvels at the gap between American radical political economy and literary theory:

> To the extent that American Marxism has itself produced major work in political economy in the quarter-century up to 1975 – as, for example, from the publishing house of *Monthly Review* – the striking feature of American literary theory of the last two decades is the paucity of influence from that tradition.

He suggests (p. 320) as evidence for 'the lack of any lived connection between the cultural radicalism of the American academy and any home-grown labour movement' the complete failure of cultural radicalism to take up the issues raised by Braverman (1974) about the degradation of work under monopoly capitalism. It is fair to add that cultural radicalism has been untouched by the mass of political economic analysis of labor that followed on Braverman's work.

Complete research is constituted by information processing and communication activities. It requires the application of tools that represent and explain social practices and conversations among speakers *and* the different ways of speaking about these practices. Research, including political economic research, is mutually constituted out of the dialectic of information and communication.

Conclusion

This chapter set the stage for the detailed examination of the political economy of communication by presenting political economy as a broad-based and variegated approach to social analysis. It started with a set of definitions that suggested how political economy developed out of practical questions of household and community management. The history of how to think about political economy is marked by differences over whether the discipline should encompass the full range of social activity or purchase a scientific warrant at the price of narrowing its scope to economic phenomena presented in the form of falsifiable propositions using mathematical discourse. The chapter highlighted two definitions which have been used in communication research. One concentrates on the social relations, particularly the power relations, governing the production, distribution, and exchange of resources; the other on broad problems of control and survival.

Following this presentation and assessment of definitions, the chapter took up central characteristics which mutually constitute a political economy approach. These include social change and history, the social totality, moral philosophy, and social praxis. Political economy has made use of these from its roots in the thinking of eighteenth-century Scottish Enlightenment philosophy. Their meaning has shifted as they have been tested against a changing world order and challenges from alternative intellectual currents.

The chapter proceeded to address the development of major schools of thought in political economy, suggesting how the discipline evolved initially out of the tensions between a classical approach established in the work of Adam Smith and his followers and challenges from organic conservative and Marxian perspectives. In the last half of the nineteenth century, this struggle grew into the differences between an increasingly orthodox economics that traded the broad characteristics of political economy for utilitarian principles and a positivist method and heterodox approaches that covered a range of conservative, institutional, and Marxian perspectives. These have levelled a wide-ranging critique at what has come to be called the neoclassical approach, a loose synthesis of characteristics that contains its own internal ferment. Recently, perspectives marked by the growth of feminism and environmentalism have joined the major heterodox approaches.

The chapter concluded by summarizing the major elements of the critique that political economy levels against conventional economics. This included a theoretical and political economic assessment of the substantive grounding that economics occupies. It also addressed the discipline's epistemological and methodological foundation. The latter took us into the domain of communication research where the dialectic of information–communication suggests an alternative for political economy. This would combine the analytic foundation of the information processing model with the rhetorical or conversational foundation of communication. The next chapter takes up the development of political economy in communication studies.

3

The Political Economy of Communication

This chapter takes up the specific ways that communication research has made use of the manifold political economy tradition. It starts with a note on the meaning of communication and proceeds to consider the social and intellectual context that gave rise to a political economy of communication. Drawing on the documentary record and on discussions with four generations of scholars, the chapter examines the development of the field and its central figures.

One of the major conclusions from this assessment is that the political economy tradition, spanning principally Marxian and institutional approaches, has produced a substantial research record, well out of proportion to the institutional support it has received. Although the number of people making use of the perspective has grown over the generations, they continue to work largely as isolated individuals. It is hard to speak of research centers, since collaborative work is largely the product of mutual interests among individuals generally in the face of, at best, tepid institutional support and often outright opposition.

The chapter focuses on what distinguishes the political economy of communication, its central areas of interest, differences of emphasis between Marxian and institutional dimensions of the tradition, and how the perspective diverges from mainstream economic approaches to communication. The chapter concludes by considering the direction of political economy research and previews subsequent chapters that constitute one view of central challenges confronting the field. This includes addressing the problems of epistemology, the processes of commodification, spatialization, and structuration, and the challenges posed by policy studies and cultural studies.

Communication

One of the challenges facing any discipline is the understandable tendency to *essentialism*, i.e., an inclination to reduce reality to the discipline's central constituents. In taking up the characteristics of political economy, Chapter 2 addressed the need to avoid reducing social reality to political economy by seeing the latter as one among several forces constituting social life. One can certainly comprehend the pressures toward essentialism. The theoretical power of Marx's *Capital*, Marshall's *Principles*, and Keynes' *General Theory* offer compelling grounds for reducing social reality to a political economic or even just an economic logic. Nevertheless, as Chapters 1 and 2 maintained, there are important epistemological, theoretical, and substantive grounds for resisting this tendency. Mindful of these, I view political economy as an entry point in social analysis, one important opening to the social field, but not one to which all approaches are reducible.

It is just as important to avoid essentialism of communication. Again, the pressures in this direction are strong, particularly in the current intellectual climate. These include calls for reconstituting epistemology by shifting from analytical methods that have guided science for three hundred years to a range of communication-based approaches centering on rhetoric and a set of standards to be found in rules of discourse (Burke, 1969a, 1969b; McCloskey, 1985; Rorty, 1979). From this point of view, the rhetoric of conversation, as much as the logic of inquiry, should provide the standards of science. Moreover, the development of cultural studies has given weight to organizing analysis around constituents of communication content such as text and discourse. As a result, one is inclined to reduce epistemology and social analysis to communication – both the act of knowing and the object of knowledge reduced to discourse, to reading texts. The analysis of McCloskey's work in Chapter 2 suggested that this approach provides powerful tools for unmasking the universalistic claims of, among other forms of knowledge, science and economics. Nevertheless, this power can overwhelm even the most skilled of users, who effectively universalize conversational epistemologies and discourse analysis. The approach taken here is to acknowledge both the strength of this perspective and the danger of creating a new essentialism that takes with it a reductionist view of communication.

Political economy offers another reason for taking care to avoid communication essentialism. Although there is understandable tension over this, political economists of communication have sought to *decenter the media* even as they have concentrated on investigating their economic, political, and other material constituents. Decentering the media means viewing systems of communication as integral to fundamental economic, political, social, and cultural processes in society. There are several ways to accomplish this, including, for example, starting from constituents of capitalism, such as capital accumulation, wage-labor, etc., and situating the media within the framework of production and reproduction set out by these constituents. According to this view, the media, in their economic, political, social and cultural dimensions, parallel education, the family, religion, and other foci of institutional activity. One distinguishes them because each is exceptional in some respects, but since all are mutually constituted in capitalism, one avoids exceptionalism, of the media, or of any other institutional activity. This is not the place to examine the debate over the difference between offering a distinguishing characteristic and exceptionalism. Rather, the point is that the political economy approach to communication places its subject within a wider social totality and therefore tends to be especially concerned about essentialism in communication research.

With these cautions in mind, it is useful to reflect briefly on the meaning of communication. My conception of communication follows from a general interest to place social process and social relations in the foreground of research. It therefore begins with the idea that *communication is a social process of exchange whose product is the mark or embodiment of a social relationship.*[1] Broadly speaking, communication and society are mutually constituted. The tendency within political economic and forms of institutional analysis is to concentrate on how communication is socially constructed, on the social forces that contribute to the formation of channels of communication, and on the range of messages transmitted through these channels. This has contributed to an important body of research on how business, the state, and other structural forces have influenced communication practices. Moreover, it has helped to situate these structures and practices within the wider realm of capitalism, trade, and the international division of labor. Nevertheless, it is also important to recognize that the social process does not end by structuring communication practices. Communication is not simply an effect of social practices, not just the cultural cartography for the social sciences – describing a cultural landscape that can only be explained by economics, political science, and sociology.[2] Because it has tended to practice this form of essentialism, social science in general and political economy specifically have neglected communication and some of the substantial changes that transformations in communication are helping to bring about in the world. It is therefore equally important to think about how communication practices construct society. Furthermore, this is *not* accomplished by arguing that the political economic is the realm of structure, institution, and material activity while communication occupies culture, meaning, and subjectivity. Both political economy and communication are mutually constituted out of social and cultural practices. Both refer to processes of exchange which differ, but which are also multiply determined by shared social and cultural practices.

The Development of a Political Economy of Communication

The remainder of this chapter takes up the body of research in the political economy of communication. It starts by examining some of the social influences that propelled the development of this tradition. There is no simple way to examine the wider influences on a field that spans at least four generations, with researchers scattered around the world, some of whom do

---

1. This appears to get at what Smythe meant when he referred to the dialectical relationship between communication and information.

2. My argument draws on the work of Massey (1992), who has applied this line of thought to space and geography.

not explicitly identify with the political economy approach.[3] Nevertheless, it is useful to begin with those broad social forces that contributed to the development of a political economy approach and take up specific influences ✓ on individuals when we move into a more detailed treatment.

One of the chief influences on the development of a political economy approach was the transformation of the press, electronic media, and tele-communication from modest, often family-owned enterprises, into major businesses of the twentieth-century industrial order. The process of change has not been an inevitable one, nor necessarily linear. Some of the major media companies, such as the New York Times Corporation, remain in family hands. Nevertheless, the development of industrial and corporate management practices familiar to most modern businesses, including the application of production, marketing, finance, and accounting processes and techniques, has extended to the full range of media businesses. Some of the early political economy work took up the task of describing the structure and practices of large communication enterprises and addressed concerns about the use of power in such large enterprises. Danielian's (1939) research on the largest such company, AT&T, exemplifies this tendency, as did Smythe's (1957) on the structure of the American media industry. This tradition has continued in later generations of research (Herman and Chomsky, 1988), although this work has also moved on to reflect the tendency to corporate integration across media industry divisions and across the range of manufacturing and, even more so, service industry lines (Mattelart, 1991; Schiller, 1973, 1984). Much of this work involved 'catching up' with historical patterns that occupied classical political economy, such as the transition to capitalism and the creation of wage-labor, and with those that led Marxian political economy, such as, for example, the transition to monopoly capitalism and the creation of a labor process that separates conception from execution. The catch-up results from the persist- ✓ ence of craft traditions in the media industry, problems with commodifying these industries (in part owing to the recalcitrance of the media commodity and the resistance from craft workers), and the relatively recent introduction of technological innovation to advance the application of market practices. Today, it is interesting to observe differences in views on corporate media structure and process played out against the background of the debate on post-Fordism and postmodernism. For example, some (Christopherson and Storper, 1989) suggest that post-Fordism means the deconcentration of media structures and a greater flexibility in structure and diversity in content.

3. One explicit example of the generational connections starts with Dallas Smythe, who taught the political economy of communication at the University of Illinois. One of his students, Thomas Guback, took a position at the Institute for Communication Research in Illinois, where he supervised Janet Wasko's thesis on the political economy of film. Wasko went on to a position at the University of Oregon, where she worked with then graduate student Jack Banks, who has now begun a research and teaching career at the University of Hartford.

Others disagree (Aksoy and Robins, 1992), contending that post-Fordist arguments miss a deeper level of concentration in global media conglomerates which are now powerful enough to control circuits of accumulation without needing to retain the risk of owning all structures along these circuits.

The political economy approach generally began with the [production] side of the communication process by examining the growth of the business and its links to the wider political economy. Nevertheless, the development of a mass consumption economy impelled political economists to take up the complete process of realizing value, including the social relations and organization of consumption. They addressed consumption by examining its growth as a *structural* response to the economic crisis of overproduction and as a *social* response to the political crisis, each arising from the mass organization of the working class in North America and Europe (Ewen, 1976). The growth of a mass circulation press, the spread of national telecommunication systems, and, more importantly, the development of radio and television broadcasting were central elements in the mix that made up specific forms of mass consumption. But this was a mixed blessing for the political economy approach. The intimate connection between mass consumption and mass communication, linked from the start, meant that a political economy of communication would not have to catch up with an earlier process, but would instead be centrally placed to examine one of the critical developments of the twentieth century. On the other hand, mass consumption and mass communication brought with them a conceptual apparatus that differed in some fundamental ways from the range of political economy traditions. Political economy was ill prepared to address activities organized around the household rather than business and equally challenged by the use of a new language that spoke of audiences who participate in the accumulation process by listening, reading, and viewing, as well as by shopping.[4] These issues are now compounded by the debate over post-Fordism and postmodernism because these approaches contain conflicting views about the significance of tendencies to flexible and specialized consumption (Harvey, 1989). One of the major issues confronting political economic research today is the significance of the tendency to organize production around specific rather than mass markets. Applied to consumption, the post-Fordist idea of flexible specialization suggests a substantial

---

4. Once again, consider the irony of a discipline founded to examine household labor, struggling over two millennia later with new processes of accumulation organized around the household as a fundamental site of productive activity. Is this just consumption? Production and consumption? Additionally, the reorganization of the basic circuit of economic activity brought with it a painful effort to literally come to 'terms.' What are the fundamental units of analysis: classes? gendered households? audiences? Debates within political economy such as that inspired by Smythe's (1977) work on the 'audience commodity' are partly a result of this understandably difficult process.

restructuring directed at the continuous production of specialized or custom-ized products for particular markets. This issue is particularly important for communication studies because communication is implicated in every part of this transformed circuit. Communication systems are central to custom-izing production lines, central to marketing these lines to customers, and central to the rapid response times necessary to translate actual purchases into new production decisions. Finally, the proliferation of channel capacity for communication and information transactions suggests that specialized and customized media products for increasingly fragmented audiences are one concrete consequence of the process. These developments lead contem-porary political economy to reflect on their pervasiveness (do they constitute another dimension of a new epochal transformation?) and their wider significance (what are the implications for power relations in the global political economy?).

Political economy studies also grew in response to the expansion of the state as a producer, distributor, consumer, and regulator of communication. Much of this activity arose from the pressures to manage the conflicting demands of growing domestic and international business. The results can be found in the expansion of government intelligence, information gathering, propaganda, broadcasting, and telecommunication systems. In particular, the relationship between the military and the media, telecommunication, and computers has occupied several generations of political economists (Mosco, 1989a; Roach, 1993a; Schiller, 1969/1992; Smythe in Guback, Chapters 7–9, 1993). In addition, the state's communication sector has grown with systems of regulation and policy-making that mediate business rivalries, respond to struggles emanating from class, gender, race, and social move-ment pressures, and coordinate long-range planning among leading fractions of capital. Political economy has taken up the role of the state in the construction of national telecommunication, broadcasting, and information systems and assessed the consequences of a range of public and market-based approaches (Garnham, 1990; D. Schiller, 1982; Smythe, 1957). Early in the development of a political economy approach to communication, the chief preoccupation was with supporting social movements for public access and control over these systems. The global pressures to privatization then led political economy to address the instrumental and structural roots of the process. More recently, particularly in response to the tendency of privatiza-tion to create disparities in access and changes in content that reflect largely market pressures, political economy has revived interest in exploring a wide range of alternative forms of the public sphere, civil society, and community communication (Murdock, 1990a, 1990b).

The growth of business and the state contributed to global upheavals as both projected their power from the Western core nations into the rest of the world. The result was a body of political economic research that sparked a widespread debate on the issue of media imperialism. Although scholars based in the developed world contributed extensively, this is an area also marked by important work from Latin America, Asia, and Africa.[5] Much of this research grew out of the global movement for decolonization that accelerated at the end of World War II. One manifestation of this was the Non-Aligned Movement, an organization of nations that sought to develop policies independent of Cold War considerations. At their own conferences and before the United Nations, the Non-Aligned Movement pressed for a New International Economic Order to rectify global imbalances in the distribution of wealth. On the heels of this was the call for a New World Information and Communication Order (NWICO), which aimed to address imbalances in the political economy of the media and information systems. The NWICO brought together most of the scholars active in the political economy of communication around the world who produced basic research (Nordenstreng and Varis, 1974), policy analyses (Somavia, 1979, 1981), and assessments of the movement itself, including how Western media worked to undermine it (Preston et al., 1989). This wide-ranging effort to integrate academic research with political activity exemplified the commitment to Gramsci's ideal of the organic intellectual. Neo-conservative governments of the 1980s, with the near complete support of the media, slammed the door on all but a few token efforts to implement the United Nations' own report on the subject (UNESCO, 1979).[6] Nevertheless, political economists continue to press for the NWICO's goals, principally through the MacBride Roundtable, an organization committed to carrying on the work of decolonizing the media and documenting the continued need for a new world order in communication and information (Roach, 1993a; Traber and Nordenstreng, 1992).

Although not an exhaustive treatment, these are the general societal forces that motivated the development of a political economy approach. In addition, there are important intellectual currents that also contributed. Every generation of political economists has been influenced by the perceived need to create alternatives to orthodox economics and, following from this, to develop media policies based on these alternatives. For the reasons discussed in Chapter 2, political economists reject as inadequate the neoclassical synthesis. They argue that the approach is particularly unsuited to the

5. This research is taken up in greater detail in the discussion of the growth in political economy across different regions. Among the representative work is that of Schiller on Western imperialism (1969, 1993); Atwood and McAnany (1986), Beltrán and Fox de Cardona (1980), Dorfman and Mattelart (1975), Freire (1974) on Latin America; Smythe (1981) on Canada; Ibrahim (1981) on Africa; and Tran van Dinh (1987) on Asia. For collections containing the work of international scholars see Mowlana et al. (1992), Nordenstreng and Schiller (1979, 1993) and Sussman and Lent (1991).

6. One sign of just how powerful the reaction against popular national sovereignty has become is the appearance of work in the mainstream elite press supportive of a return to colonialism. In one example, Paul Johnson (1993), author of the widely read history *Modern Times*, writes in *The New York Times* that 'Colonialism's Back – and Not a Moment Too Soon: Let's face it – Some Countries are just not fit to govern themselves.' He calls on the 'civilized world' to return to the colonial trusteeship system that would seize control of countries it deems unfit to govern themselves.

analysis of the communication industry because most of its fundamental characteristics occupy the area that neoclassical economics reserves for exceptional cases. Throughout most of this century, the media business has been highly concentrated with one or a few large firms controlling markets for production and distribution. Moreover, outside the United States, mass media and telecommunication networks have been organized in government-owned monopolies. Even in the United States, where only the postal service remained in government hands, the telecommunication and broadcasting networks were placed under government regulation from their early years. Furthermore, there was considerable ambiguity about the nature of what exactly was produced by these industries. Although a radio news broadcast delivered through commercial sponsorship appeared to be a standard commodity, it retained certain unique characteristics (e.g. it was not used up in consumption) that lent ambiguity to its treatment under orthodox economic approaches. Moreover, while it is the case that Smythe sparked an intellectual debate about the nature of the audience commodity, the industry, as Smythe himself recognized, understood quite clearly that it operated both in the market for programming and in the market for audiences. The point is that there was enough uncertainty about the nature of the primary commodity in the communication industry to lead one to consider alternatives to standard economic approaches. In sum, while many critics argued that much of the Western economy does not easily fit the models that neoclassical economics provides, this lack of fit appeared to be particularly pronounced in the communication industry. The drive to deregulate and privatize this sector diminishes some of the arguments about its distinctiveness. Nevertheless, there is enough uncertainty about these processes to approach such a conclusion with caution.

[handwritten marginal note: acquiesent to Smythe's partial success]

Following on this interest in alternatives to mainstream thought, over the generations political economy has constructed alternatives to orthodox communication policy. For example, Dallas Smythe, one of the founding figures in the field, pursued a career that combined academic analysis, policy research, and activism. He began it in 1937 as an economic policy analyst with the U.S. Department of Agriculture and followed this with a stint at the Department of Labor, where he worked with trade unions representing newspapers, postal, and telegraph industry workers. In 1943 he was appointed the first chief economist at the Federal Communications Commission, where he addressed the many broadcasting and telecommunication issues that had been put off during the war. After entering an academic career, Smythe's policy work continued to support public interest concerns, including support for public broadcasting, for public control over the communication satellite network, for the development of a New World Information and Communication Order, and the demilitarization of global communication systems. Similarly, a younger generation of political economists, led by Herbert Schiller and Kaarle Nordenstreng, provided assistance on the development of national communication policies in Latin America, Asia, and Africa. Thomas Guback, a student of Smythe's, applied political economy to the global film industry and carried out policy research on the industry during the heyday of UNESCO's interest in democratic communication. William Melody, a close colleague of Smythe's, trained in institutional political economy, has been active in the critique of policies inspired by neoclassical economics across North America and for major policy centers in the United Kingdom and Australia. His student Robin Mansell has carried on this work for policy centers in France and the United Kingdom. Nicholas Garnham has been a trade union activist in the British communication industry and more recently has joined with Graham Murdock, Peter Golding, Kevin Robins, and other British political economists who have attacked the deregulation and privatization of that country's broadcasting and telecommunication systems. One can find similar policy applications of the political economy perspective in the work of Oscar Gandy, Dan Schiller, Janet Wasko, Manjunath Pendakur, Gerald Sussman, and myself, among others in the United States and Canada. A newer generation including Jack Banks, Ronald Bettig, Eileen Mahoney, Robert McChesney, Colleen Roach, and Kevin Wilson have combined a strong commitment to political economic analysis with policy research and activism. Furthermore, Armand Mattelart earned a reputation as a leading scholar and policy activist on communication issues confronting the Third World and in the 1980s turned his attention to the communication policy ferment in Europe. This is simply a sampling of examples that are taken up in the more detailed analysis of political economic work below. The point is that four generations or so of people whose work has been guided by a range of political economic perspectives have used that work to engage the major policy issues in communication.

In addition to this consistent critique of orthodox economics and policy research, the development of a political economy approach responded to intellectual concerns that run deeper. The first generations of political economists tended to react against the wider *behaviorist* paradigm within which orthodox economics, as well as political science, psychology, sociology, et al., were situated.[7] Although behaviorism is still a concern for contemporary political economists, they have a greater tendency to build an approach in critical response to varieties of cultural studies.

The political economy of communication started against the intellectual backdrop of a multidisciplinary movement to apply the epistemology and

---

7. This point was brought home to me in an interview with Dallas Smythe (December 1991). Smythe was taken aback by a question regarding the tension between political economic and culturalist approaches to communication. Referring to the major intellectual divides that occupied his thinking, beginning with his graduate training in the 1920s, he saw political economic and cultural analysis as close partners in the critique of behaviorism. In his view, it was the latter that presumed to limit research to positivist methods of empirical observation. Political economic and culturalist approaches opened research to questions of meaning, dialectics, and critique. This view of behaviorism as the principal intellectual adversary for early political economy was confirmed in interviews with Herbert Schiller (January 1992) and James Halloran (April 1992).

method of the physical sciences to the social sciences. This included the goal of using empirical observation to build systems of law-like theories whose constituents were falsifiable propositions. Propositions would be continually tested against additional empirical evidence in an ongoing process of refinement. In essence, the scientific method that appeared to serve the physical sciences so well would realize the goal of creating a science of the social (Nagel, 1957).[8] Applied to the social sciences, this positivist approach to investigation was commonly known as *behaviorism*. Its exemplars can be counted across psychology (the conditioning approaches of Pavlov and Skinner), sociology (the analysis of group behavior in Homans), and political science (the public opinion work of Key). Behaviorism made its way into communication studies through several routes, prominent among them the work of Lazarsfeld and Cantril, who sought to create a social science of mass communication by examining behavioral responses to mediated messages. The point here is not to retell the history of behavioral communication research, a story that has received some interesting treatments (Buxton, 1994; Gitlin, 1979; Morrison, 1978). Rather, it is to situate the first generations of political economy opposite their principal intellectual adversary.

Early work in the political economy of communication never opposed empirical investigation.[9] Rather, it set itself apart from *empiricism* or the reduction of intellectual activity to the production of parsimonious and falsifiable statements about observed behavior. The goal was to replace this with a broad analysis based on the dialectical relationship (what I call the mutual constitution) between theory and observed behavior. Moreover, political economy aimed to situate theory about mass mediated activity within the wider framework of political economic, particularly Marxian, theory. Political economy also argued for a critical approach that examines empirical findings in the light of a critical purpose, such as the need to advance democratic communication by building public television systems. Empirical results neither arose out of a black box nor spoke to one. They grew out of a dialectical relationship with theoretical formulations and spoke to a broadly defined political interest. Finally, political economy identified the researcher as an active participant in the social process under investigation. Denying the possibility of a 'free-floating intellectual,' political economy sought to account for the relationship of the researcher to the research subject. In this respect, as Smythe has noted (interview, December 1991), this placed political economy within the range of the hermeneutic approach

8. I use the word 'appeared' because an extensive body of research has called into question just how faithfully the physical sciences have lived up to the strictures of the scientific method. (Feyerabend, 1988; Lakatos, 1978; Latour, 1987).

9. Dallas Smythe carried out one of the first content analyses of commercial television in order to make the case for a public network. This work caught the eye of *Time* magazine, which wrote a story on it. He was also involved in an attempt to secure Ford Foundation funding for a content analysis of the popular television program *The Mickey Mouse Club* (interview December 1991).

Geertz ✓

that was more fully developed in anthropology and, specifically, in the critical cultural studies work of the Frankfurt School. In essence, the first generation or two of the political economy of communication, making allowances for variation within specific work, was *allied* with cultural approaches against what they both perceived to be the essentialist account proffered by behaviorism.

The third and fourth generations of political economy continue to distinguish themselves from behaviorism. However, what was once an affinity with culturalist approaches against positivist accounts has turned adversarial. Indeed, current work in communication studies appears to indicate a major divide between two schools of thought once allied against the intellectual orthodoxy ('Colloquy,' 1995). Chapter 7 takes up this division in some detail. Nevertheless, it is useful to refer to it here because one way to comprehend current developments in political economic research is by setting it within the context of a shift from stressing differences with behaviorism, which it still addresses, to its differences with cultural studies.

✓ For contemporary political economists like Graham Murdock the cultural studies project started out as a vital effort to redefine the cultural by discarding traditional notions that equate culture with elite practices embodying a universal aesthetic. Rather, culture was to be associated with popular practices that follow a range of aesthetic and social principles, including opposition to established cultural and social practices (Murdock, 1989a, 1989b; interview, April 1992). Murdock and others take issue with some of the tendencies in contemporary cultural studies, an approach occupying an intellectual terrain that is at the complete opposite pole from behaviorism. These include giving near essentialist warrant to the subjective, the local, and the particular; privileging speech, conceptual or naming activities over all other forms; and resisting the development of explanatory schemes that unify a range of activities. Political economists recognize that there are many varieties of cultural studies with greater or lesser attention to these tendencies. Nevertheless, recalling the behaviorist effort to write a metanarrative of positivist social science, political economists raise concerns about the metanarrative, however ironic in light of its professed opposition to forms of totalizing thought, contained within the culturalist project. According to Garnham (1990: 1–2), this tendency grew out of literary and film studies, extending into the range of structuralist, post-structuralist and postmodern thought. In the course of its development, he concludes:

> It took with it the bacillus of romanticism and its longing to escape the determining material and social constraints of human life, from what is seen as the alienation of human essence, into a world of unanchored, non-referential signification and the free play of desire.

Strong language is not limited to one side of the divide. Proponents of a cultural studies view have tended to reject political economic approaches as economistic, totalizing, or simply derivative of the outmoded Marxism of *Capital* (Baudrillard, 1975). Moreover, the heat is not limited to communication and cultural studies. Just about every discipline has been occupied with concerns raised on either side.[10] In addition to engagement at the level of mutual critique, there have been some efforts to reach across the divide to comprehend the other perspective on its own terms (McIntyre, 1992; Resnick and Wolff, 1987). One can observe this in some of the communication scholarship carried out from the cultural studies perspective (Berland, 1992; Hall, 1993). Recent work in the political economy of communication has also taken an interest in exploring continuities between the perspectives (Mattelart and Mattelart, 1992; Murdock, 1989a, 1989b).

This brief review suggests that the political economy of communication defines itself in part against a range of intellectual challenges. The challenge of neoclassical economics and the policy perspectives that flow from it have historically embodied the most significant intellectual opposition and continue to do so. But the alternative that political economy has offered extends beyond the theoretical viewpoint and substantive position of the economic and policy canons to the wider behaviorist and positivist positions that provide orthodox social science with its philosophical grounding. The political economy of communication began by setting itself apart from this grounding. For contemporary political economy research, cultural studies has replaced behaviorism as a major intellectual reference point.[11] These shifting currents reflect a dynamic arena where perspectives grow and decline in the face of a changing global political economy and from alternative intellectual currents. One of the primary tasks confronting the political economy perspective is to put the range of challenges in perspective by acknowledging its own strong tradition even as it renews its philosophical roots.

The remainder of this chapter is taken up with an overview of the research tradition in the political economy of communication. It deepens and extends my 1989 overview of critical research in North America (Mosco, 1989a). Recognizing that there is no ideal way to approach this task, I settled on an assessment organized by region. The alternative, a division based on thematic content, would likely do a better job of keeping the focus on substantive matters, but runs the risk of missing regional distinctions that

10. Consider this analysis of the linguistic turn in history. After acknowledging that 'this is not an entirely pernicious development,' social historian Bryan Palmer (1990: 5) concludes:

> What I question, what I refuse, what I mark out as my own differentiation from the linguistic turn, is all that is lost in the tendency to reify language, objectifying it as unmediated discourse, placing it beyond social, economic, and political relations, and in the process displacing essential structures and formations to the historical sidelines.

11. The historical development of the political economy of communication contains both generations of scholars and generations of research. The two correspond at times, but at times they do not. It is therefore important to distinguish the two, particularly when the lack of correspondence makes a significant historical difference. For example, Herbert Schiller belongs to the first two generations of political economists in communication studies. Yet his recent work (1993) takes up the challenge of cultural studies, giving evidence of his ability to renew his own work in the face of a shifting intellectual landscape.

have important consequences for the development of the field.[12] To counter the tendency to view regions as singular compartments, I address the wide degree of interaction across regions including the genuine internationalization of research organized in professional associations and government agencies. Moreover it is essential to state from the start that generational influences do not respect regional boundaries. For example, several younger scholars in North America point to the influence of European and Third World political economy on their work.

This discussion is also mindful of Mills' (1959: 6) admonition that the 'sociological imagination' required the sensitivity 'to grasp history and biography and the relations between the two within society.' To that end the overview draws on interviews and discussions with major figures in the political economy of communication to situate their lives, their work, and the field within the wider historical context in which four generations of scholars have worked. There is another reason to accentuate individuals. The political economy approach has developed without the benefit of institutional centers that might focus the attention of more than one or two scholars. As a rule, researchers have carried out their work as individuals who rely on meetings and conferences for face-to-face exchanges.[13]

North America

The discussion of the political economy approach in North America begins with Dallas Smythe and Herbert Schiller, the two people who arguably have exerted the most significant influence on the field in this region and whose influence has been felt worldwide.[14]

Dallas Smythe began the study of the political economy of communication in the United States. He taught the first course in the field and several

12. For example, Murdock (1978) made the point in his response to Smythe's 'Communication: Blindspot of Western Marxism' that the practice of marketing audience labor is more applicable to North America, where commercial broadcasting is the dominant form. However one responds to the exchange, it reveals persistent regional differences in the mutual constitution of theory and the organization of communication practices. Nevertheless, the spread of the American commercial model may be eroding these differences. It is interesting to observe that in their recent formulation Golding and Murdock (1991: 20) refer to the 'audience's position as a commodity.'

13. There were some exceptions. These include the brief period that brought together Smythe, Wasko, Dan Schiller, and me to Temple University, during which several of our major works were produced (Mosco, 1982; Mosco and Wasko, 1983; D. Schiller, 1982; Smythe, 1981; Wasko, 1982). It was also during this time, particularly under Wasko's leadership, that the Union for Democratic Communication (UDC), an organization of critical scholars and media activists and practitioners, was created. An earlier period gathered mainly around Thomas Guback at the University of Illinois a group of graduate students who would go on to work in political economy and critical cultural studies. The group included Wasko, Eileen Meehan, Jennifer Slack, and Fred Fejes, who founded the newsletter *Communication Perspectives*, a precursor to the UDC.

14. Unless otherwise stated, material for this section comes from interviews conducted with Smythe (December 1991) and Schiller (January 1992).

of his junior colleagues and students have gone on to do prominent work. Like others who work in political economy, Smythe was influenced substantially by engagement with central political and social forces and issues. For him, these were principally the Great Depression and the rise of fascism in the 1930s. Specifically, Smythe cites three turning points that helped to transform him from someone who cast a 1928 vote for the successful Republican presidential candidate Herbert Hoover into a person open to radical ideas and political action. These include his observation of clashes between national guard troops and striking dockworkers, interviews with impoverished migrant farm workers that formed the basis of a graduate school project on agricultural extension programs, and his contact with people who had supported and fought with the anti-fascist forces during the Spanish Civil War.[15] He concludes that his Marxism grew first from the practical experience of class struggle and only later from intellectual encounters.

Trained as an economist at the University of California, Berkeley, Smythe benefited from the wider range of viewpoints then admissible in the economic canon. Though the neoclassical perspective was achieving some closure by the 1930s, challenges from institutional and Marxian sources, sustained by horrendous economic conditions, were then important components of graduate education. Specifically, Smythe read economic history and theory from people like M.M. Knight who accepted institutionalists such as Veblen and American interpreters of Marx into the economic corpus. Moreover, Smythe placed substantial emphasis on his immersion in government reports and documents that provided concrete analyses of political economic conditions. These included extensive government hearings on the economic collapse of the 1890s and the transportation literature that formed the basis of his doctoral thesis.

If the Great Depression helped to shape Smythe's thinking, the New Deal response influenced the course of his career. After being awarded his Ph.D. in 1937, Smythe went to work for the federal Department of Agriculture and later the Department of Labor, where his associations with politically progressive civil servants and trade unionists strengthened his critical thinking. Smythe's work on the media began with his job at the Department of Labor, where part of his responsibility was tracking the media and telecommunication industries, their labor practices, and trade unions. He observed first-hand the struggles between supporters of radical and company unions battling for support of workers at AT&T and Western Union. This work also brought him into close contact with the details of a changing labor process in the communication industry as skilled radio and telephone operators began to feel the effects of new technologies and deskilling.

Smythe left the Department of Labor in 1943 to become the first economist to work at the Federal Communications Commission (FCC). He

---

15. His support for the anti-Franco side would place him among those the U.S. government called 'premature anti-fascist,' a label that would ill serve Smythe in the 1950s.

arrived at the Commission to address issues of labor relations and to provide advice on rate hearings. He also participated in one of the busiest periods of spectrum allocation as the agency took up the backlog of radio license requests, the issue of FM allocations, and, arguably the most important, channel allocation for television. Smythe's future work was indelibly marked by the lessons he learned from the mobilization of commercial interests to defend private control over radio and, later, television.[16]

Smythe left the FCC in 1948 to begin an academic career at the University of Illinois where Wilbur Schramm had started the Institute for Communication Research. Opening the first Ph.D. program in communication studies, the Institute became a crossroads for several people who would leave their mark on communication studies. These include the communication psychologist Charles Osgood and, later on, George Gerbner, for a brief time Theodor Adorno, and Herbert Schiller. In the Cold War climate and with communication research so sensitive to the increasingly powerful mass media, Smythe began cautiously with a course on the economics of communication before developing the first course specifically about the political economy of communication. This period is also marked by Smythe's research on the need for public broadcasting, publication of the first political economy of the electronic media (1957), and the beginnings of his work on the audience commodity.[17]

McCarthyism did not end with the Senator's demise and, as university life in America became more repressive, Smythe decided to return to his native Saskatchewan, Canada, where he established a communication program at the University of Regina. Smythe had met Herbert Schiller at Illinois, and when he left Schiller was brought into the Institute from economics to teach the political economy of communication. Smythe's principal student, Thomas Guback, completed his dissertation on the political economy of the international film industry. Guback would eventually take a position at Illinois and teach the political economy of communication. Smythe spent a decade at Regina, where, with William Livant, he further developed the idea that the audience was the principal commodity in the mass media. In 1974 Smythe joined the faculty at Simon Fraser University in British Columbia, where he worked with the institutional political economist William Melody. Here, Smythe concentrated on telecommunication policy (the AT&T anti-trust case was a central concern), on the audience commodity paper, and on his major academic work, *Dependency Road* (1981), a dialectical analysis of monopoly capital anchored in the case of Canadian dependency. During this

16. Under the influence of pro-market Commissioners, the FCC voted to protect the largest AM radio broadcasters (whose 'clear channel' stations could cover half of the United States in nighttime hours) against the challenges from FM and public radio advocates. The Commission also limited its allocation of the first television channels to commercial interests, most of which were also powers in the radio industry.

17. Smythe dates the first formal presentation of the idea at a 1951 talk to a meeting of the Consumers' Union Institute at Vassar College.

time he travelled widely, carrying out research on the reforms Salvador Allende's Popular Unity government was bringing about in Chile, and on communication practices and policies in China, Japan, the United Kingdom, and Eastern Europe. At Simon Fraser, his work in political economy and public policy influenced a number of the leading people in the field. In addition to Melody, these included Robert Babe, Manjunath Pendakur, William Leiss, Sut Jhally, Robin Mansell, and Rohan Samarajiwa.

Smythe left Simon Fraser in 1980 to take a position at Temple University, where, for a short time, he joined Janet Wasko, who had been a student of Guback's at Illinois, Dan Schiller, and myself. Three students of this program, Eileen Mahoney, Sylvia Sholar, and Rosalind Bresnehan, have gone on to work in the political economy of communication. Smythe continued in a series of visiting appointments, eventually returning to British Columbia where he died in 1992. A festschrift volume (Wasko et al., 1993) gives some evidence of his impact on four generations of political economists around the world.

Like Smythe, Herbert Schiller attributes his political and intellectual development to the experience of transformation in the American and global political economies. For Schiller, about a half generation removed from Smythe, this meant entering his high school and university years during the Great Depression and serving in World War II. He attended the City College of New York, which provided a free education to the city's working class in what most accounts conclude was a highly politicized atmosphere. Although his interests ran to the literary, he chose to study economics, for him 'a Depression induced choice,' more likely to lead to a job. As with many people living through this economic cataclysm, Schiller was left with an intense sense that something was fundamentally wrong with the Western political economy.

The other substantial formative influence was his service in the war and his work for the U.S. military government in Germany immediately thereafter. The latter was particularly important because it gave him the opportunity to observe first-hand the imposed transformation of a nation's political economy compressed into a very short period.[18] Among intellectual influences, Schiller emphasizes the research carried out by U.S. government bodies in the 1930s on the structure of the American economy and the

---

18. His recollection deserves a lengthy quote:

In Germany, I witnessed the resurrection of economic power as a by-product of anti-communism. I saw the absolute vitiation of what was supposed to be de-Nazification. I saw the recartelization of German industry. I saw the very impressive way that every obstacle under the sun was put in the way of those Left parties that were opposed to such policies. I saw the splitting of east and west Germany which was done to prevent any real opportunity for social change in the West. This was done with very great skill and dexterity. I developed a very strong appreciation of those who administered this process. It also demonstrates that these things don't just happen randomly, that there is a class consciousness at the top.

causes of the Depression. For him, these detailed political economies provided concrete, systemic evidence of the structure and exercise of business power.

The war, economic necessity, and his own uncertainties about the academic world delayed the start of Schiller's academic career.[19] He spent ten years as an overworked sessional instructor, before receiving his doctorate from New York University in 1960 with a thesis on the political economy of post-war relief efforts. He started with a visiting position at the University of Illinois Bureau of Economic and Business Research, where his interests in economic resource allocation led eventually to work on the radio spectrum as a natural resource. Though remaining at the Bureau throughout his time in Illinois, Schiller attracted the attention of the Institute for Communication Research, where he met Smythe and took over the political economy course when Smythe left for Regina. His *Mass Communication and American Empire* appeared in 1969 to widespread attention that included growing pressure from conservatives at Illinois who did not appreciate the book's position and the author's outspoken opposition to the war in Viet Nam. These factors and the attractiveness of a proposed alternative college at the University of California, San Diego, led to a move in 1970.

At San Diego, Schiller produced a series of books that helped to define the political economy of communication in the United States and had enormous influence on the development of critical perspectives worldwide. Schiller's work has consistently aimed to situate communication studies in the wider political economic context. His second book, *The Mind Managers* (1973) offered the first sustained critique of the information society idea by documenting the growing integration and transnationalization of the information and cultural industries and the broad political and cultural power of major exemplars, such as the Gallup polling company, *Reader's Digest Magazine*, and the *National Geographic*.[20] Following this, his *Communication and Cultural Domination* (1976) addressed the question of cultural imperialism and his observation of Chile's effort to build an alternative under Salvador Allende. In *National Sovereignty and International Communication* (1979), he and Kaarle Nordenstreng produced a collection that

19. Though accused, as he puts it, of having 'an animus against business,' Schiller was awarded the master's degree from Columbia University in 1941. He was not impressed with this center of elite intellectual life:

It was a revelation because I came to realize how totally inadequate the graduate process was. The textbooks used in those days were just appalling, conservative concoctions that were presented in ways that were desiccated and abstracted from reality. Not to say anything of the theories they presented.

20. The book was published in the same year as Daniel Bell's *The Coming of Postindustrial Society*, a work that shaped the agenda for the debate on the 'information society.' Schiller attracted attention when an excerpt on polling appeared in *Psychology Today*, whose editors gave what Schiller calls the 'inflammatory' title 'Polls are Prostitutes for the Status Quo.'

addressed central issues in the New World Information and Communication Order debate.[21]

Schiller returned to issues of information control in his next two books *Who Knows* (1981) and *Information and the Crisis Economy* (1984). These examined the vital significance of information and communication systems for the general operation of transnational capital and, particularly in the second book, the role of these systems for overcoming the crisis of accumulation that continues to bedevil capitalism.

In *Culture, Inc.* (1989), Schiller revisited the cultural industries and departed from his previous work by addressing trends in academic disciplines, specifically the turn to cultural studies.[22] He returned to his long-standing interest in the transformation of international communication with *Hope and Folly* (1989), a book written with William Preston Jr. and Edward Herman that documents the demise of the call for a new information order, and a second collection with Kaarle Nordenstreng, *Beyond National Sovereignty* (1993). Along with Hamid Mowlana and George Gerbner, Schiller provided a global perspective on the Gulf War with a collection of papers from international media scholars.[23]

Schiller has been a model of the activist scholar. In addition to his enormous research contribution with editions published in most major languages, he has spoken out on cultural and information issues before a wide range of local, national, and international organizations. His work provided one of the principal inspirations behind the international call for a new world information order. He has been one of the leading figures in the International Association for Mass Communication Research, the academic

21. This book is also notable because it was the first communication volume published by Ablex, which, under the editorship of Melvin Voigt, produced many of the major works in political economy into the early 1990s.

22. Schiller explains that though 'the subject matter of my work is not a tiny academic squabble,' his analysis of the cultural industries required that he 'take into account those who say that there is no cultural apparatus, or who try to take the view that we can handle this cultural apparatus because we bring to it our own abilities in responding to and in transcending it.'

23. *Hope and Folly* documents the triumph of U.S.-led conservative forces at UNESCO. It was initially commissioned by UNESCO during a period when the organization supported many of the concerns raised by NWICO proponents. But by the time the report was completed, the agency was so concerned to transform itself, in hopes of bringing back American and British membership, that it refused to release it. The University of Minnesota Press published the book, but with a printed disclaimer that completely disassociates UNESCO from its contents.

According to Nordenstreng (1993: 253), this is not the first example of 'anti-intellectual repression' at UNESCO. In 1973, it dropped Dallas Smythe from a Panel of Experts formed to establish the UNESCO communication research program. This took place after Smythe presented two papers critical of mainstream international communication policy and its infatuation with new technologies. It also refused to publish a paper commissioned from Schiller in a 1982 collection. Finally, Nordenstreng describes how UNESCO also retreated from a commitment to follow up the Mass Media Declaration with a Symposium that would amplify its reform proposals.

association most strongly identified with international and political economic research. Though the vision of an alternative college at the University of California, San Diego, fell victim to neo-conservatism, Schiller has left his mark on students there, as well as on his and subsequent generations of communication research.[24]

Smythe and Schiller have provided considerable intellectual and political inspiration to later generations of political economists. The remainder of this section takes up some of the major themes that characterize this work. Political economists have lived up to the general interest of the discipline in historical research, a central theme of which has been the valorization of communication, information, and culture in the development of capitalism. Jhally (1990) provides an important critical evaluation of theoretical perspectives on advertising, audiences, and culture that addresses and extends central concerns raised in Smythe's (1977) seminal article on the audience commodity. Dan Schiller (1988) takes up the range of ways of thinking about information, including the valorization process.

Specific historical studies include Stuart Ewen's *Captains of Consciousness* (1976) which documents the social construction of mass consumption through the development of the advertising industry. The book, coupled with more recent work (1988), provides an important parallel to Braverman's (1974) analysis of the social construction of labor in the twentieth century. Together they offer critical political economies documenting the mutual constitution of mass production and mass consumption in the development of advanced capitalism. In related work, Dan Schiller (1981) and Elizabeth Eisenstein (1979) have produced histories that address the social relations of the newspaper, particularly the process of constructing markets first of business customers and later of mass consumers, which were vital for overcoming the crisis of overproduction that led to economic recession and depression in the last quarter of the nineteenth century.

Smythe's students have been particularly important for their work on the development of the international film industry. Thomas Guback took the lead in developing this area of political economy with his 1969 book that examines its history from the 1940s and with subsequent work on the commodification of film, the changing allocation of capital in the business, its impact on labor, and the role of the business in the wider capitalist service economy (1987, 1989, 1991, and interview October 1992).[25] Guback's student Janet Wasko (1982) has carried on this work with a book that documents the changing relationship between the film industry and the financial institutions that provide essential capital. More recently she has turned to the impact of new technologies on Hollywood and the growing integration of the international audiovisual industry (Wasko, 1994). Another

---

24. Substantial evidence of this influence can be found in a Schiller festschrift volume (Becker et al., 1986). Nevertheless, even it provides an incomplete account because Schiller maintained his prolific research accomplishments after it was published.

25. Guback (1993) has recently returned to Smythe's work to produce a collection of his papers, some of which have not been previously published.

student of Smythe's, Manjunath Pendakur (1990a), has documented the history of American film industry hegemony over the Canadian cinema. One of the central characteristics of their historical work on the film industry is its careful attention to the dialectical relationship between production and distribution. This is important in all industries, but particularly in the media, because its product is easily reproduced and because successful media companies, notably in the film industry, have, with few exceptions, depended on controlling both steps in the circuit of capital.

Historical research on the political economy of broadcasting and telecommunication has focused on the relationship between centers of political power and centers of media power. This includes Herbert Schiller's (1969/1992, 1981) work on the development of a global and heavily militarized electronic media system and Smythe's (1981) research on the evolution of Canadian dependency across publishing, broadcasting, and telecommunication. Subsequent generations of scholars have further developed and reworked several of their prominent themes, greatly emphasizing the relationship between government and corporate power. These include studies of American broadcasting (Kellner, 1990; Winston, 1986) and telecommunication (McChesney, 1993; Mosco, 1982; Schiller, 1982) as well as their counterparts in Canadian broadcasting (Raboy, 1990) and telecommunication (Babe, 1990; Martin, 1991) history. Dan Schiller's work is particularly important because it identified the development of a powerful new force in the telecommunication industry, well-organized, large business users, that signalled a significant shift in the industry power structure. Raboy's book challenged the idea that public broadcasting necessarily contributes to political democracy by documenting the ways state control of the public system has silenced the voices of community and civil society groups. Newer scholars have continued the work of documenting the history of corporate and state power in the communication systems of the United States (McChesney, 1993) and Canada (Coulter, 1992). One of the more interesting recent tendencies is the interest in examining communication power from a grass-roots historical perspective that features the role of labor and social movement organizations. For example, Montgomery (1989) takes up the recent history of the media reform movement in the United States across the political spectrum, McChesney (1992a) addresses the struggles to establish labor radio broadcasting, and Winseck (1993) considers the history of labor involvement in the development of telecommunication policy in the advanced industrial societies, particularly Canada.

One of the principal substantive themes in North American research draws from political economy's general concern with ownership concentration. This includes the vertical integration of companies that control more and more of the process of production in a specific industry sector, and horizontal integration across sectors within and outside the general communication industry. Arguably the most systematic effort to address this theme for the print industry is Herman and Chomsky's *Manufacturing Consent*

(1988).[26] They examine press treatment of international news from the vantage point of central political economic and organizational filters, starting with the 'size, ownership, and profit orientation of the mass media' (p. 3). Specifically, they provide financial data on the largest U.S. media companies, the wealth of the groups controlling these firms, and the affiliations that link external members of media boards to non-media companies. Related filters include the relationship of the media to the advertising industry, and the ability of corporations and governments to mobilize sources that provide 'bureaucratic affinity' and flak to challenge negative treatment in the media. Also concentrating on the press, Bagdikian (1992) offers a similar analysis of how media concentration, including the growing integration of the news and entertainment industries, blurs the distinction between information and commercial content.[27] Although Canadian research tends to emphasize the impact of U.S. media concentration on Canadian media, Clement (1977) laid the groundwork for the analysis of a national system of media concentration which Hannigan (1991) has extended by documenting the links between national and international media powers.[28]

North American research in the political economy of telecommunication has also given considerable attention to the question of business concentration. DuBoff (1984) documented a pattern of government-approved monopoly power in the telegraph industry that continued with the rise of the telephone (Babe, 1990; Danielian, 1939), with allocation of the electromagnetic spectrum (Smythe and Melody, 1985), and with the development of new communication and information technologies (Mosco, 1982; Mosco and Wasko, 1988; Schiller, 1982).

One of the major challenges facing telecommunication research is how to think about the changes that have taken place with the opening of markets to more than one dominant service provider, AT&T in the United States and Bell in Canada. This has led to three types of responses among political economists. One is to examine the changing industry structure and particularly the similarities between it and the cartel arrangements that characterized the early days of North American telecommunication. In addition to this, political economists have shifted attention from service providers to business and government users, arguing that their concentrated power means that whatever competition exists will be managed to benefit their needs for

26. This book is particularly important because it defines their political economic model in greatest detail. They have produced many works on the media and Chomsky is one of the world's best known intellectuals and activists. A film that addresses the ideas in this book, in the wider context of Chomsky's life story, is also called *Manufacturing Consent* and is available in film and video from the National Film Board of Canada in Montreal. In addition to his books on the media, Herman has written extensively on the general nature of corporate concentration. He also writes for critical magazines such as *Z* and *Lies of Our Times*, both of which he helped to found.

27. Bagdikian's work is one of the more important in a growing category of books written by career journalists who have experienced directly the impact of commercialization on their profession. Squires (1993) offers another, more personal, example.

28. See also Magder (1989).

efficient and cost-effective services. Finally, political economists have examined the changes in discourse that accompany structural changes, specifically by exploring the roots of a shift in the dominant rhetoric from that of 'public' service provided by regulated monopolies to 'cost-based' service offered by market competitors (Mosco, 1989a; K. Wilson, 1992).

Research on media concentration confronts an increasingly difficult task of examining the growing integration of media businesses across traditional industry and technology divisions. It was easier to address concentration in the press, broadcasting, film, and telecommunication when these were relatively discrete entities. This is no longer the case. In fact, a number of firms, such as Time Warner, are involved in each of these businesses. As a result, recent work on the political economy of international electronic media (Downing, 1990; Pendakur, 1990a; Schiller, 1989; Wasko, 1994) reflects the growing integration of film and video media that results from the application of new technologies by companies whose vision extends beyond a specific industry to the manifold media commodity. Integration is part of a more general process of *structural transformation* to which political economists are paying closer attention. One of the reasons for this is that along with *integration* that extends the direct ownership control of Sony, Bertelsmann, and other conglomerates, there is also *division* as large companies sell off units and as new companies look to fill old and new niches. The latter development attracts the attention of those who read into structural transformation the rise of a post-Fordist economy in which conglomerate power is tempered by smaller companies able to innovate and transform themselves unencumbered by the bureaucratic weight that slows down larger firms. Although they take issue with this conclusion, political economists of communication are nevertheless beginning to address how large companies gain by decentralizing operations, particularly by passing the risk on to smaller firms. Hence, what appear to be tendencies against concentration can turn out to strengthen the position of major firms (Mosco, 1992). Wasko (1984) was one of the first scholars to address the implications of this development for how we think about and measure communication markets and media concentration. The debate about whether the dramatic restructuring of long-dominant firms like IBM and Sears signals a change in the nature of capitalism (post-Fordism) or simply reflects another cycle in the development of a system that is above all else dynamic and self-transformative is likely to occupy political economy for some time. Finally, perhaps the most substantial challenge facing political economists who study ownership and control of media firms is the absence of debate on this subject in American political culture, a point taken up by McChesney (1992b), who has explored the reasons why this subject is, as he puts it, 'off limits' to general discussion. The lack of discussion in the wider culture marginalizes research on concentration and contributes to a view that the topic has little to do with the way the media actually work.

One of the central goals of the political economy tradition in North America is to understand the relationship of government or the state to the communication business. The challenge here has been to explain the role of the state without suffering the extremes of viewing it as either an independent arbiter of a pluralistic field of pressures or, alternatively, as the instrumental and dependent arm of capital. Smythe's early political economic and policy research is important here because, following themes laid out in Danielian's (1939) research on AT&T, it recognized the ongoing tensions between the state's general tendency to mediate the interests of leading corporate forces and its potential to serve as a vehicle for publicly controlled services.[29]

Schiller's *Mass Communication and American Empire* (1969/1992) brought the state into central focus as a principal user of communication services. This is especially significant because much of the communication literature on the state has tended to present it only as a regulator and policy-maker. The literature on political communication does examine the role of communication in campaigns and propaganda. However, with the exception of Herman and Chomsky's work, which sees the propaganda function as integral to day-to-day state activity, political communication research diminishes an otherwise valuable analysis by giving it an event focus (e.g. election campaigns) or by neglecting to specify the social mechanisms that mutually constitute rhetorical tendencies. Drawing on his economic background, Schiller started by thinking about communication as a resource. With this insight, he proceeded to open a field of analysis that communication research ignored: since the 1920s, the U.S. government, particularly the military, with the active support of key corporate players who benefited from military contracts, managed to control vast amounts of the radio spectrum, a central instrument for electronic communication. The government was not only the arbiter of communication resources for major business interests, it also structured the resource allocation process to ensure that government controlled fully half of the spectrum, half of which was allocated to military and intelligence agencies. With this work on the spectrum and his related analysis of the Communications Satellite Corporation, Schiller presents the state as a set of interconnected structures immersed in the social relations of capitalism – not simply the state, but the *capitalist state*. Subsequent generations of scholars gave attention to this view of the state in both its military (Mosco, 1982: Chap. 2; 1989a: Chap. 6; 1993a) and corporate dimensions (D. Schiller, 1982).

The extent of the integration between capital and the state is a source of important debate within the general field of political economy. This has led to a range of views on the so-called relative autonomy of the state (Jessop, 1990). One of the chief reasons why the debate is important is because it reflects a fundamental problem facing government in advanced capitalism: the state has to promote the interests of capital even as it appears to be the independent arbiter of the wider social or public interest. Since the definition

---

29. This is reflected particularly in Smythe's work on behalf of both a public broadcasting system and government ownership of the communication satellite system.

of these interests is contested and since opposition to unbridled accumulation is a continuous threat, it is not always possible for the state to simply equate accumulation with the general public interest.[30] Mahon's work is particularly interesting in this regard because she offers one of the few attempts from someone whose work is centrally located in Marxian political economy to apply state theory to the regulation of, among other things, communication. According to her, the starting point for understanding the state is to specifically define the production of its 'bias.' This admittedly complex process is constituted

> through the unequal structure of representation inside the state, a structure expressive of inter- and intra-class relations of power. Through this structuration of class relations 'inside' the state, the interests of various social forces are combined in a particular way – organized around the long-term political interests of the hegemonic fraction of the dominant class. (Mahon, 1980: 154)

Using the example of the Canadian Radio-television and Telecommunications Commission, Mahon (1980: 160) argues that a state regulatory agency can be understood as a 'special case' of this unequal structure of representation

> created in order to neutralize a threat to hegemony that cannot easily be contained by the normal functioning of the political and administrative apparatus of the state. It represents a 'politically insulated' framework for the ongoing negotiation of this special compromise.

Nevertheless, she concludes, the compromise itself is tentative because it may be subordinated to what is typically glossed as the 'national interest,' more appropriately the general pattern of compromise inscribed in the state.

Communication scholars in North America are beginning to address these issues from a political economic point of view. For example, Kellner (1990) examines television in the United States as a contested hegemony evidenced in both the content of news and entertainment programming *and* in the system of state regulation and policy formation. According to him, neo-conservatives succeeded in using crises in accumulation and legitimation to redefine the state's role in communications. They did so, he maintains, by eliminating practically the entire complex of policies supporting a public audiovisual space and by replacing them with policies centered on a state that manages market competition. Although a politically masterful achievement, it is hard to sustain because the underlying crises remain. The examination of contradictions facing the capitalist state has been addressed

---

30. Mainstream positions increasingly focus on problems of national interest identification. This has received widespread attention in Robert Reich's (1991) provocative question: 'Who's us?' His point is that the permeability of corporations and governments makes it more difficult than ever to define a national policy. For example, should the U.S. government retain a pro-Hollywood film policy that includes among 'us' companies like Sony and Rupert Murdoch's empire? The question is interesting but it leads one to respond: 'What's new?' Class-divided societies have continually confronted the 'Who's us?' as a matter not merely of identity but of material gain and loss. *The problem for the advanced capitalist state remains one of sharing identity without sharing wealth and power.*

in the area of telecommunication policy (Calabrese and Jung, 1992; Mosco, 1993b), copyright (Bettig, 1992) and in the development of new communication and information technologies (Gandy, 1993). Calabrese and Jung open a new area of research in the political economy of telecommunication by placing in the foreground the impact of market-based policies on rural residents and rural life and by assessing the response of movements organized around rural rights. All of this is interestingly situated within the reconstruction of the rural utopia myth, now reborn in the image of the 'electronic cottage.' Gandy's work draws on Giddens' effort to address the productivist bias in political economy by incorporating broad processes of social control. In the process, Gandy politicizes that work, Beniger's (1986) included, by addressing the capabilities of those with new technologies to commodify, control, and reconstruct personal information and personal identity.

North American political economy research has been particularly strong in combining its analysis of business and the state in the international arena. This research draws on the robust foundation established by Smythe and Schiller, as well as on the work of principally Western European and Latin American scholars whose contribution is taken up in the following sections. Much of it aims to understand the global structure of power in the media and telecommunication industries and its consequences, principally for the world's poorer societies. The research record includes extensive debate, chiefly with variations of the developmentalist approach to communication, an approach that gave academic warrant to the efforts of the U.S. and other Western governments to expand their media and information agencies under the policy banner of development assistance. But it also contains internal debate, particularly over the relationship among media producers, their messages, and audiences (Fejes, 1981; Schiller, 1993). These debates raise questions about what constitutes media imperialism, its relationship to general hegemonic processes, the significance and extent of message control, and the activity and power of receiving audiences.

One of the more significant themes in international research is the transition from America's post-war hegemony to a world communication order led by transnational businesses and supported by their respective nation states increasingly linked in continental and global structures.[31] This has led to research on both the specific characteristics of the transnational media (Wasko, 1994) and information businesses (Schiller, 1994), as well as on the rise of trade agreements (Mosco, 1990b; Samarajiwa, 1993) and on the changing character of international organizations (Mahoney, 1988) increasingly providing the major instruments for managing the contradictions that structural transformations bring about (see also Comor, 1994). Mahoney has addressed the difficult task facing transnational business and

---

31. This is a central theme for Herbert Schiller (1992) in his look back on changes in international communication since the first publication of *Mass Communication and American Empire* (1969).

national states whose managers need to coordinate global strategies and markets without also creating political structures on which the wider public might make demands, i.e., how to manage global policies without a world state.

Another important area of international research is linked to political involvement in the New World Information and Communication Order. Here, Colleen Roach (1993a), who once worked for UNESCO and was a student of Armand Mattelart's, has applied a critical historical approach incorporating class, nationality, and gender to broaden the context of the NWICO debate and renew it, demonstrating that the NWICO movement itself suffers from UNESCO's capitulation to Western pressures. McPhail (1987) has provided a political economic overview of the issues from the perspective of the government of Canada which has felt both U.S. and British pressures to broker the United Nations into a more conservative position. Mowlana (1993) on the Middle East, Lent (1985, 1990) on Asia, and Atwood and McAnany (1986) on Latin America provide important viewpoints bridging their bases in North America with extensive regional experience.

North American political economy has also been interested in situating global communication within a changing international division of labor. Sussman and Lent (1991) have taken a leading role in this area by bringing together the work of international scholars who start with a critical examination of the traditional developmentalist model of communication that linked media growth to national development. They recognize that one of the central problems with this model, and with attempts to revise and renew it (Rogers, 1976), is that it accepts the system of political and economic power that effectively defines development to meet the needs of Western media and information companies, their respective states, and a class fraction in the less developed nations that implements development programs in return for a disproportionate share of the benefits. The effective goal of 'development' is to produce an international division of labor that maintains the flexibility and control of transnational business to maximize the cost-effective use of capital, raw materials, and labor. Communication and information technology is central to this process because it provides the means to overcome space and time constraints on the ability to manage international operations and respond to constantly changing market demands and conditions. Moreover, it provides both end products (communication and information content and instruments) as well as the means to add value to all of a company's final output (see particularly Clement, 1990). In addition to this, Lent and Sussman document the conflicts and contradictions that beset national states that are organized to advance the process, but which must confront opposition from those classes and movements that bear the social and economic consequences of the 'development' process.

Although the general corpus of political economic research concentrates on how communication operates in systems of power, it does not show evidence that resistance, opposition, and efforts to create counter-hegemonic alternatives have been neglected. Most of this work necessarily considers the social relations of class, gender, and race, in order to understand the dynamics of resistance and its connections to the wider political economic field. Some of it foregrounds social class, concentrating on the resistance of organized labor in the media and information industries and its relationship to the wider needs and concerns of working-class people (Douglas, 1986; Lonidier, 1992; Mosco and Wasko, 1983; Waterman, 1992; Winseck, 1993).

This line of analysis is particularly significant because it contributes to removing a major blindspot in communication research. There is a general tendency in communication studies to define its subject as the *consumer* and action as *leisure* activity, separated from the world of work and labor. Outside of political economic research, one typically finds scant attention paid to those who work in the mass media and telecommunication industries, to the general depiction of working people in the mass media, and to coverage of labor issues.[32] This is a problem because it misses the enormous role that labor plays in social life[33] and additionally fosters the view that one can dismiss as anachronistic efforts to organize resistance around labor and the working class.[34]

Political economic research on social relations also starts from gender and looks at the specific ways women have responded to patriarchal structures of communication and information. An important example is Martin's (1991) study of the social construction of 'the women's voice' in telecommunication. She describes the changing social relations resulting from bringing women into the workforce as telephone operators and into wider communication networks as telephone users. Martin provides persuasive evidence that this 'voice' resulted from a complex process involving power, struggle, and resistance waged in the industry at the point of production and at the point of consumption in the household (see also Moyal, 1989; Steeves, 1987).

In addition to class and gender, North American political economists have addressed the significance of race in communication. One of the more significant recent examples takes up the relationship of race to social class in *The Cosby Show*, among the most popular television programs in history. In *Enlightened Racism* (1992), Jhally and Lewis review the literature on the portrayal of race in television entertainment, assess the range of responses to *The Cosby Show*, and produce an analysis that connects the show's success

---

32. See Puette (1992) for an overview of how labor is presented across the range of informational and entertainment media.

33. As Schor (1992) has documented, contrary to the expectations of the 1950s and 1960s, the average amount of time spent at work in the advanced industrial societies is growing.

34. See Luke (1989) for a representative example of an approach that dismisses movements organized around class and labor. It is important to distinguish between the hard-to-contest conclusion that class- and labor-based opposition declined in the 1980s (under furious attack from neo-conservative governments) and the conclusion that this is the permanent result of a decline in the significance of work in people's lives.

to the 'comfortable affluence' portrayed in the program, something that made it easier for white audiences to accept a nearly all-black comedy. Although they devote considerable attention to the show's cultural setting, Jhally and Lewis do not fail to situate it within an analysis of how market and production patterns constrain the quantitative and qualitative visibility of minorities in programming.

Social movements have provided an important focus for understanding oppositional practices in media and communication. Gitlin's (1980) work is paradigmatic here because it focuses on the mutual constitution of the media and social forces in a major political struggle, in this case the war in Viet Nam. Although the contradictory nature of the mass media opens spaces for oppositional groups, it also draws them into social and discursive practices that play into the hands of the other side. In short, when oppositional leaders appeal to the camera, they risk losing touch with their only real source of power, the grass roots. Examining Canadian coverage, Bruck (1992) takes this a step further by addressing how the media reprocess, reassemble, and rearrange the social and discursive practices of movements, helping to reconstitute social movements into discursive movements. Following also on the theme of the media and the peace movement, Roach (1993b) takes up the influence of feminist peace research, particularly the work of Eisler and Collins, on contemporary struggles.

Finally, for a considerable time, political economists have examined social movements organized specifically around changing the media itself (Wasko and Mosco, 1992). Haight and Weinstein's (1981) research offered an important analytical grounding to this line of inquiry – suggesting major contradictions involved in trying to challenge television ideology by organizing resistance to market-based broadcasting policy. Haight and Weinstein, along with other media reform movement analysts, could not foresee that the 1980s would be marked by the power of conservative, including religious fundamentalist, groups aiming to attack media programming and policies, a trend well documented in Montgomery's *Target: Prime Time* (1989).

Great Britain and Europe

In some respects, it is easier to chart the development of a political economy approach to communication in North America than in Europe. One reason is that in their own research and in their influence on two to three definable generations of political economy scholars worldwide, but particularly in North America, Smythe and Schiller are generally recognized as founding figures in the field. Although there are several people whose intellectual, policy and activist work have been quite influential, there are no clear generational parallels in the development of a political economy tradition between Europe and North America.

James Halloran has been a leading figure in the development of communication studies in Britain. For over two decades he headed the Centre for Mass Communication Research at the University of Leicester, where, until recently, Peter Golding and Graham Murdock produced work that helped set the research agenda for the political economy of communication. Moreover, Halloran influenced the development of communication studies worldwide with close to two decades of service as President of the International Association for Mass Communication Research.[35] The IAMCR is the professional association with arguably the strongest commitment to advance political economy research. Nevertheless, Halloran eschews identification with a political economy approach, choosing to situate his work and that of the Centre within the tradition of critical sociology and social psychology (interview, April 1992). He notes that the Centre was initiated in response to concerns raised by the Home Secretary in 1961 about problems of juvenile delinquency and the interest in assessing television's impact. Although he acknowledges the importance of political and economic research, his main scholarly and programmatic interest has been on developing a critical sociological approach.[36] Halloran distinguishes this from the work of Lazarsfeld, Klapper, Wright, and Katz, among others, whose positivist approach put data gathering ahead of 'asking the right questions.'[37]

During Halloran's tenure as Director, the Centre maintained a steady flow of research reports, several by scholars, particularly Graham Murdock and Peter Golding, who made important contributions to the political economy of communication. Nevertheless, as Halloran, Murdock, and Golding agree, the overwhelming number take up specific social problems from a sociological or social psychological perspective. Although certainly wide-ranging, the emphasis is on problems facing young people, families, and communities, including the sociological concerns and communication needs of ethnic and racial minorities. In fact, Murdock observed that the Centre received few grants for research in political economy. Most of these, such as Philip Harris' work on news agencies, Peter Hartmann's on the New World Information and Communication Order, and Murdock's on the advertising industry, incorporated several approaches along with political economy. Moreover, all of this work appeared in the 1970s and early 1980s. Sociological and social psychological research occupied practically all of the

35. See Hamelink and Linné (1992) for a collection of essays to honor Halloran.

36. A 1984 Centre planning document makes the sociological and social psychological orientation explicit:

From the establishment of the Centre it has been accepted that mass communication is a field of interest, rather than a discipline, and that several disciplines have a contribution to make to the understanding of this field of interest. Sociology and social psychology, particularly the former, are pre-eminent in the Centre's approach, but that does not imply that the potential contribution of other disciplines such as history, economics, political science, law and linguistics is not recognized. (Centre, 1984: 8)

37. He criticizes positivism directly in a 1981 work:

One may, however, criticize the primacy of this position, in which 'scientific' is defined solely or mainly in terms of method, and in which little or no attention is given to theory, concepts, or the nature of the relevant, substantive issues and their relationship to wider societal concerns. (Halloran, 1981: 23; see also 1963, 1978, 1983)

Centre's reports from 1984 (Centre, 1991; interviews with Halloran, Murdock, and Golding, April 1992). Almost all of the research and publication in political economy that people have associated with the Centre were produced outside the auspices of the Centre itself. Affirming this point, Golding concludes that there never was a 'Leicester School' of political economy in nearly the sense that one can speak of a Birmingham School of Cultural Studies under Richard Hoggart and Stuart Hall, or even comparable to a School of Political Communication under Jay Blumler and Dennis McQuail at Leeds. Following a pattern common throughout the field of political economy, what appears to be an institutionalized program of research is actually a collection of individuals, in this case Graham Murdock and Peter Golding, who, along with Philip Elliott and sporadic others, pursued political economy research.[38] They did so in a setting congenial to critical social research, but not one that gave particular attention to political economy.

Halloran is not alone in his generation of European communication scholars who have played a role that supported, if not directly shaped, the political economy approach. For example, Dieter Prokop produced studies on the political economy of the media that connected the business of communication to concerns raised by the Frankfurt School (1973, 1974, 1983). Enzensberger's 'Constituents of a Theory of the Media' (in Enzensberger, 1974) offered one of the early attempts to fill what he argues is one of the 'empty categories' of Marxist thought by producing a theory of media that accentuates class relations, conflict, and the contradictory and subversive qualities of media. The point is that, although one can identify examples of the political economy of communication in Schiller's if not Smythe's generation of European scholars, the influence on subsequent political economy work in Europe is not nearly as evident as the influence of Smythe and Schiller on the development of a political economy approach in North America. Sustained research from this perspective begins with subsequent generations of communication scholars to whose work we now turn.

For many years Kaarle Nordenstreng of Finland has played a leading role in the development of international communication studies and in the political debate over the NWICO. From the 1960s, he has taken critical issue with the positivism and technological utopianism in Western communication research (1968). Nordenstreng is best known for his work on the dynamics of global communication and specifically on the effort to redress imbalances and otherwise democratize the mass media (Nordenstreng, 1984; Traber and Nordenstreng, 1992). He has combined a strong research record in the field with persistent political activism at the national and international level, mainly, but not exclusively, in the effort to bring about the NWICO.

---

38. Golding, Murdock, and Schlesinger produced a book (1986) to honor the late Philip Elliott, an anthropologist, who made a substantial contribution to research in political communication and, with Golding, presented one of the early materialist analyses of the media (Elliott and Golding, 1972).

Nordenstreng has been particularly important for his ability to bring together scholars, including political economists and policy activists, from around the world. There are few regions of the world that have not felt the influence of his organizational acumen.

Nordenstreng's collaborations (1979, 1993) with Schiller have produced major collections in international communication that exhibit a strong political economic influence. Nevertheless, one cannot identify Nordenstreng with a political economy approach as easily as one can with Smythe and Schiller. This is not because Nordenstreng lacked interest in theoretical matters of major concern to political economists. He has made the case for a disciplinary framework that certainly overlaps Schiller's and Smythe's. For example, in a recent statement (1993) that aims to capture the paradigmatic contours of NWICO-related research, he outlines an approach founded on a realist epistemology, a holistic theory of society, and a normative view centering around the value of social equality. He has also raised concerns prominent in political economic research about 'hermeneutical solutions' and 'some postmodern streams' which 'have even gone so far that they can be seen to stand in paradigmatic opposition to the original school of thought' (1993: 271). Nevertheless, although certainly sharing values and evaluations congenial to a political economy perspective, Nordenstreng has not taken as strong a research interest in the economic dimensions of mass media and communication. Whereas Halloran chose *critical sociology* as a focus of attention, Nordenstreng focuses on a *critical politics* of communication, particularly in its international manifestations. This has provided him with a grounding for his long-standing commitment to policy research and intervention. In this fashion, Nordenstreng has influenced numerous communication scholars and activists, including political economists. However, the influence has not been as direct on the latter as that of Smythe and Schiller because Nordenstreng has not taken as sustained a research interest in the economic aspects of the political economy of communication. Choosing to concentrate on explicitly political fora, he has had less to say about the business of media and the commodification of culture and communication.

later than N.A.

The sustained development of a political economy approach in Europe emerged with the appearance between 1974 and 1982 of a set of theoretical and programmatic pieces that contributed substantially to placing the field on the European intellectual map. There are numerous parallels in theme and method between North American and European political economic research, and differences, though important, are largely a matter of emphasis, not of fundamental departure. Nevertheless one can safely conclude that there is a tendency within European political economy to adopt a more self-consciously theoretical position. The core works include Murdock and Golding's 'For a Political Economy of Mass Communications' (1974), their 'Capitalism, Communication, and Class Relations' (1979), Garnham's 'Contribution to a Political Economy of Mass Communication' (1979), and the near book-length introductions that Armand Mattelart produced for the two-volume work he edited with Seth Siegelaub, *Communication and Class*

Struggle. Vol. 1: Capitalism, Imperialism (1979) and *Vol. 2: Liberation, Socialism* (1983). These works are given particular attention because they set out programmatic positions that have significantly influenced political economy research.[39] Furthermore, though subsequent work, including their own, built on these theorizations, there have been no significant departures that fundamentally alter these original positions.[40] Finally, the continued presence of caricatures of the political economy approach (based on charges of 'economism' and 'productivism') suggests that this work has not received the sustained reflection it merits.

Trained in economics and sociology at the London School of Economics, Graham Murdock began his career by applying this background to understand cultural life. Specifically, in the late 1960s at Sussex, he wrote about the rise of New York and the decline of Paris in the elite art market. His interest in popular and youth culture took him to Leicester, where for two decades he worked in the sociology and political economy of culture and communication. He recently left Leicester to rejoin Peter Golding at the University of Loughborough. Golding moved to Loughborough after spending most of his career at Leicester. His training is also in sociology, although he has taken a stronger interest in the social policy dimensions of communication research. Garnham came to communication research from a background in film. A founding editor of *Media, Culture and Society*, he has spent his academic career at the Central London Polytechnic, now the University of Westminster.[41]

Belgian-born Armand Mattelart received his doctoral training in law and political economy from the University of Louvain and a post-graduate degree in sociology from the Sorbonne. He was a professor at the University of Chile from 1962 until the U.S.-backed military coup d'état ended the elected social democratic government of Salvador Allende and with it Mattelart's efforts to promote democratic communication. During his years in Latin America, Mattelart was influenced by and helped to shape the course of research in that region. It also brought him into contact with

39. This was an important period for the development of a political economy of communication in Europe. In addition to these works, numerous others sought to bring together political economy, Marxian theory, and the particular problems posed by communication practices (de la Haye, 1980; Hund and Kirchoff-Hund, 1985; Prokop, 1983). It is also important to mention the influence of a political economy group in Italy, including Giovanni Cesareo, Roberto Grandi, and Giuseppi Richeri, whose publication *IKON* influenced the development of political economy in Europe and North America. In Spain, a group including Madrid scholar Enrique Bustamente developed the journal *Telos*, which produced political economic and policy analyses on communication and new technology issues.

40. This conclusion, admittedly, departs from Curran's (1990) view that the recent work of political economists, particularly that of Golding and Murdock, is part of a 'new revisionism' in communication studies. Curran's position is discussed below.

41. Garnham emphasizes two primary influences on his development. The first is the tradition of British cultural studies and social history that grew out of the work of Hoggart, Leavis, Thompson, and Williams. This led him into the cultural industries, where he worked on documentary films in the 1960s, including a television program with Williams. The second is his involvement in debates on the course of British television and the role of the BBC.

Smythe and Schiller, who spent time in the region examining the impact of American media (see Schiller, 1976). Mattelart also recognizes the influence of a French 'cultural industries' approach developed by the sociologist Edgar Morin. Since leaving Chile he has been a professor at the University of Rennes.

Though differing in some respects, the early work of these scholars shares an explicit interest in making critical use of Marxian theory, in its different readings, to understand communication, the mass media, and cultural practices. Murdock and Golding's 1974 work is a ground-breaking exercise because, while admittedly 'a work in progress,' it sets out a conceptual map for a political economic analysis of the media where none existed in the British literature.[42] Using the British media as a case study, they examine the processes of consolidation and concentration at work in publishing, the press, broadcasting, cinema, and recording. In addition to addressing what have become accepted dimensions of media concentration – integration and diversification – they also take on what for that time was a new development, the internationalization of British media. Finally, they take up the wider implications, including restricted choice in entertainment and information. Though providing one of the early systematic analyses of the commercial power of the mass media, they are also careful to qualify their conclusions by situating them within an inclusive position:

> To describe and explicate these interests is not to suggest a deterministic relationship, but to map the limits within which the production of mediated culture can operate. Cultural production retains a real autonomy derived from tradition, occupational ideologies and the genuine tolerance of the liberal consensus. (1974: 226–227)[43]

Murdock and Golding's 1979 work provides an even more explicitly theoretical effort to place the political economy approach within the wider framework of critical theory. It demonstrates that, for them, a critical reading of the Frankfurt School's analysis of the cultural industries provides one of the primary links between the Marxian legacy and their application of it to communication studies. For example, Murdock and Golding start their overview of Marxian approaches to cultural analysis by noting the contribution of Horkheimer and Marcuse at the Institute for Social Research, singling out Adorno's work on the music industry. They conclude that:

> Adorno's insistence that the process of cultural domination has its roots in the economic dynamics of the 'culture industry' is an indispensable starting point for any Marxist analysis. (1979: 18)

42. They note (1974: 205) that the media, unlike the study of education, 'have gone largely unexamined' and cite a 1972 collection of writing on *Power in Britain* (ed. by Urry and Wakeford) which not only lacked a chapter on the media, but contained no reference to the media in its index.

43. It is interesting to observe this caution in one of the earliest attempts to situate the political economy of the media in a wider theoretical framework. It suggests that from the start the approach has steered clear of 'economism' and that similar caveats contained in recent work are evidence not of a 'new revisionism' (Curran, 1990) but of noteworthy consistency over two decades of research.

Nevertheless, they insist that 'it is only a starting point' and proceed to criticize that it is 'not sufficient simply to assert that the capitalist base of the "culture industry" necessarily results in cultural forms which are consonant with the dominant ideology' (p. 18).[44] Similarly, in his article of the same year, Garnham applauds the particular way the original Frankfurt School position addressed the relationship of base and superstructure in contrast to post-Althusserian tendencies. He credits the Frankfurt School with recognizing that 'under monopoly capitalism the superstructure becomes precisely industrialized; it is invaded by the base and the base/superstructure distinction breaks down via a collapse into the base.' He contrasts this with the alternative position, taken up today in cultural studies, which concludes that we are observing the 'transformation of the base into another autonomous superstructural discourse' (1979: 130). Nevertheless, like Murdock and Golding, he takes issue with the Frankfurt tradition on this point:

> the real weakness of the Frankfurt School's original position was not their failure to realize the importance of the base or the economic, but insufficiently to take account of the economically contradictory nature of the process they observed and thus to see the industrialization of culture as unproblematic and irresistible. (p. 131)

Starting from the more explicitly anti-imperialist Marxian literature, Mattelart is not as concerned to connect his approach to the Western Marxism of the Frankfurt School. This undoubtedly results in part from what he acknowledges to be one of the central problems in communication research in France. Little of the theoretical work developed by French intellectuals like Althusser and Barthes, which influenced Stuart Hall at Birmingham, was invested in the primary media research schools of France. The failure to produce French editions of Habermas' work until the 1980s also contributed to the lack of a connection to Western Marxism (Mattelart and Mattelart, 1992). Nevertheless, like his British counterparts, Mattelart steers clear of seeing power as a singularity and looks beyond it to fundamental contradictions, thereby setting aside Althusserian approaches to ideology from the start.[45]

This interest in rooting communication studies in the Marxian tradition led these writers and their counterparts to an inevitable decentering of the

---

44. In an interview (April 1992), Murdock refers to a more immediate link to the Frankfurt tradition in the early 1970s work of Dieter Prokop.

45. As he puts it:

One of the most misleading tendencies of Althusserian ideological theory is that its monolithic and vertical concept of how the dominant ideological apparatuses function does not conceive of them as being subject to class contradictions. The most concrete effect of this approach is that its field of observation marginalizes the resistance practices of the dominated classes against the dominant ideology, as well as it marginalizes the internal incoherencies which characterize the operation of these ideological apparatuses. (Mattelart and Siegelaub, 1979: 29) media.[46] True to a Marxian political economy, this meant placing in the foreground the analysis of capitalism, including the development of the forces and relations of production, commodification and the production of surplus value, social class divisions and struggles, contradictions and oppositional movements. Decentering the media actually raised the stature of media studies by moving it from an isolated, marginalized, and largely untheorized area of activity to one that is fundamental to processes of production and reproduction within the wider capitalist system. Murdock and Golding (1979) discuss this specifically with respect to the 'double vacuum' in media studies and sociology. Whereas media studies typically approach the social realm with a laundry list – the media and class, the media and youth, the media and women, etc. – which suggests a loosely articulated pluralism, sociological theory tends to ignore the media.

Sharing the view that communication needs to be situated in a wider theoretical framework, Garnham (1979: 123) argues for placing the political economy of culture within an overall analysis of capitalism with 'a political economy of mass-communication taking its subsidiary place within that wider framework as the analysis of an important, but historically specific mode of the wider process of cultural production and reproduction.' Much of Garnham's interest in this area grows out of his reading of and, later, involvement in central policy debates about the course of the mass media and telecommunication in the United Kingdom.[47] It also flowed out of his association with Raymond Williams, who aimed to secure a place for popular culture as democratic, resistant, and alternative, as opposed to the market-driven effort to align popular with mass consumption (interview, November 1993).[48] Similarly, for Mattelart (1979: 36), 'the manner in which the communication apparatus functions, which determines the elaboration and exchange of messages, corresponds to the general mechanisms of production and exchange conditioning all human activity in capitalist society.'

This process of decentering the media placed in the foreground, with different degrees of individual theoretical accentuation, capital, class, contradiction, conflict, and oppositional struggles. The analysis of capital is, for Murdock and Golding (1974), 'the obvious starting point for a political

---

46. It is not possible to discuss every one of their counterparts. Nevertheless, it is important to mention Seth Siegelaub, who worked closely with Mattelart on several projects, including co-editing the two volume *Communication and Class Struggle* and editing issues of the multi-volume bibliography *Marxism and the Mass Media*. He also founded the International Mass Media Research Center and directed the publishing enterprise International General, which is responsible for the above and other volumes of critical media research. Siegelaub's principal education was as a political activist and a manual laborer.

47. One of the more important expressions of this is his 1973 monograph (revised in 1978) on political economic and public policy issues on television in the United Kingdom.

48. Garnham is quick to emphasize that the political economy of communication is itself part of a wider process of popular cultural activity, i.e., it is one academic wing of a wider intellectual *and* popular set of movements for democratic action (interview, November 1993).

economy of communications.' Specifically, this means 'the recognition that the mass media are first and foremost industrial and commercial organizations which produce and distribute commodities' (pp. 205–206). Challenging what he refers to as the Althusser/Poulantzas theorization of social formations into relatively autonomous levels, Garnham (1979) argues for seeing the mass media 'first as economic entities with both a direct economic role as creators of surplus value through commodity production and exchange and an indirect role, through advertising, in the creation of surplus value within other sectors of commodity production' (p. 132). Rather than relative autonomy, the result is a 'close inter-weaving within concrete institutions and within their specific commodity forms of the economic, the political and the ideological' (p. 132). All of these are embodied in the generalizing and abstracting drive to reduce everything to exchange value, which Garnham perceives to be Marx's central insight into the capitalist mode of production. Drawing on *Capital*, which he argues is 'the most mature work,' Mattelart draws out specific dimensions of the mode of production of communication: first, production instruments (machines used to transmit information); second, working methods (genre specific practices, codes, etc.); and third, relations of production (property relations, transmitter–receiver relations, division of labor, organizational forms and practices).

In their view, class relations are central to political economic analysis, though they all see the articulation of class relations as a set of complex and contradictory processes. These involve principally the relationship between communication entrepreneurs and the wider capitalist class, the relationship between media industry leaders and the concrete activities of those who actually make media products (the specific form of the labor process),[49] and the dynamics of reception, i.e., how people adopt, reconstitute, and resist the range of meanings embodied, however tightly or loosely, in cultural commodities.

Notwithstanding capital's power, each of these moments in the valorization of capital is marked by contradictions. As a result, although acknowledging the power of capital to absorb social, including communication, practices into the logic of exchange value, they reject correspondence theories that unequivocally align capital logic with cultural production. Noting the tendency to see the imposition of this logic as non-contradictory, Garnham (1979: 136) concludes that:

> One must stress at the outset that this is not so. Because capital controls the means of cultural production ... it does not follow that these cultural commodities will necessarily support, either in their explicit content or in their mode of cultural appropriation, the dominant ideology.

---

49. Though they praise Adorno for his work on the influence of capitalism on the music industry, Murdock and Golding (1979: 18) take him to task for neglecting to demonstrate it with respect to the 'concrete activities of the people who actually make the products the "culture industry" sells.'

Not only can such products be, in Garnham's words, 'profoundly sub-versive,' they must be seen as the product of struggles between distinct capitalist and non-capitalist social formations, and among classes within and between these formations. For example, one can see artisanal production of books and films as congruent with a capital logic as long as capital controls mass reproduction and distribution. Artisan production provides capital with diversity and absorbs much of the risk. Nevertheless, this form of production has also been the locus of struggles against the economic logic of capitalism in defense of the public sphere and citizenship over the corporate sphere and consumerism.

Mattelart extends this research by situating contradiction and conflict within a global context. His early work is particularly revealing for the number of ideas that would later be taken up by political economists and communication scholars generally. He offers a highly nuanced perspective on cultural imperialism that, in addition to comprehending patterns of communication power, takes into account complex forms of 'secondary imperialism', e.g. in Mexico, India, Egypt, and Italy, the manifold social practices that these cultural imperialisms take, e.g. sports, tourism, etc., and various ways to conceptualize contradictory and conflictual relations of production and reception, including mass, popular, and national cultures.[50]

The remainder of this section takes up some of the major work in the political economy tradition in Britain and Europe. It is intended not to be exhaustive, but rather to identify major streams of research that attend to various of the theoretical notions addressed above.

Several works document a strong interest in historical analysis. Drawing on the strong tradition of British press history, Curran (1979, 1991) and Sparks (1985; Sparks and Dahlgren, 1991) have examined this area from a political economic framework emphasizing class analysis.[51] Curran's work has been particularly important in uncovering the history of class conflict and the rise and demise of a radical working-class press that was once central to the development of the British Labour Party.[52] Writing from a less than conventional political economic perspective, Jacques Attali (1985) has developed an historical account of music that sees this cultural form as both reflection and anticipator of social structural change. Producing a bold synthesis with admittedly little concern for fine detail, Attali identifies four

50. These ideas are presented in the 1979 volume and developed more fully in the 1983 collection. As Mattelart (Mattelart and Siegelaub, 1979: 56) notes, Michèle Mattelart (1977) provided a clear sense of the distinction between mass and popular culture. The latter is not a formal substitute for mass culture but 'a qualitatively different practice, the end of pre-history, as Marx would say, carried out by other social actors.' Specifically, popular culture embodies the experience of a people who *'become the active subject of a cultural experience linked to their own project for liberation.'*

51. As E.P. Thompson's (1963) work demonstrates, the analysis of informational and popular media has been of considerable significance in social histories of Britain.

52. It is interesting to observe that Herman and Chomsky (1988) make use of Curran's research on the history of the radical press in a book that is almost entirely taken up with the media in the United States.

networks of music (sacrificial – pre-industrial; representation – concert hall; repetition – individualized recordings; composition – self-communication) that embody and anticipate particular historical epochs.Taking a similarly integrated approach, but with greater emphasis on the political economic dimension, Flichy (1991) produced a popular history of communication that addresses the relationship of North American and European developments.

Owing perhaps to the remarkable stability of telecommunication systems across Europe, there are fewer noteworthy historical accounts than in North America that take an explicitly political economic perspective. By stability, I refer to the system of state monopolies that controlled all aspects of the production and distribution of telecommunication equipment and services. As in North America, the beginnings of significant change heightened interest in the historical development of telecommunication and this is reflected particularly in collections produced by Becker (1989, 1990).

Research on specific media, including political economic research, was slow to develop in Europe. The universities were much more reluctant than their North American counterparts to encourage the development of research and study programs in communication, journalism, and cognate fields. As a result, in the period when individual print, broadcasting, and telecommunication media flourished as separate industries, there was considerably less research from all perspectives than was the case in North America. The growth of research centers across Europe is changing this, but now they face a different media industry, one far more integrated across traditional media lines. Consequently, even when political economic research does address specific sectors, it does so with careful attention to the tendencies to integration and globalization. One good example of this is Mattelart's *Advertising International* (1991), which takes up the political economy of this industry in Europe. It does so, however, from a perspective that consistently addresses the integration of the advertising industry into all other media sectors, as well as the transformation of advertising from a commercial break in the media flow to a fundamental means of communication and an essential actor in public space.[53]

In order to develop this theme, Mattelart documents the growth of European, Japanese, and Australian firms that challenged American media hegemony. Much of this was led by the company WPP (which bought J. Walter Thompson, among others) and Saatchi & Saatchi (which bought Ogilvy & Mather), thereby reversing a trend established when the American company J. Walter Thompson set up business in London in 1899, the first of its forty foreign operations. The political economic significance of this work rests with more than the analysis of trans-Atlantic skirmishes. The very meaning of advertising has grown along with the industry's commercial linkages. In addition to buying space, advertising means market research,

---

53. A 1987 article in the Belgian trade press (Mattelart, 1991: 29) reflects the business sense of 'new times' for advertising: 'Advertising is dead, long live communication!'

opinion polling, audience ratings, consulting, design, graphics, sales promotion, direct marketing (including telemarketing with new technologies), audiovisual production, video communication, sponsorship, and public relations. Commercial linkages have expanded as advertising and media firms come together through mergers, partnerships, joint ventures, strategic alliances, and the other forms that structural transformation takes in this dynamic industry. All of this is made possible by convergences in technologies that maintain the ability to manage these organizational forms and the transitions from one to another. They also facilitate the continued, detailed tracking of consumers, suppliers, competitors, and products. With few exceptions, government policies have supported these developments, specifically by eliminating regulations that limited market entry across industries and across borders, as well as those that constrained merger activity, and by policing accounting practices to deter questionable payment practices such as hidden discounts, super-commissions, gifts, kick-backs, etc.

As he has done over the course of a prolific career, Mattelart is careful to make the links between these political economic developments and changes in contemporary culture. For him, these are more than matters of state or corporate structure. They are bound up with the reconstitution of public and human space into a private commodity – what one Omnicon executive calls 'this strategic primary material' (Mattelart, 1991: 17) – that the communication industry is free to exploit. Nevertheless, this powerful conclusion, enhanced by his use of Guattari's work on capitalist subjectivity,[54] does not entirely satisfy Mattelart. He agrees with Bourdieu that culture is a form of 'self-defense':

> this instrument of free thought, like the martial arts in other terrains, allows citizens to protect themselves against abuses of symbolic power directed against them, be they advertising, propaganda or political or religious advertising. (p. 217)

Since Mattelart does not choose to foreground the social and cultural practices that maintain the defense against capitalist subjectivity, he is not entirely clear about how this resistance operates. The outcome is a powerful political economic analysis of a complex and dynamic industry and uncertainties about the overall impact.

Mattelart's work on advertising rethinks political economy by concentrating on the variety and dynamism of its various forms. It attempts to break through the tendency to associate the power of the communication industries simply with the size of firms and the degree of corporate concentration. Although not clearly theorized in this work, it is obvious that Mattelart is aiming to broaden thinking about institutional structures, their interrelations,

---

54. According to Guattari:

Capitalist subjectivity, as it is mediated by professionals of every type and size, is manufactured in a form which pre-empts the existence of any intrusion of events likely to annoy or disturb it. Every singularity must be avoided, must be subjected to its devices, its professionals and specialized frames of reference (cited in Mattelart, 1991: 217).

and the dynamics of power in the capitalist communication industries.[55] This view is carried forward in other recent political economies of the media industries in Europe (see particularly Mignot-Lefèbvre, 1993).

Aksoy and Robins (1992) provide a political economic reading of the film and video industry that also addresses the dynamics of structural transformation, but from a more explicitly theoretical perspective. They question the claims of post-Fordist theory (Christopherson and Storper, 1989; Piore and Sabel, 1984), which observe the same types of structural changes that Mattelart describes, but conclude that they mark a major divide in capitalist development. On one side of the divide is Fordism, a system of mass production for mass consumption led by large, integrated companies whose market dominance is secured with support from the state in return for maintaining economic and, by extension, political stability. On the other side is post-Fordism, marked by specialized production for highly segmented markets, the deconcentration of business into networks of flexible producers, suppliers, investors, and by the state, whose role shifts from guaranteeing a social contract to promoting markets. Christopherson and Storper apply this view to the film and video industries by arguing that the Hollywood film industry, whose vertically integrated studio system once epitomized Fordism, is being transformed by changes in corporate strategy, communication technology, and government policy into a post-Fordist ensemble of large and small companies, producing a multiplicity of products for a wide range of markets criss-crossed by demographic and regional variations. For them, independent producers, whose flexible specialization ensures innovation, play an increasingly critical role in what have now become global audio-visual markets.

Aksoy and Robins acknowledge, with Mattelart and others, the importance of structural transformation in the communication industries, but see little evidence to support post-Fordist claims that these warrant the case for a new industrial divide. In fact, they argue that though not all large firms successfully negotiate the process of structural transformation, those doing so emerge all the more powerful. Corporate strategy, technological change, and supportive government policies permit film companies to expand more easily across media and national boundaries. The Hollywood majors are transformed into vertically integrated global media and information conglomerates like Time Warner, Sony, and the News Corp. Drawing on the work of Wasko and others, they maintain that although the number of 'independent' production companies grow, these absorb high product risks and labor costs for the giants, which maintain their control over the critical areas of finance and distribution. Aksoy and Robins conclude that Hollywood has changed: it is more differentiated and not entirely American, but the companies that now constitute 'the majors' command greater resources, markets, and revenues than was the case in Hollywood's heyday. They

---

55. This theme of rethinking is taken up more generally in Mattelart and Mattelart (1992). One foreshadowing of this is to be found in Mattelart et al. (1984).

further caution against the simple application of industrial models to the media sphere, because the latter contains unique 'logics' defined by the various forms that cultural commodities and their production and, particularly, distribution processes take.

Much of this thinking in evidenced in the work of Miège (1987, 1989) and his colleagues at the University of Grenoble. Miège departs from the broad macro-political economies of Mattelart and Schiller to concentrate on understanding differences within the cultural industries.[56] Acknowledging that the political economy of culture begins with Adorno and Horkheimer (1979, orig. 1944), Miège concludes that their work is limited by rigidities in the conception of artistic creativity in the cultural industries and by their failure to address structurally based resistances. He aims to address these shortcomings, particularly the former, by examining communication as a variegated process of commodity production.

Miège concentrates on three types of production: non-capitalist, which employs artisans in traditional craft production; capitalist, which employs wage laborers to produce surplus value; and indirectly productive cultural labor, which integrates cultural activities into the process of value realization, e.g. a musical performance at a shopping center. Though Miège agrees that communication shares with other forms of production the problem of valorization, he identifies the additional problem of reproducibility. The latter is particularly central to the cultural industries because many of their products offer an ease of reproduction that reduces marginal costs to near zero. Nevertheless, many of its products also depend on reference to an original, e.g. a concert or a painting, that provides a powerful and therefore valuable aura, to use Benjamin's term.

In his interest to improve on the standard technology-based divisions within the communication industries that distinguish print from broadcasting from telephony, etc., Miège (1987) offers an alternative based on what he calls the 'social logics' at work in the industry. These include the editorial production of cultural commodities, e.g. books; flow production, e.g. broadcasting; the production of written information; of live entertainment; and, finally of electronic information. These logics combine to form three models: *editorial*, *flow*, and *written* information models, which he uses to organize data about the industry. Miège's chief conclusion is that the flow model is becoming a dominant form in the West chiefly because of the favorable economics associated with it. An initial heavy capital investment is rewarded with low labor costs, and a range of reproduction and repackag-

56. Miège's work appears to lie on the political economy side of the boundary between the political economy of communication and institutional communication research. It shares with the latter an interest in describing the specific organizational practices that constitute communication as an institutional activity. Nevertheless, it is sufficiently interested in communication as commodity production and in the relationship of organizational practices to the wider social totality that it is fair to situate his work on the political economy side of the boundary.

ing possibilities that allow one to multiply an initial audience many times over.

This analysis certainly deepens the conception of how the communication industries are structured and the range of processes that constitute them beyond the descriptive categories that are still in widespread use. It is particularly valuable for integrating labor and the work process within the technical processes of production and distribution. His logics are social and not just technical. Nevertheless, as Miège (1989: 44–45) himself notes, political economists have raised questions about the ultimate gain from this analysis, however rich in detail. For example, Schiller has argued that Miège makes too much of what distinguishes culture from other industries in capitalism. Flichy notes that one of the chief items that appears to distinguish culture, uncertainty over valorization, is diminishing with the application of standard business practices. Rather than inherent uncertainties, we are observing the historical process of uneven development that is just now extending capitalist practices to the cultural industries. Miège counters by making the case for the inherent 'creativity crisis' in the cultural industries and for the natural tendency of culture to define divisions, a tendency that makes resistance more likely in the cultural industries than in other industrial sectors.

Although he makes the case for resistance, Miège is less interested in examining the specific forms that it takes. Nevertheless, there is a strong European tradition of examining oppositional and alternative media from a political economy perspective. Mattelart and Siegelaub (1983) brought together a substantial collection of work on the relationship of media to social resistance that includes major theoretical treatments as well as a range of international examples. Though the growth of a working-class oppositional press has been a strong interest, particularly in Britain (Curran, 1979; Sparks, 1985), one can observe a recent tendency to explore the development of local and community-based alternative electronic media (Jankowski et al., 1992). The growth of the latter is not only a result of the obvious advance of broadcasting across Europe, but more specifically results from the loosening of state monopolies on radio and television that tended to define public service as national programming with few local alternatives. As monopolies give way to commercial alternatives, primarily interested in selling products, room also opens for states and social movements to develop broadcast and cable television alternatives to this increasingly pervasive commercial fare.[57]

As in the North American literature, one does not find a substantial body of research in European political economy on the relationship of gender to the cultural industries. Gallagher (1980, 1984, 1985, 1992) offers one of the few sustained treatments that provides a general critique of leading political economy approaches and proceeds to map the terrain of a gendered political

---

57. For a political economic analysis of media that foreshadowed these developments in Central and Eastern Europe, see Szecsko (1986).

economy of the mass media. The constituents of such an approach include the positions that women have historically occupied in circuits of cultural production. Although the market for literate middle-class women has been strong almost since the invention of the press, that market has subordinated women in significant ways. For example, she documents the four-fold subordination of women in the social relations of fiction writing in the nineteenth century. Women novelists were tolerated as artisans, provided their work did not disturb their primary household duties. Moreover, women were subordinated with unskilled labor in the printing trade (along with child labor). Furthermore, the exploitation of women in domestic service freed up middle-class women to read and sometimes write. Finally, novels were saturated with content to structure and appeal to the female as consumer: romance, femininity, domesticity, and motherhood. Gallagher builds on this historical argument with an analysis that connects the structural position of women in the cultural industries – underrepresentation save for certain highly visible positions – with their portrayal across the cultural industries. This combination of historical, social structural, and cultural analysis linking class and gender offers an important model for rethinking the political economic approach to the cultural industries. Unfortunately, the literature is not as strong on a comparable treatment of the relationship between class and race, though van Dijk (1991) refers to social structural forces in his analysis of racism and the press. The reference offers little more than a suggestive gesture in an otherwise systematic analysis of news discourse.

In addition to efforts to reconceptualize the cultural industries, European political economy research has been especially active in recent years in examining telecommunication and the new computer communication technologies. This is partly the result of accelerating developments in micro-electronics and aerospace technology that have introduced a range of smaller, faster, and cheaper devices for the production, distribution, and display of communication and information. One of the major contributions of European political economy research has been to situate these technological changes within the wider context of changes in the power relations of telecommunication and new technologies. Specifically, over the past decade or so, European governments and businesses have made fundamental changes in their approach to this area. Across Europe, telecommunication was historically run by state monopolies that balanced a wide range of competing price and service demands. Led by Great Britain, most European telecommunication systems are now in various stages of privatizing state monopolies, opening their equipment and service markets to domestic and, though more slowly, to international competition, and establishing regulatory bodies to manage the transition. This marks a more significant change in direction than has taken place in North America, where competition and regulatory change were introduced into national systems that were already in private hands and already subject to government regulation.

Moreover, the transformation of European telecommunication took place as the continent moved toward transnational economic integration.

By providing a critique of technicist arguments without ignoring real changes in technology and a critique of the extremes of atheoretical description and abstract economic modelling, political economy research has addressed the social structural constituents and consequences of these changes. Hamelink (1983) provided one of the early groundwork studies that identified the relationship of finance and banking to the new information industries. More recently, Hills (1986) produced a comparative analysis of political change in telecommunication that connects a changing policy environment to changes in the relationships among the state, capital, and labor in three leading nations, each with its own unique historical variations. It remains one of the few European accounts that addresses the changing role of labor in the new telecommunication regime (see also Costello et al., 1989; Humphreys, 1986). Hills (with Papathanassopoulos, 1991) followed this with an analysis that situated telecommunication policy within the context of changes in communication technology policies across Europe and the United States, and which, she maintains, threaten democratic practices. What Hills refers to as 'the democracy gap' is a fundamental theme in much of the political economy literature. Drawing on a critical reading of theories of the public sphere, particularly the work of Habermas, Garnham (1990) examines the threats to public life that grow out of reorganizing tele-communication along strict market lines to meet the market demands of consumers rather than the needs of citizens (see also Becker, 1989; Mansell, 1993).[58]

Though much of the political economy literature takes a critical view of technology, there is some interest in exploring the possibilities of using the technology to promote democratic interests. For example, Mulgan (1991), drawing on the general thrust of the British 'New Times' movement, supports making use of new technologies to deconcentrate authority and open opportunities for public alternatives outside of the state apparatus. The general analysis of communication and information technology takes a prominent place in European political economy research, with much of it structured around a tension over the use of technology. Unfortunately, this is an area that has been too prone to caricatures of the literature. On the one hand are those who reject new technologies and earn the disparaging label of Luddite.[59] On the other are those who believe that new communication and

---

58. Though he supports the idea of using the public sphere as a critical category, Garnham is careful to criticize Habermas' uncritical acceptance of the term's historical connections to individualism, patriarchy, and the market.

59. The term 'Luddite' also tends to be misused. Historians have determined that these were not unenlightened marauders bent on stopping technology. Rather, they were by and large intelligent workers who used 'machine breaking' as one among a number of strategies to prevent wage cuts or win pay raises. In the absence of institutionalized labor–management processes, Luddism was one of the few defenses available to working people (Sale, 1995; Thomis, 1972).

information technologies are the key to realizing democracy. Neither of these images holds up well for most research in the political economy of new communication and information technologies, including the European literature. Though drawing on a tradition of technological democracy outlined in Enzensberger (1974), which leads him to support the benefits of the technology under public control, Mulgan nevertheless recognizes the anti-democratic power of transnational corporate networks, and equally the need, made all the more essential by the technology itself, to redefine both 'public' and 'control.' One finds similar sensitivity in other work that tends to emphasize the technology's benefit for more than just business and the privileged (Jöuet, 1987).[60]

This is also the case for work taking a more critical position on communication and information technology. Webster and Robins have produced a formidable body of research on the ways technology is being used to widen the control of transnational business and to deepen class and gender divisions. One of their most important contributions (Webster and Robins, 1986) takes up the provocative subtitle 'A Luddite Analysis' and is sharply critical of post-Fordism for what they conclude is a far too sympathetic account of the technology. In its place, they suggest a neo-Fordist analysis that documents how business and the state make use of the new computer communication technologies to address the crises of both accumulation and control in contemporary capitalism. In essence, one of the great benefits of the new technology is that it helps business and government to maintain hegemony without the social contract that was the price they had to absorb under Fordism. Nevertheless, Webster and Robins do not permit this powerful attack to devolve into caricature. They recognize both the contradictions and forms of resistance that the transformation to neo-Fordism brings about. Their vision of Luddism, in keeping with the historical reality, acknowledges the active agency of classes and movements that respond to technological change by defending their interests, and that use their skill, including their technical skill, to create alternative social arrangements. This is an argument mounted in other critical political economies of the new technology (Becker, 1988; Cesareo, 1992).

Before concluding the European section of this overview, it is useful to address two issues. The first is the relationship of institutional research to the political economy tradition reviewed here, and the second is the question of a 'new revisionism.' In their most recent presentation of a political economy approach, Golding and Murdock (1991: 15) distinguish their critical political

---

60. It is also interesting to observe that, particularly in France, research in the 1980s and early 1990s tended to emphasize a more supportive view of the technology than was the case in the 1970s. One can only speculate that this may have something to do with the shift from conservative to socialist rule and the commitment of the latter to the development of technology for widespread public use (e.g. upgrading the telephone system, development of Minitel, etc.).

economy from cultural studies, which concentrates on the 'construction and consumption of media meanings', and from those studies taken up with 'the economic organization of media industries.' Their departure from the latter is based on an interest in the relationship of the symbolic to the economic and on their commitment to critique or 'a theoretically informed understanding of the social order in which communications and cultural phenomena are being studied' (1991: 15–16). Although one finds examples in the North American literature (Turow, 1984), there are relatively more academic studies that address the institutional map or economic organization of the media industries in Europe.

There is no absolutely firm demarcation between political economic and organizational research on the media industries. Typical of boundary areas, this one contains enough ambiguity to suggest caution in any assessment.[61] Nevertheless, Golding and Murdock's point is important: political economy research is defined by more than an institutional map of the media industries. One way to more fully comprehend the wider dimensions of political economy is by comparison with organizational research. The latter has made a significant contribution to understanding the industry map and how it is being rewritten. Though much of this work addresses national or pan-European concerns (Blumler and Nossiter, 1991; Vedel and Luven, 1993), there are also notable examples of research on international developments (Negrine and Papathanassopoulos, 1990; Tunstall and Palmer, 1991). One can distinguish this work from the political economy tradition because it is principally interested in describing the state of the industry and its tendencies. Its concern for developments in policy and regulation, i.e., for the relationship between the state and the economic, mark a departure from treatments in orthodox economics, and its inclusion of implicit critical concerns over power constitutes another departure from the mainstream. Nevertheless, the organizational or institutional approach is not substantially interested in a theoretical understanding of these developments, i.e., with situating them within a wider capitalist totality encompassing class and other social relations. Nor is it centrally concerned with a sustained critique from a moral evaluative position which Golding and Murdock (1991: 18) suggest addresses 'justice, equity, and the public good.' Though organizational and institutional work expands the scope of research that conventional treatments narrowly confine to economic performance measures, it stops short of sustained political economy. This distinction contributes to understanding the political economic nature of Miège's work. Yes, it is the case that he departs from some political economy by concentrating on internal distinctions within the cultural industries. Neverthless, Miège is clearly interested in understanding the relationship of these distinctions to fundamental

---

61. Self-definition is not particularly helpful. One of the more substantial *organizational* analyses is titled *The Political Economy of Communications* (Dyson and Humphreys, 1990).

processes in capitalism, e.g. commodity production, and to the opportunities they present for social resistance.

Recent thinking (Curran, 1990; Curran and Gurevitch, 1991) about the state of mass communication research, including the political economy tradition, has raised questions about a 'new revisionism.' Although Curran claims the warrant carefully and with reference to important exceptions, he nevertheless concludes, referring to the general discipline of communication studies, that 'a sea change has occurred in the field':

> The most important and significant overall shift has been the steady advance of pluralist themes within the radical tradition: in particular, the repudiation of the totalizing, explanatory frameworks of Marxism, the reconceptualization of the audience as creative and active and the shift from the political to a popular aesthetic. (Curran, 1990: 157–158)

Although each of these areas is of concern to political economy, it is Curran's view of 'revisionist accounts of media organizations' that touches political economy most directly. Here Curran charges that 'disenchantment with the class conflict model of society,' influenced by the widespread impact of Foucault, led to a 'retreat from former positions.' Although these developments influenced most radical accounts in mass media research, 'the political economy approach . . . was the first to buckle' (Curran, 1990: 142). Specifically, he claims that in the 1980s Golding, Murdock, and Curran himself 'began to back off.' Golding did so by stressing ideological management and the individual values of reporters, rather than press ownership, to account for tabloid attacks on welfare recipients. Furthermore, Curran charges that Murdock did so by turning to the analysis of sources and discourses over ownership and management pressure to explain coverage of 1981 race riots in Britain.

In addition to raising critical points about the political economy perspective, Curran is interested in suggesting a convergence trend. Pluralist scholars, he contends, are shifting away from an emphasis on the individual autonomy of journalists to take up issues of structural constraint and power. They are also departing from a traditional interest in defending market neutrality to take up market deficiencies and failures. He maintains that the outcome of these reciprocal shifts is not full convergence, because pluralists and political economists continue to differ in how they theorize economic and political power. Nevertheless, 'an intermediate perspective situated between these two positions has emerged as dominant' (Curran, 1990).

Golding and Murdock, as well as Halloran, take issue with Curran's interpretation. All three agree (interviews, April 1992) that he is off the mark in claiming that the political economy interpretation can be, in Curran's description, 'associated with the Leicester Centre for Mass Communication Research,' comparable to 'an alternative, radical culturalist approach, associated with the Birmingham Centre for Contemporary Cultural Studies' (Curran, 1990: 139). As noted earlier, they maintain that the Leicester Centre never identified itself with a political economy approach in anything approaching· Birmingham's mission to promote cultural studies. According to them, political economy was a primary interest of Golding and Murdock, but had practically nothing to do with the Centre's work, which was principally taken up with traditional sociological, socio-cultural, and social problem-oriented research. This is important because the 'new revisionist' thesis implies some change in a sustained center of activity which these principal participants contend never existed.

Halloran maintains that Curran's analysis would benefit from a longer view of the Centre's activities which would reveal its long-standing commitment to a critical sociology, rather than to political economy, which appeared with Golding and Murdock, and to a lesser degree one or two others, and left with them. Golding and Murdock disagree fundamentally with Curran's interpretation of the field of communication studies, including political economy. Murdock summarizes their view by asserting that 'this is not a map of the field I inhabit.' Specifically, both contend that the suggestion of revisionism, buckling, or back-tracking fails to take into account the range of their work, which has consistently taken a broad view of Marxian theory that incorporates ideological critique, semiotics, social policy analysis, and a concern for the complete circuit of communicative activity, including production, distribution, and reception. Both note that, along with their earliest defining statements in political economy, they worked on a broad range of problems, following particularly Golding's interest in social policy and Murdock's in semiotics and discourse analysis. Curran, they maintain, mistakenly focuses on one piece of their early work, which set an agenda for political economy, and compares it to the wider range of problems they address today to conclude that they are back-tracking. Golding and Murdock conclude that, though their current work responds to new political and intellectual problems, it is consistent with their broad range of interests. Hence, even as their research leads them to address Thatcherite social welfare ideology and audience reception, they return (Golding and Murdock, 1991) to the essential principles of their political economy approach.[62] In sum, they contend that Curran's interpretation of their recent work as a back-tracking from the Leicester approach misreads Leicester, their work, and political economy.

Though the debate about Leicester, the reading of Golding and Murdock's work, and the wider interest in a 'new revisionism' are important, what

---

62. Curran appears to be of two minds about their recent map of the field. On the one hand he considers it simply a 're-presentation of a political economy perspective,' on the other an effort 'to distance themselves from simple instrumentalist and structural views of Marxist political economy, and define "economic determination" as an initial limitation and constraint' (Curran and Gurevitch, 1991: 10–11). Golding and Murdock maintain that they have consistently positioned themselves against simplistic political economic readings and argued for limiting economic determination to the 'first instance.' In their view, Curran's interpretation lives up to the popular caricature of the rigid early Marxist transformed into a more flexible, indeed revisionist, scholar, but it does not match the evidence.

makes the debate most interesting is what it reveals about different conceptions of political economy.[63] Golding and Murdock have consistently taken a broad view of the approach that, in addition to the standard interest in social class, the commodity circuit, corporate structure and the state, insists on a critical, moral philosophical understanding of the wider social totality. Regarding the latter, they see the task of political economy to 'focus on the interplay between the symbolic and economic dimensions of public communications' (1991: 15). Their vision of political economy is so broad that it appears to occupy what some, including Curran, might see as the task of communication studies in general. Although Curran does not offer an explicit definition of political economy, it appears from his assessment of the field that he would see it in far narrower terms, comprising principally the analysis of economic ownership and managerial control and the influence of these on media content. From his criticism of Murdock, one can only conclude that he does not consider the analysis of media sources to be a principal dimension of political economic analysis (Curran, 1990: 143). But source analysis is a central element of most political economies of the media, including the strongest political economy readings.[64] The debate about revisionism, at least as it applies to political economy, might better be redirected to the broader question of what constitutes the central dimensions of the discipline. At stake is more than whether we can observe backtracking and buckling. Rather, the important implication of Curran's critique is that political economy needs to reflect on its central agenda and on how the approach differs, if at all, from what should constitute the general field of communication studies.

However one responds to Curran's critique, it is important because it opens opportunities for serious debate that has been lacking in political economic analysis. There are few substantial published exchanges on central issues in the field. Nicholas Garnham's (1981) exchange with the board of *Screen* on the relationship between production and representation is one; the debate over Smythe's contention that communication was a 'blindspot' of

<hr>

63. This is not the place for an extended appraisal of Curran's thesis, which would require a detailed analysis of the evolution of positions within both the political economic and liberal pluralist perspectives, which he claims are moving closer together, if not becoming fully convergent. Nevertheless, one imagines that liberal pluralists would share some of Golding and Murdock's concerns. For example, Curran (1990: 144) claims a shift in pluralism from a focus, exemplified in Tunstall (1981), on the individual autonomy of journalists to a concern for 'the interconnections between media organizations and power centres.' In spite of its surface appeal, this thesis can be challenged by examining Tunstall's own work. Were Curran to begin in 1977 rather than 1981, he would have found Tunstall's *The Media are American*, a work that is arguably more structural and less centered on the individual autonomy of media workers than anything he produced subsequently. Testing a revisionist thesis is no simple matter. It requires a clear sense of what constitutes revision, what constituted the original vision or conceptual position, and it requires an understanding of the history that comes between original vision and the hypothesized revision.

64. For example, the analysis of news sources is a central element in Herman and Chomsky's (1988) political economy propaganda model.

Western Marxism is another. Though Curran's work addresses more than the political economy approach, it raises questions that are particularly central to it, including the relationship of political economy to cultural studies, to Marxian theory, and to the broader range of approaches to communication studies.

The 'Third World' and the Political Economy of Communication

The Third World has occupied an important place as both the subject and the source of research in the political economy of communication. The concluding section of this chapter starts with one dimension of the former and proceeds to address the contribution to research from Third World scholars and research centers. The reason for addressing the Third World as subject at this time is because its contested nature is central to comprehending the literature in this area.

The 'Third World' is one of those categories that is considerably less self-evident than it appears.[65] The appearance derives from its use as a descriptive term that makes no theoretical claims, but simply denotes the less developed or developing countries which were not part of the Second World of nations closely aligned with the former Soviet Union. The end of Soviet communism eliminates the need to refer to a Third World as distinct from a Second, but eases the use of the term simply as a default identifying what is not part of the core of developed nations. Even such a simple denotation runs into difficulty when one confronts nations at either end of the 'developing' category such as South Korea and other of the 'Newly Industrialized Countries' of Asia at the more well-to-do end and, at the other, nations such as Somalia or Haiti which are experiencing growing absolute impoverishment and marginalization, rather than anything even remotely approaching development. Nevertheless, 'Third World' has proven serviceable to categorize nations outside the highly developed core of North America, Western Europe, Japan, Australia, and New Zealand.

The term 'Third World' becomes particularly problematic, as Ahmad (1992) has documented, when it is used in the theoretical sense to define a political position within the global political economy. This is principally because the term places nationalism in the foreground and drags along with it the conflict between capitalism and socialism. The root of the term's distinction to denote a source of resistance and a real alternative was connected to nationalism, specifically to national identification with an existing state, rather than with the choice of a defining mode of production. Consequently, Third World also meant an identification with an existing

65. Reeves' (1993) overview of research in this area acknowledges that it is a 'problematic concept' but nevertheless values it enough to call his book *Communications and the 'Third World'*.

class structure, including all of its deficiencies and deformities. The Third World inevitably takes on the widely varying appearance of a collection of national states united by little more than the warrant on state power held by their respective national elites. What little coherence exists derives not from commitment to resisting a dominant mode of production, but from nationalism as an alternative to both globalization as a political economic category and to post-structuralism as its literary critical counterpart. But nationalism is, at best, a site of resistance for a range of class forces with different goals and, at worst, the ideology of a national governing comprador class. When it replaces socialism as the source of resistance to a triumphant capitalism, nationalism, including Third World nationalism, offers little more than an easy target for the inevitabilities advanced by proponents of globalization and postmodernism. These issues are addressed in subsequent chapters. Taking into account the contested nature of the subject area, including the problematic relationship of nationalism to capitalism and socialism, we turn now to a discussion of central Third World contributions to political economic research.

Third World research also departs from its counterpart in the developed world because it was forged out of a series of social struggles defined in several ways in different regions of the world. Variously identified as anti-colonial, national liberation, or socialist struggles, these eruptions of the post-World War II era helped to create an intellectual and research agenda. In fact, it was those who played a leading role in revolutionary activity, people like Mao Zedong, Ho Chi Minh, Amilcar Cabral, and Che Guevara, who were also its leading intellectuals. These leaders of the period's liberation movements are also notable in that they explicitly recognized the importance of controlling the means of communication, including radio and other electronic means, to build support for revolution. Intellectual leaders like Frantz Fanon (1965) in Algeria and Brazilian Paulo Freire (1974) throughout Latin America wrote specifically on the mass media and literacy as tools of revolutionary activity. Though a concern for communication, public opinion, and ideology had marked earlier variations on Marxian and critical thought, their work provided a departure from economistic tendencies. Forged in the 'hot wars' of the 1950s and early 1960s, Third World research took off in two related directions. First, it developed a critique of conservative and liberal developmentalist approaches, the major response of the former colonial powers to the political and military successes of anti-imperialist struggles. Second, it presented a spectrum of perspectives, best known as dependency theory, that constituted its own framework for understanding transformations in the global political economy.

The approach known as developmentalism or modernization theory was also forged in struggle. In this case, it was the recognition of the developed West, particularly the United States, that the victory over fascism left little time for triumphalism because communism and what the West perceived to be its many manifestations in wars of socialist and national liberation stood in the way of global capitalist expansion. In order to overcome these impediments, to win the Third World War, i.e. to defeat communism and pacify the Third World, the West mounted an unprecedented global military, political, economic, and ideological campaign. Developmentalism, one of its leading intellectual inspirations, brought together an elite corps of academics based in leading universities and research centers to determine how to safely secure the Third World within capitalism. Since its core notions have been subjected to a withering criticism that helped hone the intellectual strength of Third World scholars and their colleagues in the developed and socialist worlds, modernization theory is easy to dismiss as a simplistic apologia for capitalist hegemony. But that would be a mistake. There is no doubting the use of the perspective as a vehicle to defend the image of the United States as a different world power, one that helps nations beyond its shores, including those it conquered in warfare, to join the modern world. However, in addition to this, modernization theory, particularly as a theory of communication, contained a sophisticated set of tools that responded to changing military, political, and intellectual conditions in order to construct a hegemony.

Modernization theory arose out of a fundamental problem facing the United States, and to a lesser degree its Western allies, in the aftermath of World War II. The West confronted decolonization movements across Africa and Asia, and political upheavals in Latin America. Only the United States was in a position to manage these developments and bring the many newly independent nations within the evolving stratified hierarchy of the post-war circuits of capitalism. Much has been made of modernization theory as an outgrowth of classic sociological models, developed most explicitly by Tönnies, that distinguished traditional from modern, rural from urban, *Gemeinschaft* from *Gesellschaft* (Mattelart and Mattelart, 1992: 171–172). The problem with this view is the implication that modernization proponents were unsophisticated social scientists trying to apply simplistic, textbook sociology. People like Lerner, Pool, and other modernization theorists not only read their Tönnies, they also understood just how the conception of 'modern' had changed from his turn-of-the-century view.

The theory of modernization meant a reconstitution of the international division of labor amalgamating the non-Western world into the emerging international structural hierarchy. One element of this was 'nation-building,' a process of creating national elites that could effectively substitute nationalism for the alternative models of socialism on offer from the Soviet Union and, soon after the end of the war, China. Under the banner of national identity, these elite class fractions would incorporate the remaining social structural forces necessary to fend off the challenge of revolution and socialism that threatened to transcend national differences and organize the range of excluded classes and strata. Although it repeatedly attempted to do so, the United States could not achieve this goal by military means alone, nor would its own domestic pressures permit matching the Marshall Plan with a similar program for the underdeveloped world.[66] Along with military and economic weaponry, the United States made use of those communication and intelligence tools that its media and information industries had begun to hone before the war and which paid significant dividends throughout the conflict.[67] In the early years, as Samarajiwa (1985) and others (Mattelart and Mattelart, 1992; Sussman and Lent, 1991) have documented, this meant applying the methods of psychological warfare to, in the words of one of its leading figures, Harold Laswell, 'clarify the identity of genuine allies and enemies' in the struggle with the Soviet Union. Daniel Lerner's book *Sykewar* (1949) became the model for his classic work in the field *The Passing of Traditional Society* (1958). The latter used extensive interviews to map the range of attitudes and values that would support or retard modernization, understood in numerous ways, but particularly as support for those national and international forces whose goal it was to construct a market economy. Later on, particularly in the work of Schramm (1964), modernization theorists turned directly to the mass media as a vehicle to achieve this goal. In fact, the level of media development became one of the principal indicators of general societal development. Following directly from this premise, Rogers (Rogers with Shoemaker, 1971) took on the task of examining the general propensity to innovation and social change, including the introduction of modern means of communication. This was crucial because improving the general receptiveness to media technologies and media messages was vital to the wider aims of development, including the social need to change extended family structures, the economic need to create a market economy, and the political need to build a supportive class of national and local leaders. Charting the diffusion of innovation was another means to map a target, in this case a target of opportunity for the Western way of life, including its mass media.

The communication research program inspired by the modernization thesis was very influential. It provided enormous quantities of information on the behavior, attitudes, and values of Third World people and helped to shape university communication programs and research centers. Speaking about Latin America, McAnany (1986: 29) contends that the first generation or two of indigenous communication scholars were trained in the American functionalist tradition from which modernization theory descended. In a

66. Proposals for a Third World equivalent to the Marshall Plan received little serious attention, and when they did, as with President Kennedy's proposed Alliance for Progress in Latin America, the actual dollars never matched the rhetoric. It is also important to note that though the Marshall Plan involved a real economic commitment, the commitment was most important to U.S. businesses understandably eager to win access to European markets unimpeded by socialist or communist threats.

67. There is research on the links between wartime intelligence activity and the American developmentalist strategy (Samarajiwa, 1985; Sussman and Lent, 1991). But the communication strategy was not only forged in action against the enemy. In fact, some of the most significant strides in survey and intelligence research were carried out on the most substantial 'captive audience' ever marshalled in American history, its armed forces (see Stouffer, 1949).

region with scant resources, this meant that most schools, journals, and texts were funded and organized with U.S. government assistance and led by proponents of the modernization thesis.

Nevertheless, however powerful the impact on all of these levels, modernization could do little to improve the real economic conditions of Third World people. The yawning gap between prescription and accomplishment was filled by a growing number of critics, some of whom sharpened their skills in the political economy of the mass media by dissecting the modernization thesis. This was particularly the case in Latin America, partly because this region was arguably the most important target of the developmentalist project. The general problem of sharing the hemisphere with nations in poverty and social upheaval was compounded for the United States following the 1959 victory of the Cuban revolution. Partly as a result of the 'special treatment' that the modernization program brought to Latin America, critical scholarship developed relatively early there with the work of Mattelart in Chile, Freire in Brazil, Pasquali (1967) in Venezuela, and Veron (1987) in Argentina.[68] These were among the first to examine the consequences of media development programs. In their studies of literacy, mass culture, journalism, and television, they showed how Western media companies were the chief beneficiaries of modernization programs. For the people of Latin America, they were either a waste of money or the instrument to deepen inequalities and dependencies.

In the late 1960s and throughout the 1970s, the critique mounted as research expanded over the range of mass media and received significant theoretical grounding with the emergence of dependency theory (Beltrán, 1976). Political economy research received a significant boost in 1976 with the establishment in Mexico City of the Instituto Latinamericano de Estudios (ILET). ILET originally comprised a group of scholars led by Fernando Reyes Matta, Rafael Roncagliolo, Herbert Schmucler, and Diego Portales. Its principal interest has always been the study of transnational business, particularly the impact of media companies. ILET's impact was most strongly felt in international policy debates, particularly through the work of Juan Somavia, a member of the MacBride Commission (Marques de Melo, 1991: 59–73). According to Roncagliolo (1986: 79), the ILET media research agenda addressed three central questions:

1. What is the place of culture in the transnationalization process and of communication within cultural processes?

---

68. The work of Antonio Pasquali and Eliseo Veron is less well known in North America. The former made use of his training in existentialist philosophy to critique the mechanistic formulations of modernization theorists, who, he contended, were not interested in communication at all but rather with using information and technology as the means to build a mass society in Latin America. Veron was a Marxist, influenced by the structuralist work of Lévi-Strauss and Barthes, whose principal interest was the critique of ideology, including the ideological apparatus of Western 'modernization.' For an overview of the emergence of cultural studies in Latin America, see Alan O'Connor (1991).

2. What does the transnationalization of consumption consist of, if it signifies something more than the homogenization of demand at the international level?
3. Is there such a thing as a 'transnational culture,' or are there simply internationalized patterns of behavior?

This conceptual scheme situates media within cultural production and consumption and the latter within the general process of transnationalization. Moreover it places at the center of its problematic the relationship among transnationalization, internationalization, and homogenization.[69] In addition to documenting the negative consequences of media modernization projects for the people of Latin America, ILET and others contributed to and benefited from the development of an alternative theoretical framework generally referred to as dependency theory.

Among other centers of communication research, the Institute for Latin America, IPAL, founded in Lima, Peru, in 1983, stands out as a major source of research in political economy. Under the direction of its founder, Rafael Roncagliolo, IPAL has carried political economic research in two directions that are increasingly important to the approach. Going beyond the study of print and electronic media, IPAL has been particularly interested in the social relations of new communication and information technologies. This has placed it at the center of debates over what appears to be the next phase of modernization theory – the development of market-based telecommunication and telematics systems across the Third World. Furthermore, IPAL has been interested in the culture of social resistance and alternative social practices organized around popular culture and communication.

The political economy of communication has also been a prominent feature in Cuban research, led by Enrique Manet at the University of Havana. Manet (1988) has been particularly active in providing the political economic groundwork, with thorough analyses of media systems across Latin America, for his leading role in the promotion of a socialist version of a New World Information and Communication Order.

Although dependency theory was grounded in explicit theoretical concerns (Amin, 1976; Baran, 1957; Cardoso and Faletto, 1979; Dos Santos, 1970; Emmanuel, 1972; Gunder Frank, 1969), there have been enough disagreements about the meaning of dependency to warrant some caution in any brief on the perspective. There appears to be most agreement on the view that transnational businesses based in core countries, with the support of their respective states, exercise control over countries outside the core by setting the terms for market transactions over resources, production, and labor. By controlling the terms of exchange and the structure of markets,

---

69. This approach is significant because it suggests that Latin American media scholars recognized early on that the relationship between political economy and culture is not only important but also problematic. The same goes for the relationship between transnational, international, and homogeneity. Their approach to political economy was neither simplistic nor mechanistic.

transnational capital establishes the conditions of economic activity in the hinterland, including the extent of development. At best, the outcome is dependent development, at worst the development of underdevelopment. As its critics have not been hesitant to point out, the dependency approach concentrates on how external forces set the conditions for the form of social and economic development, paying less attention to the contribution made by local forces and relations of production, including the indigenous class structure.

One version of the dependency approach shifted the terms of debate to the cultural domain, as scholars whose interest was primarily in media and culture examined dependency on circuits of production, distribution, and reception controlled by transnational media firms and the state. Here was more than an empirical assessment of how well modernization theorists met their development goals. Dependency theory offered an alternative explanation that situated the practices described by modernization theorists within the wider context of transnational power and dependency, including an admittedly functional observation that modernization was an instrument to develop underdevelopment.

Dependency theory enjoyed widespread influence and equally widespread criticism. It was criticized for concentrating on the impact of transnational business on development to the neglect of internal class and power relations. Dependency theorists responded by examining the roles of comprador elites in these societies, and the roles of the richer semi-peripheral societies in specific regions, each of which played a substantial role in the core–hinterland circuit. Criticism was also directed at economistic tendencies within the perspective. Specifically, critics maintained that dependency theory tended to rest on the logic of transnational capital that appeared to capture the state, turning the state into little more than an instrument to manage the accumulation process. One response was to broaden the dependency approach by incorporating a more activist reading of the state, one which recognized the need to develop transnational state structures on the order of the European Community (now Union), the Group of Seven, etc., to harmonize conflicting economic, political, and social policies and to respond to the conflicting demands of social classes, movements, and interests. Moreover, dependency theory provided more room for the analysis of culture, a long-standing interest of critical communication research in the Third World, but an interest that had fit uneasily within the overall economic thrust of the dependency approach. Specifically, the critique of dependency theory provided some room for those who would make the case for cultural imperialism, particularly to advance an examination of the full political economic circuit and of the processes and struggles that made up the reception and constitution of culture (Mattelart, 1986). At the same time, however, the critique also contributed to the deeper attacks on political economic analysis developing in various strands of post-structuralist thought. This view rejects the value of talking about circuits of capital and linkages between political economic processes and cultural practices. Maintaining that such analysis mistakenly constructs social totalities out of at best loosely articulated, discrete, local practices, post-structuralism would do away with dependency theory as simply another attempt to create a metanarrative, a totalizing discourse unwarranted by social and cultural practices (Featherstone, 1990; Tomlinson, 1991).

Latin American scholars have been particularly strong in applying the political economy perspective to the concrete study of media structures and practices. These include studies on the political economy of advertising (Janus, 1986), international news systems (Reyes Matta, 1979), television (Beltrán and Fox de Cardona, 1980), and the general role of the media in the transformation of Latin American politics (Fox, 1988). In addition to these works, which are taken up with the explicit development of hegemony, there is also a strong tradition of examining social resistance and the construction of popular culture (Mattelart, 1986; Reyes Matta, 1983; Simpson Grinberg, 1981).[70]

Recent political economic analyses by Latin American scholars have concentrated on struggles over the extension of dependency through the use of new computer communication technologies. These studies are particularly important because they demonstrate how new technologies are central to the hemispheric integration of business activities as well as to the production of commercial culture. As Oliveira (1992) has indicated, harmonization has been a central goal of trade agreements within and between countries in North and South America and the integration of telecommunication is an essential first step. This is because telecommunication provides all businesses with the essential means to integrate their operations internally and externally. Moreover, the development of these technologies strengthens media dependency as well. Responding to those who claim that the growing power of national elites and their media operations counters the conclusions of dependency theorists, Oliveira (1991: 211) argues that the thesis 'is alive and well':

> underdevelopment appears to be a synergistic process involving dependent industrialization, mass media, global advertising, imported consumption patterns, and income concentration. Media and advertising . . . promote a consumeristic climate that materializes by increasing wages for a few and repressing the earnings of most.

Based on his research in Brazil, Oliveira concludes that national media systems are controlled by national elites with close ties to Western capital, depend on it for technology, and support it through programming that largely promotes consumerist values that the overwhelming majority of the

---

70. As Siegelaub (1983: 11) notes, 'One of the most "popular" misconceptions is the "popular" conception of the popular.' Siegelaub joins those cited here in defining the popular as a culture largely constructed by social groups themselves to meet their own needs, rather than by corporations using wage labor to produce culture for the marketplace (as in one dictionary definition of the popular song as 'a song written for its immediate commercial potential').

population cannot attain. Although their analysis of telecommunication and media policies in Brazil leads Fadul and Straubhaar (1991) to see nationalism as a progressive force, they agree with Oliveira that the United States and the International Monetary Fund remain major threats that require alliances and trade agreements within Latin America rather than between Latin nations and the United States.

Though Latin America has taken the lead in developing and applying a political economy perspective, there are important exemplars of the approach, rooted in specific regional concerns of Africa and Asia. As in Latin America, political economy perspectives have responded to extreme social necessity and the failures of modernization theory and developmentalist projects. This is particularly the case in Africa, the site of Lerner's earliest work and of continuing efforts to apply development approaches in communication (Head, 1974; Wedell, 1986). One of the leading figures in black Africa to take up the political economy of communication, S.T. Kwame Boafo (1991: 103), describes the present as a

> seemingly intractable liberation struggle against an inadequate supply of food, water, shelter, and clothing; an ever increasing population growth rate; low life expectancy; high infant mortality; and continuous political and economic strife, creating millions of political and economic refugees . . . .

Africans have taken a leading role in the movement for a New World Information and Communication Order. In spite of intense attacks from Western governments and media, Amadou Mahtar M'Bow, then Director General of UNESCO, with the overwhelming support of member states in the Third World, led the effort to promote the movement. Nevertheless, as Boafo suggests, the outcome reflects not only the power of the West to overturn reform, but also the limits of reform efforts based almost entirely on national sovereignty considerations. Along with Boafo, Ugboajah and Uche, among others, have been leading figures in the application of a political economic approach to communication in Africa. Their work has ranged widely over popular culture (Uche, 1986) and the new technologies (Ugboajah, 1986), as well as the traditional problem of understanding the media industries (Boafo and George, 1992). They have produced sharp critiques of the consequences of colonial rule, neo-colonial media systems, and the need to develop popular forms of resistance, as well as intervention in the policy arena. Nevertheless, their work can be distinguished from an earlier tradition that took a more explicitly socialist stance toward media and development (Ng'wanakilala, 1981). Today this latter position is evident in South Africa, where the African National Congress has adopted a Media Charter (1992: 41) that includes a commitment to modernization but starts from the premise that democracy, made up of full and equal participation of citizens, is the core value in any national strategy. Eschewing the language of class in favor of addressing citizens, the Charter nevertheless calls for the development of strong public media systems, controlled by communities and workers, organized to provide for the widest possible participation in the production, distribution, and exchange of communication and information.

Although there is research applying the dependency model in the Asian context (Tang and Chan, 1990), the principal focus of those working on the political economy of communication in Asia has been on the new communication and information technologies. Among the major reasons for this are the overwhelming leaps taken by Japan in the development of these technologies and the important role that several Asian nations have played in the application of these technologies to reconstitute the international division of labor. The former has given rise to a significant literature in Japan chiefly interested in articulating the social relations of computer communication based on the ideas of the 'information society' (*joho shakai*) and informatization (*johoka*) (Ito, 1989). Much of the research in this area is derivative of the early work of Machlup, Porat, and Bell. However, starting in the early 1960s, Umesao (1963), apparently independently, began his work on the development of the information industries in Japan for Japanese publications. Although Masuda's (1970, 1981) work is better known in the West, chiefly because it was published immediately in English, Umesao had an important influence on the development of social science research on the subject in Japan. This is important because, for a Western reader, his work resonates with the organic evolutionary perspective of the social Darwinists (Ito [1989: 206] notes that 'Umesao's theory reminds us of Spencer') that is reflected most recently in the work of Beniger (1986). Though later work softened the organic metaphor, much of it continues to reflect orthodox economic, political, and social theory. One of the chief exceptions is to be found in the work of Morris-Suzuki (1986, 1988, 1989), who writes with a critical eye on the political economy of computerization, the development of economics in Japan, and the social consequences of experiments making use of computer communication to restructure social activity. Morris-Suzuki's research is particularly important to a discussion of communication research in the Third World because it provides an important bridge to the second major influence on the development of research in Asia, the incorporation of poorer Asian nations into a new international division of labor organized around computer communication.

Admittedly, developmentalist communication and research tended to concentrate on Latin America, but it did not ignore Asia. In fact, one of the most substantial modernization strongholds is the East–West Center in Hawaii, which principally supports communication development projects promoting linkages between the United States and Asia. Over the past decade, along with a spectrum of development scholars, it has celebrated what appears to be the triumph of development programs among the NICs or Newly Industrialized Countries led by Singapore, South Korea, Taiwan, and Hong Kong (Jussawalla, 1986). Chiefly touting levels of economic growth and the development of the high (mainly communication and information) technology sector, supporters cite these nations as the major success stories of developmentalism. Morris-Suzuki and several Western political economists of communication, among them John Lent, Lenny Siegal, Michael Traber, and Gerald Sussman, have attacked this view and, in the process, brought to Western scholars a range of critical research in Asia that has received very little general circulation.[71] Lent (1985, 1990) has written extensively on the media in Asia and compiled documentation on research in the region that has highlighted critical scholarship. Through his Pacific Studies Center and its *Global Electronic Information Newsletter*, Siegal has documented the progress of the microelectronics industry in Asia and its ties to the United States. Based at the World Association for Christian Communication in London, Traber has supported critical work on Asia particularly through the magazine *Media Development*. Sussman (1984, 1991) has written extensively on communication, informatics, and development in Asia. Drawing in part on a critical Asian literature that includes local journals, magazines, reports, and working papers, these scholars focus on several critical points. The levels of economic growth are substantial but fragile because they depend on the general state of economies in the core countries, particularly those of Japan and the United States, especially their demand for advanced technological products. Moreover, even when demand is high, comparative advantage is difficult to sustain because it requires widespread control over a labor force in order to enforce low wages, long work hours, poor working conditions, detailed surveillance, and restrictions on the formation of trade unions. As Lee (1988) among others (see also Heyzer, 1986) have documented, women have faced the harshest control measures. Moreover, critics (Bello and Rosenfeld, 1992: 92–112) point to the destructive economic consequences of development programs in agriculture, manufacturing, and microelectronics, as rapid economic growth has taken complete precedence over environmental protection. The early triumphalism over the progress of the NICs has been substantially muted. Economic stagnation in the core has slowed demand in the high technology sector. Moreover, labor unrest, including the formation of unions, and demands for higher wages and better working conditions have sent core transnationals searching for new sites of low-cost production and have encouraged them to automate fabrication and assembly processes once reserved for low-wage labor.

Although political economy research in this region has concentrated on communication and information technologies, there is also evidence of this tradition's influence in research on the mass media as well. This is particularly the case in India, which has established one of the largest film and video industries in the world, resulting in the development of an Indian mass media research tradition that chiefly makes use of conventional British and American sources, with some Indian influence, to produce a local version of communication orthodoxy, including general support for the developmentalist thesis (Kumar, 1989). Admitedly far from numerous, political economists have challenged this mainstream orientation. From within India, P. Sainath (1992a, 1992b) has made use of a class analysis to

---

71. For a general review of critical research on the Asian NICs, see Bello and Rosenfeld (1992).

examine Western influence and internal elite accommodations in the production and distribution of news and developed a critical analysis of Western attempts to incorporate India within its trade-in-services regime. The Indian émigré Manjunath Pendakur (1990a ,1990b, 1991, 1993) has made use of his multiple national locations (the United States, Canada, and India) to produce political economies of film and video that address similar themes of reconstituting forms of dependency. It is his contention that the cultural industries play a particularly significant role in the neo-colonial period, especially for countries like Canada and India which contain a well-developed national elite that now face significant crises. Having made the necessary accommodations that required substantial sacrifices in national autonomy to achieve a privileged place in the global hierarchy, they now confront challenges from international capital, which has less need of their services, and from indigenous working class and social movements that attack national elites for declining standards of living and for the loss of national economic, political, and cultural autonomy.

Defenders of the developmentalist view have revised the perspective to better respond to their recognition that the outcome of years of promoting development has resulted in little success and that the political economic critique struck a chord in the Third World. Specifically, this revisionist version of the developmentalist view shifts enthusiastic support from mass media to new communication and information technologies, acknowledges the popularity of critical perspectives, and absorbs some of their ideas to create what amounts to a neo-developmentalist view. Equating progress with urbanization and mass media, the early modernization literature concentrated on the need to build the mass media infrastructure, including newspapers, radio, television, and cinema. One response to critiques of the recommendations and programs built on this view was to shift attention to new technologies, arguing that development actually required the construction of a telecommunication and computer communication infrastructure. This revisionist argument maintains that business leads the modernization process and that, while nothing should be neglected, it is more important to establish an advanced telecommunication and computer infrastructure for business than it is to create mass communication systems. The new version calls for the establishment of state-of-the-art digital communication systems that make it possible for businesses operating in the developing world to participate fully in the international division of labor (UN, ITU, 1985).

The second element of this revisionist response is the acknowledgement that critical perspectives, including indigenous ones, have enjoyed widespread success. Reporting on the results of a survey of Latin American and U.S. communication scholars and a citation analysis of Latin American communication journals, Chaffee et al. (1990) conclude that North American scholars do not sufficiently appreciate the influence of critical scholars, particularly Armand Mattelart, in Latin America. According to their results, Americans perceive that Latin American scholars continue to rely, in large part, on what they call 'empirical' schools of thought, operationalized as those who have advanced a developmentalist view. Contrary to this view, Latin American scholars and their journals reflect the overwhelming influence of political economic and semiotic schools of thought.[72] Though they give precedence to an explanation based on cultural factors ('The Luso-Hispanic cultural heritage is quite distinct from the northern European institutions that took root in North America'), Chafee et al. (1990: 1023) come close to admitting that critical approaches are more useful in explaining reality in Latin America:

> Theories of society that flow from a highly stratified socioeconomic order, such as the Marxist viewpoints that have been flourishing in Latin America, are a much better fit to the realities of life in that region than in the more affluent U.S. (1990: 1024)[73]

Acknowledging the popularity of the 'critical' school, modernization theory makes its own adaptations, revising some of its own orthodoxy to win back those Third World scholars who had been part of its primary audience. With considerable foresight about the need for a revision, Rogers laid the groundwork in 1976 by acknowledging the failures of technicist approaches to development and by calling for an incorporation of local cultural practices into the modernization mix. The outcome of this revision or co-optation is to expand the perspective without changing it in any fundamental way. Its essence continues to include exporting Western technology, now with greater stress on telecommunication, and incorporating Western media models, if not specific Western programming. What differentiates this revisionist tendency is a greater reliance on local social structures and cultural practices to carry out the process. Departing from earlier strategies, based on the view that people had to incorporate Western values before they could industrialize, this view now calls for using local culture as well as critical approaches to achieve the result. In essence, it concludes, one can adopt the methods of Paulo Freire to market the Western political economy.

In recent years, the rise of perspectives influenced by post-structuralism has offered a form of support for this revisionist position by arguing against the prevailing political economy view that capital, class, and the state are central forces capable of mobilizing action with broad and deep consequences for social and cultural life. In the extreme, it rejects the view that political economic forces exist in any degree of articulation holding significance for the ways people conduct their lives. Post-structuralism defends,

---

72. The survey suffers from an unusual conceptual scheme that applies Rogers' distinction between 'empirical' and 'critical' research. Since most of the latter employ research techniques that philosophies of the social sciences would describe as empirical, the scheme simply does not work. In practice, their 'empirical' category comprises the leading defenders of the developmentalist approach; the 'critical' school contains those who do not.

73. This amounts to an admission that the 'empirical' approach has failed to do what it is supposed to do, i.e., describe reality, and that critical approaches, which are, by their definition, not empirical, have accomplished precisely what empirical methods set out to do. What better test of the value of a research approach than that it provides 'a much better fit to the realities of life'?

with the modernization school, the position that political economic power has dissipated to the point of limited relevance in a world of loosening articulations, multiple subjectivities, and increasingly random readings. In essence, there is no 'map' that would link Time Warner or Matsushita to a village in Peru or Indonesia. One might talk about about the multiplicity of maps subjectively produced in the minds of corporate planners and village elders, but to conclude the conversation and suggest that one map is more useful renders one guilty of historicism, rationalism, empiricism, totalizing discourse, and other sins of the Enlightenment.

Such an approach favors the developmentalist critique of political economy, particularly its claims about the relative power of core capital and the consequences of its use for the rest of the world. Nevertheless, modernization theory flirts with post-structuralism at the peril of its own methodological and political programs. Post-structuralism does not look with much favor either on the possibility of making use of conventional scientific techniques to know what development and modernization mean or on claims for the need to modernize. Post-structuralists who have spoken on these issues (Tomlinson, 1991) favor the view that Marshall Berman (1988) offered in *All That is Solid Melts into Air*: the only meaning that modernity conjures is the tendency to eliminate structure, solidity, substance, and meaning itself. In a position that echoes the 'iron cage' sociology of Max Weber, what links Time Warner and the village is not a system of power but a process of globalization which sends both hurtling into the unknown and the unknowable.

Substance and Challenge

The political economy of communication covers a wide intellectual expanse and faces numerous challenges. It is an approach that brings together an international collection, if not a community, of scholars united not so much by a singular theoretical perspective or problematic, as by an approach to intellectual activity.

One cannot say that the approach is constituted by a community of scholars because most work as individuals who come together informally and at the meetings of associations such as the International Association for Mass Communication Research.[74] There are numerous thematic interests

74. The IAMCR has supported political economy research in several of its sections, but particularly in the section on Political Economy. According to Professor Robin Cheesman of Denmark (letter, July 1993), the section was formed at the 1976 IAMCR meeting in Leicester as the 'Materialist Theory Group' with some 25–30 persons involved, including Robin Cheesman, Nicholas Garnham, Fernando Perrone, Roque Faraone, Herbert Schiller, Graham Murdock, Peter Golding, and Janet Wasko. The group began meeting as the Political Economy section in 1980 under the headship of Cheesman and Tamas Szecsko of Hungary. The section has met at every IAMCR conference since that time. Zoltan Jakab of Hungary was appointed to the section headship in 1987 and I headed it from 1990 to 1994. In 1994 Manjunath Pendakur was elected the next section head.

that link political economists within and across regions. These include the business of communication, the role of the state, the connections between the corporate and state sectors, and the linkages between the political economy of communication and the wider global and national political economies. These concerns are often framed in the language of power, for some as institutional power, for others as class power. New themes have emerged: connections between production, discourse, and reception; the relationship of class power to gender and race; the significance of structural change within and across the communication industries; the consequences for labor and the labor process; the relationship among private, state, and public communication.

These and other substantive concerns are important for an understanding of what frames agreements and debates in the political economy approach. Beyond these, however, there is a shared sense of intellectual attitude that more or less distinguishes the approach. Acknowledging the critiques of historicism, of meta-, mythic, and simple narratives, political economists continue to maintain that history matters, that analysis requires both diachronic and synchronic methods. Similarly, although it recognizes the limitations of systems thinking, particularly in the more rarefied forms of disembodied and ahistorical functionalism, political economists generally agree that social totalities exist, that, among other forces, the means of communication are making them both stonger and more complex, and that political economy needs to situate communication within the wider social totality being forged in the global political economy. The challenge here is to comprehend the social totality without resorting to a revisionist correspondence theory that reads the cultural directly from the social or vice versa.

Political economists are also in general agreement that, however important it is to eschew moralizing, understood as the unquestioned insistence on a specific value stance, it is necessary to incorporate a moral philosophical dimension. The latter means understanding the role of moral positions in social action and recognizing that intellectuals are more than disembodied wisdom, but are social beings who make moral judgements. As intellectual social actors, they interrogate the range of moral stances and incorporate these questionings into their analyses. Finally, political economists also tend to see themselves as more than members of a community of scholars. Following Gramsci's notion of the organic intellectual, they are motivated by a sense of praxis, by the need to act on the world as well as to explain it. Nevertheless, by virtue of their commitment to research, they recognize that explanation *is* a form, though admittedly only one among many, of social action. Rejecting dichotomies that would distinguish thought from action, analysis from politics, they nevertheless do not rest on their research but see it as one tool, one form, of social transformation.

These elements of an intellectual self-definition tend to bring political economists of communication together. As the foregoing chapters emphasized, there are also numerous areas of difference. These include the degree of emphasis one places on the elements that comprise this self-definition. For example, there are important areas of difference between research that takes a value position, such as one organized around democratic communication, and those that concentrate on mapping the existing political economy of communication. Again, these differences tend to be matters of emphasis, of decisions about relative explicitness. Nevertheless, one would be remiss to neglect noting that such differences have research consequences. Beyond this, there are a wide range of substantive perspectives within political economy that constitute areas of contention about what the approach should place in the foreground of analysis. For example, there are noteworthy differences between approaches that concentrate on the global political economy, stressing for example the power of transnational communication conglomerates, and those that look at how the logic of capital is contested within the internal operations of a media firm, such as at the point of production. There are also important differences between research that insists on the centrality of social class and those that foreground gender or race within an overall political economic analysis. Moreover, one observes a range of views about the relative positioning of institutional structure, text, and the social relations of reception within this perspective.

These and other differences suggest a discipline with a wide range of standpoints, interests, emphases, and tensions. The foregoing suggests that in its diversity political economy belies attempts to reduce it to an essentialist formulation that, in the extreme, would dismiss the approach as economistic. This charge is doubly problematic. First, it misreads the depth and range of political economy, which, if nothing else, has demonstrated a profound sense of the need to push beyond economic orthodoxy. Second, it fails to appreciate the real, if not deterministic or essentialist, power of the economic in social life. This is particularly remarkable since it comes at a time when most of the world's people face the bleak reality of economic deprivation.

PART II
Rethinking and Renewing the Political Economy of Communication

Notwithstanding its strength in diversity, political economy, like other intellectual standpoints, faces a number of challenges, which the following chapters address. Since they are concerned with *rethinking* the political economy of communication, it is useful to define the term, particularly since the world's political and intellectual upheavals have given it a cachet that is not entirely conducive to understanding.

Rethinking needs to be distinguished from *revision* and *repudiation*. A revisionist view provides minor modifications, such as the use of more fashionable language or the incorporation of peripheral notions from an adversarial position, that give the perspective a new look without much substantive modification. For example, a revisionist view of the modernization approach uses the language of, for instance, sustainability or decentralization, without challenging the fundamental premise that equates modernization with capitalism and private control over the means of communication. On the other hand, repudiation rejects the basic premises of a perspective, aiming to dispose of it in favor of a distinctly different alternative or to transform it in fundamental ways. The functionalist critique of behaviorism is a good example of the former. Mounted across the social sciences in the 1950s, particularly in sociology, where Parsons sought to replace the physicalist models of Anglo-American psychology with goal-oriented action theories that took into account subjectivity and consciousness, functionalism sought, with some success, to sweep away the behaviorist tradition.[1] Althusser's project is an example of an effort to

---

1. This is particularly evident in Parsons' work (Parsons, 1966; Parsons and Shils, 1951) on a general theory of action and on cybernetic approaches to social structure. The latter is reflected in the major work of Herbert Simon (1957), whose influence has been felt in most every area of social science research, including communication and information studies (Beniger, 1986). The work of Parsons and other functionalists has been largely read as a conservative alternative to Marxian theory, its major structural alternative. This is accurate though partial, neglecting the major rift between functionalism and the behaviorism of Skinner in psychology and of Homans in sociology.

transform Marxism by eliminating elements like history, humanism and the centrality of the political economic which left other elements of the Marxian approach intact but in such a condition that the outcome represented more of a repudiation than a fulfillment or reformation of the Marxian legacy.

Rethinking lies somewhere between the opportunistic tinkering of the revisionist and the transformation that results from a *de facto* repudiation. It starts by critically acknowledging the central principles and diverse renderings of the approach. By critical, I mean coming to a deeper understanding of a perspective and its various offshoots by comparing them for their differences and similarities with one another and with alternative perspectives. Second, rethinking requires that one approach a perspective with the self-consciousness and self-reflexiveness necessary to take stock of its fundamental epistemological and conceptual foundations. This is particularly important for the political economy of communication because it has rarely engaged in this sort of activity, admittedly understandable considering that the problems it has addressed, such as the tightening concentration of media ownership, are of such substantial political significance. This drive for engagement has meant that its practitioners have lived up to the goal of praxis, but it also means that, by placing in the foreground a tendency to look outward into the world, political economy has rarely looked inward to what makes it a central perspective in communication research and a vital set of tools for understanding the global political economy. In this respect, rethinking means taking stock of accomplishments, but also reflecting critically on the relationship of these accomplishments to the fundamental characteristics of the perspective. Finally, rethinking means directly addressing streams of thought that depart in some degree or fundamentally from the political economic approach. One does this not to dress up an old perspective, as a revisionist would attempt, nor to repudiate its central tenets. Rather, the goal is to assist the process of self-reflection, to help one to sense what is most fundamental in the approach, and to influence debates about those alternative perspectives, at the very least by reminding their defenders that political economic considerations are significant.

Epistemology

In its tendency to look outward, the political economy of communication has tended not to pay much attention to its own theory of theory or epistemology. Before addressing the substantive elements that constitute this rethinking, it is useful to recapitulate briefly the elements of epistemology that were discussed in Chapter 1. The approach adopted here begins with a *realist* epistemology that understands reality as the mutual constitution of sensory observation and explanatory practices. Avoiding the extremes of subjectivism and idealism, it maintains the possibility of comprehending reality through a combination of empirical and theoretical methods. In addition, this epistemological view takes an *inclusive* and *non-reductionist* approach to understanding. This means that, without arguing for a pluralist theory of knowledge which accepts the validity of any interpretive model, this approach is open to a range of explanatory approaches and rejects the view that all reality is reducible to one specific causal force.

The goal is to steer a course between relativism and essentialism, between, for example, the conversational epistemology of Rorty (1979), which translates 'accurate representation' into whatever is 'helping us do whatever we want to do,' and those approaches that would reduce social and cultural practices to a core essentialism, whether economic, political, social, or cultural. It eschews reference to causality because the term excessively constrains social analysis.[2] Use of the term 'causality' channels thinking into identifying how a thing, viewed as a singular entity (or things viewed as a set of entities), acts directly to transform the state of another thing or things, also seen as a singular whole or wholes. The term makes it considerably more difficult to think about how things work their component parts into one another. More significantly, it resists shifting our thinking from things to processes, and from linear to non-linear relationships among them. I am also reluctant to make use of the language of determinism because its stronger manifestations suggest that one unchanging thing brings about change in another. The use of determinism to mean setting limits (Williams, 1975) is √ more acceptable, but nevertheless maintains the mental map of traditional physics which spoke of unchanged wholes changing, whether through causality or by setting limits, other wholes. The concept of overdetermination, which began with Freud and achieved singular prominence in the work of Althusser, marked a step toward a language that comprehends the social as determined by each and every other social action, process, and structure. Rather than singularities, as part of a social field that contains contradictions and conflicts as well as unities, each contained contradictory and conflicting forces which work on one another in mutual effectivity. The result is a dynamic social field irreducible to any particular essences and comprised of manifold articulations and fractures.

This reading of epistemology broadens the knowledge process from simple determination to multiple, dynamic interactions. However, the price of doing so is to shift the burden of specificity, of determining precisely how some as opposed to other articulations and fractures are realized, to the specific juncture of conceptual and empirical reality.

The language of overdetermination provides a useful step forward to a theory of knowledge that satisfies the criticism that traditional deterministic approaches oversimplify the dynamic, complex, and often non-linear relationships that comprise a social totality without eliminating determinism entirely. Though certainly a useful step, one still wonders about the need to rescue determinism at all. The need to do so is sufficiently questionable that

---

2. One hastens to add that this conclusion is not limited to the social sciences. Practitioners and philosophers of the social sciences (Resnick and Wolff, 1987) are tending to view causality as a constraint on forms of explanation that require non-linear, process-oriented thinking.

it is worthwhile to bracket determinism and consider the value of alternative formulations. Among these, *mutual constitution* contains several advantages. Suggesting interactions among elements that are themselves in the process of formation and definition, the term *constitution* foregrounds the *process of becoming* within all elements of the social field. No thing is fully formed or clearly defined, but one can specify processes at work within and between them that define the nature of the constitutive process and the relationships among the elements. 'Mutual' is preferred to 'over' because it maintains the sense of manifold without the connotation of excessive which 'over' conveys.

In this view, the social field is comprised of *processes* that mutually constitute relationships among elements. The latter include structures like the social, political, and economic institutions that are the stock in trade of social scientific analysis, the articulations and fractures between and within them, as well as the thinking, the mental maps, the conceptual schemes, and the investigatory processes of the researcher trying to make sense of these structures and relationships. What we call the results of research are made up of the mutual constitution of the object and the subject of the research process; specifically, constitutive social processes that include the active process of research itself.

This epistemology is further defined as *critical* because knowledge is produced through a process of comparison, between alternative theoretical formulations, between subsets of a particular formulation, and between two components that mutually constitute intellectual praxis. These are the commitment to understand the world and to transform it.

Ontology

Connected to this epistemological approach is an ontology that foregrounds social change, social process, and social relations against the tendency in social research, particularly in political economy, to concentrate on structures and institutions. This means that research starts from the view that social change is ubiquitous, that structures and institutions are in the process of constant change, and that it is therefore more useful to develop entry points that characterize processes rather than to name institutions. Guided by this principle, I develop a substantive map of political economy with three entry processes, starting with *commodification*, the process of transforming use to exchange value. From this, the analysis moves on to *spatialization*, the transformation of space with time, or the process of institutional extension, and finally to *structuration*, the process of constituting structures with social agency. Foregrounding social change with these processes does not replace structures and institutions, something that would substitute one form of essentialism for another. Rather these are entry points that constitute a substantive theory of political economy, one preferred choice among a range of possible means of understanding the social field.

Theoretical Parameters

These processes are referred to as *entry points* because they open the analysis and help to frame a political economy, but are not considered to be essential singularities to which all other social processes, or structures for that matter, can be reduced or which exhaust the application of a political economy approach to communication. In fact, each is marked not only by its own articulations, but by fractures, disjunctions, as well as by oppositional and alternative processes. Finally, they are mutually constituted by one another and by every other process at work in society. Among the many processes that one might choose, these are considered the most useful for developing a broad-based, inclusive political economy of communication that can address concerns raised about the approach and that enable it to confront the challenges posed by the major perspectives on its borders, namely policy studies and cultural studies.

Commodification refers to the process of transforming use values into exchange values, and the manifold ways this process is extended into the social field of communication products, of audiences, and of labor, which has been given less attention than one would expect from a political economic analysis. Conversely, Chapter 4 addresses processes that Offe awkwardly refers to as decommodification which emanate from forms of resistance in public and private life. Comprising globalization, or the worldwide agglomeration of the communication industries, and industrial restructuring, or their manifold integration, *spatialization* is the process that Marx, Harold Innis, and others referred to as the transformation of space with time. The processes of nation-building or nationality and citizenship are sources of division and opposition to spatialization. Finally, *structuration* describes the process whereby structures are mutually constituted with human agency, or, to put it more specifically, structures are constituted out of agency even as they serve as the very medium for that constitution. The outcome of structuration is a set of social relational and power processes organized around class, gender, race, and social movements that both correspond to and oppose one another.

Having begun with a discussion of the broad sweep of the general political economy literature, the book turns inward to rethink the political economy of communication. Finally, it concludes by moving outward again to approaches on the boundaries of the political economy of communication, namely *cultural studies* and *policy studies*. The aim here is to deepen the understanding of political economy, and, in the process, assess the strengths and shortcomings of these alternative perspectives by observing what defines their boundaries and by considering some of the major border exchanges that take place among political economy, cultural studies, and policy studies.

4

Commodification

The wealth of societies in which the capitalist mode of production prevails appears as an 'immense collection of commodities'; the individual commodity appears as its elementary form. Our investigation therefore begins with the analysis of the commodity.

(Marx, 1976a: 126)

the exercise of borrowing a banal statement from economic discourse and conferring meaning on it by associating with every 'market,' 'capital,' or 'profit' the qualifiers 'linguistic,' 'symbolic,' or 'of distinction,' is not so much a metaphor as it is a parody, according to the definition of Louis Marin – that is, a strategy of description and analysis involving the displacement of terminology and notions from the domain in which they were produced, their dissociation from the epistemological and methodological acts that gave birth to them, and their deployment on a different stage.

(Cot and Lautier, cited in Mattelart and Mattelart, 1992: 16–17)

The first chapter to describe the substance of rethinking political economy begins with the commodity and commodification for several reasons. The process of commodification describes the way capitalism carries out its objective of accumulating capital or realizing value through the transformation of use values into exchange values. Moreover, following Marx, who began *Capital* with a discussion of the commodity form, it is largely through 'the immense collection of commodities' that capitalism presents itself, its most common embodiment. Finally, starting with this idea suggests the need to make an adjustment in the conceptual balance of political economic analysis in communication. As this chapter documents, the latter has certainly addressed the commodity and the process of commodification. However, political economy has tended to give considerably greater weight to those business institutions and structures that produce and distribute commodities and to government bodies that regulate the process. This is partly to correct the tendency in communication studies to focus on the content and the range of ways to understand it, rather than on the structures responsible for its production. The correction is warranted, but the shortcoming of concentrating on structure is to cede content to those with little or no interest in political economy. Rather than paying too much attention to the text, political economy might better argue that it needs to pay more attention, but by attending to the text within a thorough political economic analysis.

Adam Smith and classical political economy distinguished between products whose value derives from the satisfaction of a specific human want or

need, i.e. use value, and those whose value is based on what the product can
command in exchange, i.e., exchange value. The commodity is the particular
form that products take when their production is principally organized
through the process of exchange. *Commodification is the process of trans-*
forming use values into exchange values.

Marx began *Capital* with an analysis of the commodity because he found
it to be the most visible form, the most explicit representation, of capitalist
production. Capitalism literally *appears* as an immense collection of commodities. Though this appearance did not go unnoticed in classical political
economy, the tendency was to naturalize it, a point that marked a critical
departure in Marx. What for the classicists was 'a self-evident and nature-
imposed necessity' was for Marx the product of 'a social formation in which
the process of production has mastery over man, instead of the opposite'
(Marx, 1976a: 175). One of the keys to Marxian analysis and a legacy that
has influenced all subsequent political economy is to interrogate the commodity to determine what the appearance means, to uncover the social
relations congealed in the commodity form. As Jhally (1990) has documented, in one of the few sustained analyses of the commodity form in the
communication literature, Marx took a broad view of both the commodity
and the meaning of use value. For Marx (1976a: 125), commodities ensue
from a wide range of needs, both physical and cultural ('from the stomach,
or the imagination, makes no difference') and whose use can be defined 'in
various ways.' The commodity could arise from a range of social needs –
including satisfying physical hunger and meeting or contravening the status
codes of a particular social group. Moreover, contrary to some interpretations, use value is not limited to meeting survival needs but extends to
the range of socially constituted uses.

Some critics have not been satisfied with this formulation, arguing that the
distinction between use and exchange value obscures more than it illumi-
nates. For example, Sahlins (1976: 15) contends that Marx acknowledges the
social character of all value but tends to *naturalize use value*, 'to trade away
the social determination of use-values for the biological fact that they satisfy
"human wants".' Baudrillard (1981) extends this critique by maintaining that
use value is ultimately left outside the sets of structures and codes that
constitute specific exchange values. This critique reminds us that Marx's
chief aim was to interrogate capital and, given the primacy of this interest,
he neglected detailed treatment of ideas that embody the fundamental
negation of capitalism, including use value and the contours of a socialist
society. Nevertheless, the cultural critique also defines a boundary that
political economy would have difficulty crossing because the critique aims
to do more than suggest lacunae: it substitutes an idealist relativism that
defines value as whatever the code specifies and, as suggested in the
variability of human cultural practice, this can amount to practically anything. Political economy admits to variability, but bounds it by the understanding that uses are conditioned (in Marx's language) or limited (in the

language of Raymond Williams) by the structural properties of the commodity and take their existence from them. Drawing on Rubin, Jhally (1990) suggests the language of 'partial necessity' to deal with Marx's recognition that 'usefulness does not dangle in mid-air.' Alternatively, one might suggest the multiple determination and mutual constitution of use values and retain the distinction between socially constituted use values and values which arise from a specific set of social arrangements, namely the market, which produce exchange values.

Peeling back what Marx called the 'onion skin' of the commodity appearance reveals a system of production. There are two general dimensions of significance in the relationship of commodification to communication. First, *communication processes and technologies contribute to the general process of commodification in the economy as a whole*. For example, improving the channels of communication in the clothing business, particularly with the introduction of global computer and telecommunication technologies, expands information about the entire circuit of production, distribution, and sales, which improves inventory controls thereby saving on space and increasing the likelihood that stores stock only what customers want. Second, *commodification processes at work in the society as a whole penetrate communication processes and institutions, so that improvements and contradictions in the societal commodification process influence communication as a social practice*. For example, the international tendencies to liberalization and privatization of enterprises, which picked up steam in the 1980s, were felt by public and state-run media and telecommunication institutions throughout the world.

Given the interest in situating communication within a general political economic analysis, it is useful to start from the general process of commodification and examine how it relates to communication. From the point of view of capital, the production process begins with the capitalist's purchase of the commodities *labor power* and *the means of production*. The total output is sold for more than originally invested, the addition is called *surplus value*, which may itself be invested to expand the accumulation of capital. In essence, capital is value that expands through processes of production and exchange. Marxian theory takes this analysis one step further by concluding that these are *exploitative* processes because the expansion of capitalist control eliminates alternative systems of production and forces labor into a social relationship wherein it takes on the status of a commodity, or a factor of production, along with land and raw materials, and is made to give up its control over the means of production. As a result, workers are made to exchange their labor power for a wage that does not compensate fully for the labor sold. The commodity labor is reproduced through processes of absolute (extending the working day) and relative (intensification of the labor process) exploitation that intensify the extraction of surplus value. Exploitation is a *sine qua non* of the capitalist labor process, but the degree of exploitation depends on the state of class struggle. Thus, the commodity, whose appearance fills the image space of capitalism, is also a congealed set of social relations that connect capital to the commodity labor in a struggle for control over the value generated from production and exchange.[1]

In the Marxian view, the commodity objectifies exploitative social relations by presenting them in a congealed form that naturalizes them. Hence a computer appears to us as a commodity with a defined set of use values and a specific exchange value marked by its price. Its value in use and in exchange tends to mystify the ability to comprehend the computer as the embodiment of an international division of labor that stratifies productive relations along class, gender, national, and spatial dimensions. A deeper level of mystification is revealed in Marx's analysis of *commodity fetishism*, according to which the commodity not only congeals social relations and contains the struggle over value, but takes on a life and a power of its own, over that of both its producers and consumers, which, for Marx (1976a: 165), was once largely reserved for religion:

> In order, therefore, to find an analogy we must take flight into the misty realm of religion. There the products of the human brain appear as autonomous figures endowed with a life of their own, which enter into relations both with each other and with the human race. So it is in the world of commodities with the products of men's hands. I call this the fetishism which attaches itself to the products of labor as soon as they are produced as commodities and is therefore inseparable from the production of commodities.

In fact, for him, the commodity fetish is more powerful than its counterpart in religion because commodities have a material embodiment that presents itself directly to the senses more readily than do religious beliefs.[2] In this view, the commodity contains a double mystification. First, it naturalizes the social relationship between capital and labor. It is the computer that appears and not a struggle at the point of production. Second, the commodity is reified, i.e., it takes on a life of its own that stands against the social realm and governs it. The first point sees the commodity as the natural outcome of a production process, rather than the social consequence of a fundamental social struggle; the second point completely cuts the tie to a production process and situates the commodity in its own realm controlling social life. The computer appears as a power over people, as the force that shapes, determines, constrains, or otherwise controls social development. The outcome of this double mystification is that the product of a social process is given an existence of its own and the power to shape social life.

Commodification refers to the process of turning use values into exchange values, of transforming products whose value is determined by their ability

1. My epistemology precludes the essentialism that would reduce the appearance to a social relational essence. Eschewing the language of essence, I view the commodity as mutually constituted out of both its appearance (as automobile, situation comedy, or news broadcast) and the social relations that bring it about.

2. One might dispute this contention as an unwarranted conflation of the real and the material. Nevertheless, the argument for commodity fetishism does not rest on agreeing that the commodity is somehow more real than religious faith.

to meet individual and social needs into products whose value is set by what they can bring in the marketplace. Owing in part to the emphasis on structures and objects over processes and relations in much of political economic thought, the term has not received substantial explicit treatment. Nevertheless, it is implicit in discussions of the process of capitalist expansion, ranging widely to include the global extension of the market, the privatization of public space, and the growth of exchange value in interpersonal life. Some of the leading work in the political economy of communication has taken up these themes (Ewen, 1988; H. Schiller, 1981, 1989).

This analysis distinguishes commodification from commercialization and objectification, processes with which it tends to be associated. Commercialization is a narrower process that specifically refers to the creation of a relationship between an audience and an advertiser. For example, the commercialization of the airwaves means the growth of broadcast advertising and the development of programming to deliver audiences to advertisers. Since the market encompasses more than commercialization, e.g. the commodification of labor, we view commodification as a broader process. Objectification is a still broader notion that is often conflated with commodification. For example, in his work on reification, Lukács (1971) describes the process whereby the relations between people 'take on the character of a thing and thus acquire a "phantom objectivity".' Commodification is a specific form of this process whereby the 'thing' that acquires phantom objectivity is a commodity, i.e., an object whose value is established in the marketplace. Although Lukács is careful, he tends to conflate the processes, as do those writing today from what is referred to as a post-Marxist position (Luke, 1989). One can understand the position of those who 'recognize how completely commodification has come to dominate every aspect of culture' (Luke, 1989: 10). Nevertheless, such an argument leaves one in the difficult position of either arguing for practical surrender to commodification, since it is such a totalizing process, or, conversely, uprooting the concept from its original meaning in market exchange to encompass any process of depersonalization or objectification. Admittedly, the latter strategy opens the analysis to forms of resistance, but it does so at the price of abstracting the term into so malleable a form that it loses the ability to point to something specific. As Marx understood, when he carefully distinguished between the religious and the commodity fetish, the latter is a specific historical development and not simply the latest manifestation of the forces of anti-humanism. Nor is it satisfactory to agree with Marx but argue that since the time of his work the forces of production have so developed that commodification has become the equivalent of objectification. Again, one cannot hold this position and retain the original meaning of commodification without resorting to a strong reductionist and totalizing analysis. Yielding the original meaning removes the ability to distinguish the market from non-market forces and processes.

The Commodity Form in Communication

The political economy of communication has been notable for its emphasis on describing and examining the significance of those structural forms responsible for the production, distribution, and exchange of communication commodities and for the regulation of these structures, principally by the state. Although it has not neglected the commodity itself and the process of commodification, political economy has tended to foreground corporate and state structures and institutions. When it has treated the commodity, political economy has tended to concentrate on its embodiment in media content, to a lesser extent on media audiences, and paid surprisingly little attention to the labor process in the communication industries. Emphasis on the first two is understandable, in light of the importance of global media companies and the growth in the value of media content. Tightly integrated transnationals like Time Warner are able to create media products with a multiplier effect embodied, for example, in the tiered release which starts, for example, with a theatrical film released in U.S. and foreign theaters, followed in six months or so by a video, shortly thereafter released on pay-per-view, pay-cable, and perhaps, finally, aired on broadcast television (see Table 4.1). Notwithstanding the importance of institutions, emphasis on their activities has meant less than adequate attention to the commodity form of the mass media and, particularly, to the commodification of audiences and of labor.

Table 4.1   *The process of commercialization, 1983 and 1990*

Commercialization phases in 1983:	
t0	Film release in U.S. cinemas
t0 + several weeks	Film release in world cinemas
t0 + 4 months	Sales of video cassettes in U.S.
t0 + 1 year	Pay television in U.S.
t0 + 1 year (approx.)	Re-release in cinemas
t0 + 2 years	Broadcast on terrestrial television
t0 + 2/3 years	TV broadcast outside the U.S.
Commercialization phases in 1990:	
t0	Film release in U.S. (this phase no longer exists for many independent productions)
t0 + several weeks	Film release in rest of world (this phase no longer exists for many independent productions)
t0 + 3/6 months	Video cassettes in U.S.
t0 + 3/6 months	Pay-per-view broadcast in U.S. (transmission authorized 15 to 18 times in a 12-month period)
t0 + 6/12 months	Video cassettes in rest of world
t0 + 9/15 months	Pay television in U.S.
t0 + 1 year	Cable and terrestrial television outside U.S.
t0 + 30 months	Networks in U.S. (2 broadcasts in 3 years or 3 broadcasts in 4 years)
t0 + 36/42 months	Syndicated television in U.S.
t0 + 36 or 42 months	Repeat on pay television

Source: IDATE, 1992: 62

The Commodification of Content

When political economists think about the commodity form in communication, they have tended to start with media content. Specifically, from this point of view, the process of commodification in communication involves transforming messages, ranging from bits of data to systems of meaningful thought, into marketable products. For example, consider a newspaper reporter whose job it is to apply professional skills to produce stories that contain use values, of varying degrees of practicality. The history of newspaper production in capitalist society has involved numerous processes, including commodification, which makes the story teller a wage laborer who sells her labor power, the ability to write stories, for a wage. Capital turns that labor power into a newspaper article or column which, along with other stories and advertising, forms a packaged product. It sells the newspaper package in the marketplace and, if it is successful, earns surplus value, a profit, which it can invest in expanding the newspaper business or in any other venture that promises additions to capital. Marxian political economy views this as the realization of surplus value because the control that capital wields over the means of production (ownership of presses, offices, etc.) enables it to receive in labor more than it pays out in wages.

The extent of surplus value realization depends on numerous factors in labor, consumer, and capital markets. With respect to labor, Marxian political economy has examined the process of creating absolute and relative surplus value. The former involves extending the working day for the same wage; the latter to intensifying the labor process through greater control over the use of work time, including work measurement and monitoring systems to get more labor out of a unit of work time. The success of these strategies depends on the ability of labor to resist, something that rests on the strength of its organization, and on more general social conditions, such as capital's ability to replace the workforce with new workers and new technologies.

Capital also aims to control consumer markets through a range of tactics that amount to achieving the status of 'natural' or taken-for-granted provider of the product. These include building a market monopoly or controlling an oligopoly arrangement, using advertising to create product identification with the company, and diversifying its product line to achieve the flexibility to overcome product-specific changes in market demand, among others. As with labor, the ability to realize surplus value also depends on the extent to which consumers are able to resist, a consideration that also depends on its history of organization and the general social conditions that enable or retard the ability to substitute products and services. Finally, realization depends on the state of capital markets, specifically on the cost of capital, which permits the replacement of labor with capital and the expansion of the commodity form (from, for example, the newspaper format to an all-news pay cable channel).

This schematic description suggests that the process of creating exchange value in the content of communication draws an entire complex of social relations into the orbit of commodification, including labor, consumers, and capital. The general tendency in communication research has been to concentrate on the content as commodity and, by extension, to identify the connections between the commodity status of the content and its meaning. As a result, communication is taken to be a special and particularly powerful commodity because, in addition to its ability to produce surplus value (thereby behaving like all other commodities), it contains symbols and images whose meaning helps to shape consciousness. Numerous studies have documented the value of this approach and its conclusion that the mass media in capitalist society have expanded the process of commodity production by, *inter alia*, producing messages that reflect the interests of capital and, through however circuitous, contradictory, and contested a process, advancing support for the interests of capital as a whole and for specific class fractions (Herman and Chomsky, 1988; Schiller, 1973, 1984, 1989, 1969/1992). Although they have concurred in general terms with this conclusion, some political economists, notably Garnham and Smythe, have suggested alternative formulations. Both raise concerns about the tendency to emphasize the meaning or ideological dimension of media production. Throughout his career, Garnham has directed his strongest salvos against those who would, in effect, jettison the economic for the analysis of 'autonomous discourses.'[3] Nevertheless, he is also concerned about the tendency within political economy to address the message, its meaning and ideology, to, as Jhally puts it, adopt a 'consumer model of communications,' without adequately addressing the mass media as 'economic entities with both a direct economic role as creators of surplus value through commodity production and exchange and an indirect role, through advertising, in the creation of surplus value within other sectors of commodity production' (Garnham, 1979: 132). In this reading, the mass media are important because they are the immediate site of commodity production *and* because they play an important, if indirect, role through advertising media, in the process of commodification throughout the economy. The point is not that the ideological is less than significant, rather that it is thoroughly integrated

---

3. In his influential 1979 'Contribution to a Political Economy of Mass Communication,' Garnham wrote:

> Thus economism, the concern for immediate physical survival and reproduction within the dominant relations of exchange is an immediate and rational response to the determinants of social being. What E.P. Thompson has recently dubbed 'lumped bourgeois intellectuals' too easily forget this, both because their material conditions of existence are often less immediately determinant and also because of a guilty conscience concerning the subjective relationship of exploitation in which they stand *vis-à-vis* productive material labour. (p. 126)

And in his more recent *Capitalism and Communication*, he attacks first 'the tendency which privileged the text' (structuralism and post-structuralism), for its unanchored romanticism (a 'bacillus'), a view 'perfectly designed as an ideology of intellectuals or cultural workers for it privileges their special field of activity, the symbolic, and provides for cheap research opportunities, since the only evidence required is the unsubstantiated views of the individual analyst' (Garnham, 1990: 1–2).

within a process of production that is too often treated as instrumental to (in some political economy) or autonomous from (in structuralism and post-structuralism) ideology.

The Audience Commodity

Garnham thereby gives us two principal dimensions of media commodification: the direct production of media products and the use of media advertising to perfect the process of commodification in the entire economy. Smythe (1977) took these ideas in a different direction by advancing the claim that the audience is the primary commodity of the mass media. According to him, the mass media are constituted out of a process in which media companies produce audiences and deliver them to advertisers. Media programming is used to attract audiences; it is little more than the 'free lunch' that taverns once used to entice customers to drink. From this vantage point, audience labor or its labor power is the chief product of the mass media.

Smythe's analysis provoked one of the more interesting and well-examined exchanges in the political economy literature (Livant, 1979; Murdock, 1978; Smythe, 1978). Rather than review the debates on the primacy of the audience as commodity and as labor, exchanges that have been recounted more than once in some detail (Jhally, 1990), it is more useful to take up the wider significance of Smythe's argument.[4] Neglected in the debate about whether the audience labors, or whether it is the sole media commodity, is arguably the central contribution that Smythe made to our understanding of the media commodification process. For him, the process brought together a triad that linked media, audiences, and advertisers in a set of binding reciprocal relationships. Mass media programming is used to construct audiences; advertisers pay media companies for access to these audiences; audiences are thereby delivered to advertisers. Such an argument broadens the space within which media commodification takes place beyond the immediate process of media companies producing newspapers, radio broadcasts, television programs, and films, to include advertisers or capital

---

4. The dispute over the audience commodity has lost some of its edge partly because one of the central arguments levelled against it has diminished in importance. Murdock and others claimed that Smythe's contention was more appropriate to North America, where advertiser-supported mass media predominated by comparison with Western Europe. This view was not shared by all European political economists. Miège (1989: 30), for example, notes that it is impossible to make a clear distinction between a profit-seeking private sector and its public counterpart in the cultural industries because 'the public sector plays not only a very important part in creating and developing cultural markets but, in addition, contributes directly to the financing of the conditions of production of cultural commodities.' Moreover, the global advance of privatization and of the advertising industry weakened this case for North American exceptionalism. Finally, without reference to the debate, Golding and Murdock's 1991 assessment of political economy advances the view that the mass media produce the audience commodity. Additionally, Smythe's argument was alternatively too strong and too weak. Founded on the materialist contention that eschewed content, Smythe argued that audience labor was the only commodity that the media produced. Nevertheless, as Livant noted, Smythe insisted on discussing the ideological influence of media messages.

in general. The process of commodification thoroughly integrates the media industries into the capitalist economy not primarily by creating ideologically saturated products but by producing audiences, en masse *and* in specific demographically desirable forms, for advertisers. Smythe thereby aimed to rescue the materialist analysis of the media by demonstrating that it is the production of audiences for the general capitalist economy that is central to the commodification process rather than the production of ideology.

Putting aside the contentious and doubtfully productive argument about whether audiences constitute labor as it is generally understood, Smythe's use of the labor process concept is useful as metaphor or analogy because it provides a way to think about the triad without submitting to the mechanistic thinking that such a structural argument invites. Bracketing the question of whether audiences work in the traditional sense of the term (with all of the implications for the labor theory of value), it is useful to think about analogies between audience activity and the labor process because the latter is a dynamic activity involving complicity and contestation between capital and labor over control of the process and the product. This is considerably more valuable than addressing the audience as the inert mass that so-called mass society theorists, dating from Ortega y Gasset (1957), have conjured, or, alternatively, as the co-producers of media products, the view on offer from pluralists like Fiske (1989) and Ang (1991), who respond to traditional criticism of the mass society by going to the other extreme. The latter are correct in pointing to the co- or mutual constitution of media products, *but* they neglect to situate this within a structure of decision-making that places in the hands of capital most, though not all, of the levers on control over decision-making processes regarding production, distribution, and exchange.

Capital, in its own various and contested manifestations, must actively construct audiences as it constructs labor, but even as it does so, both audiences and labor construct themselves by deciding, within a social field whose terms of engagement are primarily set by capital, how to activate their audience and labor power. For the audience, this means attending or watching as capital would like, interpreting programming in oppositional or alternative ways, or simply not watching at all. As with labor, which the literature on work demonstrates brings a wide range of responses to the point of production, from full compliance to withholding labor power, the audience exercises power, but also, like labor, it is power circumscribed within terms largely, though not entirely, set by capital. One can extend the analogy further by noting how the conflict between capital and audience at the point of media reception is carried on over the general expansion of commercial broadcasting, the restructuring of commercial time, the use of new technologies to expand the process of measuring and monitoring audience activity, the introduction of pay-per-channel and -per-view services and, conversely, through the use of illegal satellite receivers, decoding boxes, cassette recorders that time shift, zip, and zap commercials, etc. There is considerable room for a fruitful marriage of political economic and ethnographic analysis here.[5] Political economy has begun to address this area with important research (Jhally, 1990; Meehan, 1984), but there is a tendency for it to stall over the issue of whether audience activity is not just like labor but *is* labor. One result of this is to incur attacks from traditional Marxian theorists, who, in their understandable rush to defend materialism and the labor theory of value, end up by dismissing, however unintentionally, the field of media analysis (Lebowitz, 1986). Jhally (1990) has determinedly pressed to find the positive dimension of this exchange, e.g. rethinking the notion of differential rent. Nevertheless, on balance it confirms the primary intent of Smythe's original article on the subject – to suggest that the media constitute a blindspot in Marxian theory. Taking into account simply the growing size and scope of the media industries, ranging across publishing to electronic information services, it is difficult to comprehend the reluctance of Marxian analysis to find more than marginal room for a materialist analysis of the media. Nevertheless, this remains one of the more important challenges facing the political economy of communication.

The Cybernetic Commodity: Intrinsic Commodification

Meehan (1984) offers an alternative way of thinking about the audience as commodity which centers on the audience ratings services. Since 'neither messages nor audiences are exchanged: only ratings,' she maintains (p. 223) that these reports on audience size, composition, and patterns of media usage constitute the primary commodity in the media system. Meehan's research makes a significant contribution to several dimensions of political economic analysis, including the materialist history of an industry, led by the A.C. Nielsen Company, and the social construction of a statistic, the rating, whose exchange value barely resembles its use as an empirical marker for actual audience characteristics. For the purpose of this analysis, her work is particularly valuable because, when combined with work in other areas, it points to the increasingly *cybernetic* nature of the commodification process. This dimension of the *ratings as commodity* argument has been overshadowed by the interest in finding the Holy Grail of a 'real' commodity in the media–advertiser–audience relationship. As a result of the attention directed to whether audiences, audience labor, audience attention, audience power, audience time, or ratings constitute the essential commodity, a vital element of the commodification process has received little attention.

Commodification demands the use of measurement procedures to produce commodities and monitoring techniques to keep track of production, dis-

---

5. There is an understandable tendency to skepticism about a struggle at the point of reception over something like television, which is associated with leisure and entertainment, by comparison with labor, which is essential for earning a living. Nevertheless, the media industry spends considerable money and expertise on surveillance systems which precisely measure who is watching and for how long and on advertisements that resist zipping through channels with slow motion and zapping ads by placing them on the screen with the program. Audience purchases of dishes, decoders, and sophisticated remote control devices suggest the struggle is mutual (see Larson, 1992).

tribution, exchange, and consumption. An example of the former is the precise length of an advertisement or amount of commercial time produced for sale to advertisers. Monitoring is exemplified by a range of practices including traditional business accounting, marketing studies, capital cost assessments, wage and benefit studies, customer surveys, and more recent innovations like data bank matching systems that link a credit or debit card purchase to demographic and attitudinal information. These practices are part of the commodification process because the information they produce is used in the production of commodities, like newspapers or television situation comedies, and are cybernetic because the outcome of the information production process is the production of a new commodity. In this respect, ratings are cybernetic commodities because they are constituted as commodities in the process of contributing to commodity production. Specifically, they are produced as an important element in the commodification of television programming and are themselves the central commodity of the ratings industry. This makes the ratings services important not because they are *the* media commodity, but because they represent one rather advanced stage in the process of media commodification, the development of the cybernetic commodity. They are part of a family of such commodities that grow out of the development of generalized monitoring and surveillance procedures that make use of advanced communication and information technology.[6]

In this respect, audience ratings are as important, though not inherently more so, than commodities produced and marketed from data automatically gathered on consumer purchases. Both are cybernetic commodities containing a secondary order of exchange value that depends on a first order. Although he confuses original exchange value with use value, the head of a major company which markets such cybernetic commodities recognizes their significance (DeSimone, 1992). They shift the commodification process

> from the value that is *intrinsic* in the product to values associated with the knowledge of who needs it, who supplies it and what it does. You buy a magazine and pay for it with a credit card. A simple transaction? Hardly. The *information* about who you are and what magazines you prefer – recorded by a computer – is

6. Giddens' work has been undoubtedly valuable in calling our attention to the development of institutional surveillance systems. Nevertheless, by locating surveillance in an institutional realm occupied with the 'control of information and social supervision' and separate from capitalism, which he describes as primarily taken up with 'accumulation in the context of competitive labor and product markets,' he misses the central contribution that the accumulation process makes to the development of surveillance systems and the necessity of these systems for the expansion of capital accumulation. Giddens is careful to speak of interpenetration, but they remain separate realms, their boundary reinforced in his *identification of surveillance with the nation state*. The latter is certainly implicated in the constitution of surveillance, but, by locating surveillance in the state, Giddens forgoes the point that surveillance, in the form of rationalizing production, distribution, and consumption, is integral to and propelled by the commodification process (see, *inter alia*, Giddens, 1990: 55–63). For a thorough analysis of corporate and state forms of measuring and monitoring transactions see Gandy (1993).

quote

worth as much as the return on the sale of the magazine. The information can be variously packaged. It can be marketed to others. Moreover, all the internal processes are affected by your decision – from marketing to purchase to finance. Today, all organizations are in the information business.

Notwithstanding the need to discount for the hyperbole that typically accompanies emanations from the corporate center of the information industries, one is left with the view that it is essential to move beyond the notion of finding *the* commodity in the media. It is more significant to foreground a process of commodification that connects a range of practices in a spiral of expanding exchange value that, as DeSimone concludes, draws all organizations into the orbit of the information business. It is within this general framework of commodification that it becomes useful to examine the application of new measurement and surveillance technologies to expand the production of media commodities. These would include, among others, pay-per-view programming, 'people meters' and room scanners that monitor specific program choices and attention, and so-called smart cards that are used to activate television receivers and to purchase products. These produce new products, in the form of reports on viewing and shopping, containing demographic detail that is linkable to a range of data bases. But these new products are more than discrete units. They are part of a commodification process that connects them in a structured hierarchy.

One can also say that cybernetic commodities are principally part of an *intensive* commodification process because they are the direct product of refining the process of production in a specific area. Cable television, pay-per-channel and -per-view television intensify the packaging of programming in increasingly customized forms from the original broadcasting form, which, by comparison, produced programming with limited specificity for a mass audience. The former intensify the commodification process by linking increasingly specific kinds of programming to increasingly well-defined audiences. For example, the Time Warner magazine division, which represents 20 percent of all advertising placed in consumer magazines, created Target Select, a system that customizes and personalizes ads, using computer-controlled selective binding and ink-jet printing, to produce issues targeted to individual subscribers (Wasko, 1994). One company, Lotus Marketplace, using information acquired from a major credit bureau, has already proposed to market profiles on 80 million American households. Citicorp has announced plans to sell marketers access to its files on 22 million credit-card customers. Even the tradition-bound newspaper is learning about the value of selling customer data. According to the press observer Alex S. Jones (1991), 'Americans are only beginning to realize that when they call a newspaper's sports line to get a score or send for a free brochure about car maintenance, they are probably also entering a data bank as a prospect for advertising about golf clubs or tires.' As a result, he concludes, 'privacy looms as a potential land mine.' According to the vice president for advertising of the *Atlanta Journal and Constitution*, which has one of the most sophisticated systems, 'It's part of the future of the newspaper business.' Surveillance systems, whether required for billing or for audience surveys, intensify the process by producing marketable products out of the information gathered on viewer choices. Telephone systems that shift from gross categories of payment for unlimited monthly use to specific payment by the call or by time of use, what is called local measured service, similarly intensify the commodification process by refining the constitution and packaging of the message commodity and by using technologies that, in the process of producing the communication link, compile marketable information on the person initiating the transaction. One can say the same thing about the general category of payment systems, such as credit and debit cards, which intensify the exchange process and create marketable information about users (Gandy, 1993).

The Cybernetic Commodity: Extensive Commodification

One can also observe a process of expansion that extends commodification to areas that, for a range of social, political, and economic reasons, were only lightly touched, if at all, by the process. These include numerous information and cultural areas that have been taken up prominently in communication studies (Garnham, 1990; Schiller, 1989), geography (Harvey, 1989), urban studies (Davis, 1990), and cultural studies (Davis, 1986). This work describes how the process of commodification has been extended to institutional areas such as public education, government information, media, culture, and telecommunication that were certainly created out of a range of contested forces and motives, but which nevertheless preserved principles of universal access, irrespective of one's marketplace power. The manifestation of extensive commodification takes many notable forms, though this is not the place for a detailed discussion of each. Declines in economic growth and the rightward shift in political power have prompted funding cutbacks for public information institutions, such as libraries and public schools, prompting a turn to once unthinkable alternatives such as the widespread introduction of mandatory commercial television in American classrooms. We have also witnessed the broad-based privatization and commercialization of public information, postal, broadcasting, and telecommunication systems and the introduction of the neoclassical economic logic of 'cost-based' pricing or what amounts to governance in the interests of those with market power. Extensive commodification also includes the transformation of common spaces, from public parks to privately governed shopping malls, and the increasing reliance on commercial sponsorship of museums, sports, and festivals. The growing tendency for people to wear clothing and adornments that advertise products commercializes the body and the identity. These developments suggest that the process of commodification has extended into places and practices that once tended to be organized according to a different social logic, one based on universality, equality, social participation, and citizenship, which, for all of its well-chronicled shortcomings, broadened the grounds of social action now increasingly reduced to a market logic that equates rights with market power.

One of the important contributions of a political economy perspective has been to document the process by which state and corporate power extend commodification. What this perspective needs to address more substantially than it has is how the process is linked to what takes place, as it were, at *the point of extension*. The use of political and economic power holds considerable explanatory value for understanding the success of commodification. The process reduces the resources, the time, and the space available to alternatives, so that commodification is perceived not as a process of power but as the natural order, common-sense, taken-for-granted, reality of social life. This argument for *hegemony* is an important one, but the process of arriving at it forgoes an important step that takes us to the border of political economy and cultural studies. Institutional power, promoting one logic and eliminating alternatives, is central to the construction of hegemony. But there is also the question of the link between institutional power and the power that works on the multilayered relationship between use value and exchange value. For exchange value expands not only by undermining use or non-commodity values but also by using these values to enhance its own attraction and, in the process, by transforming use to exchange values.

Drawing on the work of Sennett (1976), Crawford (1992) describes how this process works in the shopping mall. Research based in political economy documents the use of institutional power to change transportation, land use, investment, and other structural policies to reconstruct patterns of shopping and, more generally, of social interaction around the shopping mall. Crawford gestures to this literature but concentrates on how the process of commodification works *inside* the mall. She offers an example from a shop window display that sets an ordinary pot in a Moroccan harem scene. This, she argues, decontextualizes the pot, thereby turning it into something unanticipated, exotic, and, hence, stimulating. As she puts it:

> This logic of association allows noncommodified values to enhance commodities, but it also imposes the reverse process – previously noncommodified entities become part of the marketplace. Once this exchange of attributes is absorbed into the already open-ended and indeterminate exchange between commodities and needs, associations can resonate infinitely. (Crawford, 1992: 15)

The reference to infinite resonance exaggerates by turning a cybernetic process necessarily into runaway feedback. Numerous processes, including the recollection of our mundane experience with pots, can short-circuit this one. Moreover, the description of the process as 'retail magic' idealizes something that is mutually constituted out of material use and images of association. Nevertheless, Crawford's description gives texture and nuance to the process of commodification. It suggests one means to deepen the analysis of a process whose general structure has been well described by political economists.

If Crawford's example suggests a useful broadening at the boundary of political economy and cultural studies, two other tendencies are less productive. Since these bear directly on the process of commodification, it is useful to address them here rather than wait until Chapter 7, which takes up general challenges on political economy's borders. One unproductive tendency is to conflate commodification with universal tendencies to social reciprocity. The latter refers to a generalized sociality that binds people in exchange relationships. Proponents of this view (Davis, 1992; Schudson, 1984) tend to reference the anthropological literature on gift exchange rituals, such as the potlatch, which suggests that the construction of markets and the development of exchange value are deeply rooted in more general processes of social group formation. From this vantage point, rather than a principal entry point for comprehending the social field, commodification is merely one among many expressions of a universal tendency to social exchange. This view is valuable in that it directs attention to the layers of ritual that adhere to social processes and contributes to their constitution (Davis, 1992). In political economy, Veblen (1934) put this approach to use in what are best appreciated as the anthropological insights of an ethnographer among the leisure and business classes. But Veblen recognized and steered clear of the temptation to conflate the general tendency to ritual exchange with its specific manifestation in the commodification process. He recognized that the former is an idealist trap suggesting, in its abstract universality, that the dynamic processes of social transformation, which gave rise to capitalism, are less important than the general similarities among tribal, feudal, and capitalist societies. Veblen would appreciate this powerful irony: today academics aim to de-historicize exchange, diminish the concrete significance of the transformation to capitalism by referencing tribal practices in societies that capitalism has all but eliminated. Political economy acknowledges that the process of commodification involves ritual practices that can serve to tighten or loosen social bonds. Indeed, one of its primary criticisms against orthodox economics is the tendency to eliminate the power of custom and morality in economic life. However, political economy also aims to avoid idealism by focusing on the power contained in the historically specific substance and form that the process takes in mutual constitution with a capitalist social formation.[7]

Another problematic tendency does the reverse by arguing for the universality of commodification in a form that replaces its traditional connection to the transformation of use to exchange value and the production of goods with the production of codes and the hegemony of sign value (Baudrillard, 1981). Offering the converse of an approach that would fold commodification into tribal ritual, Baudrillard proposes a radical mitosis in which objects and the labor process that gave rise to them break off and dissolve before the free-floating power of the sign. All is absorbed within a transformed process of commodification. He could not be more emphatic:

7. For an analysis that treats reciprocity in a specific political context, see Rucinski (1991).

The super-ideology of the sign and the general operation of the signifier – everywhere sanctioned today by the new master disciplines of structural linguistics, semiology, information theory and cybernetics – has replaced political economy as the theoretical basis of the system. (Baudrillard, 1975: 122)

This is not the place to examine the debate over Baudrillard's position (see Kellner, 1989). Rather, it is more useful to consider the implications for the specific process of commodification. Here Baudrillard appears to support the view that the commodity has swept aside alternatives to its universal power and won out – a view that is shared by political economists of communication. However, political economists take issue with two fundamental dimensions of the argument. First, whether framed in the modernist discourse of universal contamination or the triumphalism of post-structuralist thought, the argument for the emergence of commodification suggests one-dimensionalism, essentialism, and what can only logically inspire fatalism about alternatives to this all-encompassing process.[8] It lacks a sense of the contradictions that emerge in the process of commodification and of alternative processes. Second, it is not clear what the victory of the commodity actually means because the sense of the term changes fundamentally in Baudrillard's analysis. Particularly in his later work, Baudrillard replaces the process of using commodified wage labor to turn use into exchange value with a generalized social process that creates sign value. But to the extent that it holds a specific meaning, sign value is limited to the needs of capital to produce a dense, hierarchical system of meanings, of status identifications, in order to cement its power. However warranted as one reading of political economy, it purchases this partial warrant by eliminating two fundamental considerations of political economy – the existence of human needs, which emerge in use values and which constitute the standpoint of political economy from the viewpoint of the working class, and an institutional system organized around transforming use into exchange for the purpose of producing surplus value or political economy from the standpoint of capital. Consider, once again, Veblen, whose influence Baudrillard acknowledges but whose analysis of status he treats as an independent ground of social organization without what Veblen saw as its fundamental foundation – the existence of human need and an institutionalized political economy that subverts it. The process of commodification is reduced to the free-floating circulation of symbols, an outcome obscured by the misappropriation of political economy's conceptual apparatus, itself reduced to a set of free-floating terms, torn from their historically constituted and specific meanings, to add weight to an otherwise light argument.

---

8. One of the difficulties with some of the work in cultural studies is that it accepts Baudrillard's argument about commodification, but proceeds to ignore the logical implications by turning to social forces like the new social movements, which tend to appear *sui generis* as the central locus of opposition.

The Commodification of Labor

There are two sets of related processes at work in the commodification of labor that are relevant to communication studies. The first refers to the use of communication systems and technologies to expand the commodification of all labor processes, including those in the communication industries, by increasing the flexibility and control available to employers. Second, political economy has described a double process whereby labor is commodified in the process of producing goods and services commodities.

In the interest of examining the commodification of goods, there is a tendency to neglect the labor commodity and the process that takes place at the point of production. Braverman's (1974) work gave rise to an intellectual drive to end this marginal status by directly confronting the transformation of the labor process in capitalism.[9] According to him, labor is constituted out of the unity of *conception*, or the power to envision, imagine, and design work, and *execution*, or the power to carry it out.[10] In the process of commodification, capital acts to *separate* conception from execution, skill from the raw ability to carry out a task, to *concentrate* conceptual power in a managerial class fraction that is either a part of capital or represents its interests, and to *reconstitute* the labor process to correspond to the redistribution of skills and power at the point of production. In the extreme, this involved the application of so-called scientific management practices, pioneered by Frederick Winslow Taylor.[11] Braverman documented the process of labor transformation in the rise of large-scale industry, but he is particularly recognized for producing one of the first sustained examinations demonstrating the extension of this process into the service and information sectors. Braverman's work gave rise to an enormous body of empirical examination and theoretical debate, the latter focusing principally on the need to address the contested nature of the process and the active agency of workers and the trade union movement (Burawoy, 1979; Edwards, 1979). Much of this work constituted what Kuhn would call 'normal science,' i.e., working through and expanding upon the wide range of problems and implications contained in Braverman's contribution. This included mapping the contested terrain at the point of production, its history, and specifically how the transformation of the labor process was experienced differently by industry, occupation, class, gender, and race. Recent work, including scholarly assessments and business press accounts, has tended to incorporate an interest in how the

9. Braverman's work was especially timely in that it appeared at the start of the economic decline following the sustained post-war boom, the peak of Fordist prosperity. It also corresponded to the accelerated application of integrated computer communications systems in the factory and the office. For a critical evaluation of his work in comparison to that of contemporaries in political economy, see Hillard (1991).

10. The distinction between conception and execution corresponds to the view of Marx that the unity of the two distinguishes the human architect from the bee.

11. In the hands of Lilian Gilbreth (whose husband, a follower of Taylor, developed the unit of worktime measurement, the 'therblig'), this process of taylorization was applied to the home, to manage the household 'scientifically.'

means of communication, sharpened by steady improvements in techno-logical proficiency, have enhanced the commodification of the general labor process (Ansberry, 1993; Berberoglu, 1993; Ehrbar, 1993; Zachary and Ortega, 1993).

Communication studies, including the political economy approach, con-tributed fewer than its share of analyses on the changing labor process in the media industries. There are several reasons for this less than thorough treatment. Despite a strong political economy tradition and a broad interest among economists and policy-makers in the cultural industries, communica-tion studies has tended to situate its object within the sphere of consumption and this has contributed to a focus on the relationship of audiences to texts. Political economists of communication have paid considerable attention to the institutional control over media production and to the extent of the impact on audiences, including the conception of audience labor. Arguably more attention has been directed to the labor of audiences than to the traditionally understood labor process in the media industries. Another reason for the shortcoming is that the media industries carried strong craft, professional, and artisan traditions that continue, even as the labor process is transformed.

There is an understandable tendency to emphasize the individual creative dimensions of media production which distinguish this sector from the many occupational sectors that share the characteristics of industrial production. Authors write books, some directors are the *auteurs* of film, stars make movies or television programs, etc. There are substantial grounds for this view, principally based on the relatively high level of conceptual thought that this industry requires. This is the chief reason why print workers and their trade unions have historically occupied a privileged position in the workforce. But the emphasis on individual creativity only obscures a complex process of production, one that, however unevenly, has come to look more like the labor process in the general economy.

Organizational communication and sociology have provided some of the better insights into the bureaucratic structure and production processes in the media industries. The work of Tuchman (1978), Fishman (1980), and Gans (1979), among others, examines the system of bureaucratic controls that manage the complex process of, principally, news production. Their work highlights those simplifying routines such as beat reporting, a detailed division of labor, and regularized features that establish a template for what is potentially an open-ended production process. This body of research demonstrates that a substantial amount of organizational planning and pre-processing are used to gather, package, and distribute news and information on a routine basis. This line of research is important for a political economy that would address the labor process because it describes in rich empirical detail the socio-technical processes that help to constitute the production process. However, though this work gestures to political and economic influences, these are left untheorized in favor of a framework based on theories of bureaucracy and organization that foreground abstract administrative needs and functions. Notwithstanding nods to power and profit, this approach concentrates on how the structural pressures of bureaucracy, following on a literature originating in the work of Max Weber and Robert Michels, rationalize production in the cultural industries, just as they do throughout an economy managed by complex bureaucracies.

From a political economic perspective, the organizational literature contributes rich empirical detail but rests on an idealist foundation that substitutes an administrative essentialism for what it perceives to be the economic essentialism of the market. It places, as Weber suggested, the determining influence of the *means of administration* over that of the means of production. This has not been a central issue in the political economy of communication because it has concentrated on the institutional level where the corporation, the state, and their relationships constitute primary units of analysis. The challenge that the organizational literature poses to political economy is to develop a position that examines the process of production foregrounding political and economic power, specifically the commodification of labor. This would constitute an important link between institutional and textual analysis that retains the materialist strength of a political economic approach. The point is not to reclaim ground lost to one essentialism by restoring another, but to theorize the commodification of labor in the process of media production.

The political economy literature has taken some steps in this direction, particularly by examining the introduction of new communication and information technologies. Research has addressed the transformation of work, including patterns of employment and the changing nature of labor in the media and telecommunication industry. Decrying the absence of a labor perspective in journalism history, Hardt (1990) integrates what is primarily a political economic perspective with a cultural history of the newsroom that focuses on the introduction of new technologies deployed to carry out work processes described by Braverman. This extends the pioneering work of political economists working outside communication studies who have studied the labor process in the newsroom (Zimbalist, 1979).[12] More recent work that, *inter alia*, addresses the commodification of labor in the newsroom looks to the application of new technologies to reduce employment in the industry and to restructure the work of editors by implementing electronic page layout or *pagination* and, to a lesser extent, by transforming reporters' jobs with electronic news gathering (Russial, 1989). These are specific applications of the labor process view that points to the use of

12. Following a useful overview that situates current conflicts over electronic news production technologies in the context of over one hundred years of struggle in which 'newsrooms, like factory floors, have been a laboratory for technological innovations and a battleground of economic and social interests,' Hardt (1990: 355) offers a political economic perspective to explain the neglect of labor:

under prevailing historical conditions that privilege dominant visions of the press, press histories ignored working-class issues and questions of labor practices (reflecting the anti-labor attitudes of publishers).

communication and information technologies to shift the balance of power in conceptual activity from, in this case, professional newsworkers, with some control over their means of communication, to managerially controlled technological systems. Similar work has begun to address the transformation of the labor process in film (Nielsen, 1990), broadcasting (Wasko, 1983), telecommunication (Mosco and Zureik, 1987), and the information industries (Kraft and Dubnoff, 1986).

Miège (1989) offers a variation on this analysis by suggesting that there is a connection between the type of media product, the structure of corporate control, and the nature of the labor process. What he calls Type One products, mainly hardware like television receivers and recorders, are characterized by a simple process of production and little intervention of creative or artistic workers. According to Miège, these media products lend themselves to industrial concentration and a detailed labor process, including an international division of labor that takes advantage of low-wage areas with predominantly non-unionized workers subjected to a regime of authoritarian control. At the opposite end of the spectrum, Type Two products, art prints and what he calls 'réalisations audio-visuelles,' are produced almost solely with artisanal labor, are not easily reproducible, and require relatively low infusions of capital. This supports a sector dominated by small businesses and enables widespread producer or labor control. Miège identifies a final or Type Three product as a principal site of struggle and conflict, because it is both easily reproducible and requires some degree of artistic contribution. This sector contains growing, but far from complete, monopoly control and a wide mix of labor that makes for tensions and conflicts within, as well as between, capital and labor.

Miège's analysis is important because it offers one of the more detailed accounts of labor commodification in the media industries, as both a general political economic process and a process contingent on the relationship among products, industry structure, and the demand for skilled and unskilled labor. Nevertheless, the analysis is limited by a conceptual scheme with three categories, one of which (Type Three products) contains most of the variation. It is also the case that this variation is diminishing, as industry concentration and the rationalization of the labor process, features of the highly standardized Type One product area, come to characterize Type Three products. Furthermore, by giving determinant power to the structural demands of various product types, the scheme rules out such variables as levels of unionization and militancy and the extent of state regulation or general control of the sector. Notwithstanding these shortcomings, this is an important start toward the systematic analysis of the labor process in the media industries.

A start has also been made on political economic work that addresses the international division of labor and labor internationalism. The former results from the pressures to rationalize production and the opportunities that technologies, particularly in computers and telecommunication, provide to overcome space and time constraints on the ability of business to do so. The next chapter addresses globalization, but it is useful to note here a few points on the significance for labor. The development of global labor markets is one consequence: business can take advantage of differential wages, skills, and other important characteristics on an international scale. Much of the early political economic work in this area concentrated on the spread of the hardware (Southeast Asia) and data entry (the Caribbean) businesses into the Third World, where companies were attracted by low wages and authoritarian rule (Mosco, 1989b; Sussman, 1984). More recently, the scope of research has expanded to address capital's growing interest in looking to the less developed world for sources of relatively low wage but skilled labor, needed in such areas as software development (Vijayan, 1996), and also to the developed world, where a prime example is the growth of U.S. film and video production in Canada.[13]

The growth of the international division of labor in communication has sparked an interest in labor internationalism. Specifically, this involves making use of the means of communication, including new technologies, to forge close links among working-class and trade union interests across borders (Waterman, 1990). Again, like much of the literature on the commodification of labor in communication, it has only begun to address what is a central focus of attention in other fields of political economy.

Alternative Processes in Private and Public Life

Critics of political economy, including those who resist its use in communication studies, have consistently raised concerns about essentialism. The argument is put in many ways, but with respect to communication research, it rejects the idea that one can reduce all communication and cultural practices to an underlying or more fundamental political economic reality which encompasses the process of commodification. Chapters 2 and 3 offered evidence that this view is overstated. Both general political economy and its application in communication contain rich, diverse, and comprehensive bodies of research that are not at all reducible to simple categorizations or simplistic charges. Nevertheless, one of the valuable consequences of the critique in communication studies is the beginning of an effort to reflect on some of the basic epistemological and ontological principles that guide the perspective.

As a part of a process of self-reflection and disciplinary renewal, this book has responded with a realist, inclusive, non-essentialist, and critical epistemology and an ontological position that foregrounds social process and social change. The latter is embodied here by entry points that inform the social field, but which also constitute alternative and oppositional social

---

13. These developments are also the consequence of explicit government policies in the host country. Nevertheless, in the case of Canada, there seems to be no discernible positive impact on the growth of local production (see Salutin, 1993).

processes. Hence commodification is identified as the entry, rather than the essential, standpoint from which to examine the relationship of exchange to use value in communication. Commodification transforms media content, but does not reduce it to a singularity that would allow one to interpret media content directly from the commodification process. By beginning with commodification, the chapter establishes a theoretical frame of reference, even as it recognizes the multiple determination and mutual constitution of all processes. The chapter now proceeds to identify additional processes and their accompanying structures that are made up of alternative and opposi-tional practices.

One of the more valuable theoretical suggestions in this area addresses the role of the state in what Offe (1984) calls the process of 'administrative recommodification.' According to him, this is the most recent point in a process that has characterized political economic development in advanced capitalist societies. For Offe, a period of laissez-faire was followed by *decommodification* or the 'socialization' of political economic life, in response to instabilities and conflicts brought about by failures in the overwhelming reliance on the market mechanism. Decommodification involves the creation of social policies and programs to protect the economic existence of social actors, in the ranks of both capital and labor, including those who are by and large incapable of participating in commodification or who are unable to do so. However, the transfer payments and other sources of income that prevent these people from 'dropping out' of the process prove to be fiscally unsustainable in the longer term. Moreover, Offe (1984: 35–64) maintains, the process proves to be politically unsustainable because it is practically impossible to politically regulate the economy without materially politicizing it. As a result, Offe sees capital responding with *recommodification*:

> since the mid 1960s the increasingly dominant and exclusive strategy of the capitalist state is to solve the problem of the commodity form by politically creating conditions under which legal and economic subjects can function as commodities. (Offe, 1984: 124)

Specifically, this calls for a set of programs that intend to enhance the market value of labor, integrate and concentrate transnational capital, and permit the exclusion of those who fail the market test. However, according to him, these are only partially successful because the state is caught up in trying to use non-market means to advance the market and must pay, however indirectly, the price of exclusionary practices, e.g. crime control and prison expansion. Moreover, as critiques of bureaucratization dating back to Max Weber have demonstrated, the result is often that non-market mechanisms, initiated as a means, become ends in themselves and under-mine the recommodification process. This brings about its own government response, particularly prominent in the 1990s, which amounts to the applica-tion of market principles to the state in the expectation that if the state took on the look of a market enterprise, it would advance market principles. The problem, one that Offe returns to time and time again, is that though the state can be made to *look* like a market enterprise, there are fundamental limits on its ability to *act* like one, primarily because the state is ruled out of direct accumulation.

Offe's arguments, echoed in others (see O'Connor, 1987), take a step toward correcting the essentialism inherent in the assertion of a simple, deterministic process. Nevertheless, because it defines alternatives negatively, i.e., that which is not commodification, or in terms of constraints like fiscal limits, bureaucratization, or politicization, it does not go far enough.[14]

Social Process in Private Life

The remainder of this chapter draws out tendencies in contemporary social thought and communication scholarship that, for a range of reasons and from different theoretical standpoints, point to alternatives to commodification. They suggest that commodification, though powerful and pervasive, is not a singularity. Although not exclusively the case, these alternatives are each generally linked to use value and specifically to what we typically call private and public life. Private life refers specifically to the process of face-to-face interaction, which has alternatively been referred to in Habermas (1989) as the domain of the life-world (*Lebenswelt*) or, in phenomenological sociology, as that of intersubjectivity. Processes based in private life are typically affective ones that revolve around identity formation, friendship, and kinship. The emphasis is placed on how people and objects, both material and symbolic, are valued as ends in themselves and not for their market value. Those that emanate from public life tend to be civic processes that bring people together to exchange ideas, govern themselves, support, resist, oppose, and attempt to create alternatives to what Habermas (1989) calls the organization of power and money in the 'system' world. One of the central alternatives to the process of commodification in the private sphere is the constitution of friendship, in the public sphere, citizenship.

One of the challenges facing the attempt to address the relationship between commodification and social processes at work in private and public life is overcoming the inclination to mechanized thinking. First, there is the general tendency to reduce the discussion simply to the dichotomy between private and public. One of the major problems with this is that the term 'private' has taken on the burden of including both the most intimate of human experience and the market behavior of the transnational business

---

14. Offe (1984) is aware of this limitation and also writes suggestively of the need to expand the general conception of crisis from the view that it simply emanates in the economic to one that finds crisis in the relationship among three organizing principles in society – the family–normative, business–calculative, and state–coercive.

system.[15] It is easy for the idea to collapse under such weight. More substantially, it seriously constrains the ability to comprehend the wider implications of commodification. When the concept of the private is effectively constituted as a type of default option for non-state activity, as in Giddens' (1991: 153) view of 'privacy as the "other side" of the penetration of the state,' we are left with no room to think about the intimate connection between commodification and surveillance and about privacy as the other side of the penetration of the market. But even when we expand the framework to include the market, it is easy to think about these as three separate spheres of activity that tend to be rooted in a well-defined place: private life in the home, public life in the state, and commodification in the marketplace. As Sennett (1976) has demonstrated, this view has always been a problematic reflection of social life, and has never been more so than today, when the lines between what constitutes public, private, and market places are blurred to the point of practically eliminating the value of territorial and object distinctions. One increasingly questions the value of thinking about them as *things* operating a zero-sum game in which more of one constitutes less of another. Rather, following my preferred onto-logical strategy, it is more useful to consider them as mutually constitutive social processes. These processes form relationships that vary according to specific historical circumstances. Again, the tendency to mechanism leads us to locate the constitution of, for example, friendship in private life and citizenship in public life. Furthermore, these are seen as directly opposed to commodification, vectors that each take off into a completely different direction. But this form of thinking about processes is also to be avoided because the relationships among them are more complex and wide-ranging. Complete opposition is one among many possible configurations of a relationship among different processes.

The structure of communication studies, reflecting divisions within the social sciences, makes it particularly difficult to conceptualize the relation-ship between private processes and commodification, as well as those that mark public life, because the discipline tends to be organized along levels of social complexity which set apart interpersonal from organizational and institutional communication. Though there are exceptions, it is generally the case that interpersonal communication, like microsociology, is set apart as the sphere within which one can examine affect and intimacy. These gradually lose their significance as one leaves the interpersonal level of

15. One of the conceptual difficulties that this discussion faces is the general confusion in the meaning of the private sphere. One perspective sees the private as constituting all activity outside the state sphere. According to this view, referred to in broad conceptions of civil society, *interpersonal life* (as in private life) and *business* (as in private sector) are both a part of the private sphere. I take a different approach that distinguishes between interpersonal private life, the subject of this theme, and the private sector, which comprises a fundamentally different domain of life that takes up the market and commodification. We would benefit from an alternative to the term 'private sector', perhaps 'commercial', 'market', or 'audience sector' would be more appropriate.

analysis. By the time one reaches political economy, located at the upper levels of social complexity, the issues taken up at the micro or interpersonal level virtually disappear. This is significant for the broadest conception of political economy's mission because it restricts both theoretical comprehensiveness and social praxis. Without a direct encounter with the interpersonal, political economy has little to say about that realm of experience, the realm of affect, and therefore little to say about the consequences for action among people who experience an enormous gap between what takes place at the institutional level of power, the traditionally central focus of political economy, and their daily existence as a series of encounters in small groups, with mediated presentations of word and image, and with themselves.

Over the years, the concern over mediating the institutional and the personal has taken up considerable theoretical reflection, though the growth of work within social science on identity, including the politics of identity and self-identity, leads one to conclude that we are now observing a sustained effort to break new ground (Giddens, 1991; Hall, 1989b; Meyrowitz, 1985; Sichterman, 1986; Turkel, 1984). There are numerous reasons for this, including particularly a tendency which Hall (1989b: 12) observes, that 'the great social collectivities which used to stabilize our identities – the great stable collectivities of class, race, gender, and nation – have been, in our times, deeply undermined by social and political developments.' The rise of feminism, especially the political and intellectual drive to overcome the prominent division in social thought under patriarchy which separates the personal from the political, has played a leading role in the ensuing ferment over these developments and the process and possibility of reconstitution.

There is considerable room to debate the issues raised by this literature. For example, one can understand how, in one sense, Hall is correct to call attention to the destabilization of subjective identities, but it is also the case, as political economy has demonstrated, that *capitalism has always destabilized identities* and that, in terms of education, income, power, and general life chances, class, race, and gender now matter as much or even more than they ever have. While the criticism reminds us of Pêcheux's warning to avoid narcissism of the subject, it should not divert attention from the need to address private life and to do so without resorting to essentialism of the commodity. Giddens' recent work is suggestive here, particularly his analysis of the relationship between what he calls personalized versus commodified experience (1991: 196–201). Nevertheless, he is acutely aware of a shortcoming: 'I have not sought to trace out in a detailed fashion the impact of capitalistic production on modern social life.' Notwithstanding this shortcoming, he does provide a clear sense of the power that commodification extends over personal life. For this Giddens draws explicitly on Bauman (1989), but reminds the communication scholar of Schiller and Smythe. His brief overview of the process suggests some of the major ways in which it advances the 'continuous reshaping of the conditions of day-to-day life.'

This extends to the mass media, including a mini-industry promoting self-therapy that, in books, videos, etc., aims to oppose commodification, 'yet in so far as they become marketed in pre-packaged theorems about how to "get on" in life, they become caught up in the very processes they nominally oppose' (Giddens, 1991: 198–199). Yet, Giddens also notes that there are grounds for resistance that emanate from private life, including the process of creating a self-identity and a social identity based on some sense, however tentative, conflicted, and difficult to articulate (particularly relative to the naturalistic certainty of mediated word and image), of moral and aesthetic value.

Political economy departs from Giddens by placing more weight on the division between the private and the commodified experience. He sequesters it at the end of a book on identity, the last of four 'tribulations of the self,' offering a powerful, but marginalized, argument. One reason for doing this is understandable. Giddens aims to create a language of the self and identity that can stand on its own to participate in an intellectual *and* an existential project: to explain the condition of private life and 'to provide the moral resources necessary to live a full and satisfying existence' (1991: 9). Notwithstanding the need for such a language, it raises a fundamental problem for the political economist. Giddens offers a liberal version of an argument that Lasch and Bell have made on the conservative side. The self is battered by social and institutional forces and it does not have the resources to mount a successful response. Whereas conservatives would have us draw on tradition to strengthen the self, the liberal response is to give legitimacy to a modern language of the self and use it to create a more open moral and aesthetic life – in essence one that, following Habermas, is more communicative. The problem for the political economist, as O'Connor (1987: 175) puts it sharply, is that these theories are 'ideological':

> They are backward-looking and naturalistic respectively. They ignore the question, *what is a specifically capitalistic personality crisis in the epoch of the universalization of the wage and commodity form?* (emphasis mine)

This is not a central question for Giddens because he chooses to situate private life in what he calls 'the late modern age,' rather than in capitalism. Nevertheless, he offers a set of conceptual tools for thinking about private life that one finds lacking in most political economic thought.[16]

One goal of political economic analysis is to make critical use of these tools to think about the relationship of private life to the specific experience of commodification and to the experience of self- and social identity in capitalism. This would enable political economy to speak of a contested terrain in which the moral, libidinal, and aesthetic processes at work in private life meet commodification in a contested terrain of recursive crisis – whereby the very commodification of private disorder poses another crisis to

---

16. Marcuse offers one formulation in *Eros and Civilization*, but Connell (1987: 201), among others, notes that it is founded on a nature-induced crisis tendency in the pressure limit that the instinctual character of sexuality can reach before inducing a social crisis.

private life. Furthermore, one can push beyond the mapping of crisis to the point of resistance, which O'Connor (1987: 181–182) describes in this way:

> This moment of crisis is precisely when transformation into a social individuality becomes possible. . . . At this moment, one can externalize the internal struggle, or know and feel that the ways in which one suffers are also the ways in which others suffer, grasp suffering as a social process, externalizing suffering through social and political struggle.

Two problems confront the political economist of communication regarding this resistance. How is it organized and how is it expressed? Chapter 6 takes up these issues by addressing the meeting point of identity and structure in social class (Aronowitz, 1992), race (Sivanandan, 1990), gender (Connell, 1987), and the range of oppositional social movements (Bruck, 1992; Luke, 1989) that cut across these categories to foreground central social issues and their specific media embodiments in the creation of oppositional and alternative media. Some media analysts have made the case for audience resistance (Ang, 1991; Fiske, 1989). This work raises the important question of the differential impact of media messages and the range of reactions they bring about. But, as critics have noted (Schiller, 1989), the approach tends to ascribe the weight of social and political resistance to what turn out to be opinions about what a television program means or about its value. Just as significantly, it gives the concept of the audience an unmerited social structural status practically on a par with class, race, and gender. This results, in part, from the reduction, particularly in Fiske, of the social class category to what is essentially a continuum of status attributes rooted in functionalist theories of stratification. Weakening traditional social categories permits raising the analytical position of the audience. As has already been noted, given its long-standing consumptionist bias, it comes as no surprise that communication research would give this attention to the audience. But a problem arises when one attempts to transform a thought-provoking trope into a major social category. Audience resistance, like audience labor, inflates the status of the audience by juxtaposing it with a concept of central social significance, but it does so at the price of deflating the specific and powerful meanings of both resistance and labor.

Social Process in Public Life

Social theory and communication research have taken up public life as a form of resistance to commodification and of alternative social practices.[17] The work of Habermas (1989) on the public sphere is particularly important because it has interrogated the idea critically and has provided the conceptual tools that help to restore an historic debate on public life and

17. I agree with Keane (1984), who prefers the term 'public life' over public sphere because, for reasons outlined below, it avoids treating the public as the description of a specific space. My inclination is to think about public life as a set of processes that advance fundamental characteristics of democracy, i.e., equality and participation.

citizenship. His work attracts the attention of communication scholars partly because he concludes that communication, or the 'ideal speech situation,' provides the foundation for a successful public sphere. He also concludes that the contemporary commodified mass media, along with the general expansion of consumerism and of the bureaucratic state, are root causes of its decline. Among the criticisms of Habermas' conception of the public sphere, what is most pertinent here is that his public sphere was overwhelmingly male, bourgeois, and white and, therefore, hardly democratic or very public.[18]

The responses take several turns. Some would discard the notion as hopelessly compromised, reduced, as Derrida (see Keenan, 1993) says of public opinion, to the 'silhouette of a phantom.' Some aim to rescue and breathe new life into the idea by addressing the public sphere of women (Peiss, 1991) or the proletarian public sphere (Negt and Kluge, 1972). Another attempt to critically advance the idea foregrounds the public sphere as a set of principles, including democracy, equality, participation, and citizenship, that point to an alternative to the set of practices bound up with commodification. The latter has been the most prominent position taken in communication research, in particular by those with an interest in political economy (Garnham, 1986; Murdock, 1990a; Sparks and Dahlgren, 1991).[19] This work addresses the use of the press, telecommunication, and electronic media, as well as systems of regulation and policy, to create oppositional spaces for the development of a public sphere. Communication research has also been interested in the concept of the *public interest*, a term with roots in the law governing regulation of the communication industries.[20] The notion has received extensive treatment, including criticism for ambiguity, particularly when set against the seemingly clearer test of the marketplace. It nevertheless survives in law, though the process of commodification has weakened its standing.[21] It also survives in research as an extension of the

18. The more generous of these critics acknowledge that Habermas intended to write about one specific historical manifestation of the public sphere, as the subtitle of his book reads: 'An Inquiry into a Category of Bourgeois Society' (Fraser, 1993; see also Peters, 1993).

19. Writing from an Islamic perspective, Mowlana (1990) offers a critique of the Western concept of civil society that applies to the notion of the public sphere as well.

20. For example, the U.S. Communication Act, the statute governing the regulation of broadcasting and telecommunication, calls for regulation 'in the public interest, convenience, and necessity.'

21. According to Anthony Smith (1989: 12), for example, 'the discourse of consumerism has replaced in arena after arena the discourse of public interest.' He sees this process leading to a new definition of the public good:

The new public good is an economic one: we all benefit from living in a competitive and updated economy and the degree of benefit we gain from government intervention designed to free the market is greater than the gain from society continuing to pursue a welfarist view of provision.

Actually there is nothing terribly new in this view. Another Smith (Adam) identified the public good and public welfare with expansion of the market.

public sphere notion to refer to those interests that transcend commercial gain and consumerism (Melody, 1990).

The debate on the public sphere is undeniably one of the more significant intellectual currents in social thought today (Peters, 1993). This is partly because it constitutes a widespread movement to develop substantial alternatives in social life to the market and the process of commodification. But it is also an exasperating debate because the public sphere umbrella covers the widest range of definitions and positionings. For some, it opposes both the state and the market; for others it is aligned with one or the other.[22] Depending on the theorist, the public sphere encompasses civil society, is encompassed by it, or is distinct from it. It can occupy physical space, institutional space, or electronic cyberspace. It includes the widest range of social behavior from debate on central public issues to shopping and music videos. The public sphere contains such a wide range of meanings and positionings that one is tempted to agree with a recent assessment (Robbins, 1993) that the public sphere is little more than a 'phantom,' or, better yet, a 'phantasmagoria' – the Greek *agora* mythologized. Notwithstanding the merits of this critique, the alternative, scrapping the idea altogether, is less appealing. It is, as Robbins (1993: x) suggests, a powerful 'discursive weapon' without which we enter social struggles 'inadequately armed':

> If the phrase 'phantom public' still has the power to startle and disorient, if there is some reluctance to see the public melt conclusively into air, the cause may not be vestigial piety so much as the fear that we cannot do without it.

The problem is how to address whatever *it* is? Or, since it is popular to think of it as a sphere, *where* is it? My view is that the latter question raises a critical problem with the notion of a public sphere. The tendency is to think of it as an object that occupies a specifiable space, whether physical, social, electronic, or phantasmagorical. Defenders of the public sphere sound like they are protecting a territory from a powerful, hostile invader whose goal is conquest. The analogy works to help one comprehend how the market and the public are opposed. But it suffers when it leads one to think of the market and the public as objects that occupy specific places, that are themselves difficult, if not impossible, to pin down. As a result of this difficulty, positions change about what is in or out of the public sphere. The term 'public' is far from unambiguous, but the problem appears to be less with it than with the idea of a sphere, however it is specified.

Tempting as it is to leap from the difficulty of seeing the public sphere in locational terms to seeing it as simply phantasm, the leap is hardly necessary. One can avoid both the idealism of the phantasm and the false materialism of the public sphere as a space to be defended *by defining the*

---

22. For example, Herbert Schiller (1989) offers a powerful critique of the state, but has also pointed to the value of government-operated public institutions, like public libraries and public education, that have suffered from the attacks of commercialism. On the other hand, Andrew Ross (1993) has made the case for viewing the market as an oppositional force to repressive forms of regulation.

public as a set of social processes that carry out democracy, namely advancing equality and the fullest possible participation in the complete range of economic, political, social, and cultural decision-making. These processes are distinct from those centered in private life, which advance interpersonal intimacy, and from those of the marketplace, which promote the creation of exchange and surplus value. The value of thinking in process terms is that, while there may be a greater likelihood that equality and participation adhere to some institutional forms and spaces rather than others, it does not rule out, by definition, any structural embodiment or location. The latter are better viewed as contested terrains, whether the state, the marketplace, or those structures, such as social movements, that manage to distance themselves from state and market, in which the processes of commodification and social equality and participation contend. All can be sites of the struggle between one's identity as, for example, consumer and as citizen, what Murdock (1993: 527) has concluded to be 'one of the central tensions of modern experience.'

Thinking in terms of a public process is difficult because the alternatives, clearly distinguished institutions and structures, give a concrete sense to what can otherwise be viewed as an idealist abstraction. More than that, they provide a road map which, however often it needs to be revised, offers guidance on getting from one point to the next, suggesting what course to follow and what to avoid. Nevertheless, institutions and structures can also offer false security. It is now fashionable to argue that the state in advanced capitalist societies, to which many once turned for alternatives to commodification, is irredeemably compromised, if not thoroughly market-contaminated and bureaucratized beyond much hope of realizing anything more than formal democracy. As a result, the search for oppositional and alternative forms, including media and culture, must be found outside, in places that have managed to maintain some distance from both state and market. There is considerable substance to the charge against the state and much to be said about finding uncontaminated spaces, what Aufderheide (1992: 53) describes as 'a living reality in "free spaces" in which people both discuss and act on their own conclusions.' Depending on how you define free, i.e., how much contamination can be absorbed before free space turns into market or state space, the free spaces in communication include traditional forms, such as the alternative press, public service (as opposed to state-controlled) broadcasting, as well as new forms, like public access cable channels and computer networks that open an electronic meeting place. The problem with seeing these as embodiments of free space is that, in non-trivial ways, they are neither free nor spaces. The alternative press may be the most free but, depending on state practice, makes use of mail subsidies and direct government grants, as well as market support mechanisms that include subscription fees, advertising and commodified labor processes and distribution networks. Again, depending on the jurisdiction, public service broadcasting depends on user fees, government grants, commercial advertising, and government appointment of major management personnel, who are often required to demonstrate their ability to meet either political or market criteria of success. Public access cable channels produce demonstrably more diverse content but they are limited to those who can afford a cable subscription fee (in 1996 about two-thirds of American homes subscribed to cable) and, again, depending on the jurisdiction, are subject to the oversight of both the cable operating company and state regulators. Interactive computer networks are particularly constrained by market and class considerations. They require access to computers and to telecommunication, and either the ability to pay for communication charges or the privileged access of the university professor whose charges are underwritten by the state, by universities (which are the recipients of considerable state support), or by companies trying to create a market in new forms of communication.

It is important to emphasize that these media provide major forms of alternative and oppositional communication. Nevertheless, by looking at them as free spaces, we tend to miss the significant ways in which the unequal structure of representation, of hierarchies organized according to class, gender, and race, are replicated, admittedly with specific variations, within each of these media forms.[23] Additionally, it also draws attention away from struggles that take place over resistance to commodification in both state and market. Here is where the contributions of Schiller (1989), Golding and Middleton (1982), and Ewen (1988), in particular, are so telling. Schiller and Golding have addressed media, communication, and information issues in the contested terrain at the heart of state activities, including public education, public libraries, government information, and the social welfare system. Furthermore, Schiller's work on commercial speech and Ewen's on style describe the contested nature of the commodification process within the innermost regions of the market. It is, above all, research that starts from the lived experiences of people who today confront the clash of opposing processes in schools, malls, social service agencies, and on the job, more than they do in alternative media and computer networks. Moreover, one of the central lessons of this work is that the market, the state, and the public are, in a real sense, located everywhere and therefore have no fixed coordinates. This should discourage the tendency to think about finding free space, or about looking for that ideal social form, whether located in a privileged class, or in a new social movement, that might represent a particularly privileged or purer manifestation of social opposition.

This should also encourage thinking about social processes, those vectors of social action that form different relationships in different dimensions of social life. The public sphere is more usefully conceptualized as a set of processes constituted out of the agency of social agents organized and

23. This misconception is prominent in the literature on new social movements, where we find the tendency to define them as part of a free space, free from state contamination and, though this is less explicit, the market. Such analyses often gesture, or refer substantially, to civil society, as the free space locus for these movements. For a critical analysis, see Wood (1990).

identified as citizens, and which promotes equality and participation, the core of democracy. These processes exist only in relation to a social field whose primary entry point, commodification, gives it pattern and initial shape, but a relation that is nevertheless continuously reconstituted out of the interaction between commodification and social process in public and private life. It is a social field from the standpoint of commodification, but a standpoint that is mutually constituted by private and public life. What we call the public media is public not because it occupies a separate space, relatively free from market considerations, but because it is constituted out of a particular patterning of processes that privilege the democratic over commodification. To the extent that it does not, the expression *public media* diminishes in value.

This chapter has argued that commodification is the entry point from which to begin rethinking the political economy of communication. It patterns a social field, but only in mutual constitution with processes at work in private and public life. The next chapter takes up a second set of entry points, led by spatialization, the process of overcoming the constraints of space and time.

5

Spatialization

Marx argued that the development of capitalist relations had the effect of overcoming all spatial barriers; hence to 'annihilate space with time'. Now, although this is a fundamental *objective* of capitalist production, what Marx (and some other Marxists) ignored is that this annihilation can only be achieved through the production of new, fixed and relatively immobile spatial configurations. As Harvey puts it, 'spatial organisation is necessary to overcome space'.

(Lash and Urry, 1987: 85)

The new territorial dynamics ... tend to be organized around the contradiction between placeless power and powerless places, the former relying upon communication flows, the latter generating their own communication codes on the basis of an historically specific territory.

(Castells and Henderson, 1987: 7)

Commodification is the starting or entry point for the political economy of communication. As such, it opens a field of analysis that includes processes emanating from private and public life which relate to one another and to commodification. The latter is a starting point and not one to which all others can be reduced. This chapter takes up the entry point of spatialization, a term introduced by the social theorist Henri Lefebvre (1979) to denote *the process of overcoming the constraints of space and time in social life*. There are two reasons why spatialization holds special significance for the political economist of communication. First, communication processes and technologies are central to the spatialization process throughout the wider political economy. Second and partly because of this, spatialization is particularly significant in the communication industries.

Although there is growing general interest in spatialization, social scientists, including political economists, have paid attention to it for some time. The question of how to measure the value of land and labor time, as well as the relationship between the spatial extension of markets and the division of labor, were central issues for Smith, Ricardo, and other classical theorists. We find a closer approximation to the concept of spatialization in Marx, who in the *Grundrisse* remarked on the tendency of capitalism to 'annihilate space with time.' This refers to the growing power of capital to use and improve on the means of transportation and communication, to shrink the time it takes to move goods, people, and messages over space, thereby decreasing the significance of spatial distance as a constraint on the expansion of capital. Among political economists who developed this theme, Harold Innis (1972) stands out for his sustained effort to establish the connections among forms of media, time and space, and structures of power.

Recent work in political economy (Lash and Urry, 1987) amends the Marxian view by suggesting that rather than annihilate space, capital transforms it, by restructuring the spatial relationships among people, goods, and messages and, in the process, transforms itself.[1]

The use of the term 'spatialization' draws on concepts and arguments increasingly central to the work of geographers and sociologists with an interest in political economy. For example, Giddens (1990) has made use of the term *time–space distanciation* in order to examine the decline of time–space dependency and to suggest a focus on the growth of time and space as elastic resources. Harvey's (1989) description of *time–space compression* strikes a similar chord, though with a greater interest in the political economic implications, such as for an international banking system that, among other things, manages capital flows amounting to about one trillion dollars (U.S.) a day over electronic highways that transcend time and space limitations. Castells (1989: 348) draws attention to the declining significance of physical space relative to what he calls *the space of flows*:

> the deployment of the functional logic of power-holding organizations in asymmetrical networks of exchanges which do not depend on the characteristics of any specific locale for the fulfilment of their fundamental goals.

Castells' work provides an active sense of space, viewing it as more than, as Massey (1992) reminds us, the traditional, gendered conception of space as simply the absence of time, 'the slice through time, Mother Earth dependent on time's dynamism for its ability to change.' Moreover, Castells (1989: 348) places communication at the center of the spatialization process, because communication maintains the dynamic balance between differentiation and reintegration:

> The new industrial space and the new service economy organize their operations around the dynamics of their information-generating units, while connecting their different functions to disparate spaces assigned to each task to be performed; the overall process is then reintegrated through communication systems.

Finally, his conception is important because it retains a sense of differential power which, in some conceptions of globalization, tends to dissipate in networks of mutual interdependence. Making this more explicit, Massey (1992) refers to space in relational terms, comprising sets of dynamic social relations organized in a 'power-geometry.' Their work suggests that the political economy of communication can benefit by taking up spatialization as a means of understanding the relationship of power-geometries to the

1. We should not make too much of Marx's reference to *annihilating* space. He recognized (in *Grundrisse*, de la Haye, 1980: 156) that in practice this meant a shift in the balance of attention that capital would direct to different spaces, specifically to new markets:

> the opportunities created by the development of transport and communication facilities make it imperative, conversely, to work for evermore remote markets, in a word – for the world market.

Recent critics (Lash and Urry, 1987) describe the shifting, multilayered nature of the spatial consequences that Marx began to describe.

process of constituting space, particularly the space through which communication flows.

Communication and Concentration: Space as Institutional Extension

In general terms, spatialization research has taken up the geographic and institutional extension of organizational activity. The political economy of communication has specifically addressed spatialization chiefly in terms of *the institutional extension of corporate power in the communication industry*. This is manifested in the sheer growth in the size of media firms, measured by assets, revenues, profit, employees, and share value. Political economy has specifically examined growth by taking up different forms of *corporate concentration*. Although both growth and concentration are central features of the contemporary communication map, concern about the social consequences of these developments is not new. For example, a century ago, Honoré de Balzac criticized the Charles Havas' monopoly on French wire service copy because it led to a decline in information sources.

The simplest form of concentration takes place when a media firm buys a controlling interest in a company operating principally in the same business.[2] *The New York Times* purchase of the *Boston Globe* newspaper is a prime example of this basic form. Traditional thinking examines the major different types of concentration according to their *horizontal* and *vertical* forms. Nevertheless, although terms are used widely, it is important to underscore the point that there is less than complete agreement on concepts, definitions, and applications in this area. This is partly due to the underdeveloped state of research on media concentration, which, in some measure, results from the media industry's ability to influence the research agenda, leaving us with more studies on how to market products than on the nature and implications of media concentration. The lack of conceptual agreement is also partly the consequence of a rapidly changing industry. Changes in industry structure, technology, services, as well as in state policy and regulation (which typically lags these changes), have made it difficult to provide a generally agreed upon language for mapping media concentration.

Taking into account the limited agreement on terminology, we can consider some of the major ways people have thought about media concentration. Horizontal concentration takes place when a firm in one line of media buys a major interest in another media operation, not directly related to the original business, or when it takes a major stake in a company entirely

2. The definition of a controlling interest or major stake varies widely, from as little as 2 percent in a company with widely dispersed shareholders to 51 percent or more, which gives a company majority control of stock and consequently of the board of directors.

outside of the media.[3] The typical example of the first or *cross-media* concentration is the purchase by a firm in an older media line, say a newspaper, of a firm in a newer line, such as a radio or television station. This is one way an industry like newspaper publishing is able to remain profitable in the face of newer media forms, exemplified in the purchase of the Twentieth-Century Fox Film Corporation by Rupert Murdoch's News Corp. Horizontal concentration also takes place when a media firm moves on a company entirely outside the media business or when a media firm is swallowed up by a non-media business. The former took place when the Radio Corporation of America (RCA), the parent firm of the NBC television network, purchased the Hertz rental car company. An example of a non-media takeover occurred when the General Electric Co., an electronics firm and a major defense contractor, purchased RCA, a company it actually first owned in the 1920s. Additionally, the Fininvest Group, an Italian company led, until early 1994, by Silvio Berlusconi, who used his media holdings to help him lead a rightist coalition to victory in national elections, provides one of the clearer examples of building a media empire from a non-media base. Starting in construction and real estate (Cantieri Riuniti Milanesi), the company has created seven additional divisions in the mass media and financial services.[4] This form of horizontal concentration results in the creation or expansion of *conglomerate* ownership, a product of the amalgamation of firms in different lines of business.

Vertical integration describes the concentration of firms within a line of business that extends a company's control over the process of production. MCA's purchase of Cineplex-Odeon gave the former, a major Hollywood producer, control over a major film distribution company. This is also referred to as forward integration because it expands a firm further along the circuit required for the realization of value. Backward vertical integration took place when *The New York Times* purchased paper mills in Quebec, thereby expanding the company down the production process. Depending on its ability to manage the flows among stages in production, a company can gain a competitive advantage from the opportunities that vertical integration

3. The phrase 'not directly related' is significant for more than definitional reasons because the purchase of a related firm could diminish the degree of competition in one (if the firms operate in the same market) or more markets (if they operate in different ones). Conversely, one could argue that the purchase of a related firm is more likely to increase market efficiency because it would enable the purchaser to rationalize operations.

4. At its peak in the 1980s, Fininvest's sprawling empire included holdings in property, publishing, leisure, financial services, retailing, and broadcasting, most of which were accumulated rapidly and with borrowed money. The company ran into trouble in the early 1990s, when Italy's booming economy slowed. In 1994, Fininvest sold $1.3 billion of its assets to pay down debt. Mr Berlusconi stepped down from Fininvest in January 1994 in order to participate in the rightist coalition of parties mobilizing for the next country-wide vote. He had been criticized for holding on to the media conglomerate, even as his direct involvement in Italian politics mounted. Exemplifying the shifting tides in this industry, in May 1995 Rupert Murdoch's News Corp. bid $2.8 billion for 51 percent of Fininvest's three national television networks.

offers to rationalize its operations. By owning program production companies, television networks are guaranteed a supply of product at prices that offer few surprises. This holds as well for telephone companies that own equipment suppliers and for film companies whose control over exhibitors provides a guaranteed outlet for their products.

These forms of integration are essentially means of controlling uncertainties that arise when a company has to rely on external markets to complete the circuit of production. Business historians have long recognized the significance of this process in the development of, depending on the interpretation, corporate, managerial, organized, or monopoly capitalism. For example, Chandler (1977) has documented management strategies that produced integrated companies, such as DuPont, General Motors, and Sears, which succeeded in dominating industries over several decades. According to him, what stands out in their success was a management strategy to seal off the company from many external market uncertainties produced by, for example, several strong competitors along the circuit of production. Just as important, they created markets within this protected environment by requiring competition among product line divisions. General Motors succeeded where others failed, in part, because vertical and horizontal integration protected it from competition *and* because it created an internal market in which its Oldsmobile, Pontiac, Chevrolet, and Cadillac divisions competed as independent product lines responsible for meeting individual growth targets. The Executive Committee of the corporate board served as the manager and banker to this integrated multi-divisional corporate form, assessing success and shifting resources accordingly (see Figure 5.1).[5] According to Chandler, companies that instituted this structure enjoyed many of the benefits of internal market competition even as they reduced the uncertainties of hostile competition from outside the corporation. He, along with other business historians (see also Brunn and Leinbach, 1991; Pred, 1966; Yates, 1989), also acknowledges that communication and information technology, as well as transportation systems, have been central to these processes, because they have given management the tools to control the speed and the form of integration. Rapid and efficient communication systems are essential for a company to manage the multiplicity of exchanges that flow within an integrated, multi-divisional corporate form whose success depends on timely assessments of relative performance, e.g. which division has the best return on capital and why (Chandler, 1977, especially Chap. 6; see also Malone and Rockart, 1991).

One of the leading multi-divisional firms in the media business, Time Warner, demonstrated the value of this organizational form in its handling of

5. Chandler contrasts successful firms which tended to make the shift to a multi-divisional quasi-market arrangement with those firms, such as Ford, which were less successful, in spite of a significant measure of integration. In his view, the latter neglected the internal market by retaining a functional corporate structure divided according to traditional finance, marketing, production, and accounting lines, which precluded, or made much more difficult, intra-corporate competition.

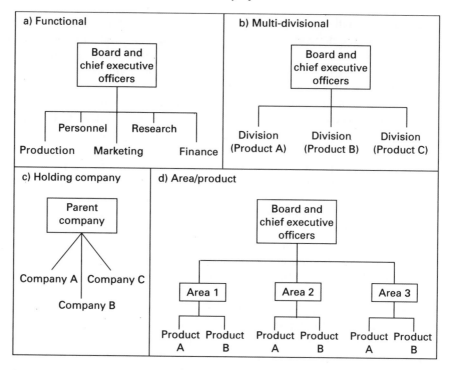

Figure 5.1   *Corporate structure types (Chapman and Walker, 1987: 115)*

the best-selling novel Robert James Waller's *The Bridges of Madison County*. The Warner Books division published the book, which, by July 1993, had sold 2.5 million copies. Time Warner's Atlantic Recording division produced a recording of songs inspired by the novel and sung by the author, as well as a music video. Both the novel and album, the first of a five-album deal with Atlantic, have been written about and advertised in Time Warner's magazines, and the company has produced a short spot for Time Warner cable systems that features the author turned balladeer promoting his work and providing an 800 number for phone orders (Cox, 1993).[6] By 1996 Warner Bros. had turned it into a film and video hit.

The post-World War II acceleration in *multinational* enterprises introduced another form of media industry growth that increasingly occupies

6. Though not a primary consideration, one of the reasons why the major U.S. television home shopping channel, QVC, made a strong bid to take over Paramount Communications is that QVC has demonstrated a remarkable ability to sell almost any consumer good, including books. In one thirty-minute period of televised home shopping, the company sold 15,000 copies of a novel. In 1993 Paramount bought Macmillan Publishing for $553 million from the dying Maxwell empire, giving it control over a dozen or so houses including Simon and Schuster, Prentice Hall, Touchstone, Scribner's, and Pocket Books (Mehegan, 1994). But before the sell, the restructuring. Early in 1994 Paramount Publishing announced that the merged companies would drop 1,100 jobs from their combined workforce of 10,000 and eliminate some specialized units such as the 35-year-old Atheneum unit (Cox, 1994).

communication scholars. As Smith (1991) and Tunstall (1977) have demonstrated, transnational media enterprises are as old as the mass media themselves. The production and distribution of news in the nineteenth century was controlled in large measure by three international press conglomerates – the British Reuters, the French Havas, and the German Wolf – which divided the world's markets into monopoly zones that, for a considerable time, kept out the competition.[7] This tendency has expanded in recent decades as communication firms seek out new markets for products, low-cost labor, and areas with minimal government oversight and regulation. The media industries have been particularly important to the general process of transnationalization because media, directly through advertising, but indirectly as well in all forms of media, call attention to products in general, in addition to the specific media product for sale. Moreover, the means of communication, including new technologies such as communication satellites and high-capacity cables, have made it cost-effective and easier for firms, including most of the communication industry, to operate efficiently across several borders. It remains the case that the largest transnational media firms retain a base in one generally identified nation. Nevertheless, they are increasingly able to use the genuine multinational dimensions of their product, marketing, labor, and financing to transcend the legal, regulatory, cultural, and financial constraints of their home base.

One obvious consequence is the rise of what Anthony Smith (1991) calls the 'behemoths': Time Warner, Matsushita, Bertelsmann, News Corp., Fininvest, Hachette, Disney, and Sony, among others. These firms integrate vertically by securing control over production, distribution, and exhibition; horizontally across a range of media products, including hardware and software; and globally by taking advantage of an international division of labor that makes possible the flexible and cost-effective use of labor, capital, research and development. They embody enormous concentrated economic power. Nevertheless, you do not need to be a former employee shorn of a pension from Robert Maxwell's crumbled empire, a creditor hoping for a few cents on the dollar, or a Time Warner investor wondering if the company will ever get out from under its debt load to recognize that the conglomerate form is not the only or even the most effective form of corporate response to global restructuring. The integrated conglomerate benefits from competition within, as it flexes its market power without. But it does so at a price. The Time Warner merger resulted in a company weighed down with over $10 billion in debt. Rupert Murdoch built his News Corp. empire on $8 billion in short-term debt. Admittedly, the conglomerate form provides for enormous flexibility, but it can also develop bureaucratic

---

7. Herbert Schiller (1976: 26–29) reminds us that the United States chafed the most under the worldwide press cartel, demanding, as many of the world's poor nations would demand decades later of the U.S., that size and assets alone should not be permitted to determine who controlled the production and distribution of information (see Cooper, 1942).

tendencies that restrict more innovative units, as the conglomerate ITT learned in the 1970s and IBM in the 1980s.

As the significance of the national base declines, some wonder about what this means for the interests of transnationals and the ability of the nation state to control them. Robert Reich (1991: 8) asks,

> So who is us? . . . Neither the profitability of a nation's corporations nor the successes of its investors necessarily improve the standard of living of most of the nation's citizens. They are becoming disconnected from their home nations.[8]

This view is disputed by those who find that the economic power-geometry of transnational business is skewed in favor of the workers and consumers in the home countries of multinational firms (Thurow, 1992). Others conclude that states continue to retain power over all firms in their jurisdiction, whatever home flag they happen to fly, so that a world made up of powerful nation states and powerful multinational firms can coexist (Strange, 1988). Although certainly arguable, Reich's point does raise important questions about who is served by policies aiming to protect 'national' companies. Still acting on the view that though they are multinationals, at least they are *our* multinationals, U.S. policy-makers worry about the consequences of having almost half the Hollywood majors under foreign control – rather than asking what makes the rest American. Or why the United States should continue a decades-old practice of permitting 'our' Motion Picture Export Association to avoid anti-trust oversight when it operates in foreign markets.[9] Furthermore, U.S. telecommunication policy-makers worry about the loss of its manufacturing market share to Northern Telecom, a 'Canadian' company headquartered in the United States with more of its workforce based there. Americans rarely question the national identity of IBM, half of whose revenues are earned outside the United States, or what makes Ameritech, which has used its regional monopoly to buy half of New Zealand's

---

8. Reich (1991: 166) turns to the media industry, countering the claims of Time Warner that the creation of the conglomerate 'will make America better able to challenge foreign media companies':

> Why such a merger would help the United States in particular, relative to what the nation gained from Rupert Murdoch's News Corporation (which included 20th-Century Fox, Fox Broadcasting, *TV Guide*, and Harper & Row), or West Germany's Bertelsmann's media empire (including RCA Records and Bantam, Doubleday, and Dell), or France's Hachette (*Women's Day* and Grolier's Encyclopedia), or Sony (CBS records and Columbia Pictures), remained a mystery. American writers, editors, directors, musicians, and cinematographers were involved in all these global media companies, as were their foreign counterparts.

9. Wasko (1994) refers to Hollywood as a 'three tier society.' At the top are the largest studios: Paramount, Twentieth-Century Fox, Warner, Universal, Disney, and Columbia. Of these, three are under non-U.S. ownership. Rupert Murdoch's News Corp. owns Fox, Matsushita, the Japanese electronics conglomerate, owns Universal, and Sony owns Columbia. The second tier includes what she calls 'minor/majors,' including MGM/UA, Orion, Carolco, and New Line Cinema. The smallest firms, often referred to, with dubious accuracy, as independents, occupy the third tier.

Table 5.1 *Top twenty-five audiovisual companies worldwide by sales*

Rank	Company	Country	Total audiovisual 1991 (in millions of US dollars)
1	Time Warner	USA	7,391
2	Sony	Japan	5,702.6
3	Capital Cities/ABC	USA	4,329.7
4	NHK	Japan	4,039.8
5	Matsushita[1]	Japan	3,951
6	ARD	Germany	3,730.4
7	PolyGram	Holland	3,379.7
8	Fininvest	Italy	3,331
9	Fujisankei	Japan	3,259
10	BBC	UK	3,237.6
11	Bertelsmann	Germany	3,159
12	RAI	Italy	3,125
13	General Electric/NBC	USA	3,121
14	CBS	USA	3,035
15	News Corp.	Australia	2,750.6
16	Walt Disney	USA	2,593.7
17	Thorn EMI	UK	2,497.5
18	Paramount	USA	2,380.2
19	Tokyo Broadcasting System	Japan	1,581
20	Ashai National Broadcasting	Japan	1,570
21	Nippon Television Network	Japan	1,544
22	TBS	USA	1,433.9
23	Viacom	USA	1,370
24	PBS	USA	1,320
25	CLT	Luxembourg	1,305

[1] Matsushita 1990 (pro forma) = MCA 1990 + JVC Entertainment, 1990/1.
Matsushita 1991: 25% + 80% of MCA.

Source: IDATE, 1992: 6

telephone system and the German publisher of Yellow Pages, American. Nevertheless, many firms *are* reluctant to give up the national base because it provides considerable support, often in the form of preferential legal, regulatory, and investment policies that afford an essential cushion in the face of an often hostile international environment. Preferential government treatment in their home countries enabled companies like Matsushita of Japan, Time Warner of the United States, and the Canadian Northern Telecom to expand into international markets with considerably reduced risk. The point is that Reich's question 'Who is us?' is relevant whether or not companies retain a national base, because, from a societal viewpoint, the issue is not where is the base, but, wherever it is, do companies create jobs, produce socially useful products and services, and can their behavior be regulated in the public interest?

Political economists have been interested in a wide range of forms of concentration. Nevertheless, there has been an overwhelming interest in

Table 5.2   *Market concentration in the international record industry, 1990/1*

Company	Turnover (in millions of US dollars)	Market share
Sony Music Entertainment	3,274	20.60
Time Warner	2,931	18.50
PolyGram	2,884	18.20
Bertelsmann	2,219	14.00
Thorn EMI[1]	1,814	11.40
JVC[2]	815	5.10
MCA	764	4.80
Virgin	567	3.60
Other (estimate)	600	3.80
Total	15,868	100.00

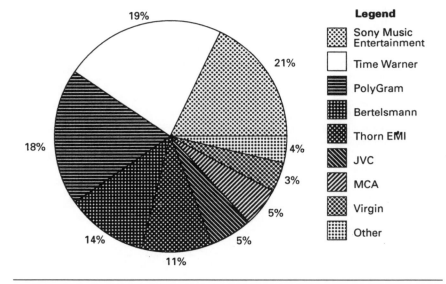

[1] Thorn EMI acquired Virgin in 1991.
[2] JVC and MCA turnover is for 1989.
Source: IDATE, 1992: 31

ownership as the primary defining element in media concentration. This is chiefly because of the concern that ownership concentration can restrict the flow of communication and information by limiting the diversity of producers and distributors. Hence, research on the variety of vertical, horizontal, and transnational forms of concentration tends to emanate from debate on the consequences of ownership concentration. There are, however, significant differences in the measurement of concentration and in the assessment of its significance. For example, Compaine et al. (1982) distinguish between the traditional anti-trust definition, which looks at market share, and broader conceptions that address firm size and the diversity of products in the market. The former definition tends to be used in regulatory and legal proceedings and a range of measures have been developed to test

Table 5.3 *Top ten entertainment companies by revenue, 1992*

Company	Country	Revenue (in millions of US dollars)
Time Warner	USA	7,957
Sony	Japan	5,775
Matsushita	Japan	4,709
Philips	Netherlands	3,700
Walt Disney	USA	3,115
Paramount Communications	USA	2,657
Thorn EMI	UK	2,463
Bertelsmann	Germany	2,219
Fujisankei	Japan	2,100
News Corp.	Australia	1,858

Source: *The Wall Street Journal*, March 26, 1993, p. R16.

the degree of market competition.[10] The approach focuses on the market and aims to determine how open it is to a multiplicity of products, such as television programs or newspapers. Nevertheless, the unit of analysis is the firm, under ownership that is discernibly different from that of other firms in the market. For example, in a newspaper market, a daily owned by Murdoch's News Corp. and one under the Gannett banner would be considered competitors; two Gannett papers would not. Though the market is foregrounded, the unit that provides the test of concentration remains the firm.

A broader conception of concentration (Wasko, 1984, 1994) takes into account the market, but shifts attention to the degree of ownership concentration that enables firms to make use of resources based on operations in a *range of markets*. Moreover, it shifts the focus from the sheer multiplicity of product to its *diversity*. For example, this approach weighs more heavily the ability of Manhattan Cable, the unit of Time Warner that provides cable television to part of New York City, to draw on the resources of the various divisions of the parent company for product, financing, and political lobbying power. Manhattan Cable is thereby a fundamentally different firm from one that lacks these connections. Yet, for the purpose of a market-specific analysis, it is treated like any other discretely owned entity. Moreover, the broader form of concentration analysis shifts attention from the sheer number of conduits into a market, to the diversity of content provided by whatever number of channels. It follows from this view that one cable firm with an ownership monopoly in a market, but also with a wide range of different voices reflected in its various channels, constitutes less concentration than a market with several newspapers that, though under different

10. The U.S. government has used concentration indices to determine the extent of oligopoly control of a market. For example, the Herfindahl–Hirschman Index is the sum of the squared market shares of all firms in a market. A market with two equal-sized firms would have an index of 5000. An index below 1000 is considered unconcentrated, 1000–1800 a 'gray area', and over 1800 highly concentrated (see Levy and Setzer, 1984: 209).

Table 5.4   *Top fifty communication users in the United States, 1994*

Rank 1994	Rank 1993	Company	FY '93 revenue (in millions of US dollars)
1	1	General Motors Corp.	135,696
2	3	Ford Motor Co.	108.448
3	2	Exxon Corp.	97,825
4	8	Wal-Mart Stores Inc.	67,345
5	4	AT&T	67,156
6	5	IBM	62,716
7	7	General Electric Co.	59,827
8	6	Mobil Corp.	56,576
9	9	Sears Roebuck & Co.	50,838
10	10	Philip Morris Co. Inc.	50,621
11	15	Chrysler Corp.	42,260
12	11	KMart Corp.	34,353
13	14	Texaco	33,245
14	13	EI DuPont de Nemours & Co.	32,732
15	12	Chevron Corp.	32,123
16	18	Procter & Gamble Co.	30,433
17	16	Citicorp.	28,868
18	17	Boeing Co.	25,438
19	20	Amoco Corp.	25,336
20	22	Pepsico Inc.	25,021
21	23	ITT Corp.	22,762
22	21	Kroger Co.	22,384
23	25	Conagra Inc.	21,519
24	28	American International Group Inc.	21,155
25	24	United Technologies Corp.	21,081
26	39	Hewlett-Packard Co.	20,317
27	NR	Allstate Corp.	20,228
28	27	GTE Corp.	19,748
29	29	JC Penney Co.	19,578
30	33	Dayton Hudson Corp.	19,233
31	30	American Stores Corp.	18,763
32	32	Cigna Corp.	18,402
33	31	Dow Chemical Co.	18,060
34	38	United Parcel Service of America Inc.	17,782
35	NR	Atlantic Richfield Co.	17,189
36	35	Aetna Life & Casualty Co.	17,118
37	41	Salomon Bros. Inc.	17,107
38	53	Motorola Inc.	16,963
39	51	Merrill Lynch & Co. Inc.	16,588
40	26	Eastman Kodak Co.	16,364
41	37	Xerox Corp.	16,193
42	196	USX Corp.	16,137
43	45	Federal National Mortgage Assn.	16,053
44	62	Super Value Stores Inc.	15,937
45	44	Bellsouth Corp.	15,880
46	46	AMR Corp.	15,701
47	128	Price/Costco Co.	15,476
48	43	Safeway Inc.	15,215
49	40	RJR Nabisco Inc.	15,104
50	54	Sara Lee Corp.	14,580

Source: *Information Week*, October 10, 1994: 38

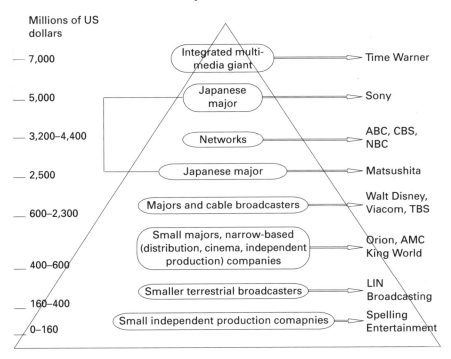

Figure 5.2 *A structural view of the U.S. communication industry (IDATE, 1992: 44)*

ownership, offer essentially the same point of view. Proponents of the broader view grant the difficulty of measuring such forms of concentration, but argue that the more narrow view, with its indices of market share, provides a mechanistic and inadequate barometer of concentration.[11] Moreover, they also maintain that the narrower view falls short on how to expand access to the widest range of information and opinion, one of the major policy goals of concentration analysis.

McLaughlin with Antonoff (1986) provide one of the more recent efforts to remap industry space by examining changes in communication technologies and services within the context of changes in the economy. They created a series of maps providing variations on a view of the information business that distinguishes between products and services, on one axis, and form (conduits) and substance (content), on the other (see Figures 5.3–5.6). As their historical overview suggests, the major areas of growth have taken place in the center of the map, where products and services, conduit and content converge. Taking a more ambitious approach that draws on social

11. Orthodox economists explain their reluctance to address the broader view of diversity, whatever its merits, because it cannot be measured empirically. They tend to equate program diversity with the number of competitors and production quality with the size of program budgets (Owen and Wildman, 1992: 146).

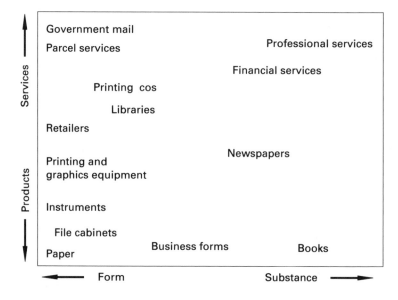

Figure 5.3   *The information business in 1790 (McLaughlin with Antonoff, 1986: 18)*

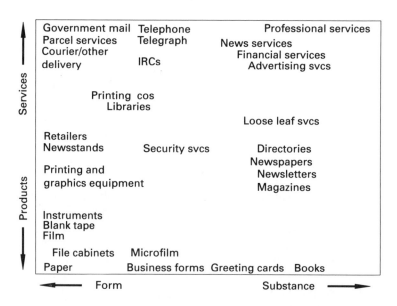

Figure 5.4   *The information business in 1880 (McLaughlin with Antonoff, 1986: 19)*

network analysis, Burt (1992) produced a topological map of the American economy that aims to determine clusters of business activity distinguished principally by the emphasis on inorganic and organic products and by the

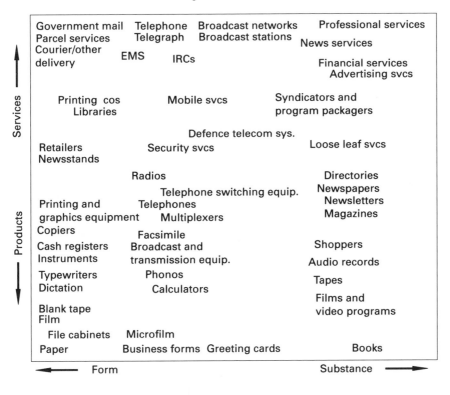

Figure 5.5   *The information business in 1930 (McLaughlin with Antonoff, 1986: 20)*

use of older or newer technologies (see Figure 5.7). Interestingly, one of Burt's major conclusions (p. 88) is that the map, which makes use of the U.S. *Survey of Current Business* input–output tables, is fundamentally stable since 1960, except for 'a pocket of instability at the bottom of the map created by change over the two decades in transactions defining the ordnance, computers, and communication equipment markets.'

However differently approached, the narrow and broad views of concentration share a primary focus on ownership as the central measure. One major exception to this tendency is the broader view's interest in the analysis of *corporate boards of directors*. Rather than examine who owns the media, the goal of this approach is to map relationships among members of the body holding primary responsibility for corporate performance. Although the law governing corporate boards of directors varies from jurisdiction to jurisdiction, most firms carry out this responsibility by selecting the highest level of management, including the chief executive officer, and by deciding on major budget allocations, such as capital outlays and retrenchments. The latter include decisions to build or to close plants and offices. Boards are formally selected by shareholders, but, in practice, it is the board itself that generally succeeds in determining its own composition. Board size varies

Services

Products

Form	Substance

Government mail	Mailgram VANs Broadcast networks	Data bases Professional services
Parcel services		Broadcast stations Videotex
Courier/other	Telex DBS	
delivery	EMS Intern., long dist.	News services
	and local telephone service	Teletext Financial services
	Cable networks and operators	Advertising svcs

Multipoint distribution svcs

Digital termination svcs

Printing cos
Libraries

Mobile svcs	FM subcarriers	Time sharing	Service bureaus
Paging svcs	Billing and	On-line directories
metering svcs	Software svcs
Multiplexing svcs

Bulk transmission svcs

Retailers	Industry networks

Newsstands	Defence telecom sys.	Syndicators and
program packagers

Security svcs	CSS svcs	Loose leaf svcs

Radios	PABXs	Computers	Software packages

Directories

TV sets

Telephone switching equip.	Newspapers

Printing and	Telephones
graphics equipment	Modems

Newsletters

Copiers	Terminals	Concentrators	Magazines

Printers
Facsimile	Multiplexers

ATMs, POS equip.

Cash registers	Broadcast and	Shoppers
Instruments	transmission equip.	Audio records

Typewriters	Word processors	Tapes

Dictation	Video tape recd.	Films and
video programs

Blank tape	Phonos, video disc players
Film	Calculators

File cabinets	Microfilm	Microfiche

Paper	Business forms	Greeting cards	Books

ATM	Automatic Teller Machine	IRCs	International Record Carriers
COS	Companies	PABX	Private Automatic Branch Exchange
CSS	Carrier 'Smart' Switch	POS	Point-of-Sale
DBS	Direct Broadcast Satellite	Svcs	Services
EMS	Electronic Message Service	VAN	Value-added Network

Figure 5.6 *The information business – present (McLaughlin with Antonoff, 1986: 4)*

with the size and diversity of the company, with a range of fifteen to forty members common. The chief distinction within the board of directors is between *inside* members, who are part of management, and *outside* directors, who are generally executives with other firms, though this category might also include token representation from civil society groups. For example, the 1991 board of Time Warner contained thirty-five members, twenty-three of whom were company executives. Outside directors were major executives with financial and industrial companies, including the chairman of Xerox and the chair of the executive committee of IBM (Dun's Marketing Services, 1991).[12]

Studies of corporate boards examine the ties that connect board members to a common fiduciary responsibility. Analysts distinguish between *direct* interlocks, which link two firms through the membership of an executive from one company on the board of another, and *indirect* interlocks, which connect two companies through common membership on a third board. IBM and Xerox are each directly connected to Time Warner through the common responsibility that their representatives on the board have for the performance of Time Warner. IBM and Xerox are also indirectly linked to each other through their common membership on the Time Warner board. Media concentration is thereby extended through the shared responsibilities for performance among companies that compete in some markets. The analysis of company boards developed with some rigor through the application of common statistical measures, network analysis, and matrix algebra (Burt, 1992; Scott, 1991). The central point of the analysis is that overlapping board structures provide the opportunity and the responsibility for close cooperation among the representatives of firms, some of which are competitors (Coulter, 1992).

Social scientists (Clement, 1975, 1977; Domhoff, 1978, 1990; Useem, 1984) have documented many other places that afford opportunities for elite corporate interaction and planning. These include private clubs, associations, and professional organizations which serve as nodes in networks of class power. Nevertheless, the corporate board stands out among these venues because of the added legal, fiduciary responsibility demanded of its members. The Time Warner board offered more than the opportunity for David Kearns of Xerox and John Opel of IBM to meet and discuss common concerns. They, along with their fellow board members, had a legal responsibility to act on behalf of Time Warner and, according to those who argue for the significance of indirect interlocks, for one another. It is through this process that concentration achieves a texture comprised of both the opportunity and the responsibility for cooperation and planning that overcomes differences and tempers competition. This texture, made up of the many daily occasions for contact and interaction, gives concentration the quality of *hegemony*, a taken-for-granted belief in the right to use power.

Recent research opens up new directions in the analysis of concentration which, though rooted in understanding the power of ownership, look to forms of corporate interaction that build powerful relationships without actually merging businesses. These forms encompass a range of 'teaming arrangements,' including *corporate partnerships* or *strategic alliances* for specific projects such as media co-productions or for the development of

12. In addition to company annual reports and the Dun's *Directory, Standard & Poor's Register of Corporations* is an excellent source of data on company boards.

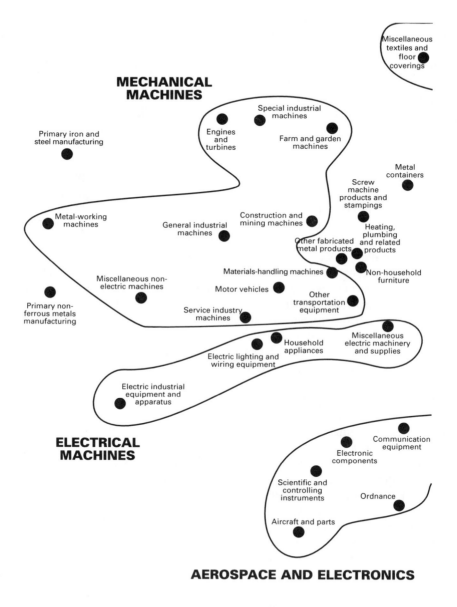

Figure 5.7   *Topological map of the US economy (Burt, 1992: 86–87)*

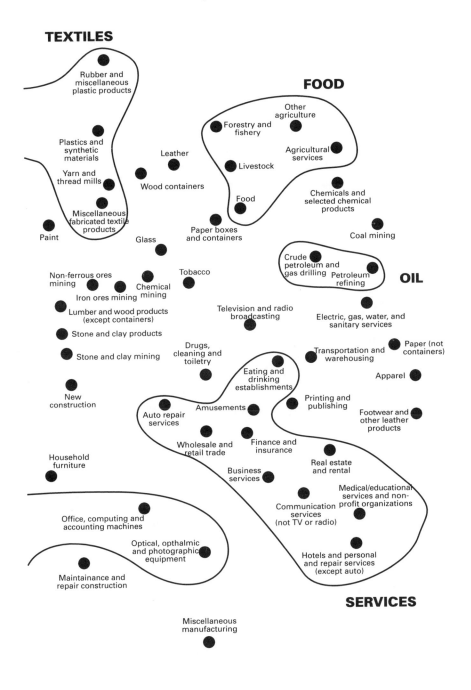

Figure 5.7 *continued*

new technologies.[13] They also include *merchandising arrangements* that link media companies with marketing and merchandising firms.[14] These practices are not new to corporate practice, including media firms, but they have grown more common in recent years. This is partly because the process of spatialization enables companies to restructure internal operations and their external relationships for a specific period of time, such as the duration of one project, without incurring organizational disruptions that ruled out these arrangements in the past. Whether or not the project succeeds, companies can reconstitute to carry out their major businesses. Moreover, they can cooperate and compete at the same time.

One caveat for understanding these developments is that the language used to describe them, e.g. 'synergy,' is formulated for its public relations, as much as for its analytical, value. As a result, terms like strategic alliance and synergy, which offer rhetorical weight, also carry different meanings.[15] In the pure sense, a strategic alliance brings together two or more firms, or specific units of these firms, for one or more projects, without any change in ownership or investment of one in the other. Alliances may involve the creation of a new company, though this is not essential to the alliance. Media co-production arrangements constitute a good case of the pure form. Prompted by compelling economics that promise, and regularly deliver, lower production costs, this form of alliance has grown to dominate video and film production in Europe.[16] International alliances are also influencing significantly the once insular American production industry. For example, in 1991, the Warner film division of Time Warner reached a co-production agreement with Canal+, one of the largest private broadcasters in Europe, to make twenty films, the first fruit of which was the box-office hit *JFK*. In this

13. Pogorel (1991: 104) defends the value of alliances in the new information and communication technologies (NICT):

> The spread of 'alliances' during the last few years, has exemplified NICT favoring 'externalisation.' This illustrates the existence of forms in between markets and hierarchies and of the influence of NICT [which] finds here a spontaneous and imaginative answer. Between the ever-spreading and longlasting hierarchies, and Brownian markets, where only stochastic, instantaneous transactions could take place, there are all kinds of combinations.

Various types of alliances including independent profit centers, spin-off partnerships, spin-in partnerships, licensing, and pure brokerage are discussed in Reich (1991: 91–94).

14. Merchandising, as Wasko (1994) notes, is formally the mechanical act of creating and selling a product based on a copyrightable product. Licensing is the legal mechanism by which a copyright trademark holder receives a royalty for the use of a name, a likeness, or an image.

15. For Schiller (1993), 'synergy' is a glossy term for corporate control over the entirety of consumer images and products. Drawing on Meehan's concept of the 'cultural fund,' Wasko (1994) refers to cultural synergy as the set of overlapping cultural images produced by these companies.

16. According to Strover (1993), of fifty-four films made in the United Kingdom in 1991, twenty-one were co-produced and another seven were entirely foreign made. Supporting co-production agreements with forty-five countries, nearly half of the films produced in France in 1991 took this form.

case, Warner and Canal+ contractually agreed to an alliance for a specific product, twenty films, that does not involve the exchange of stock or any commitment at all beyond the agreement. Such activities have also brought companies together in the area of new communication technologies, where, for example, two fierce competitors, IBM and Apple, have formed an alliance to develop specific new-generation components, such as the Power PC computer system.

These limited contractual arrangements sometimes take the form of a new company which gives greater substance to the alliance. In one of the more significant such developments in recent years, Time Warner, the world's largest entertainment company (and owner of one of the largest cable television systems), Tele-Communications, Inc., the largest cable television company, and Microsoft, the world's largest software producer, formed an alliance to establish standards for distributing new generations of interactive programs, largely through cable television systems. The alliance is crystallized in a joint venture company, Cablesoft, which manages the alliance and produces the system. Another example brings together the two largest telecommunication companies, AT&T and Japan's NTT, the three largest consumer-electronics concerns, Sony, Matsushita, and Philips, as well as Apple Computer and Motorola to form General Magic, which aims to create intelligent, interactive products that integrate different technologies for electronic information access and communication. The development of High-Definition Television systems brought together global competitors in what the popular press referred to as a 'grand alliance' of global firms, including AT&T, General Instruments, Philips, Thomson, and Zenith, among others. These are some of the more significant examples of alliances among telecommunication companies, cable television firms, entertainment conglomerates, and computer firms that aim to take advantage of market position and expertise to create specific products out of the much-heralded promise of technological convergence. They are particularly notable not only because they cut across technologies, but also because they bring together some of the traditionally fiercest competitors.

The term 'strategic alliance' is also used when one company buys an interest, if not necessarily a controlling one, in another company. Prominent recent examples include AT&T's 1992 announcement that it would purchase a one-third stake in MacCaw Cellular Communications for $3.73 billion, a deal that positions the company to re-enter the local telephone service market. In 1993 the telecommunication firm U.S. West agreed to take a one-fourth stake in an entertainment subsidiary of Time Warner, a deal worth $2.5 billion, and British Telecom announced a deal worth $4.3 billion to take a 20 percent share of MCI Communications. Not all proposed deals see the partners make it to the altar. Such was the case when in the largest proposed merger in U.S. communication history, Bell Atlantic, another of the regional Bell operating companies announced in 1993 that it planned to buy Tele-Communications, Inc., the largest U.S. cable firm, with over 13 million subscribers and an ownership stake in Turner Broadcasting and the

Home Shopping Network, for $12 billion plus $9.6 billion in corporate debt. Nevertheless, this was followed by completed mergers between the telephone company Nynex and the television production company Viacom ($1.2 billion), between BellSouth and the television shopping company QVC ($1.5 billion), and between Southwestern Bell and the cable firm Cox Enterprises ($1.6 billion).

A major reason for the recent wave of mergers and alliances across media is that companies are eager to take advantage of converging hardware and software systems that enable them to control major pieces of the entire circuit of production, distribution, and exhibition or display. Specifically, companies want to be indispensable participants in the reconstitution of entertainment and information networks, euphemistically dubbed the 'information superhighway.' For example, in 1995 Time Warner agreed to pay more than $7.5 billion for the 80 or so percent of Turner Broadcasting that it did not already own. Westinghouse offered $5.4 billion to buy CBS and Disney agreed to pay $19 billion for the Capital Cities/ABC conglomerate. These and other takeovers have raised the specter of monopolization to a new order of magnitude as one or a few integrated conglomerates might gain substantial control over the production and flows of communication, information, and entertainment.[17] On the other hand, doubts have been raised about whether there is significant enough household demand to justify the multi-billion dollar investments and about whether newly merged companies can fit together their different parts to produce smooth-functioning operations (Miller, 1994; Ries, 1993; Tierney, 1993).[18]

Networks of corporate power are also constituted out of merchandising agreements which connect companies that market a specific media product, such as a feature film or an athlete. These agreements are different from the expansion of advertising into the communication industry, e.g. through the use of product placement ads in feature films and videos, and through tie-ins that promote a specific film with products unrelated to the movie. In merchandising agreements, a media company licenses the right to use the name of the media product to a company that then uses it to create trademarked products. For example, Universal Pictures and producer Stephen Spielberg created such a network for the blockbuster hit *Jurassic Park*, which turned out over one thousand trademarked products bearing the

17. Concerns such as this have led to the creation of a coalition of non-profit groups, one of whose leaders, Jeffrey Chester of the Center for Media Education, says: 'Unless there is a public outcry and it becomes a populist issue, we won't be able to prevent these media monopolies from controlling the paths to the home' (cited in Aufderheide, 1994: 21).

18. Robert Lucky, then executive director of AT&T Bell Laboratories, put the sceptic's view this way: 'The business is not in global networking but in private networks. Every big corporation has its own network, because that's where the densest traffic flows. About 95 percent of all calls are made within those small islands.' To build a universal network, 'you'd have to set up a network for millions and millions of people to route 5 percent of the calls' (Wright, 1990: 93).

movie's name. These range from major deals with McDonald's restaurants,[19] Choice Hotels, and Nintendo, to licensing agreements for lip balm, bubble bath, candy dinosaur eggs, and bedspreads, among many others.[20]

Sport is one of the fastest growing merchandising sectors. Here, athletes, linked through a range of contractual agreements with their league and a major advertising/management consulting company, use images that are carefully cultivated across the range of media to create a lucrative business, the entirety of which brought in $12.1 billion in 1992 (Wasko and Philips, 1993). Twelve athletes earned over $5 million, with former basketball star Michael Jordan topping the list at $25 million. Jordan's network of endorsed companies includes Nike, Quaker Oats, Gatorade, Wilson Sporting Goods, Sara Lee, Chevrolet, General Mills, McDonald's, and several lesser companies. In addition to these direct links, Jordan filled the coffers of the television networks (principally one national broadcast network and one national satellite 'superstation') that aired his games, his league, the National Basketball Association, and his employer, the Chicago Bulls basketball team.[21]

The pure form of strategic alliance, involving contractual arrangements to cooperate without a complete or partial ownership takeover, breaks some new ground in corporate practice. But there is nothing new in communication industry alliances that bring about a new entity or which result in one company taking a position in another. Nor is there anything new in alliances that cut across industry sectors or technologies. It was a strategic alliance that brought about the creation of one of the most powerful companies in electronic media history, the Radio Corporation of America. In the 1920s, RCA was founded out of a strategic alliance among major corporate forces

19. The McDonald's connection raised questions about the impact of merchandising on content. Feeling bruised by its promotional connection to the film *Batman Returns*, which many agreed was too gory for a McDonald's tie-in, the company demanded to know more about *Jurassic Park* before it committed. MCA cooperated by providing company executives with storyboards that led McDonald's to skip a youthful 'Happy Meals' promotion in favor of a more adult tie-in (King, 1993).

The link between sponsorship and content is not easy to establish. It is nevertheless interesting to observe that one of the most significant changes in story line from Michael Crichton's novel to the screen is the transformation of the multi-millionaire creator of the Park. Crichton's unrepentant capitalist who meets a violent end is transformed in the film into the kindly old man who learns the lessons of greed and is spared the wrath of his creatures.

20. Considering the extent of alliances across the industry, it is inevitable that we begin to see products resulting from intersecting alliances. In 1992, Matsushita joined a transnational alliance of industry leaders to form the 3DO Co., a firm aiming to create new generations of interactive home entertainment for which Matsushita is developing digital hardware. Matsushita, which at the time owned MCA, the studio producing *Jurassic Park*, created 'Jurassic Park' software for the 3DO system. Matsushita also displayed trailers for the film on each of the television sets for sale in the 24,000 stores in Japan that carry its Panasonic label.

21. Though the multiplicity of network connections creates incentives for harmony among the many parties, they also multiply the potential for disruptive squabbles over rights to the product, in this case, to the image of the athlete. One such dispute between Jordan and NBA sportswear took a year to settle and resulted in the league subsidiary retaining control over Jordan's image.

in the early development of electronic media: AT&T, Westinghouse, General Electric, and the United Fruit Company (which invested heavily in radio to build a communication grid for its U.S. and Latin American operations). In the 1960s, the U.S. Communication Satellite Corporation, Comsat, the institution responsible for creating a U.S.-led global satellite system, was formed out of a strategic alliance among AT&T, RCA, and the International Telephone and Telegraph Company. These are far from exceptional examples of alliances among leading forces in different segments of the communications industry that built corporate success stories out of some of the same, and some very different, communication technologies.

The RCA and Comsat cases are powerful reminders that there is nothing particularly new about the dynamism of capitalism. Today's alliances, as Vernon (1992: 16) suggests, are not all that much different in function from jointly owned oilfields and mines that competing refiners and marketers, such as ARAMCO in Saudi Arabia, Southern Peru Copper in Peru, and HALCO in Guinea, once shared. Change, including structural transformation in business, has always been a constant. Nevertheless, there are several dimensions of the current wave of restructuring that mark a departure from the established pattern. First, it is arguably accelerating in both time and space. The pace of corporate restructuring, the process of formal and informal coupling and decoupling, has speeded up and become more unstable. For Vernon (1992: 16), this is the principal departure from the historical alliance pattern:

> In industries with rapidly changing technologies and swiftly changing markets, the interests of the participants in any given alliance are likely to be relatively unstable: such firms will be constantly withdrawing and regrouping in order to satisfy their rapidly shifting strategic needs.

Furthermore, the spatial agglomeration of such activity knows fewer constraints. Whereas alliances once would only rarely cross borders, today such developments are commonplace in both the pure form of alliance, through co-productions and contractual agreements to work together on a common project, as well as in the various forms of ownership, ranging from the creation of a new company, to taking a position in another, to a complete takeover.

In addition to these considerations, the role of the state has changed substantially. This is a subject to be taken up at greater length below, but it is important to highlight here the significant alteration in state activity. Although this varied by nation and historical circumstances, the state used to occupy a considerably different role in the process of structural transformation in the communication industries. This is because, unlike many other economic sectors, the communication industry was owned outright by the state or, if not completely a part of the state apparatus, was closely integrated into wider state functions through processes of budgetary allocation, policy oversight, and regulation. To return to the RCA example, the strategic alliance that constituted the company did so with complete U.S. government participation, as the next best alternative to government ownership of radio, and at the price of government participation at the board and management levels. Similarly, the alliance that formed Comsat came together at the specific request of government, under the threat of outright government control over the company, and the outcome was an organization subject not only to government regulation, but also to its representation on the company's board. Admittedly, it is still the case that states own communication facilities and continue to provide services, particularly telecommunication and broadcasting, in much of the world, but this role is diminishing. Moreover, though states still play a role in cross-border alliances, such as the regulation of co-production agreements, this too is changing. It is more typically the case for the companies themselves to negotiate deals directly, whether within a country or across borders. States may intervene to assess anti-trust or trade implications, but today they are more likely to take the lead in encouraging such arrangements, rather than in seeking to regulate them or in demanding a stake. Strategic alliances, which were once more likely the result of an effort to create what have been called *chosen instruments* of state policy, are now typically the result of corporate policy to expand into new areas with partners who are willing to pool expertise and risk.

Furthermore, the current form of alliances exhibits a greater tendency to include the best organized among the major *users* of communication. Again, as United Fruit's participation in the RCA alliance suggests, there is precedent for this in communication history. However, the recent involvement of users, particularly banks, investment companies, and other large corporate communication customers, suggests that a standard has grown from what was once an occasional practice. Recognizing the importance of communication and information technology for growth and control, companies outside the formal boundaries of the industry use their individual and combined power, in large user associations, to steer the development of the communication industry to meet their interests in the creation of high-quality and low-cost networks and services. The growing involvement of large users in the spatialization of the communication industry suggests an important power shift that brings to the center of the industry a new set of participants to join the traditional companies that produce and distribute hardware and services. Led by the financial services sector, this increasingly includes traditional industrial powers (e.g. General Motors), retail firms (e.g. Sears), and even resource companies, such as hydroelectric and integrated energy companies, whose business it has been to structure the space of energy flows, and who now aim to use that expertise to manage the space of communication flows. In addition to marking an important power shift, this development points to the remapping of the communication industry from a highly differentiated sector, whose boundary with the rest of the economy was easily delineated, to one that is so increasingly dedifferentiated or integrated into the wider economy that it is becoming difficult to identify clear boundary distinctions. Private data networks, in-house video services, and just-in-time inventory control systems are just a few of the rapidly growing business sectors that have turned traditional consumers of services into major producers. In essence, traditional categories and the legal, regulatory, and policy apparatus that came with them are eroding. What separates an American from a Japanese company, or a telephone from a cable from a computer company, or a producer from a consumer? All of these differences are tending to disappear as we move into a global *electronic services marketplace.*[22]

These developments are part of a wider process in which companies adopt *new organizational structures* that combine the power to command resources and the flexibility to respond to changing markets. According to the economic geographer David Harvey (1989: 147), this form of restructuring 'rests on flexibility with respect to labour process, labour markets, products and patterns of consumption.' It results in 'entirely new sectors of production, new ways of providing financial services, new markets, and above all, greatly intensified rates of commercial, technological, and organizational innovation.' Finally, it leads to what he calls a new round of 'time–space compression' – the time horizons for decision-makers shrink while declining transport and communication costs make it possible to spread decisions over a wider and more diverse space. Economic restructuring sometimes leads to the conglomerate, but this is not essential to success. It is more important to develop flexible structures that can take on new forms rapidly to meet changing demands.

In conclusion, rethinking political economy includes recognizing that, though important, corporate size and concentration are just starting points for understanding the transformation of the communications business. Global restructuring offers numerous opportunities to expand control from the conglomerate form to the range of flexible alternatives. The chief requirements include controlling central points in the production, distribution, and exchange process (outright ownership is one among numerous alternatives) and remaining flexible to respond to changing markets and technologies.

Changes in corporate and spatial structures prompt some analysts to different interpretations of remapping the space that business occupies. The growth of strategic alliances and other forms of corporate linkages that do not require ownership changes, or even a significant investment, suggest the need to rethink traditional concentration research. Firm size and market control remain important indicators of concentration. But corporate restructuring also creates forms of concentration based on dense networks of

22. It may be the case that much of the heat coming out of the battles among media firms results from an understandable tendency to cling to old categories, as they puzzle over how to think about this new reality.

connections among producers, suppliers, and customers. According to Soja (1989: 185),

> Added to the corporate conglomeration of ownership has been a more techno-logically-based integration of diversified industrial, research, and service activities that similarly reallocates capital and labor into sprawling spatial systems of production linking centers of administrative power over capital investment to a constellation of parallel branches, subsidiaries, subcontracting firms, and specialized public and private services. ... the spatial scope of these production systems has become global, but they also have a powerful urbanization effect through the local agglomeration of new industrial complexes. ... Here again there seems to be a paradoxical pairing of deconcentration and reconcentration in the geographical landscape.

In addition to corporate restructuring, changes in the spatial patterning of business activity also prompt a rethinking of business concentration. Specifically, and contrary to forecasts that telecommunication would necessarily decentralize business activity, the concentration of business activity in New York, London, Tokyo, and other international cities provides grounds for thinking about spatial agglomeration as a major form of business activity. Economic restructuring and spatial agglomeration are central features of a resurgence of interest in the discipline of geography. Though these developments have been taken up across the social sciences, they have had the most pronounced influence on geography, which now addresses central issues in political economy, including the relationship of spatial structures to accumulation, class, gender, and race (see especially Castells, 1989; Harvey, 1989; Massey, 1984; Sassen, 1991; Thrift, 1987).

This line of spatialization research suggests the value of breaking new ground in the analysis of media concentration. Spatial agglomeration, as well as ownership agglomeration, is a significant form of business concentration. It brings together companies, whether connected or unconnected by ownership ties, in dense networks of producers, suppliers, and customers whose mutual dependence, consolidated geographically in global cities and dispersed electronically across the globe, creates significant forms of concentrated economic power. This development is especially important for the communication and information industries because they are central to the producer services sector, which is primarily responsible for spatial agglomeration today. Communication and information processes, and the industries in which they are organized, contribute fundamentally to a principal form of economic restructuring in the global political economy: the rise of concentrated economic power in the spatial agglomerations of business.

Research on spatial agglomeration shares with the more traditional forms of media concentration research an interest in providing ways of seeing a dynamic industry within a dynamic economy. Admittedly, ownership research tends to pay greater attention to mapping corporate power within the industry and its extension into the social field. Nevertheless, although both types of work take an interest in the state, each tends to see it as either reactive to corporate power or responsive to cross-pressures (Mosco, 1995).

The State

There is certainly ample evidence to support the view that the contemporary state has reacted to changes in corporate and industry structure, as well as to changes in technologies and services. Nevertheless, there is also support for the view that these changes have come about with the active legal, regulatory, and policy direction of the state. In fact, there is enough support for the latter to warrant the conclusion that political economy would benefit from a greater emphasis on the *political*, calling for attention to the *constitutive* as well as the reactive role of the state in the communication industry. This has been difficult to accomplish because much of the literature on the role of the state in the communication industries provides narrow descriptions based on the language of policy-makers. The tendency is understandable because mastering legal, regulatory, and policy processes, and their various languages, is difficult. The problem for political economy is that explaining the role of the state and situating the state–media relationship in the wider political economy requires a transition, without losing a sense of material practice, from the epistemic community of policy action, to that of political economy.

There is a tendency to think about spatialization as an economic or technologically driven process whereby business, equipped with computer communication systems that overcome the constraints of time and distance, erodes fundamental political processes led by the nation state. On the other hand, processes of *nation-building* are viewed as occupying a political space either supporting or resisting the economic imperative. There is some substance to this view, as suggested by those who argue, for example, that economic logic calls for a united Europe. But it oversimplifies. Both spatialization and nation-building are political economic processes. Spatialization involves, among other things, both the logic of production in the contemporary global economy, and a logic of power concentrating some measure of control over economic decisions in those who, directly or indirectly, hold substantial sway over the political decision-making of nations, regions, and localities. European, as well as North American and Asian, union is influenced by both an economic drive for capital accumulation and a political drive to control the spaces through which accumulation flows. In fact, the distinction between the economic and political is an analytical one that obscures and obfuscates more than it enlightens (Wood, 1981). Similarly, nation-building is more than a political process led by government bureaucracies, trade unions, or social movements, among others, who want to retain, or simply to gain, power. It is also an economic process based on views about the appropriate political unit required to accomplish economic goals. One of political economy's major contributions is to overcome the tendency to distort complex social processes by sorting them out into the economic and the political.

Furthermore, it is important to emphasize that the national unit is not the only force operating in an uneasy relationship to processes of spatialization.

As was noted above, there are nationalisms within nationalisms. Moreover, like globalization, nationalism is far from a unitary process, bound up, as it has been, with a wide range of political practices and ideologies that include both support for and opposition to the nation state. What these nationalisms tend to hold in common is an identification with the idea of the *local* that tends to oppose the logic of spatialization.

The problem, and the significance of addressing it, are exemplified in the concept of *regulation*. There is an extensive literature on regulating the communication industries and, though some variation exists, one finds consistency in the view that regulation is a government reaction to market problems. Explanations certainly range widely, including the presence of natural monopoly conditions, industry pressures on the political apparatus, public interest pressures from citizen groups, etc. The definition of the problem *is* significant, but each tends to be couched within a conception of regulation as something governments do in reaction to perceived problems. As a result, when policy-makers and academic analysts review industry regulation, they tend to examine government practices and contend over whether more or less regulation is needed. Hence, debate on the role of the state in the communication industries frequently comes down to the choice between regulation and deregulation.

A political economy approach, particularly one that reflects fully on its constituent terms, sees this quite differently. Political economy takes the entire social field, including the pattern of industry activity, as a form of regulation.[23] For example, a social field primarily influenced by industry decisions, rather than by state intervention, can be characterized as a form of *market regulation*, as opposed to *state regulation*, which takes place when government plays the prominent role.[24] From a political economy perspective, the policy debate over deregulation is disingenuous at best, because deregulation is not an alternative. Rather, the debate comes down to the choice among a mix of forms that foreground the market, the state, or interests that lie outside of both. Eliminating government regulation is not deregulation but, most likely, expanding market regulation.

Political economy avoids the language trap, concentrating on assessing the merits of different forms of regulation, such as market and state, for different groups in society. This reassessment of regulation is necessary for

23. The so-called Regulation School has taken the lead, though other political economy approaches have also developed this formulation. According to Lipietz (1988), one of the leading advocates of the Regulation School position, regulation is an adjustment of contradictory tendencies within a social field. See Chapter 2, p. 59.

24. Depending on the market structure, several types of regulation exist within the market form. These range from monopoly through oligopoly to fully competitive forms of regulation. What tends to be called 'expanding competition' in the communication sector actually means the addition of one or more companies that permits a shift from monopoly to duopoly or oligopoly regulation. This hardly justifies the description 'expanding competition' and the policy conclusion that warrants a decline in government oversight.

considering the constitutive role of the state, which the concept of deregulation masks. It suggests another step in the political economy approach to the state, namely, how it actively constructs forms of regulation. Nevertheless, great care and caution are warranted because there is little agreement here on the meaning of terms and central concepts.[25]

One starting point is to consider four processes characterizing current state-constitutive activity that emanate from both spatialization and commodification. The first, or *commercialization*, takes place when the state replaces forms of regulation based on public interest, public service, and related standards, such as universality, with market standards that establish market regulation.[26] Commercialization applies to both public and private sector organizations, though it is more significant in the former because it can serve as a step toward privatization. In communication, this has meant greater emphasis on market position and profitability, even among state and public service broadcasting and telecommunication firms. Specifically, it leads to greater emphasis in broadcasting on audience size and advertising revenue, producing programming that anticipates an international market and linkages to other revenue-generating media. In telecommunication, commercialization means building and organizing networks and services with a greater concern for those customers, principally business, likely to increase revenue, even if that means greater attention to linking metropolitan centers in global networks, rather than to extending networks into rural and generally underserved regions. Commercialization has led state communication authorities to separate telecommunication and other revenue-generating activities from postal and other services, which are mandated by constitution or legislation. Defenders of commercialization argue that it does not preclude and may even enhance public service goals, such as universality (Noam, 1987). Conversely, opponents contend that it is a means of transforming the space of communication flows, which, in a world of limited resources, inevitably means supporting one class of users over others and relying on 'trickle-down' economics to overcome class divisions (Castells, 1989).

Liberalization is a process of state intervention to expand the number of participants in the market, typically by creating, or easing the creation of, competing providers of communication services. This typically involves the creation of a private competitor in a state or private monopoly marketplace.

---

25. However one feels about the content of arguments, one is struck by the difference between the precision applied to economic models of industry performance and the imprecision in political analysis.

26. More specifically, this amounts to redefining the public interest as an advance of the marketplace. For example, until the early 1980s, U.S. government regulations restricted the amount of advertising on television because excessive commercialization violated the 'public interest' criterion in the Communication Act. These restrictions were relaxed in the 1980s. In July 1993, the Federal Communications Commission ruled that the public interest *requires* cable companies to carry local channels that air the Home Shopping Network, a 24-hour advertising and shopping channel, even if that means dropping some cable programming.

Unlike commercialization, which aims to make business practices the standard for the communication industry, with or without competition, liberalization aims specifically to increase market competition. Over the past twenty years, states have changed the communication industry in most parts of the world by introducing private competitors over a range of broadcasting and television services. Supporters contend that liberalization lowers prices, expands services, and generally speeds up the process of innovation (Owen and Wildman, 1992). Critics counter that it substitutes private oligopoly regulation for state regulation, carrying out price, service, and innovation mandates that advance the interests of an oligopoly cartel and its more privileged customers (Mosco, 1989a).

Third, *privatization* is a process of state intervention that literally sells off a state enterprise such as a public broadcaster or a state telephone company. Privatization takes many forms, depending on the percentage of shares to be sold off, the extent to which any foreign ownership is permitted, the length, if any, of a phase-in period, and the specific form of continuing state involvement, typically constituted in a regulatory body, in the aftermath of privatization. This process has accelerated for several reasons, including the rise of governments ideologically committed to private control over economic activity, the attraction, if for one time only, of fresh revenues for government coffers, and the pressures of transnational businesses and governmental organizations, such as the International Monetary Fund and the World Bank. For its supporters, privatization is necessary because commercialization is, at best, an inadequate first step toward market control. Critics see in privatization the elimination of the primary alternative to complete market regulation, the loss of sovereignty for nations selling off to foreign firms, and the consequent loss of local control over national policy.

Finally, states are also creating their own wide range of teaming arrangements or strategic alliances that integrate them in different degrees of *internationalization*. These include regional trade alliances, such as the North American Free Trade Agreement, 'trade plus' (such as financial, political, and social links) arrangements like the European Union, as well as institutionalized planning organizations, exemplified in the Group of Seven. Internationalization also brings about specific state organizations, such as the GATT, the World Bank, and the International Monetary Fund, which, though not new to the global political economy, have taken on increasingly powerful roles in managing relations among the most developed nations and negotiating the terms of development (and underdevelopment) in the rest of the world.

This process has been particularly important in the communication arena because the transnationalization of communication networks requires some degree of interstate coordination. Again, this is not new to the industry – the International Telecommunication Union (ITU) began to bring together governments to coordinate telegraph policy in the 1860s. In recent years, states have developed new arrangements that enable the richest nations to exert tighter control over global communication policy. These have brought about significant changes in international policy-making, including the decline of UNESCO, site of the major support for the NWICO, and the opening of the ITU to considerably greater private sector participation. These organizations are either less powerful or are transformed to reflect new power balances that all but eradicate equal representation among the world's nations. It has also meant the growth of short-term, function- or technology-specific sites for meeting and planning that bring together government and corporate decision-makers who, largely outside the formal and publicly accessible traditional sites of regulatory activity, coordinate technologies, services, and pricing. The rise of associations representing large business and government users, such as INTUG, the International Users' Group, has provided one important opportunity for such activity.

Commercialization, liberalization, privatization, and internationalization are among the more significant examples of the state's constitutive role. More importantly, they suggest the value of a political economy approach which starts from the mutual constitution of the industry and the state in the creation of forms of regulation. These reflect the needs and interests of capital and the nature of opposition at a particular historical period. This does not mean that the industry and the state are therefore *equally* responsible for the resulting structure and practice of communication, just as it does not suggest that different industry forces are equally responsible. Rather, historical practice leads a political economic analysis to conclude that both the industry and the state are primary forces in the development of communication, that their relationship is mutually constitutive and variable. Furthermore, political economy argues against an analysis that concentrates solely on one or the other. Both industry and state are central to a political economic analysis, specifically important for creating the form of regulation that governs the industry and the social field, including oppositional forces with a relationship to the industry. Finally, the active state cannot guarantee its own success. In fact, the sheer growth in the number of participants in the communication arena and the rise of *ad hoc*, flexible mechanisms to manage this growth create significant problems of coordination and control that make success far from guaranteed. This is partly because the recent expansion in state activity has not included any growth, in fact has come about along with a noticeable decline, in the direct participation of the state in the accumulation process. This accentuates a long-term problem in capitalism: the state is necessary to manage the multiplicity of short-term specific interests of capital, but is not permitted to participate fully in the process of capital accumulation itself. This results in what many conservative critics of the state have been stressing for years: the state tends to follow a bureaucratic logic of organizational self-perpetuation that acts like a drag on, thereby weakening, the accumulation process. Their solution, to cut back on the state, leaves the problem of coordination. Only those societies where socialism is on the agenda of acceptable, if marginalized, debate have addressed the alternative of stronger, direct state participation in the accumulation process.

Globalization

This conclusion holds important implications for the specific form that the process of spatialization takes today, widely discussed under the heading of globalization. As Ferguson (1992) has demonstrated, globalization is not an easy term to examine, because it has already been mythologized in terms like cultural homogeneity, planet earth, worldwide media democracy, and the New World Order.[27] Notwithstanding the difficulty, it is useful to address globalization because the term resonates with popular views about social change and because, when demythologized, it suggests one dimension of a process within the wider movement of spatialization. Specifically, from a political economic perspective, globalization refers to the spatial agglomeration of capital, led by transnational business and the state, that transforms the spaces through which flow resources and commodities, including communication and information. The outcome is a literal transformation of the geography of communication and information that accentuates certain spaces and the relationships among them. For example, the New York–London–Tokyo axis anchors a map of communication and information services that extends secondary connections to Frankfurt, Paris, and Los Angeles, and so on, to form a network grid of worldwide linkages. Like any map, it cannot be drawn with absolute precision (Hall, 1992). New York's place on the grid does not extend to the entirety of the city but includes lower Manhattan, the center for financial services, mid-Manhattan, where we find the headquarters of communication and entertainment conglomerates, and parts of the New Jersey, Connecticut, and New York suburbs, where companies like AT&T, IBM, and facilities such as Teleport, a hub of telecommunication facilities, are located. Large parts of the city and surrounding areas may benefit, but only indirectly, from this activity. Globalization is a process of transforming these spaces, not, as the mythology suggests, of eliminating them. Communication and information technology expand the range of locations that can link people to the primary axis, but they also intensify the importance of central nodes because, at the center, one has direct access not only to the technology, in multiple forms, but also to the principal people and organizations that have the power to constitute

27. She also eloquently affirms the need to discard the myth that globalization leads to overcoming rather than to transforming time and space:

> The mobility of commerce, organizations, information and people does *not* make time and space irrelevant, rather, it highlights the extent to which these areas of experience have become more, not less, multilayered, interrelated and complex. For the uprooted, the restless or the peripatetic, the business of 'living life' (family, friends, work) in three or four time zones requires new negotiating skills in a perceptual world of spatial indeterminacy and temporal recalculation, a world of 'time without time' and 'space without space.' (Ferguson, 1992: 79)

the network of flows (Sassen, 1991). This conclusion supports a speculation that Raymond Williams offered in 1983, namely that 'it is now very apparent, in the development of modern industrial societies, that the nation-state, in its classical European forms, is at once too large and too small for the range of real social purposes' (p. 197). Global cities and regional blocs rise in prominence at the expense of a nation state that is, at once, too large to provide the concentrated personal and information power of the global city and too small to govern continental blocs. These transformations create hierarchies of control over which the term 'globalization' can serve as a mystifying gloss.

One would also contribute to the mythology of globalization by suggesting that this is a fundamentally new process. The mythology grows out of a deeper resistance, beyond the level of surface acceptance, to the view that space, and not just time, is dynamic, that what we map, whether physical or political space, or the space of human communication flows, is constantly changing (Massey, 1992). The choice of the term 'spatialization' is precisely intended to point to this process of constant spatial change, which geography has documented over the range of configurations of absolute space, time–space, cost–space, and social space, among others (Abler et al., 1971). The process popularly referred to as globalization identifies the current patterning of spatial change. The departure which fuels the mythology is the real expansion in the ability of those people and organizations with the power to command political economic resources to make greater use of time and space as resources by altering the space of flows to their benefit. Giddens (1990: 53) refers to this as expanding indefinitely the scope of 'time–space distanciation' which 'provides means of precise temporal and spatial rezoning.' Although a political economist can admire his analysis for capturing a sense of spatialization, political economy departs from it because, rather than viewing spatialization as one of the 'consequences of modernity,' it starts from the political economy of capitalism, which constitutes the process of rezoning, in part, by stratifying and concentrating the power to do so along class, race, and gender lines.

Nationalism, Localism, and Socialism

The mythology of globalization is also founded on a reductionist view of spatialization. Understandably taken by the spatial transformations that make up the process of redrawing the map to take into account the space of flows, proponents tend to miss other related processes, including oppositional ones. One of the chief reasons for this is the tendency to treat contemporary capitalism as a distinct set of relations among the advanced societies *alone*, rather than as a set of *hierarchical* political economic and cultural relations articulated and disarticulated within and across all nations. The tendency is understandable because the capitalist core has assumed enormous power over the global political economy and culture.[28] But it has not abolished class, imperialism, nor nation, in their varied forms. These are arguably more vital than ever in the global political economy. Moreover, though the world of 'actually existing' socialisms hardly exists, the principles of socialism, of democratic control over production, distribution, exchange, and use, live on in a wide range of political, economic, social, and cultural movements. Globalization is a contradictory unity that continues to live up to that much used and abused term 'uneven development.'[29]

The map is therefore not only being redrawn to account for the space of flows. It is also being transformed by a resurgent nationalism that has added a score of new nations to the world atlas. Many of these result from the breakup of the Soviet Union, itself partly the victim of national, ethnic, and racial upheavals. Moreover, as the Québecois, Azerbaijani, Bosnians, and many others know very well, there are nationalisms within nationalism. The process of what may still appropriately be called nation-building is doing remarkably well despite the power of spatialization to make physical boundaries seemingly inconsequential for economic, political, social, and cultural practices. The media are unquestionably enmeshed in this process of nation-building[30] (Schlesinger, 1991). One of the major projects of new nations, and of people anticipating or promoting nationhood, is to develop national media, telecommunication, and information systems. The international movement to create a New World Information and Communication Order was largely based on building a coalition of nations united principally by their lack of power to control their own communication systems, to influence their own position in the transforming space of flows, and to create their own national communication policies. At its most oppositional, this meant using the levers of national power and combining these across nations, to create a standpoint of popular democratic control and citizenship over the Western-controlled marketplace. Until defeated by the military, economic, and political power of core powers, led by the United States, the Popular Unity government of Chile and the Sandinista government of Nicaragua were major exemplars of oppositional nationalism. Today, in spite of massive positive trade balances in communication products, the United States remains deeply concerned about the range of efforts to exert some degree of national or local independence from the world communication marketplace, including what copyright holders refer to as video piracy.

28. To cite one example, according to a UNESCO report (1989: 160-161), the United States, France, Italy, the United Kingdom, and Germany supplied 80 percent of all film exported to non-socialist countries before the collapse of the USSR.

29. For an interesting review of the many uses of uneven development and an effort to reconstruct the term along non-essentialist Marxian lines, see McIntyre (1992).

30. 'Nationalization' would be a better term were it not for the generally accepted view that the term means a state takeover of an economic activity.

Nevertheless, the relationship of spatialization to nation-building is complex. The latter process can be strongly influenced by both commodification and spatialization, as, for example, when national and transnational businesses see the market potential in building media that reflect national concerns. For example, the steps taken by the European Union ostensibly to build alternatives to powerful U.S. television companies also provide a convenient vehicle for strengthening the hold of home-grown monopolies (Papathanassopoulos, 1990). Moreover, the political economic meaning and significance of nationalism is itself unclear, for, as Ahmad (1992: 11) concludes, it is not 'some unitary thing, always progressive or always retrograde':

> What role any given nationalism would play always depends on the configuration of the class forces and sociopolitical practices which organize the power bloc within which any particular set of nationalist initiatives become historically effective. (See also Greenfeld, 1992)

Nationalist movements in what, after World War II, was called the Third World began generally in opposition to capitalism, seeking a variation on socialist alternatives to what were widely agreed to be the imperialist foundations of Western capitalism. As a result, the nationalism that issued the call for a New International Economic Order, followed by the NWICO, was built on opposition to the marketplace and aimed to create national democratic alternatives. However, the relationship of nationalism to socialism was never this clear precisely because there were always class fractions within Third World countries, typically led by the civil service and the nascent business community, whose links to the former colonial power gave their nationalism a more self-serving and generally conservative character. With the assistance of Western governments, businesses, and the growing international infrastructure built on the World Bank, the International Monetary Fund, and capital's other coordinating instruments, these class fractions rose to greater prominence in the 1980s and largely triumphed in the Third World by the early 1990s. Nationalist opposition to the West lost much of its socialist character and took on the meaning of uniting the nation to create a local form of successful Western capitalism that might retain cultural forms of oppositional identification, but contained these within a capitalist political economy. Oppositional politics increasingly meant that, in the face of what appeared to be the choice between succeeding at building a capitalist economy or marginalization and exclusion, one could only choose the former, even if that meant, as it typically did throughout the Third World, that the fruits of any success would be concentrated at the top of the class ladder. The socialist alternative of growth *and* the redistribution of power in land, industry, communication, and culture all but disappeared. Anti-imperialism, which once meant a socialist political project, to be brought about by mass movements of the lower classes, has been redefined as a developmentalist project to be realized by the weaker states of the national bourgeoisies in the course of their collaborative competition with the more powerful states of advanced capital. (Ahmad, 1992: 293)

This reduced mass social movements to a state of dependency on the national government, whose ability to keep a lid on revolutionary activity strengthened its negotiating hand with the power centers of advanced capital.

The consequences for the communication industry were significant. It meant the decline and general abandonment of the global movement to create a NWICO, in favor of negotiating national and regional relationships with the global media powers. Specifically, some nations, Singapore is a good example, diverted resources to build the infrastructure for tele-communication and information systems that would enable them to achieve, at least for a short term, a favorable position in global networks. Others, like Mexico, gave up national control over their telecommunication industry, relying on foreign capital instead, but aiming to take on the role of regional power in the production and distribution of mass media, chiefly film and video. However the relationship to the major powers is negotiated, it reflects a nationalism largely purged of socialist content.

Nevertheless, however essential it is to acknowledge these developments, only a dogged positivist would eliminate principles because it is difficult to find current empirical referents. Consequently, it is also important to raise the principle of socialism in relation to nationalism. But this is difficult to do, not only because of capitalist triumphalism. Although the mixed character of nationalism is not lost on contemporary scholarship, determining whether nationalism is progressive or retrograde seems to matter less than the need to debunk the idea of nationalism, to interrogate its ontological status as a *myth of origins*. The leading critical standpoint is no longer *socialism*, which attacks the tendency in nationalism to ignore capitalism, class, and gender, but *post-structuralism*, which attacks nationalism, as it does capitalism and socialism, as just another totalizing narrative. Specifically, post-structuralism aims to eliminate such totalizing thinking by revealing the textual illusions that sustain such narratives, myths, and discursive formations. Despite criticism for its reactionary cast of mind which refuses history, incidentally protecting itself from critical assessment of its own material, narrative story, and the very notion of a political project, post-structuralism maintains a hold on academic intellectuals. Its influence has been felt in communication studies, including critical assessments of the political economy of international communication and calls for research on the micro-reception of media texts (Ang, 1991; Tomlinson, 1991). Although he commends this line of thinking for reminding political economy to avoid reductionism, Schlesinger (1991: 149) finds this a meager payoff for the price paid in the failure to 'offer an especially good vantage-point for examining how large cultural collectivities constitute their identities.' The point, however, is that post-structuralism rests on a philosophical foundation fundamentally at odds with the view that identities are constituted in anything resembling large cultural collectivities.[31] Successful treatment of this issue requires an openness to what are rejected as totalizing narratives and material practices, openness to what constitutes political economic analysis. This includes a critique of capitalism, a recognition of the checkered history of nationalism that leads one to reject the view, as does Ahmad (1992: 11), 'that nationalism is the determinate, dialectical opposite of imperialism, that dialectical status accrues only to socialism.'

This is difficult to do because socialism has been identified with nation states which, with few exceptions, no longer identify with socialism. But the qualitative difference between capitalism and socialism is not based on spatial differences between nation states, but between differences in processes of production and distribution that compete in the same space. Specifically, as Chase-Dunn (1989: 30) puts it:

> Socialism is a mode of production which subjects investment decisions and distribution to a logic of collective use value, and, as such, socialist movements reintroduce non-commodified relations into the interstices of capitalist relations.

The very same institution, in the very same space, may promote both capitalist and socialist processes. Chase-Dunn cites the example of trade unions that promoted mechanization, even as they struggled for restraints on surplus value production. Similarly, one can cite movements that advance public broadcasting systems, even as they accept forms of its commercialization. But such a view also requires a critique of socialisms, not in order to serve capitalist triumphalism, but to recognize the living qualities of democracy, including participation and equality, citizenship, cooperation, and collective participation in a political project that inspired so many, from Indochina to Nicaragua, to struggle against not just the totalizing discourse, but the totalizing military, economic, and political power of imperialism and class rule.

One can conclude from this that nationalism is a form of local opposition that gives priority to a resistance based on spatial identification over the general tendency of globalizing capitalism to rationalize and homogenize spatial difference, thereby undermining the grounds for such identification. Though it can succeed, and has succeeded, in slowing down the process of globalization, and in shaping capitalist development by forcing transnational actors to address the national, nationalism is inadequate to the task because it neglects the relationship between space and commodity or, more formally, the mutual constitution of commodification and spatialization. As a result, nationalism tends to accept local control, whether or not that comes with

---

31. It is important to distinguish between the philosophical opposition to political economic, as well as macrosociological, approaches, and the use of ethnographic methods in much of this research. There is nothing in the nature of ethnography that is inherently opposed to political economy. In fact, recent work (Pendakur, 1993) aims to integrate political economic and ethnographic research. The difference between this and research inspired by post-structuralist thought is that post-structuralism uses ethnography to dis-integrate the social whole, to suggest the ineffable subjectivity of all social analysis, and the futility of viewing social categories, like class, as anything more than discursive constructs.

deepening commodification. The socialist critique of nationalism is largely founded on the failure to recognize that, though commodification may not destroy nationalism, may not annihilate space, it transforms nationalism into a site of struggle among competing capitals for control of space. On the other hand, the failure of socialism to acknowledge the constitutive power of spatialization has led it to reject the power of nationalism to buttress the commodification process, as a form of local control, which diminishes opportunities for promoting non-commodified or use value practices. The mutual constitution of commodification and spatialization therefore embodies political as well as theoretical consequences, some of which are pursued in the next chapter, which takes up the process of structuration.

6

Structuration

OTA found that changes in the U.S. communication infrastructure are likely to broaden the gap between those who can access communication services and use information strategically and those who cannot. Moreover, the people most likely to be adversely affected will be those for whom the new communication technologies are held out as a means to improve their circumstances – the poor, the educationally disadvantaged, the technologically isolated, and the struggling small business.

(U.S. Congress, Office of Technology Assessment, 1990: 243)

During the past decade, debates provoked by commercial and military designs for a coming 'information age' or 'information society' have become prime sites for international political, economic, and cultural struggles. These struggles, in turn, have provided the auspices and impetus for ambitious agendas of politically engaged critical communications research. . . . Nevertheless, this body of theory and the empirical assessments it has produced have remained largely silent about a crucial dimension of the power–knowledge of the information age: its gender politics.

(Jansen, 1989: 196)

This chapter takes up the process of structuration, a subject developed most prominently in the work of Anthony Giddens (1984). Giddens presents the theory of structuration in an effort to bridge what he perceived to be a chasm between theoretical perspectives that foreground structure and those that emphasize action and agency. This encompasses the gap between, for example, the range of structural theories found in the work of Durkheim, Lévi-Strauss, and Althusser and those action-theoretic perspectives that span sociologists, including Max Weber, and phenomenologically oriented theorists, such as Schütz and Gadamer.

To accomplish this, Giddens proposes that we consider structure as a duality including constraining rules and enabling resources. No longer the rigid scaffolding that controls and gives form to social life, structure both constitutes action and is reproduced by it. In this respect, structure and action are interconnected in the ongoing patterning of social life. Structuration therefore describes a *process by which structures are constituted out of human agency, even as they provide the very 'medium' of that constitution.* Social life is comprised of the mutual constitution of structure and agency. As Giddens himself recognizes, the concept of structuration is not new to social thought. It is certainly a central component of Marx's historical work, featured most prominently in his *Eighteenth Brumaire of Louis Bonaparte*, where he elaborated on the now well-worn phrase that people make history, but not under conditions of their own making.

One of the important characteristics of structuration theory is the prominence it gives to social change, seen here as a ubiquitous process that describes how structures are produced and reproduced by human agents who act through the medium of these structures. The concept of structuration responds to criticisms directed at functionalist, institutional, and structuralist thought arising out of their tendency to present structures as fully formed, determining entities. These approaches have made important contributions to understanding the operations of structures, but they have given an inadequate accounting of the process of structural formation, as well as of social action and human agency. As Hobsbawm (1973: 280) has argued:

> a structural model envisaging only the maintenance of a system is inadequate. It is the simultaneous existence of stabilizing and disruptive elements which such a model must reflect. . . . Such a dual (dialectical) model is difficult to set up and use, for in practice the temptation is great to operate it, according to taste or occasion, either as a stable functionalism or as one of revolutionary change; whereas the interesting thing about it is, that it is both.

This chapter suggests how structuration theory might join with the processes of commodification and spatialization to advance a political economy of communication. Specifically, structuration balances the tendency in political economic analysis to feature structures, typically business and governmental institutions, by addressing and incorporating the ideas of agency, social relations, social process, and social practice. At the same time, joining with Garnham (1990) among others, it rejects as extreme the notion that one can analyze agency in the absence of structures. This is because structure provides the medium out of which agency operates. Consequently, while political economy is aligned with Laclau and Mouffe when they maintain that 'the social itself has no essence,' it takes issue with their conclusion:

> In order to place ourselves firmly within the field of articulation, we must begin by renouncing the conception of 'society' as founding totality of its social processes. We must, therefore, consider the openness of the social as the constitutive ground or 'negative essence' of the existing, and the diverse 'social orders' as precarious and ultimately failed attempts to domesticate the field of differences. . . . There is no sutured space peculiar to 'society' since the social itself has no essence. (Laclau and Mouffe, 1985: 95–96)

Structuration theory is an approach to social life that aims to address goal-oriented, reflexive human action, without giving up on understanding the 'sutures' of power that mutually constitute social action.

A major problem with structuration theory in Giddens, as Thompson (1989) has maintained, is that it tends to accentuate agency, leaving us with a conception of structure limited to a set of *operating rules* and a *store of resources* which individual agents use to meet their needs. Rather than elaborate on Thompson's detailed critique, suffice it to say that Giddens' chief conception of structuration (one source of criticism is that he has several conceptions) relies on terms that disincline thinking about *power* and generally stand back from a critical approach to social analysis (see also

Bernstein, 1989). There are many different kinds of operating rules, including, as Thompson (1989: 63) notes, 'moral rules, traffic rules, bureaucratic rules, rules of grammar, rules of etiquette, rules of football.' Admittedly aware of this confusing range of possible referents, Giddens does not provide a satisfactory response, does not offer a clear sense of what are distinctly *social* rules, perhaps because such specificity would make it more difficult for him to establish the *transhistorical* theory essential to his opposition to Marx (Giddens, 1981). One can say the same about resources, which can include everything from the counselling services of a welfare office to the commodity futures traded at the Chicago Mercantile Exchange. Again, arranging resources in a particular form would privilege one type, such as power resources, over others, thereby turning a general theory of social life into a specific, perhaps historically specific, reading of one among many manifestations. A political economy reading of structuration is more inclined to accept the necessity of historical specificity. It therefore is comfortable with retaining Giddens' general notion of the duality of structure and action, but gives greater weight to *power* and to the incorporation of structuration into a *critical* approach to social analysis.

Such a focus deepens the substantive and methodological approach to power in political economy. As earlier chapters have suggested, the latter has made a substantial contribution to social research, including the explanation of communication practices, with a sustained analysis of the commodities, institutions, practices, and consequences that comprise the production, distribution, and use of power. Political economy has accomplished this with concepts and methodologies particularly suited to the large-scale or macro-analysis of power. This has enabled it to examine, for example, how mergers, acquisitions, labor practices, and borrowing have enabled Rupert Murdoch's News Corp. to amass the power to expand the production of media and information commodities and to influence government regulatory policies. The methodology used to carry out such research concentrates on the summary data on revenues, organizational structure, employment, as well as submissions to government bodies such as regulatory agencies.

The emphasis on agency that informs the structuration approach suggests expanding on this conception of power by examining how it operates at the constitutive, interactive, or micro-level of power. For example, from among the range of macro-pressures that confront the board of Time Warner, how does it constitute an agenda of priorities that lead it to enter one specific market rather than another, buy one rather than another company, and invest in one rather than another new technology? These decisions tend to be normalized as the objective assessments of the bottom line, which is, in effect, a measure of the balance of macro-pressures. But objective assessments are also glosses on a set of micro-power struggles that can grow out of the narrow interests of specific executives or board members. Construction of the assessment is itself a contest over control of symbolic resources. Those whose field of analysis is broadly economic have only started down this road to power (Tinker, 1985). To do so involves equipping oneself with different research tools from those political economists are trained to operate. These include ethnography, ethnomethodology, participant observation, and other means of observing the social practices that constitute the meaning of power for a particular set of actors (Pendakur, 1993).

The emphasis here is on the *social* as well as the micro. One of the problems with some current conceptions of agency is that they tempt one to introduce the individual into social analysis. Nothing could be further from the meaning of structuration, including Giddens' conception of it. Agency is a fundamentally social conception that refers to individuals as social actors whose behavior is constituted out of their matrix of social relations and positionings, including class, race, and gender. Nevertheless, though structuration addresses agents as social, rather than individual, actors, it recognizes the significance of a social process of individuation. The concept, taken chiefly from Poulantzas (1978), refers to the practice of redefining social actors, capital and labor particularly, as individual subjects whose value is connected to individual rights, individual expression, the individual exercise of political rights in voting, and individual rights of consumption. These actions, taken in the name of the state, but bound up with the exercise of class rule, isolate individuals from one another, from their social identities, and from those with the power to carry out individuation. One of the central tensions within the process of structuration is between these social and individuating tendencies. Structuration is therefore an entry point to examine the mutual constitution of structure and agency in political economy. It is a starting point for expanding the conception of power and, in addition, it provides a lever for understanding the forms that social relations take in political economy.

When political economy has given attention to agency, process, and social practice, it has tended to focus on *social class*. There are good reasons for considering class structuration to be a central entry point for comprehending social life, as studies documenting the persistence of class divisions in the political economy of communication attest. Nevertheless, there are other dimensions to structuration that complement and clash with class analysis, including gender, race, and social movements that are based on public issues like environmentalism which, along with class, constitute much of the social relations of communication.

From this use of structuration theory, one might think about society as the ensemble of structuring actions initiated by agents that mutually shape class, gender, race, and social movement relations. According to this view, society exists, if not as a seamless, sutured whole, at least as a field on which various processes mutually constitute identifiable social relationships. The focus on class, gender, race, and social movement relationships is not intended to suggest that these are essential ones to which all others can be reduced. Rather, this formulation suggests that these are central gateways to the analysis of structuration and that the social field is not merely a continuum of subjectivities denoted by categories whose value is purely nominal. Social class is real as *both* a social relationship and an instrument of analysis. The process of structuration constructs *hegemony*, defined as the taken-for-granted, common-sense, naturalized way of thinking about the world, including everything from cosmology, through ethics, to social practices, that is both incorporated and contested in everyday life. Hegemony is a lived network of mutually constituting meanings and values, which, as they are experienced as practices, appear as mutually confirming.

This chapter contributes to the analysis of class, gender, race, and hegemony by demonstrating how these terms have been used in political economic research with the goal of moving beyond the notion that these are simply categories on which the media have impacts. It proposes to examine them as means of describing the *social relations of communication practices*, including how they serve to organize the agency of individuals who produce them. Out of the tensions and clashes within various structuration processes, the media come to be organized in their full mainstream, oppositional, and alternative forms.

Social Class

Class analysis is one of the more well-trodden fields in social science.[1] Williams (1976) begins his analysis of the concept by recognizing that it is an 'obviously difficult' one, both in its range of meanings and in the specific application to a social division. The term appears in the Latin *classis* to describe a division according to property among the people of Rome and made its appearance in sixteenth-century English in a reference, which Veblen would appreciate, to the various forms of vanity. One of the problems with the term is that it evolved in a very general sense to indicate groups of plants and animals, as well as collections of people, without specific social implications. The modern division among types of social classes such as lower, middle, upper, and working arose with the Industrial Revolution and particularly superseded other notions of division (such as estate) with the increasing awareness that social divisions are created, rather than simply inherited.

Much of the contemporary debate on the concept revolves around distinctions among categorial, relational, and formational dimensions of social class (Miliband, 1989). Social class is *categorial* in the sense that it defines a category of people who occupy a position in society by virtue of their economic standing measured by wealth and/or income.[2] Seen as a *relationship*, social class refers to the connections among people based on their relationship to the primary processes of social production and reproduction. In this sense, class is not a position that adheres to an individual or group, but a relationship that exists, for example, between capital and the

1. For an overview of debates see Giddens and Held (1982).
2. The tradition set out chiefly by Max Weber responded to what he considered Marxian economism by expanding the categorial notion of class to incorporate political power and social status (the general *perception* of one's ranking).

working class, based on ownership of the means of production. According to the relational view, capital does not exist without the working class and vice versa. Class is therefore embodied in the shifting ties that connect and divide them. Finally, class is also, as Williams (1976: 58) notes, 'a *formation* in which, for historical reasons, consciousness of this situation and the organization to deal with it have developed.' According to this view, class exists to the extent that people are aware and act on their class position, are a class *for* themselves, not just a class *in* themselves.

Though distinguishable as such, these ways of thinking about class also overlap considerably. For example, much of the work of the social historian E.P. Thompson (1963) is about social class as relational and formational. There is also a long-standing debate about specific dimensions of these definitions. What marks a class category – income, wealth, power, status, some combination? What defines the relationship – the means of production? of reproduction? or the means of administration? What constitutes class consciousness – individual awareness? social communication? organized resistance? Widespread differences about these dimensions and about the compatibility of various positions mark contemporary debates about social class.

The political economy of communication includes a literature on social class, principally from a categorial perspective, exploring the significance of class power. This includes studies demonstrating how media elites produce and reproduce their control over the communication business, including analyses of its class composition, as well as forms of integration and division within the media elite. Early studies include Mills' (1956) research on media and entertainment elites in the United States and Clement's (1975) assessment of media elites in Canada. More recent work pays greater attention to media outside of North America (Tunstall and Palmer, 1991) and to the growing networks of class rule that link mass media to new communication and information technologies (Mattelart, 1991). Second, there are studies that examine the dense web of connections between media entrepreneurs and the rest of the elite class, through the range of connections on corporate boards, business associations, civic organizations, and private clubs (Dreier, 1982; Herman and Chomsky, 1988; H. Schiller, 1981). Finally, there are studies that concentrate on the process by which class rule takes place in policy-making and regulation (Coulter, 1992; Mosco, 1982: Chap. 2; Rideout, 1993; D. Schiller, 1981).

These studies contribute to understanding the structure and process of elite rule. Political economy has directed some attention to the consequences of this rule for the remainder of the class structure, by, for example, addressing the relationship of social class to communication access throughout the class structure. This area of research is particularly significant today, for several related reasons. The last fifteen years have brought about deepening class divisions as neo-conservative governments introduced austerity policies that reduced spending for social services, education, and health care, as they lowered taxes for the upper classes and generally promoted budget austerity (euphemistically referred to as 'structural adjust-ment' measures) for much of the less developed world. The drive to commercialize, liberalize, and privatize public institutions, including public service communication systems, has accentuated the significance of austerity policies because these policies have made market power more significant than ever for determining access to services, including communication. Finally, there is the development of ever more refined user-pay services, again, including communication systems, such as cable and satellite tele-vision, that charge by the month, channel, and, increasingly, by the program. These contribute to the formation of communication hierarchies, increas-ingly based on the ability to pay.

Drawing on the work of Oppenheim (1990), Golding and Murdock (1991: 28–29) identify growing income differentials in Britain, with wage increases for the highest paid fifth of male workers 42 percent greater than for the lowest fifth. Gaps between households dependent on social security have also widened. As a result, between 1977 and 1987 the after-tax income share of the poorest fifth fell from 6.4 percent to 5.1 percent while that of the richest fifth grew from 40 percent to 45 percent. One of the consequences of class division in communication is presented in Golding's analysis of the relationship between income, one traditional (and modest) indicator of class divisions, and ownership of a telephone, television, and home computer.[3] As the data indicate, there is a consistent relationship between income category and ownership of these communication goods.

These data are consistent with the U.S. experience. According to the Congressional Budget Office, from 1977 to 1989 the pretax income of the top 1 percent of U.S. families grew by 77 percent and by 29 percent for the top fifth. The second fifth saw its income grow by 9 percent, followed by a 4 percent gain for the third fifth. Meanwhile the fourth and bottom fifths saw their income decline by 1 and 9 percent respectively. According to 1992 U.S. Census Bureau data, after five decades of stability in income distribu-tion, the top fifth income category went from earning 40.9 percent of national income in 1970 to 44.3 percent in 1990; whereas the middle fifth dropped from 17.6 to 16.6, the second poorest fifth from 12.2 to 10.8, and the poorest fifth from 5.5 to 4.6 percent of national income. Moreover, in spite of an ostensibly progressive tax system, the richest kept most of the income after taxes. Over that period, 60 percent of the after-tax income gain went to the top 1 percent of families. Thirty-four percent of the gain went to the top 20 percent and the bottom 80 percent had to settle for the remaining

---

3. Income generally refers to salary, wages, rent, interest, and dividends. Wealth, which is a better indicator of class position, because it encompasses the value of all family assets (e.g. home, car, stocks, bonds, etc.), is nevertheless difficult to analyze because, measurement problems aside, data on wealth are not gathered nearly as systematically as they are on income.

6 percent of increased income. Back in 1959, the top 4 percent of U.S. wage-earners received the same in wages and salaries as the bottom 35 percent. By 1989, the gap had widened to the point that the top 4 percent took in as much as the bottom 51 percent of workers (Bartlett and Steele, 1992: ix).[4] In part because of this U.S. pattern and, in part, because its government of the 1980s shared the neo-conservative perspective of its southern neighbor, Canada experienced comparable growth in class divisions. These were cushioned to a degree by a more substantial social welfare system, but this too met with regular attacks from business and government.[5] The class character of these societies is reflected in patterns of media access and use. For example, there is a clear correspondence between income and the likelihood of a personal computer in the home.[6]

Changes in U.S. communication policy in the 1980s also demonstrate greater class power. This was reflected in non-commercial electronic media as government funding for public broadcasting eroded, forcing the system to greater reliance on corporate support that introduced a significant degree of market power (including the first real advertisements) to what was largely a system whose program decisions, though regularly contested, nevertheless reflected public concerns that addressed people as citizens and not just as consumers. With a greater reliance on corporate and charitable giving, public broadcasting came to embrace the programming interests of those class constituencies that took up more of the funding responsibility. In commercial electronic media, the U.S. government ended regulations that limited the amount of commercial time permissible on the air. As a result, one of the largest communication networks was formed in 1993, when the

4. Recent data indicate that poverty in the United States is becoming both more pervasive and more spatially concentrated. The Census Bureau reports that 1992 marked another in a series of years in which the number of poor people rose, reaching 36.9 million or 14.5 percent of the population. Furthermore, the number of people living in concentrated poverty areas, or places with more than 40 percent of poor residents, rose to 10.4 million in 1990, up from 5.6 million in 1980 and 3.7 million in 1970. (U.S., Department of Commerce, Bureau of the Census, 1993)

5. According to a Statistics Canada report for 1991, only the top fifth, which received 40 percent of total family income, increased its share of national income. In that year, the bottom fifth received 6.4 percent, unchanged from the previous year. The government's poverty measure added 400,000 people to stand at 16 percent or a total of 4.23 million Canadians, up from 14.6 percent in 1990 and 13.6 in 1989 (Canada, Statistics Canada, 1993).

6. Krueger (in Nasar, 1992b) makes the connection between computer use and pay disparities. He concludes that workers who use computers, but are similar in every other respect to those who do not, earn an additional 10 to 30 percent. Furthermore, those who use computers tend to be white, female, and well educated. Those who do not are disproportionately black, male, and high-school dropouts. Additionally, Piller and Weiman (1992) maintain that computer use in poor school districts tends to differ substantially from its more affluent counterparts. Whereas the latter tend to use computers for creative exploration, such as designing multimedia presentations, the former concentrate on drill and practice routines. They conclude that 'instead of becoming instruments of reform, computers are reinforcing a two-tiered system of education for the rich and poor.'

Table 6.1   *U.S. media penetration by gender, race, education, and income, 1989*

Characteristic	Total population (1,000)	Television viewing and coverage (%)	Television prime time viewing and coverage (%)	Cable viewing and coverage (%)	Radio listening and coverage (%)	Newspaper reading and coverage (%)
Gender						
Male	85,035	91.8	75.1	50.7	87.1	85.7
Female	93,246	91.6	77.7	45.3	83.6	84.6
Race						
White	154,028	91.2	75.9	50.2	85.4	86.5
Black	19,599	95.5	80.3	32.7	84.5	78.8
Other	4,653	93.2	79.7	34.6	85.0	66.3
Spanish(-speaking)	10,301	91.0	74.7	38.9	90.8	76.7
Education						
Not high school graduate	45,389	91.8	75.9	36.7	75.2	71.9
High school graduate	69,392	91.8	77.8	49.7	86.7	86.6
Attended college	32,228	91.5	74.5	54.8	90.5	91.6
College graduate	31,271	91.4	76.3	53.0	91.3	94.2
Employment						
Full-time	101,695	90.8	75.8	51.8	91.1	87.7
Part-time	11,602	89.9	72.6	50.4	90.3	88.1
Not employed	64,984	93.4	78.2	41.3	75.2	80.5
Household income ($)						
Less than 10,000	19,644	91.6	74.4	27.4	70.9	66.6
10,000–19,999	31,564	94.2	79.4	38.0	80.5	79.3
20,000–29,999	32,361	91.7	77.0	47.5	84.2	84.8
30,000–34,999	16,105	93.3	78.6	49.1	89.1	87.1
35,000–39,999	14,391	91.5	77.5	55.7	88.9	89.4
40,000–49,999	24,001	90.6	75.2	54.4	90.8	90.8
50,000 or more	40,215	89.8	74.2	58.8	90.7	93.1

Source: US., Department of Commerce, Bureau of the Census, 1990: 550

Table 6.2 *UK ownership of communications equipment by income, 1989*

Weekly income (£)	Phone (% owning)	Video (% owning)	Home computer (% owning)
46–60	64.3	13.9	0.8
81–100	73.9	25.9	6.2
126–150	83.9	42.6	6.9
151–175	83.9	55.4	11.2
176–200	87.2	65.5	14.1
226–250	96.2	75.4	25.8
276–325	96.2	80.5	29.4
376–450	98.6	85.2	33.1
Over 450	99.7	77.7	34.3
All households	86.2	56.6	16.6

Source: Golding and Murdock, 1991: 29

two leading home shopping channels (QVC, or Quality Value, and Convenience, and the Home Shopping Network) merged to produce a major power in television, whose success depends on its freedom to do nothing more than sell throughout the broadcast day. The government also eliminated the fairness doctrine, which, however meekly enforced, put pressure on broadcasters to provide balanced coverage of issues in the public domain. Now stations are not only free to cover the issues they choose, however they choose, they are also under no obligation to cover any issues at all. In addition to this, government loosened ownership concentration regulations, and even made it easier for local monopolies, such as telephone companies and cable franchises, to charge whatever a nearly captive market can afford.

The elimination of requirements to program news and information has shifted that burden to cable television, where CNN, C-Span, and other news networks have taken over from the broadcasting networks, which have cut back on news, the coverage of such political events as Presidential conventions, and almost completely ended documentary public affairs production. But a combination of mainly high prices and some unwillingness on the part of cable companies to wire low-income areas has meant that in 1996 only two-thirds of American households subscribed to cable television.[7] As a result, a large percentage of viewing households do not have access to the primary carrier of electronic news and information in the United States. The practical end of rate regulation for what are local franchise monopolies, combined with the growing concentration of market control in the hands of

7. Under common carrier regulation, telephone companies were required to make their service accessible to all customers at reasonable rates subject to regulations which, even if weak in the eyes of most public interest advocates, nevertheless, were stronger than anything that cable television companies now have to face. This is particularly the case in recent years because most cable rate regulation has been eliminated.

Table 6.3 *U.S. media use by household income, 1992*

Household income ($)	Total population (1,000)	Television viewing and coverage (%)	Television prime time viewing and coverage (%)	Cable viewing and coverage (%)	Radio listening and coverage (%)	Newspaper reading and coverage (%)
Less than 10,000	20,273	93.7	82.7	41.8	77.4	64.9
10,000–19,999	29,823	95.2	84.2	45.1	79.1	73.8
20,000–29,999	30,266	94.1	81.5	52.6	82.5	82.2
30,000–34,999	14,976	94.8	83.6	58.9	87.9	85.7
35,000–39,999	13,113	92.2	78.3	63.1	89.3	89.8
40,000–49,999	22,008	94.0	81.2	64.0	91.1	90.5
50,000 or more	54,703	91.7	78.1	69.9	91.6	92.8

Source: U.S., Department of Commerce, Bureau of the Census, 1993: 561

Table 6.4 *Telephone penetration rates in the United States by selected socio-economic characteristics, 1992 (%)*

Characteristic	All races	White	Black	Hispanic
Total	93.9	95.3	83.8	86.6
Age of householder				
16–24	82.0	85.3	63.1	78.0
25–54	93.2	94.7	82.9	85.8
55–59	96.2	97.0	91.2	91.3
60–64	96.6	97.6	90.1	92.2
65–69	95.9	97.1	85.8	90.3
70 and over	97.6	98.3	92.0	95.4
Household size (persons)				
1	91.9	93.8	80.1	79.6
2–3	95.3	96.5	86.2	88.5
4–5	93.5	95.0	83.3	87.2
6 or more	90.6	91.8	85.2	86.6
Labor force status				
Total population	94.7	95.9	86.5	88.5
Employed	96.0	96.8	89.8	90.2
Unemployed	88.5	90.0	82.8	85.9
Not in labor force	93.4	95.1	82.8	86.0
Income level ($)				
Less than 5,000	71.7	76.0	63.0	66.9
5,000–7,499	83.7	85.9	76.7	72.8
7,500–9,999	88.3	90.4	79.3	78.4
10,000–12,499	90.0	91.0	83.5	81.2
12,500–14,999	91.2	92.3	85.4	84.1
15,000–17,499	93.2	94.3	86.4	87.3
17,500–19,999	95.6	96.4	89.7	91.6
20,000–24,999	97.2	97.8	91.5	96.0
25,000–29,999	98.2	98.4	96.9	96.1
30,000–34,999	98.6	99.2	95.7	96.7
35,000–39,999	99.0	99.3	96.4	96.0
40,000–49,999	99.5	99.5	98.9	99.1
50,000–74,999	99.4	99.4	98.7	100.0
75,000 or more	99.4	99.5	95.3	99.1

Source: U.S., Department of Commerce, Bureau of the Census, 1993: 563

mainly two integrated conglomerates, Time Warner and TCI, led to mounting protests which resulted in the reintroduction of some oversight for basic cable rates in 1992.[8]

In telephony, class power amounted to the redistribution of billions of dollars from local residential subscribers to corporate users. This resulted from a series of decisions that shifted the burden of paying for the system to

8. However, these new rules are so weak that approximately 30 percent of cable subscribers are paying higher bills. As a result, the FCC revisited its cable rate policy in 1994 and introduced reductions of about 7 percent in basic cable charges. The 1996 revision of the Communications Act calls for a gradual elimination of most cable rate regulations.

local subscribers and small businesses (Ramirez, 1991).[9] Indeed, the cost burden reflects what are effectively decisions to make residential subscribers pay for the construction of an infrastructure (the so-called electronic information superhighway) and new services, for which there is little demonstrable demand, but which business has argued are essential for its future operations.[10] As a result, although many policy analysts have declared universal telephone service a *fait accompli*, the 20 percent of low-income Americans, including about 15 percent of all black and hispanic households, without telephone service would disagree. As a report of the congressional Office of Technology Assessment (1991) has concluded, so too would rural Americans (for the United Kingdom, see Hepworth and Robins, 1988). Indeed, pressured by people who have seen their telephone bills increase, and, interestingly, at about the time that the United States reached a consensus that traditional welfare programs are not the best way to deliver services to the needy, the FCC and state regulators stepped in to start a national telephone welfare program. Packaged in euphemisms like Link-up and Lifeline, they amount to a national patchwork of state and federal programs that will subsidize a phone hookup and monthly bill provided the applicant can pass a means test that differs in every state. For example, in 1991, those living in South Carolina were only eligible for Link-up, had to be receiving one of four types of welfare assistance, and also pass an income test administered by the phone company. Alternatively, Oregon residents were eligible for both Link-up and Lifeline, but had to be receiving Food Stamps and pass an income test administered by the state (U.S., FCC, 1991). The pattern of means tests, policing, bureaucracy, and underenrollment (by January 1991, 3 percent for Link-up and 32 percent for Lifeline) contains all of the characteristics of welfare programs, whose major outcome it has been to maintain a permanent welfare class, economically and psychologically excluded from opportunity and access.

Similar developments are taking place across the electronic services marketplace. In the name of 'paperwork reduction,' the U.S. federal government has cut back on data collection, has privatized, for commercial use, data that were available free to a public that paid for their collection, and has

9. In its December 1991 report, the Consumer Federation of America concluded that the monopoly Baby Bells have overcharged their customers by about $30 billion since the 1984 breakup of AT&T.

10. It is common to justify regulatory changes because they ostensibly align prices with costs. In effect, this means eliminating what are considered subsidies from long-distance to local telephone customers. This view has been challenged chiefly from two perspectives. One (Oettinger, 1988a) holds that there is no economically certain way of determining the one best costing procedure because definitions of terms (what is a local loop?) are subjective and, more importantly, *politically* determined. In this view, cost-based pricing is, in Oettinger's formulation, little more than a fairy tale that rationalizes whatever the balance of industry power determines. Another view (Aufderheide, 1987; Denious, 1986; Melody, 1984) holds that the subsidies go in the other direction, from local to long-distance users. Their view is supported by evidence that local subscribers are paying disproportionately for infrastructure and services that long-haul users have demanded.

shifted much of its information to on-line data banks accessible only to those who can afford access to computer technology. According to its biannual publication *Less Access to Less Information by and about the U.S. Government* (1988: Preface), the American Library Association reports on the trend to 'cost–benefit analysis of government activities, maximum reliance on the private sector for the dissemination of government information, and cost recovery through user charges. The likely result is an acceleration of the current trend to commercialize and privatize government information.' The Association also reports that the American public library system is in worse condition than at any time since the Great Depression (*The New York Times*, July 8, 1991: A1). Librarians and others fear that the development of fee-for-service policies will, according to the deputy director of the American Library Association, 'skew how future services in the library are developed.' Understandably attracted to services that would raise much-needed funds, libraries could lose sight of their principal mission of providing access to all users, notwithstanding the ability to pay (De Witt, 1993). Finally, the U.S. public school system is in such desperate straits that 12,000 schools, representing nearly half of America's 12 to 17 year olds, now *require* their students to view Channel One, a commercially sponsored television news summary. In return for making students view Channel One, the schools receive what they consider to be much-needed video technology.[11]

Class power has also influenced the shape of the contemporary workplace as numerous studies point to the development of a massive service sector divided into two distinct tiers. Highly skilled people are trained to use information technologies that, in the words of Zuboff (1988), enrich or 'informate' their work. But more people tend machines that simply automate it. The exercise of class power in the workplace has a long history in political economy, with much of the debate in the nineteenth century centering on Marx's brief discussion of the separation of conception from execution at the point of production and invigorated in contemporary debates with the work of Braverman (1974).

This work suggests ways of thinking about the exercise of class power in the communication workplace through the elimination of labor and through the exercise of surveillance-based control over the remaining workforce. Today, no sector of the occupational structure is free from restructuring. Though considerable attention has been directed to the manufacturing sector, today the service sector, which some considered the 'engine for boom' of the 1980s, is experiencing at best slow growth and massive transformations. The communication industries are centrally placed within the services sector and are feeling the bite of job loss and restructuring (Nasar, 1992a; Zachary and Ortega, 1993).

---

11. The focus on communication technology and such notions as computer literacy misses the severity of the problem of general literacy in the United States, where, according to a 1993 Department of Education study (U.S., Congress, Senate, Subcommittee on Education, Arts and Humanities, 1995), 90 million of the country's 191 million adult citizens are not minimally proficient in English.

The print and publishing industry has experienced waves of technological change over the years, but the introduction of computer-controlled production methods is unprecedented in its impact on whole categories of both blue- and white-collar workers. Among the former, the application of computerized typesetting has eliminated the work of typesetters and compositors. Pagination systems give much of the responsibility for page layout and design to editors, who find that they spend less time on shaping stories and more on learning how to fit them onto a page. Technological change has also brought about cutbacks in broadcast news, where portability and automation have reduced the number of people assigned to produce stories. Special effects are also playing a role here. For example, the BBC was able to cut back its studio production staff by creating an automated, 'virtual' studio that presents to the viewer an image of the studio four times its actual size and whose most expensive props (cut crystal bearing the BBC coat of arms) exist only on the laser disk that contains the expanded studio (Drohan, 1993).

As in print journalism, video journalists are being given jobs that once belonged to technicians and graphic artists. Providing journalists with the ability to call up moving pictures and graphics on a single computer screen, including space alongside to write a script, reduces from three to one the number of people required to create a news item. The trade press now foresees that these 'Desk Top Video' systems will substantially alter work in video news. Similarly, major television networks have cut back sharply on expensive foreign bureaus and now rely on independents like WTN and Visnews. In addition to externalizing risk, restructuring by streamlining enables companies to rely on a small collection of highly skilled workers and avoid the range of costs that come with a large group, including unionized employees.

Automation has substantially reduced employment in the telecommunication industry, where computerized systems for handling long distance and directory assistance, among other services, have reduced the ranks of telephone operators by 20 percent over a ten-year period (see Table 6.5). Similar systems have cut into the work of telephone maintenance, engineering, and clerical workers (Moody, 1993).[12] Nielsen (1990) and Wasko (1994) have documented the impact of technological change on work in the film industry, where a host of technologies has restructured practically every production job, eliminating work for projectionists, lab technicians, and film exchange workers, among others.

Class power is also exercised in tighter *control* over the contemporary workplace. Companies use the very telephones and computer terminals that people work with to measure worktime (calls taken per minute, keystrokes per hour, groceries scanned in a shift, etc.) and performance (number and duration of break times) (Clement, 1992; U.S., Congress, Office of Technol-

---

12. Challenger et al. (1994) report that 41 percent of all layoffs announced by U.S. firms in January 1994 were in the telecommunication industry.

Table 6.5 *Elimination of jobs in the U.S.*
telecommunication industry 1992–4
(announced and planned job cuts)

Company	Jobs cut
IBM	35,000
AT&T	26,000
GTE	20,000
Nynex	17,000
Ameritech	11,000
Pacific Telesis	10,000
BellSouth	10,000
U.S. West	9,000
Apple	2,500
Southwestern Bell	1,500
AST Research	1,000
Compaq	1,000
Total	144,000

Sources: Andrews, 1994: D1; Mandel, 1994: 26

ogy Assessment, 1987). Again, the temptation is strong to measure and monitor whatever the technology makes feasible, marketable, and controllable. Although accounts on the subject often summon the specter of Big Brother, in most cases there is no irrational drive to heavy-handed domination. In some respects, this is a new form of power, one that does not physically coerce but rather insinuates almost naturally into what Michel Foucault (1982) has called the capillary system of the body politic. Monitoring is seen as an extension of normal business practices in a competitive environment. For example, the airline TWA monitors its reservation agents and distributes weekly and monthly report cards on computer-measured time spent on the phone and on a supervisor's assessment of phone conversations. According to a company executive, 'I don't think we're different from any other type of workplace. From the standpoint of productivity, we believe it's possible for all agents to maintain the benchmarks. We want to make sure the customers, paying hard-earned dollars, are getting what they paid for' (Kilborn, 1990: 8).

These forms of class analysis are important because they demonstrate that class tells us a great deal about the production, distribution, and consumption of communication in society. Nevertheless, they treat social class largely in *categorial* terms. The primary interest is in determining membership position in a category and in describing related behavioral patterns, including those responsible for the reproduction of class categories. They foreground class as structure and treat the process of class formation largely as a problem of reproduction. This work has been essential to the critique of liberal pluralist views that deny or ignore the existence of a class structure and which view the production, distribution, and consumption of media as the natural outcome of a democratic marketplace. According to liberal pluralism, the market may need some adjustment but, because the primary unit of analysis is the individual consumer (defined as a person or a business), the adjustments amount to improved market functioning for the individual, rather than the amelioration of fundamental class divisions.

Categorial class analysis provides a powerful critique of the liberal pluralist view, but its critical warrant can be strengthened by greater attention to three points. First, class analysis in communication would benefit by placing greater weight on *relational* and *formational* conceptions of social class. Second, it would be strengthened by addressing the connections between social class and other entry points in the structuration process, particularly *gender, race,* and those *social movements* that organize the energies of resistance to class (and other forms of) power. Finally it needs a tighter link to the construction of *hegemony*, or the social constitution of 'common sense.'

Whereas a categorial approach defines class by what is contained within a specific category, i.e., wealth or income, a relational method looks for the connections or links between categories. According to this view, social class is designated not by what a class contains or lacks, but by its relationship to other classes. There is no ruling class without a working class, and vice versa. What principally counts about class is what defines the relationship between classes, e.g. ownership and control over the means of production, reproduction, communication, etc. The relationship can be characterized in numerous ideal types, including *harmony*, where classes are integrated and mutually accept the class relationship, *separation*, where classes are largely excluded from one another, and *conflict* or *struggle*, where class relations are regularly contested.

In actual research practice, categorial and relational approaches overlap because one cannot speak of a category without some reference to the relationships that different categories form, and vice versa. Hence, even research that focuses almost complete attention on the communication elite will likely include material on the impact of this elite on its workforce and on consumers. Similarly, relational approaches necessarily refer to the categories that different relationships connect or divide. Even though the differences amount in practice to matters of degree or emphasis, these can be significant for the overall analysis of social class. One of the important consequences of a categorial emphasis in political economy is a specific view of class that foregrounds the resources that give class power to the top categories and what, as a result, those categories at the bottom lack. Findings based on this view are significant, but incomplete. It makes an important difference in the meaning of resource distribution to determine the nature of the relationships among classes that sustain or disrupt it.

Of equal significance is the problem of defining a class by what it lacks. Again, it is important to acknowledge the significance of a lack of control over the means of production, reproduction, and distribution, of lack of wealth, income, and the opportunities that go along with them. In communication, it is equally significant to document the consequences of a lack of access to the means of communication, mass media and telecommunication. However, such a categorial view is limited to the conclusion, however important, that the lower classes are defined by the absence of power-generating resources. Some sociologists have addressed this problem by viewing class structure as a continuum of categories (upper-upper, lower-upper, etc.) in which, as one moves down the continuum, classes exhibit diminishing resources. In communication, Fiske (1989) is most notable in his development of the categorial continuum approach to specifically cultural resources. Though this expands the class structure and recognizes some of the fuzziness at the borders of class categories, it does more to obscure real categorial and relational class differences than it does to advance either approach. A social relational approach rejects the calls for eliminating categories because it rejects the conclusion that they are merely artifacts of a real continuum and insists on specifying real relations among categories and on addressing class *formation*.

The concept of class formation is central to a structuration approach because it refers to the process by which social agency creates class through the medium of class structure. From this vantage point, one views class as an active process of social formation that makes use of, and is constrained by, the resources available in the class structure. Class is therefore less a category relatively full or empty of resources, including communication resources, and more appropriately the set of changing social relationships resulting from the actions of social agents making use of, and limited by, the very structure of those relationships. In the process of social action, people constitute themselves and their class relations. This approach is less mechanical than one concentrating on categories, structures, and social reproduction because it permits one to see social class as both a central material force in social life and the product of social action carried out by people on all sides of class relations.[13]

Given the importance of a categorial view, one does not find many examples of social relational and formational approaches to social class in political economy research. This is understandable considering the ability of class power to deepen a sense of alienation, which Bourdieu argued rests on 'a force of something said with authority' by which subaltern classes are

> Unceasingly asked to accept the point of view of others about themselves, to bear in themselves the viewpoint and judgment of others, they are always exposed to becoming strangers to themselves, to cease being subjects of the judgment they bring to bear on themselves, the center of the perspective of the view they have of themselves. (Cited in Mattelart, 1983: 19)

One finds a starting point for the formational approach in the communication research of Mattelart, who calls this task the search for a 'lost paradigm' containing the ways subaltern classes constitute themselves, both in relation to dominant classes and from a self-conscious sense of their own needs and interests. Acknowledging the difficulties of moving beyond a categorial

13. Katz et al. (1982) offer a good exemplar of a formational approach to social class.

view, Mattelart (1983) addresses the use of the mass media and popular cultural practices outside the West and the tradition of rank-and-file communication among workers in the West. He does so to suggest how these people built their own means of communication, developed their own languages, and their own common sense and popular hegemony, which, though constituted along with, alongside, and in conflict with a hegemony of the ruling classes, nevertheless provided independent grounds for social action, including class struggle. Political economists have responded tentatively to this call for a class formational approach, though a literature on the working class and labor has begun to address this area more forthrightly (see, e.g., Bekken, 1990; McChesney, 1992a; Ross, 1991; Waterman, 1990). This begins to examine working people as more than passive receivers, or even as, in Ross' words 'creative receivers, but as actual producers of mass culture' (Ross, 1991: 336). There is a pressing need to examine oppositional and alternative class-based movements, ranging from revolutionary struggles in Latin America, Asia, Africa, and Eastern Europe, where the creation of mass media was part of the revolution, to alternative media in the West, which provided a trade unionist, rank-and-file, or socialist alternative to capitalist 'common sense.' The point of this work is not to engage in romantic celebration, but, at the very least, to demonstrate how classes constitute themselves, how they make history, in the face of well-researched analysis of the conditions that constrain history-making activity.

Gender

A political economic perspective makes use of social class as its entry point for examining structuration. The preceding section recognized the value of a categorial conception of social class and described its use in communication research. It also suggested how to build on this conception by incorporating relational and formational conceptions of social class. Such a turn strengthens the political economy of communication by deepening the meaning of social class that underlies so much of its work. Notwithstanding the importance of this project, the analysis of structuration calls for reference to additional conceptual coordinates.

Although social class is a necessary entry point for political economy, it is not a sufficient condition for addressing structuration and its relationship to communication, in part because it leaves the question of gender, in the words of Jansen (1989), 'a socially structured silence.'[14] As Chapter 3 demonstrated, unlike other approaches, political economy has not been entirely silent on the issue of gender, though it typically addresses the subject as a dimension of social class relations. For example, political economic research on information technology and the international division of labor describes the double oppression that women workers face in the

14. Jansen is particularly concerned about the absence of attention to the issue of gender in the study of new communication and information technologies. For further explorations of this issue, see Friesen (1992); Rakow (1988); and van Zoonen (1992).

microelectronics industry, where they experience the lowest wages and the most brutalizing working conditions. Nevertheless, even though political economy has made important gestures to gender, it has not aimed to incorporate gender relations as fully as possible within the limits of the political economy perspective (Connell, 1987). Some leading political economists are beginning to recognize this shortcoming. For example, Golding and Murdock (1991: 30) conclude their assessment of the field with a call for political economic research on women and the media:

> we need to go on to explore other links between people's location in the productive system and their communicative activity. In pursuing this project, it is important to remember that 'production' is not the same thing as paid employment, it also includes domestic labor. Women's prime responsibility for the 'shadow work' of shopping, cleaning, cooking, and nurturing has fundamental consequences for their relation to the mass media.

Notwithstanding this concern, and discounting for the low level of conceptual development within the entirety of the political economy of communication, one observes remarkably little effort to theorize gender within a political economy approach to communication. Such work is long overdue, in part because of the enormous growth in the general literature on gender and mass communication (Lent, 1991). What follows is a set of starting points to move this work along.

One obvious task is to consider the range of social perspectives on gender and assess their compatibility with a political economic framework. This is important because the goal is not to find a place for gender, or, specifically, for women, in political economic analysis. This sort of 'search for women's place' is very much part of the problem. Rather, the goal for political economy is to determine how best to theorize gender within a political economic analysis, i.e., to suggest areas of agreement and, where these are not possible, to identify terms or zones of engagement between the frameworks. It is also important to emphasize that these efforts join those of Dervin (1987), Gallagher (1992), Jansen (1989), Martin (1991), Moyal (1989), Roach (1993a), and others, whose work has begun the project of bridging perspectives. Moreover, it also recognizes the significant contribution of explicitly feminist scholarship that starts from the need to address the specific concerns of feminism before beginning to think about connections to alternative perspectives (Dervin, 1987; Kramarae, 1989: 157–160; van Zoonen, 1991).

Political economic perspectives are most compatible with gender theories that foreground social, rather than biological or psychological categories. Moreover, on a spectrum comprising those social viewpoints most to least tied to a political economy perspective, we find gender approaches that start with *social class as an entry point* to examine, for example, gender and power, next, those that concentrate on *social reproduction*, and finally, those focused on the *duality of gender and class*, or the mutual constitution of patriarchy and capitalism.

Perspectives that start with social class foreground the system of production and tend to locate gender within it. This point of view considers, for example, how the international division of labor, whether defined in Fordist, post-Fordist or neo-Fordist terms, creates labor hierarchies that locate women predominantly at the bottom, a reserve army of low-skilled, dependent, and flexible workers. A class analysis of communication similarly examines labor hierarchies in the business of producing and distributing media and information, addressing the presence of significant gender divisions within an overall class-divided system (Gallagher, 1985, 1992; Martin, 1991). Moreover, such an analysis considers the consequences for media access as it situates gender relations within a communication system that stratifies access opportunities by class. For example, class analysis documents diminished access among the poor, but the system of gendered power locates women disproportionately within this category, leaving women in the more marginal position for access to media, telecommunication, and information technology.

Theories of social reproduction move political economy closer to gender analysis because these shift the locus of attention from the production of media, or, in the case of access, from the production of audiences, to the reproduction of social relations. Concretely, this means a tendency to shift the center of attention from the workplace to the home, the family, and sexuality. Though operating on the territory that typically occupies gender analysis, political economy takes a major role because the analysis of social reproduction tends to examine the functional connections between the reproduction of capitalism and class structure and the reproduction of social relations in the home and family. From this point of view, the media serve to tie the home, particularly through the activities of women, to the system of production and consumption by replenishing the energies of workers and connecting people to networks of consumption that thicken with each wave of new media and information technology. To complete the cycle, needs, interests, and desires emerging from the process of social reproduction become the source of entertainment and information programming which are used as direct and indirect vehicles for promoting consumption.

Explicitly functionalist analyses of social reproduction persist, but most acknowledge the presence of contradictory tendencies and forms of resistance that loosen the link between capitalism and gendered power. For example, as Adam Smith, Marx, and other classical political economists recognized, capitalism tends to move in different directions with respect to gender (as well, *vis-à-vis* race and ethnicity). Even as class power constitutes hierarchies of production that keep women out or, at best, marginalized, it erodes many of the traditional practices that limited the available human resources. Hence, although capitalism continues to constitute job ghettoes for women, in part as a result of political struggle, it also loosens restrictions on education, occupation, and other forms of women's social activity and social mobility. Similarly, systems of communication that tighten the connections to consumption also provide instruments for breaking with traditional roles, practices, and values. These are further instances of the view that capitalism is both dynamic and contradictory. Moreover, as again is evident in Marx, capitalism creates conflict across the range of social relations, including class and gender. Capitalism uses class power to structure the social relations of production and consumption, but it cannot guarantee their *realization*, principally because the people who participate in these structuring practices are self-reflexive and able to act socially on their own needs and interests, however distorted and partially formulated. One consequence is that people recognize the opportunity in the erosion of traditional bonds and take an active role in the process of restructuring them. As a result, the process of reproduction is contested and the sources of social resistance to capitalism are multiplied, but also dispersed. Both class and gender become grounds for opposition and resistance, acting sometimes congruently, as when telephone operators, overwhelmingly women, organize feminist caucuses within telephone worker unions to fight for better wages and working conditions. But, as debates within feminist movements indicate, this is not always the case. One source of tension reflecting, perhaps more intensely, fissures within the wider society is between class and gender solidarity, manifested in debates over the relative emphasis that one should place on overcoming class divisions by, for example, providing the poor with greater access to and control over the means of communication, or on overcoming gender divisions within classes, for example by opening more positions within the executive ranks of media companies to women.[15] Social reproduction is contested, but so too are forms of resistance.

Alongside perspectives that begin with class and those that foreground social reproduction are another set that view gender and class as *independent* categories, each of which provides a grounding for power relations in society. According to this position (Hartmann, 1979), society is *both* a patriarchy, i.e., gender-divided, and capitalist, i.e., class-divided. These coexist independently within the social field, sometimes interact, and, at times, are mutually constitutive. Gallagher (1985, 1992) and Steeves (1989) illustrate this position within communication research. Steeves sets out an agenda of 'global gender issues' suggesting both the independence and interconnection of patriarchy and capitalism. These include the transnational corporation as an instrument of both, the relationship of advertising to

[margin handwritten note: multiple deter-mination]

---

15. For an overview of women in the mass media professions, see Creedon (1993).

editorial and entertainment content promoting ideas and images of class and gender, and the presence and absence of women in media organizations and in the process of media production. She concludes by addressing forms of resistance to both class and gender divisions and the problems and opportunities presented by new information and communication technologies.[16] An approach based on the duality of patriarchy and capitalism has the advantage of providing a broad field of analysis because it permits one to concentrate on a specific grounding without ignoring the other, as in studies of capitalist patriarchy or patriarchal capitalism. The approach faces some of the same challenges of any framework based on mutual formation, such as how to characterize the field they occupy – patriarchal or capitalist, which is adjective and which is noun, and how to characterize the nature of their interaction. It faces the additional problem of aiming to address mutual formation without a specific entry point such as class or gender.

These three approaches suggest ways to think about gender within an overall political economy of communication. Their major strength is that of all categorial approaches: they are relatively simple to apply to specific structural problems in communication studies, such as access to media, to power in media organizations, and to the policy-making process. Their weakness is also that of categorial approaches: they tend to pay less attention to the process of social formation, specifically, to how people actively constitute gender in relation to the mass media, to social class, and to the range of choices within gender (e.g. heterosexuality and homosexuality).

A *formational* approach concentrates on the process of creating a gender identity through the mutual formation of social structures, the means of communication, the product of communication, and the agency of individuals who act as social beings in social relationships. For example, such a perspective examines the formation of gender through the relationships among media institutions, which are situated in a wider political economy, the medium of television, the programs it broadcasts, and the way individuals, who come to the mass mediated experience with specific, though dynamic, social roles and relationships, understand and act on this programming. Examples of this sort of analysis are difficult to find, partly because they require that rare transdisciplinary perspective, spanning political eco-

---

16. In another article Steeves (1987) offers a critical evaluation of liberal, radical, and socialist feminist perspectives on the media. She concludes that liberal perspectives tend to 'speak only to white, heterosexual, middle and upper class women.' Radical, including structuralist, perspectives tend to concentrate on texts, to the neglect of the wider social framework. Socialist feminism is most promising, because it is capable of addressing the linkages between the economic and cultural positions of women, i.e., the mutual constitution of class and gender.

nomic and cultural analysis. Some of the closest approximations lie in social history, where commitments to either of these approaches take a back seat to a social understanding of a particular period (Peiss, 1986).[17] This approach concludes that the term 'social reproduction' is at once too simple and too blunt to describe this process because it implies a 'copy' theory of social development and assumes a linear relationship between texts and social experience. Analysts of culture have made progress by reminding us of the polysemic nature of texts, broadly understood to include the full range of media products, but they have tended to fall victim to their own form of simplification, namely a consistent neglect of the relationship between media products and the institutional processes of production and distribution that bring them into being, as well as a tendency to ignore the social embeddedness of individual agency. Furthermore, institutions and social roles are not mere contexts for texts and individual agency, a suggested solution to the institutional and social category blindspot in cultural research. They are full participants in a process of mutual formation. Social histories of mass communication technology, such as Douglas' (1987) work on the mutual constitution of technology and gender in the relationship of 'amateur' radio to the formation of masculinity, Spigel's (1989) and Altman's (1989) on television and femininity, and Martin's (1991) on the relationship of the telephone to gender and social class, have begun to document this complex process.

critique (margin annotation)

Race

The powerful and multifaceted effort to theorize gender within areas largely dominated by class analysis holds out the prospect for a renewed political economy of communication that encompasses broader and deeper dimensions of social experience than traditionally understood in the discipline. Nevertheless, class and gender, individually or in tandem, do not exhaust the categories that are vital to an understanding of the structuration process, in part because, on their own, they do not leave sufficient room for understanding the power of race.

17. Amott and Matthaei (1991: 6) make the case for this approach by noting that 'the gender, racial–ethnic and class hierarchies in any period are inherited from the past, and hence cannot be adequately grasped without an historical perspective.' Nevertheless, they recognize that history can constrict the development of what they call 'liberatory knowledge': 'Can we use the liberatory knowledge of these different histories to create liberatory practice, and in so doing, take control of our joint destinies … can we seek beyond history for a new and more possible meeting?' (p. 356). For an overview of feminist historiography in journalism, see Nesmith (1991).

In 1903, the American black nationalist W.E.B. Du Bois said that the 'problem of the twentieth century is the problem of the color line.'[18] For him, the color line was drawn within and across nations as a principal source of divisions within societies and between the rich and powerful nations of the predominantly white West and the poor and dependent rest of the world. Although, as we have seen, communication studies has addressed the question of imperialism extensively, principally by examining the role of the media and information technology in its formation, the discipline has done so to extend a sense of the world as class-divided and, though less frequently, as gender-divided (as in the case of studies on women in the international division of labor), rather than to understand it as *race-divided.* But one does not have to focus on South Africa to recognize that racial divisions are a principal constituent of the manifold hierarchies that make up the contemporary global political economy, and that race, as both category and social relationship, contributes fundamentally to individual and collective access to national and global resources, including communication, media, and information technology.

A categorial understanding of race, like that of class and gender, addresses the differential access to communication that racial divisions bring about. This includes access to ownership and control of communication companies (Tabor, 1991), to jobs in the media, communication and information technology industries (Honig, 1984; Sivanandan, 1989), to the means of communication and information (e.g. see U.S., FCC, 1991, for data on access to telecommunication), and to media presentations of the range and diversity of minority images (MacDonald, 1983; Silk and Silk, 1990; Staples and Jones, 1985; van Dijk, 1991; Wilson and Gutiérrez, 1985). Tabor (1991: 612) documents the historical tolerance of racism in American broadcasting, including numerous cases that demonstrate how the broadcast regulator, the Federal Communications Commission, tolerated explicit racism in television:

> in the mid-1960s, white supremacists, who managed Jackson, Mississippi television station WLBT, covered the screen with a 'Sorry Cable Trouble' sign whenever network programming featured an African-American. Clergy and local citizens banded together to challenge the lack of access given African-Americans on the Jackson station. But the FCC denied the clergy and citizens' standing and conditionally renewed the station's license.

When a federal court overturned the Commission's decision, the FCC ignored the court and renewed the station's license for a full three-year

18. Repeating Du Bois' phrase, Sivanandan (1990: 13) gives warrant to its continuing centrality and to its intimate connection with the lines drawn by social class:

Today the colour line is the poverty line is the power line. We are non-white, we are poor, we are powerless. And that which establishes the connection between them is capitalism; that which perpetuates it is imperialism. Except for a handful of black elites who are doing pretty well, the majority of non-white peoples of the world are poor, and powerless to do anything about their poverty. And they are kept that way by imperialism. That is why you cannot fight racism without also fighting imperialism. You cannot fight for the cause of black people without fighting for the cause of working people.

period. A federal appeals court finally directed the FCC to vacate the license grant to WLBT (*United Church of Christ* v. *FCC*, F.2d 543, 549–50 [D.C. Cir. 1969]). Despite 1968 regulations, embraced by the FCC, to eliminate employment discrimination in broadcasting, it was not until 1989 that the Commission upheld a complaint of employment discrimination against a licensee. In fact, there is evidence that the ratio of blacks in the professional ranks of American broadcasting actually declined between the early 1970s and 1980s (Honig, 1984: 861).

From a global perspective, race is a central force in the formation of the international divisions of labor, whose hierarchies include class and gender, but also, vitally, race, in the organization of skills and control set within a world political economy increasingly defined by the production of micro-electronics and information (Sivanandan, 1989).[19]

Racial divisions persist in access to the means of communication. Many analysts conclude that, with the telephone in 92 percent of U.S. households, universal service is all but accomplished. Nevertheless, according to the FCC's own data, almost 20 percent of black and hispanic households lack basic telephone service (U.S., FCC, 1991). Political pressures arising from the failure to extend service to many poor blacks and hispanics have prompted the federal government to initiate the first nationwide social welfare program in American telephony (see p. 224). Finally, numerous studies (Downing, 1988; Jhally and Lewis, 1992; Staples and Jones, 1985; UNESCO, 1983) document the narrow range of images and role models available to minorities in the media.

The racial division of access is not without its problems for capitalist development. As Gutiérrez (1990) has noted, deficiencies in the incorporation of minorities into communication networks represent missed opportunities for broadening consumer markets. As is the case with class and gender, one of the principal fault lines in the construction of markets is the trade-off between incorporating new people and the ground that must be given up with new messages and images that potentially challenge the dominant audiovisual space.

The categorial approach to race and the media documents the significance of race across the various forms of media access. There are fewer studies that address the social relational and formational dimensions of race and the media (Barlow, 1989; Dates and Barlow, 1993; Silk and Silk, 1990; Wilson and Gutiérrez, 1985). These demonstrate that one cannot comprehend the

---

19. In addition to taking the lead in the analysis of race and the changing international division of labor brought about, in part, by new information technologies, Sivanandan (1990: 47) has taken a strong position in defense of materialist analysis:

But what 'social signs' do 'today's goods' have for the poor in 'poor societies' except that they have not got them, the goods? And what 'meaning' or 'energy' do they produce except that those who have do not give and those who have not must take? Who are these people who, in our own societies – 'with however little money – play the game of using things to signify who they are' unless it is those who use cardboard boxes under Waterloo Bridge to signify that they are the homeless?

structuration of race in the media without taking into account how it operates through the struggles of minorities to gain access to jobs in the mass media, through the creation of alternative media reflecting the lived experience of minorities, and through pressure to change the presentation of minority information and entertainment in the mass media. As in the case of those studies which foreground gender, some of the most interesting work in this area tends to concentrate in social history. Saxton (1990) demonstrates this in a history of white racism in the United States by identifying those economic levers, from the slave trade to a segmented job market, as well as those cultural instruments, including academic analyses of racial inferiority and popular entertainments like minstrel shows, that reproduced a set of race (and class) relations. These are considerably more than embodiments of white racism. They are a set of social practices that are constantly put to the test, challenged, revised, and reformulated in the context of racial conflict and wider political economic change. The practices themselves thereby contain evidence of social contestation, as when, for example, black minstrelism became a force of social satire directed at attacking, however gingerly, the very racism it traditionally reinforced. People as diverse as Lincoln, Mark Twain, and Eugene Debs, who, in Saxton's assessment (p. 390), were 'not so much dissenters as collaborators in the midst of white racial politics, . . . nonetheless projected broader visions of human possibility.' In addition, at every stage in the construction and reproduction of white racism, oppositional forces like African-American abolitionists who produced a voluminous anti-racist literature struck at the heart of racist premises. These embody Sivanandan's (1990: 3) conclusion about racism and colonialism:

> I think that it's a mistake to think of colonialism as a one-way street, as something that is done to you, as something that takes you over, something so powerful you can't resist it. There is always a resistance somewhere that comes out of your own culture, your language, your religion. And that resistance first takes the form of an existential rebellion − a rebellion against everything that goes against your grain.

Social Movements

The mutual constitution of class, gender, and race is an important dimension of the overall structuration process. A complete analysis of this process would include generational and other processes, though there is the danger that this can all too easily devolve into a pluralistic compilation of equally influential social categories. A political economic approach identifies structuration as a social process which starts from class, as category, relationship, and formation, and examines how it is constituted principally with gender and race. Notwithstanding the value of this approach, it contains the added risk of mechanistic thinking about how these terms operate in practice and how they should be brought together in praxis. Arguing from a feminist perspective, Haraway (1991: 129) reflects on the difficulty of connecting class, gender, and race and suggests the need for new geometries of social relations:

> It has seemed very rare for feminist theory to hold race, sex/gender, and class analytically together – all the best intentions, hues of authors, and remarks in prefaces notwithstanding. In addition, there is as much reason for feminists to argue for a race/gender system as for a sex/gender system, and the two are not the same *kind* of analytical move. And, again, what happened to class? The evidence is building of a need for a theory of 'difference' whose geometries, paradigms, and logics break out of binaries, dialectics, and nature/culture models of any kind. Otherwise, threes will always reduce to twos, which quickly become lonely ones in the vanguard. And no one learns to count to four. These things matter politically.

Haraway's point is important for a political economy of communication, if only because it questions all essentialisms, whether based on class, gender, or race. However, her argument goes beyond these in its pessimism about those approaches, like the one taken here, which eschew essentialism by offering an analysis based on entry points and multiple determinations. Though the thrust of this book is more optimistic about examining the social relations of class, gender, and race, it is useful to consider additional formulations within the general political economy framework. Two possibilities focus on *social movements* and the social relations of *hegemony*.

An analysis organized around social movements holds out the advantage of transcending traditional social categories by concentrating on social agency and social action. Social movements bring together people from a range of social identities who are, more or less, united by a specific interest which includes opposing and seeking to transform established dominant power relations. Social movements can bring together people identified with a particular class position, such as trade unionists, the poor, or business elites. They can also unite people around gender, as do the range of feminist movements, or around race, e.g. the U.S. civil rights and black power movements. Furthermore, they can mobilize people based on other categorial identities, such as age or nationality. However, the success of social movements typically depends on their ability to transcend particular social categories by uniting a diverse collection of people around a specific interest or cause.

In recent years, considerable attention has been directed to movements emphasizing identification with interests and causes that, while not omitting a concern for social categories (the feminist movement is probably the most strongly categorial), are nevertheless chiefly taken up with specific goals. These 'new social movements' include preeminently the many environmental, peace, health (especially anti-AIDS), sex (gay liberation), and other movements that unite people across traditional categories and establish the grounds for greater attention to non-traditional categories.

The line between old and new social movements is not firm, though considerable heat has been expended in defending one or the other as politically superior. Some argue that the global political economy makes class-based movements more important than ever and others attack this position by claiming that a post-Fordist or postmodern information economy diminishes the significance of such categories in favor of movements that unite diverse people behind a general cause, such as global ecology. Old social movement approaches tend to be linked to traditional political economic concerns, while those that call our attention to the new movements tend to place greater emphasis on cultural identification, including the power of various media (television, rock concerts, fanzines, etc.) to forge new cultural links and propel some of these into full-blown movements. Unfortunately, although the literature on new social movements has broken new ground, so much attention has been taken up with the *break* from the old that common ground has been underemphasized and consequently so too the political potential of forging alliances across old and new movements. There is no doubt that concerns over ecology, peace, gender, and sex have provided the basis for major social movements of the late twentieth century. Nevertheless, this does not mean, as some have suggested (Luke, 1989), that society is any less class-divided, that labor is no longer a central social activity and a force in social organization, and that trade unionism is politically spent. In addition to focusing on the process of political action, a social movement approach is valuable specifically because it rejects categorical imperatives of both old and new varieties.

Social movements are particularly important for a political economy of communication because they have influenced the development of the means and content of communication. In facing up to the inevitable question of how to organize internal and external communication, all of the major social movements have developed communication strategies and policies. Among the most prominent issues are how *democratic* should be the lines of internal communication, the extent to which a movement should adopt mainstream forms of external communication, and the degree of specialized or expert attention a movement should devote to media activity. Gitlin's (1980) work is particularly important here because it suggests that a movement's media policy cannot be distinguished from its fundamental goals. The American student anti-war movement lost some of its democratic moorings when it permitted leaders to become media personalities. The political economy of the mass media itself has contributed to the formation of social movements organized principally around media production and policy. Alternative media movements worldwide have challenged dominant media forms, technologies, images, and messages. These include labor-intensive literacy campaigns, street theater, alternative newspapers, video, and film production, cartooning, public access cable programming, alternative computer networks, video piracy, computer hacking, and others. They differ in how they challenge established forms of media. Some, like the literacy movements in Cuba and Nicaragua, contested, out of political philosophy and practical necessity, technology-intensive forms of communication and education (Mattelart, 1986). Others, such as video piracy and hacking, challenge concentrated control over the means of communication (Balka, 1991; Hafner and Markoff, 1991; Rheingold, 1993; U.S., Congress, Senate, Committee on the Judiciary, 1991). Still others, such as the alternative press and public access radio and cablecasting, offer fundamentally different messages and images to those of the mainstream (Goldberg, 1990; Jankowski et al., 1992; Pizzigati and Solowey, 1992; Ryan, 1991).

Social movements have also been prominent in organized challenges to dominant media policies. The movement organized around a New World Information and Communication Order was arguably the most significant international effort to take on dominant forms of media policy-making, particularly the control that Western transnational businesses held over the production and distribution of the major mass media (Traber and Nordenstreng, 1992). The movement continues today in the MacBride Roundtable and in the effort to enshrine the right to communicate among fundamental human rights accepted by international organizations.

Numerous social movements have taken on national and local policy-making processes, including efforts to democratize decisions about licensing, spectrum allocation, industry structure, and media content. These movements have been particularly strong in the United States, which saw intense struggles over the development of the telegraph and telephone, with groups led by trade unions and rural political organizations calling for public ownership or, at least, social control over the development of telecommunication along the model of the public postal service (DuBoff, 1984; Stone, 1991). The development of radio and television broadcasting brought about similar struggles with new organizations, such as trade union and educational interests, in the forefront of efforts to promote public broadcasting and strong regulation of commercial channels (McChesney, 1993).

The growth of the civil rights and feminist movements unleashed new energy into the broadcasting reform movement. The former used the courts to gain standing for groups representing the general public interest before the Federal Communications Commission, the federal regulator which had ruled out such standing as a usurpation of its powers. Feminist groups joined their civil rights counterparts to attack established hiring practices and degrading programming (Creedon, 1993). Learning from these left of center movements, the right wing organized a strong media movement of its own to attack what it claimed were morally offensive programs (Montgomery, 1989). Contemporary interest in the development of interactive media, particularly the ferment over U.S. policy on the development of a national information 'superhighway,' has breathed new life into the public interest media reform movement. In 1993, a coalition of more than sixty non-profit, consumer, labor, and civil rights groups announced the formation of the Telecommunications Policy Roundtable. Groups including the American Civil Liberties Union, the American Library Association, the Association of America's Public Television Stations, the Center for Media Education, the Consumer Federation of America, Computer Professionals for Social Responsibility, and Ralph Nader's group Public Citizen have come together to promote universal access to the information infrastructure, freedom to communicate, democratic policy-making, and privacy protection.

Hegemony

Hegemony, the process of constituting the common-sense, taken-for-granted reality in society, provides another dimension to the process of structuration. The term achieved prominence in the West principally through the work of Gramsci, who made it a central feature of his intellectual project – to understand the specific contours of advanced capitalist societies, particularly their capacity to base control on *consent* more so than on physical coercion. The concept of hegemony is situated between *ideology*, which typically refers to the deliberate distortion or misrepresentation of social reality to advance specific interests and maintain hierarchies of power, and *values*, which denote those shared social norms connecting the wide range of differently placed people and strata in society. Unlike values, hegemony is politically constituted, but, unlike ideology, it does not reflect an instrumental distortion of image and information. Rather, hegemony is the ongoing formation of both image and information to produce a map of common sense sufficiently persuasive to most people that it provides the social and cultural coordinates that define the 'natural' attitude of social life. Hegemony is therefore more powerful than ideology because it is not simply imposed by class power, but constituted *organically* out of the dynamic geometries of power embedded in social relations throughout society.

Arguably the most powerful of hegemonic ideas is the notion that hegemony itself can be brought about, because this suggests that there is a set of cultural and social practices, ideas, and interpretations that can be recognized as naturally occurring, not socially constituted, *givens* in social life. These tend to be presented as essential elements in the formation of the self, in developing a relationship between self and society, and in locating both on cognitive maps of socio-historical experience. The notion of *tradition* is a powerful instrument in the construction of hegemony. In his attempt to remove the naturalistic gloss that gives the very idea of hegemony its transhistorical quality, Hobsbawm (1983: 1) describes 'invented traditions' which, like the ceremony surrounding the British monarchy, appear 'ancient and linked to an immemorial past.' These are, in fact,

> a set of practices, normally governed by overtly or tacitly accepted rules and of a ritual or symbolic nature, which seek to inculcate certain values and norms of behaviour by repetition, which automatically implies continuity with the past.

Tradition roots people in a past that achieves a mythic status, setting it beyond reality tests, thereby giving it a transhistorical quality. The invention of tradition is one of the central social processes in the creation of hegemony, one component of which, what Poulantzas (1978) called *individuation*, takes on a life of its own outside of tradition. This refers to the tendency of capitalism to transform collective categories and identities into individual ones, thereby diminishing the social power of class, gender, race, and other forms of collective energy. The working class, women, and blacks are thereby reconstituted as individual subjects.

Hegemony is also embodied in a range of substantive ideas such as the widespread acceptance of the marketplace as the cornerstone of a productive economy, of voting as the primary means of carrying out democracy, and of journalistic objectivity as the product of two views on an issue of the day (Goldman and Rajagopal, 1991). These and other hegemonic views (free markets, free elections, a free press, the free flow of information, etc.) are neither politically neutral values, nor ideological instruments of control imposed from above. They constitute the common-sense currency of every-day life, developing out of those social relationships that make up hier-archies of class, gender, race, etc.

Gramsci's analysis of hegemony was inextricably bound to his political project. This was to redirect opposition to capitalism and the development of democratic socialism away from the view that placed revolutionary action, direct military attack, and vanguard leaders at the center of political strategy. Rather, in this view, the transition to socialism required the development of an oppositional and alternative hegemony, which would constitute a new common sense, a new currency of everyday life that, over the many struggles or 'wars of position,' would replace the natural attitude of capitalist hegemony. Gramsci's alternative did not *replace* a political with a cultural strategy, it broadened the conception of revolutionary politics to encompass the social struggle over cultural and linguistic space.

Given the power of hegemonic ideas, how is it possible to accomplish Gramsci's transformation? The task is all the more daunting when one recognizes the dynamic power of a dominant hegemony, as it responds to changing political and social relations to take on new forms, such as, for example, the expansion of national into continental and global hegemonic blocs, the incorporation of what were once oppositional notions, such as formal gender equality, into the dominant hegemonic constellation, and the reconstruction of ideas about social welfare and private charity (Golding et al., 1986).

Notwithstanding the power of a dominant hegemony that has led some to envision 'the end of history' (Fukuyama, 1992), there are good arguments to be made for the view that hegemony does not present an impregnable barrier. Yes, hegemony is stronger than ideology because it is based on consent, rather than coercion. But consent is very demanding, calling as it does for the ongoing formation of widespread, willing agreement to accept the dominant view as natural. Unlike formulations based on the logic of capital, of a dominant ideology, or of values embedded in the natural right to rule, hegemonic power is built from social relationships requiring complicity across class, gender, race, and other hierarchies. Once achieved, consent is a powerful form of control; but a process that *requires* consent implies resistance and the potential for alternative forms of common sense. Hence, though hegemony is a central means of accomplishing the structura-tion of social relationships, it does not guarantee their reproduction. Hegem-ony is carried out over a contest for consent which, though situated within what Mahon (1980) calls an 'unequal structure of representation,' is sufficiently unstable to admit oppositional and alternative hegemonies.

Two major tasks for political economy are to identify the sources of instability in the dominant hegemony and to assess the range of forms taken by oppositional and alternative hegemonies. The former include gaps between what passes for common sense and lived experience. One of the central problems of capitalist hegemony has been to constitute consent for the idea that capitalism produces widespread material abundance in the face of a lived experience of poverty, even in its heartland. Numerous defenses offer alternatives to the conclusion that it is the economic system itself which produces poverty. These include references to the *culture of poverty*, which takes the comprehensible notion that classes produce their own cultural and social practices and turns it into the defense of an economy that would otherwise produce effectively and distribute equitably, were it not for a culture of poverty that instills in the poor the wrong values, work habits, family and sexual practices, and attitudes toward money. In the extreme, the culture of poverty argument amounts to an academic gloss on racism: blacks, hispanics, and indigenous people would advance if only they were able to overcome their own social and cultural tendencies.

Another favored defense is the 'trickle-down' view that, over time, an economy and economic policies favoring the rich will inevitably trickle down to benefit the entire class structure. This is a variation on the general defense based on the distinction between the short and long run which, in the face of evident short-term consequences (a decision favors one group over another), claims that, in the long run, the consequences will even out. Compaine (1986) offers a trickle-down view to defend the current distribution of communication and information resources. His reading of technological history leads him to conclude that the long run will see access even out across class and other social divisions.

Alternatively, the dominant hegemony defends itself with an ironic wink, i.e., with the stylistic detachment that knows full well that major gaps exist between what passes for common sense and lived experience. As Miller (1988), among others, has documented, television has perfected this form of irony, creating a bond between cynical narrator or plot line and viewer that responds to the gap with knowing recognition that, yes, it exists, but more importantly, 'no one is pulling the wool over our eyes.' Finally, another major defense relies on no direct defense at all, but rather defends indirectly through the production of entertainment and information that is largely about something else, about attractive distractions that suggest, among other things, that it is better to think about something else, or not to think at all.

Williams (1980) drew on Gramsci's notion of hegemony to develop the ideas of *oppositional* and *alternative* hegemonies with respect to cultural and media practices. Either form requires the development of a new intellectual leadership which departs from both establishment and revolutionary traditions by rejecting divisions between analysis and political practice, between conceptual and technical knowledge, and between thinking and working. For Gramsci, these leadership qualities constitute 'organic intellectuals' who use them to advance the development of oppositional and alternative hegemonies. As a long tradition of informational, dramatic, comedic, and other forms demonstrates (Buhle, 1987), oppositional hegemonies attack the shortcomings in the dominant form by peeling back the glosses that mask its contradictions. These cultural practices of opposition and resistance do not necessarily presume an alternative hegemony but, depending on their success, make it easier to create one. Alternative hegemonies, in varying degrees of explicitness and over a range of forms, describe the substance of different ways to make common sense of social life, suggesting that it is worthwhile and realistic to think about these differences and to act toward their realization. In this way, the concept of hegemony serves as a broadly based organizing principle or process providing another way of thinking about structuration, one which overlaps, complements, and departs from the processes of constituting class, gender, race, and social movements.

Conclusion

This brings to a conclusion the discussion of different ways of rethinking and renewing the political economy of communication organized around the three entry processes of commodification, spatialization, and structuration. The discussion broadened the grounds for thinking about communication from a political economic perspective, but it looked outward only within the neighborhood of political economy. The next chapter concludes the book by moving beyond the neighborhood to those disciplines which, though on the boundaries of political economy, nevertheless constitute different intellectual regions. Specifically, it takes up the challenges which policy science, specifically public choice or positive political economy, and cultural studies pose for the political economy of communication. By no means an exhaustive summary of these approaches, it is rather an attempt to identify zones of useful exchange that suggest additional lessons for rethinking and renewing the political economy approach to communication.

7

Challenges on the Borders:
Cultural Studies and Policy Studies

Must there be some wider reorganization of the received divisions of the humanities, the human sciences, into newly defined and newly collaborative arrangements? This is what now must be faced in what is also, for other reasons, a frozen – indeed a pinched – climate. All that we can be certain that we can and must do is to clarify, very openly, the major underlying intellectual issues.

(Williams, 1981b: 65–66)

We may now be observing a curious convergence between two apparently antithetical tendencies, the super-rationalism of Rational Choice Marxism and post-structuralist irrationalism. RCM's abstractions, so typical of analytic philosophies which pride themselves on their empyreal detachment from the uncertain flux of historical process, paradoxically come together here with the irrationalist dissolution of history from the opposite direction. Both are impelled toward a politics detached from the anchor of history, as game-theoretic choices join post-modern contingency in a contradictory amalgam of political voluntarism, where rhetoric and discourse are the agencies of social change, and a cynical defeatism, where every radical programme of change is doomed to failure.

(Wood, 1989: 88)

Introduction: Borderlines

The last three chapters provided a view on how to rethink and renew the political economy of communication from the inside, by assessing the state of the discipline's central questions and ideas. Rethinking and renewing political economy also requires one to look outward, at the relationship between the discipline and those on its borders. Admittedly, one can map the universe of academic disciplines in innumerable ways. Political economy can be situated opposite sociology, political science, and economics, among other approaches. Taking into account the central problems we have identified in a political economy of communication, it is particularly useful to situate the discipline opposite cultural studies, on the one side, and policy studies, on the other. On the understanding that no borders, whether physical, social, or cognitive, can be identified with certainty, the concluding chapter examines policy studies and cultural studies as two very different approaches to communication which provide alternative ways of seeing on the borders of political economic research. It would be undoubtedly presumptuous for this chapter to attempt a full-blown critique of these perspectives. The literature in both fields contains excellent maps, analyses, and critiques. Rather, starting from a political economic perspective, the chapter aims to open a conversation with each, principally in order to enrich the process of rethinking and renewing political economy. In addition to this primary goal, the chapter also contributes to identifying strengths and weaknesses within and between cultural studies and policy studies that are elements of an ongoing process of rethinking these approaches.[1]

Over the years, communication scholars have identified the disciplines' principal fault lines in different ways, including the distinction between behavioral and normative, and between administrative and critical approaches. More recently, the distinction between political economy and cultural studies has attracted considerable attention. This is understandable since cultural studies has grown substantially over the past three decades, has influenced communication studies significantly, and raises fundamental questions about the assumptions, methods, and conclusions offered by alternative approaches, including political economy (During, 1993a; Grossberg, 1991; Grossberg et al., 1992; Johnson, 1987). Moreover, since communication studies has tended to take root in the arts and humanities divisions of universities, the discipline understandably gravitates to a dialogue with cultural studies. It is therefore essential to take up the challenge of cultural studies in order to establish a sound political economy approach to communication studies.

Nevertheless, without taking anything away from the need for a systematic dialogue with cultural studies, it is equally important for political economy to critically evaluate its relationship to policy studies, where, in spite of a substantial increase in the attention of communication scholars, little systematic reflection has taken place. One can define policy studies in different ways, but this chapter specifically views the field as an amalgam of pluralist political and neoclassical economic approaches whose goal extends beyond explaining behavior to a normative interest that evaluates and recommends policy courses of action. The pluralist wing has occupied the orthodoxy of political science and public policy research. More recently, neoclassical economists have made use of central assumptions, categories, and theories to shift the center of gravity in policy studies. As a result, approaches variously labelled public choice theory and positive political economy now occupy an important place at the center of policy studies, several of whose practitioners have achieved worldwide notoriety by winning the Nobel Prize in economics, including one, Ronald Coase, who worked on central issues in communication policy.

Cultural studies is a broad-based intellectual movement which concentrates on the constitution of meaning in texts, defined broadly to include all forms of social communication.[2] It has grown from many strands, including

1. Following Grossberg (1991: 155), 'The point is not so much to choose between them, although one inevitably must do so, but define new forms of alliance and cooperation amongst them.'

2. See Burgess (1990) for a telling example of how cultural studies has influenced the core agenda of the traditional discipline of geography, a development repeated in most every academic pursuit.

one based on the drive to oppose academic orthodoxies, particularly the tendency to organize knowledge in disciplinary canons such as English Literature.[3] The approach now contains numerous currents and fissures that provide considerable ferment from within as well as without.[4] From the beginning, especially in the British context, cultural studies has been strongly influenced by Marxian approaches. This includes the tendency to see the cultural as intimately connected to social relations, particularly as organized around class, gender, and race, especially their asymmetries and antagonisms. Furthermore, Marxian concerns with power, particularly the power to define and realize needs and interests, influenced the development of cultural studies, as is evidenced, for example, in the work of Thompson (1963) and Willis (1977), which brought to the fore the cultural construction of class relations. Marxian concerns are also exemplified in the work on gender that grew out of, and in response to, the research program carried out at the Centre for Contemporary Cultural Studies in Birmingham (CCCS Women's Studies Group, 1978). Finally, there is the view, prominent in the work of Hall (1980, 1982, 1989b) and others, that culture is neither independent nor externally determined, but rather is best viewed as the site of social difference, struggle, and contestation. Indeed, commentators have noted that one of the significant differences between British and American approaches to cultural studies is that the former has adopted a more explicitly Marxian and generally political position. Cultural studies in the United States also contains numerous divisions, but one can conclude that there is a greater tendency for it to draw inspiration from a pluralist conception of society and politics which sees power as widely dispersed, from functionalist anthropology and sociology which concentrate on how cultural practices maintain order and harmony in social life, and from symbolic interactionist social psychology which uses the language of ritual

3. One of the distinguishing characteristics of cultural studies is the tendency to back off from characterizing the field as an academic discipline, in part because it is interested in questioning the foundations of disciplinarity and, in particular, the tendency to create fixed canons of knowledge. As Johnson (1987: 38) puts it, 'cultural studies is a process, a kind of alchemy for producing useful knowledge; codify it and you might halt its reactions.' Raymond Williams (1981b: 53) identified the intellectual origins of cultural studies in questions raised about the canon of English literature:

> So you have in sequence, first, a restriction to printed texts, then a narrowing to what are called 'imaginative' works, and then finally a circumspection to a critically established minority of 'canonical' texts. But also growing alongside this there is another and often more potent specialization: not just Literature, but English Literature.

4. See for example, Long's (1989: 427) critique of what she observes as a tendency to diminish the centrality of feminism in British cultural studies:

> I am struck by the ways in which the summary or presentational statements about British cultural studies that have been made in this country [the U.S.] have already practiced an exclusion that seems to have marginalized its feminist practitioners, ironically the strand of that tradition that has arguably the best chance of maintaining a critical stance in its appropriation by feminist scholars in America, both because of their connections with a broad social movement and because of the nature of their practices within the academy.

and drama to examine the production and reproduction of symbolic communities (Carey, 1979). Cultural studies in the United States has been singled out for its 'affirmative character,' essentially offering apolitical, affirmative assessments of the cultural landscape, and particularly of its audiences (Budd et al., 1990).[5]

Cultural studies can contribute to the process of renewing political economy in several ways. It has taken the lead in constructing a broad-based critique of positivism that foregrounds the subjective and social constitution of knowledge. Starting from the work of Raymond Williams (1961) and Richard Hoggart (1957), cultural studies propelled the shift in literary criticism from the analysis of canonical literature to everyday life.[6] Specifically, these authors aimed to broaden the sense of what comprises the substance of cultural analysis by starting from the premise that culture is the product of ordinary, everyday life, produced by all social actors, rather than only by a privileged elite. Moreover, though this view is contested and emphases shift, cultural studies has maintained that the social is constructed out of gender and nationality divisions and identities as much as by social class.[7]

Political economy can learn from these departures, but it can equally contribute to rethinking cultural studies. Even as it takes on a philosophical approach that is open to subjectivity and more broadly inclusive, political economy insists on a realist epistemology that maintains the value of historical research, of thinking in terms of concrete social totalities, moral commitment, and overcoming the distinction between social research and social practice. It therefore departs from the tendency in cultural studies to what Pêcheux refers to as 'the narcissism of the subject,' as well as the inclination to reject thinking in terms of historical practices and social wholes. Political economy also departs from the tendency in cultural studies to employ a specialized language that belies the original view that cultural

5. In their view, American cultural studies contains five fundamental flaws:

First, it overestimates the freedom of audiences in reception. Second, it minimizes the commodification of audiences as analyzed by a political-economic approach. Third, it fails to differentiate between mass advertising and specialized media. Fourth, it confuses active reception with political activity. Finally, it takes the exceptional situation of progressive readings promoted within oppositional subcultures as the norm. (Budd et al., 1990: 169)

These criticisms are an extension of a century-old debate between historical political economy and interpretivist perspectives within sociology. Carragee (1990) reviews some of its recent manifestations in the work of Gouldner and Giddens, among others, and applies it to debates in communication studies. For a descriptive account of different strands of audience research, see Lindlof (1991).

6. Williams (1981b: 65) squarely attributes the shift to Marxism, 'which instead of privileging a generalized Literature as an independent source of values insists on relating the actual variety of literature to historical processes in which fundamental *conflicts* had necessarily occurred and were still occurring.'

7. Affirming a sociological tradition that replaced class as a fundamental social antagonism with a spectrum of categories, Fiske (1989) provides a list of 'subjectivity positions,' including self, gender, age-group, family, class, nation, and ethnicity.

analysis should be accessible to those ordinary people who are responsible for its social constitution. Finally, it eschews the propensity in cultural studies to reject studies of labor and the labor process in favor of examining the social 'production' of consumption and the consequent tendency to reject labor as holding any value in contemporary movements for social change (Luke, 1989).

Political economy can also learn from the development of a policy science perspective. The latter encompasses a wide range of thinking with two centers of gravity around which orbit a number of diverse perspectives associated with and reacting against these two leading foci. One center privileges a political analysis that places the *state* in the forefront of analysis. The other gives weight to *economic* arguments that aim to extend the application of primarily neoclassical theory over political, social, and cultural life (Posner, 1992; Stigler, 1988). Traditionally, political economy has tended to 'read' the state and other 'superstructural' forces from the specific configuration of capital dominant at the time. It therefore can benefit from an approach that takes seriously the constitutive role of the state. Moreover, political economy shares with policy science the interest in extending analysis over the entire social totality, with an eye to social transformation. Nevertheless, political economy departs fundamentally from the policy science tendency to a pluralist political analysis that views the state as the independent arbiter of a wide balance of social forces, none of which holds sway. Against this, political economy insists on the power of capital and the process of commodification as the starting point of social analysis. Furthermore, political economy rejects the policy studies tendency to build its analysis of the social totality, and of those values that should guide its transformation, on individualism and market-rationality. Against this, it insists on what Garnham (1988: 124), commenting on Raymond Williams, calls 'a concept of social totality in process,' which starts from social processes, such as class formation, and on setting community and public life against the market and against a rationality that actually reproduces class power.

Lessons from the Borders: Cultural Studies

Cultural studies has broadened the range of epistemological approaches beyond positivist and essentialist perspectives to encompass social constructivist approaches to knowledge that have been discussed in earlier chapters and therefore require little further discussion here. Suffice it to say that in the extreme, and post-structuralist work certainly tests the limits of the extreme, social constructivism turns into a relativism that admits of little, if any, analytical or empirical certainty.

From a substantive point of view, cultural studies has sided with the view that culture is ordinary, a product of everyday life that is widely produced, distributed, and consumed. Culture is therefore not limited to those elite practices that have established the cultural orthodoxy for many years. This perspective opened the full range of entertainment and information media, including television sitcoms, mass circulation tabloids, Harlequin romances, and Hollywood blockbusters to legitimate critical analysis. More importantly, it distinguished between *mass*-produced and distributed material and *popular* culture or work created and disseminated under relatively democratic conditions (stressing widespread participation and equality) to achieve democratic goals. Ironically, cultural studies often presents itself in an academicized, i.e., relatively inaccessible, idiom that creates an unnecessary gap between the analysis of culture and those cultural workers and consumers who might benefit most from the analysis. There is no gainsaying the need for conceptual sophistication and certainly no need to apologize for acknowledging that research often requires the use of complex theoretical formulations. But, as numerous commentators have noted, some cultural studies work is so inaccessible, so limited to a specialized academic audience, that any democratic inspiration or aspiration seems to be irretrievably lost.[8] Notwithstanding this problem at the margin, cultural studies reminds political economy that the substance of its work, the analysis of communication, is rooted in the needs, goals, conflicts, failures, and accomplishments of ordinary people aiming to make sense of their lives, even as they confront an institutional and symbolic world that is not entirely of their own making and which, in fact, appears more often than not as an alien force outside of their own control.

Cultural studies has also contributed to the expansion of critical work beyond class analysis to include research inspired by feminism and those newer social movements committed, for example, to peace and environmentalism. This work has served to remind political economy that, though social class is a central dividing line, or, from the perspective adopted here, a starting point, multiple overlapping hierarchies constitute the process of

8. Consider this critique from Harvard Professor of African-American Studies Henry Louis Gates, Jr (1989: 44–45), in which he considers the pitfalls of formal cultural analysis, their 'alienating strategies,' by recounting a painful experience in trying to pass along the canon in the classroom. It is worth a rather lengthy quote:

One of the first talks I ever gave was to a packed audience at a college honors' seminar, and it was one of those mistakes you don't make twice. Fresh out of graduate school, immersed in the arcane technicalities of contemporary literary theory, I was going to deliver a crunchy structuralist analysis of a slave narrative by Frederick Douglass, tracing the intricate play of its 'binary oppositions.' Everything was neatly schematized, formalized, analyzed; this was my Sunday-best structuralism: crisp white shirt and shiny black shoes. And it wasn't playing. If you've seen an audience glaze over, this was double glazing. Bravely, I finished my talk and, of course, asked for questions. 'Yeah, brother,' said a young man in the very back of the room, breaking the silence that ensued, 'all we want to know is, was Booker T. Washington an Uncle Tom or not?'

Later on, Gates realized that this was a very interesting question, 'a lot more interesting than my talk was.' It raised questions about the politics of style, about what it means for one person to speak for another, and about how one distinguishes between co-optation and subtle subversion. In essence, it awakened Gates 'to the yawning chasm between our critical discourse and the traditions they discourse upon,' to the gap between the text and the experience to which it gives rise.

structuration. Moreover, though its extreme formulations celebrate the politics of contemporary life as a search for particular identities that fragment oppositional politics, cultural studies has recognized the energizing potential of multifaceted forms of social agency, each of which brings with it dimensions of subjectivity and consciousness that are vital to political praxis and which have received too little treatment in political economic analysis.[9] Political economy has been understandably preoccupied with the multifaceted ways in which culture is produced or structured as a result of dynamic imperatives to commodification. Cultural studies reminds political economy to incorporate, in Johnson's (1987: 55) words, 'the indirect results of capitalist and other social relations on the existing rules of language and discourse, especially class and gender-based struggles in their effects on different social symbols and signs.' Cultural studies approaches implicitly recognize the futility of relying on the outcome of the logic of capital or of organizing resistance solely around class divisions. Unfortunately, in its haste to turn to new forms of social geometry and resistance, cultural studies has tended, with important exceptions, to simply reject outright those older forms, based on class and, specifically, wage-labor, whose centrality for comprehending and transforming social life political economy quite rightly warrants.

   Political economy has concentrated on the macrosocial organization of power and has developed the methodologies to address it. Though cultural studies has, with exceptions, not given the same consideration to power, when it does so, the approach tends to shift attention to the local organization of power, concentrating on how power mutually constitutes inter-subjectivity. Moreover, though some streams of cultural studies focus almost exclusively on texts, choosing to 'read the social' from its textual embodiments, others have drawn from traditional ethnographic methodologies to understand, particularly, the social relations of textual, including media, reception and use (Morley, 1986; Radway, 1988). This observational turn has not gone without criticism, particularly for inadequacies in the application of ethnographic techniques and for generalizing from limited evidence. For example, Evans (1990: 154) argues that much of this research 'typically does not stem from traditional ethnographic techniques.' Rather, he maintains, it 'consists of one-time, open-ended interviews of the self-report variety, infrequently accompanied by any systematic observation of the anthropological variety.' Moreover, Carragee (1990) takes ethnographies to

---

9. Cultural studies is often defined specifically in these terms. According to Johnson (1987: 43), for example, 'cultural studies is about the historical forms of consciousness or subjectivity, or the subjective forms we live by, or, in a rather perilous compression, perhaps a reduction, the subjective side of social relations.' Johnson goes on to make the connection between this definition and the Marx–Engels tradition, particularly the early work such as *The German Ideology*. Later on (p. 62), he notes, in a formulation quite congenial to my conception of political economy, that 'the ultimate object of cultural studies is not, in my view, the text, but *the social life of subjective forms* at each moment of their circulation, including their textual embodiments.'

task for leaping from what he agrees is less than systematic methodology to the conclusion that viewers and audiences are as much the producers of texts as are the companies that originate and distribute them. Notwithstanding this valuable critique, by reminding us that power is also local and inter-subjective, and, as well, accessible through observational techniques, cultural studies enriches the political economic understanding of power.[10] Furthermore, it is evident that some who advance an ethnographic approach to cultural studies recognize its limitations and call for making connections between the global and the local:

> an ethnographic perspective suitable for and sensitive to the peculiarities of our contemporary cultural condition needs to move beyond the restrictive scope delimited by the boundaries of the local, and to develop an awareness of the pertinent asymmetries between production/distribution and consumption, the general and the particular, the global and the local. (Ang, 1990: 251).

Lessons from the Borders: Policy Studies

Policy studies has drawn primarily on pluralist political science and neo-classical economics research to analyze and evaluate alternative courses of action, including communication. A leading wing of this approach, *public choice theory*, known also as *positive political economy* or the *rational expectations* approach, is an explicit attempt to apply the tools of orthodox economic research to political science with the aim of creating a policy science (Alt and Shepsle, 1990; Brennan and Buchanan, 1985; Buchanan, 1986; Buchanan and Tollison, 1984; Posner, 1992; Stigler, 1988). Specifically, public choice aims to constitute a science whose coordinates are the market, individual choice, and private self-interest. The market provides the structural model for all collective activity, including that of businesses, governments, voluntary associations, interest groups, and families. Normative judgements are based on how well such activity models the maps of perfect markets featured as ideal types in economic theory. Collectivities are reducible to the sum total of individual choices which, notwithstanding how they are described, explained, and justified, reflect private self-interest. There is no society or social group *sui generis*, no sum greater than the parts. Studying individuals therefore yields data on the behavior of collectivities because structures are nothing more than convenient fictions for individuals pursuing similar interests. Finally, the approach privileges private over public interests because it starts from the view that people are, above all else, pursuers of private self-interest. According to Buchanan's (1986: 6) assessment of the primary 'teachings of public choice theory': 'persons in politics are like persons elsewhere, including the market, ... they remain pursuers of their own private and individualized interests, despicable as these might be.' Accordingly, he maintains that social order results from the ongoing process of individual utility maximization realized through the choices of

---

10. For a political economic reflection on ethnography, see Pendakur (1993).

participants across the range of relatively imperfect markets that constitute social life. Public choice theory impels policy studies to take up the normative or moral warrant in order to improve the marketness of social life because this is how people best realize self-interest. For example, from this point of view, policy studies should be taken up with producing strategies for the reduction of those transaction, information, and opportunity costs incurred in the process of choice (Alt and Shepsle, 1990).[11]

Public choice theory has grown across a range of disciplines and achieved a significant measure of general attention as a few of its leading practitioners have been awarded the Nobel Prize in economics.[12] Its success has emboldened leading proponents, such as Mancur Olson, to call for the development of a unified social science, collapsing all traditional disciplines into public choice theory (Olson, 1990). Generally aligned with conservative viewpoints, public choice theory has impressed a diverse collection of scholars, including those advancing a Marxian analysis.[13] The approach is increasingly applied to empirical studies of general social behavior, including studies of the family and sexuality (Posner, 1992). Consequently, though public choice theory is only one of several ways of thinking about policy, in the view of some, it is now, or is on its way to becoming, the leading approach in the field.[14] Over the years, the approach has exerted an influence on communication studies through the application to policy questions bearing on such subjects as the value of the radio spectrum and appropriate policies to distribute it, the extent of staff 'capture' of regulatory agencies, and the costs and consequences of deregulation (Coase, 1991; Crandall, 1991; Derthick and Quirk, 1985; Stigler, 1971; Wilson, 1980).

Policy studies can offer several lessons to a political economic approach to communication. Drawing on the tradition of pluralist political science, most applications of policy studies start from the view that a multiplicity of relatively equal participants are directly involved in the policy process and that one needs to address the specific interests and actions of each to present a full picture of how policy is formed.[15] It tends to resist arguments that maintain, for example, that the logic of capital (or any other singularity) drives policy and therefore reduces particular interests and actions to the

11. Transaction costs are those incurred in the process of exchange such as the costs of bringing together a buyer and seller. Information costs are those associated with securing knowledge about products, people, and markets necessary to make the best choice. Opportunity or 'sunk' costs are those incurred in previous choices which constrain present choices.

12. Recent public choice theory winners include George J. Stigler, James M. Buchanan, Ronald Coase, and Robert E. Lucas.

13. Leading examples of what is best known as 'rational choice Marxism' include the work of Elster (1985), Przeworski (1986) and Roemer (1982). For critical overviews see Kieve (1986) and Wood (1989).

14. There are several journals that feature public choice research. In keeping with the goal of replacing heterodox political economy with a contemporary version of classical economics, a leading outlet is called *The Journal of Political Economy*.

15. For an application to communication studies see Derthick and Quirk (1985) and Krasnow et al. (1982).

level of necessary articulations of that logic. Policy studies does tend to the extreme of a pluralism subject to no overall tendencies, a kind of interest group anarchy which political economy, quite correctly, takes to task. However, recent work has aimed to correct this, in part by introducing a wider theoretical framework such as, for example, in well-known pluralist Charles Lindblom's incorporation of the insights of critical theorists like Habermas. The goal, as de Haven-Smith (1988: 120) concludes, is to strengthen the base of policy studies by interrogating what policy analysts once took as self-evident:

> In designing the methodology of policy research, policy analysts made a funda-
> mental error. They assumed that the subject matter of policy research could be
> identified independent of a theoretical framework. This methodological assump-
> tion enabled policy analysts to set as their goal the evaluation of 'program
> performance.' What it ignored is that neither programs nor performance indicators
> are self-evident.

[handwritten margin note: masked moral assump.]

Hawkesworth (1988) takes this a step further by calling on policy studies to overcome the fact–value dichotomy that 'sanctions a clear division of labor between the policy analyst and the political decision-maker' (p. 4) chiefly because it has reduced much of the field to a 'depoliticizing scientism' (p. 10). The alternative, he maintains, is a 'post-positivist' analysis that engages in a 'sustained, critical examination of the political implications of contestable policy presuppositions' (p. 9), thereby creating a 'democratic science' in which 'more is examined and less is assumed' (p. 191). Just how policy studies resolves these issues is not central to this chapter. It is more important to recognize that the overall commitment to specific, concrete analyses of clashing interests offers important lessons for a political economy that sometimes reads specific outcomes simply from a thought-experiment on the logical outcome of capitalist processes.[16]

The political wing of the policy studies approach contains a strong pluralist tendency to address the state as a complex apparatus of competing interests, actively involved in the policy-making process. For example, it mattered to a policy studies approach that in the United States the White House created the Office of Telecommunication Policy in 1970, partly out of concern in the Nixon Administration that the communication regulatory authority, the Federal Communications Commission, was not responding sufficiently to its conservative agenda. Nixon people wanted to end what they perceived to be a liberal bias in public broadcasting and, more generally, to reconstitute the established public interest standard along technocratic and market lines. The cooperation and conflict between government agencies helped to shape the state's response to the transformation of media and telecommunication in the next two decades (which saw upheavals that influenced the structure and power of these agencies as well). Again, there is a tendency for policy studies to overemphasize the state and,

16. For another effort to broaden this area of policy studies applied specifically to communication studies, see Brennan (1992).

particularly, the formal legal-regulatory system for addressing policy issues. This tendency to formalism and an 'end-game' approach neglects the wide-ranging sources and uses of power outside the legal-regulatory apparatus and the extensive incubation and development process that shapes issues before they reach the formal stage of state consideration. Nevertheless, policy studies is instructive for political economy because it reminds the latter to resist the tendencies to economism that would read policy decisions from industry structure alone.

There are also lessons to be learned from the public choice, or economic wing, of policy studies, particularly from its enthusiastic embrace of a broad range of significant questions that have traditionally occupied psychologists, sociologists, political scientists, as well as economists, but which have fallen out of favor as these disciplines have pursued a limited warrant. Not content to remain within the traditional domain of economics, public choice theory has taken the methodological individualism and positivism of traditional economics and applied it to understand decision-making processes in the family, the state, and religious organizations over the widest range of questions, encompassing sexuality, bureaucracy, family structure, budgets, etc. Moreover, this approach has not shied away from normative and moral questions that, not too long ago, would have been off limits for mainstream social science, but which today take center stage for policy analysts, particularly those in the public choice school. Returning to the values, if not to the precise methodological strategy, that impelled Adam Smith and other classical political economists to take up a wide scope, including central moral issues of their time, they approach the social with the spirit of pioneers who challenge the timidity of social scientific modernism and the consequent failure to address many of the major social and moral issues of our time.[17] Though open to criticism for how they approach these issues, e.g. taking methodological individualism to the extreme and viewing the state as an independent arbiter of competing interests, the policy studies approach speaks to a political economy of communication that would reverse research tendencies that reward ever-narrower projects and build walls between social science and moral philosophy.

There are important political consequences that stem from efforts to stress universalism and commonality over fragmentation and division. Gitlin (1993), among others, has noted the proclivity among those associated with left of center political movements to concentrate on the politics of identity, which tends to accentuate those characteristics that distinguish groups marked by gender, race, ethnicity, age or sexual preference. This understandable effort to overcome second-class status within society, and within the Left, has resulted, according to Gitlin, in 'a politics that is rooted more in group self-assertion than in attempts to create broad alliances.' Identity

17. This pioneering spirit is particularly evident in the work of Brennan and Buchanan (1985), who view their project of moral reconstitution as nothing short of aiming to create a new 'civic religion' in America.

politics has energized a wide range of diverse political and intellectual movements. But it has also helped to reverse traditional Left–Right politics. The Left, which once stood firmly behind universalism, however flawed, now promotes a range of fragmented interests. Whereas the Right, which traditionally advanced what amounted to the particularistic standards of elites, now, with a firm base established in the Reagan–Thatcher era, confidently promotes a universalistic conservative populism.

Responses from Political Economy

Political economy offers important lessons that apply individually to policy studies and cultural studies, but it is particularly valuable to begin with those it has to offer both, starting with the centrality of *power* in the analysis of communication. Political economy departs from policy studies and cultural studies in several ways, particularly by giving considerable weight to power, understood as both a resource to achieve goals and an instrument of control within social hierarchies. Pluralism, the central political tendency within policy studies, treats power as a widely dispersed resource that is more or less accessible to all interests operating within the political arena (Derthick and Quirk, 1985). The distribution of power may be significant for particular cases, favoring, for example, broadcasters in some issues, telecommunication firms in others, and consumer groups in still others, but, according to this view, there is no structural tendency for power to be concentrated in one group or interest. From the pluralist viewpoint, it follows that power, generally diffused throughout society, is not at all a central formative influence.

Political economy agrees that it is useful to think of power as a resource, as well as a form of control, but differs significantly on the place of power in its overall analysis. Political economy thinks of power as a resource that is *structured* or rooted in what Mahon (1980) has called an 'unequal structure of representation,' a feature built into a system that rewards market position with privileged status within social hierarchies. Moreover, power is more than a resource – it is also a form of *control* that is used to preserve such privileged status against challengers. Though, in practice, policy studies and political economy overlap, it is intellectually clarifying to suggest an essential ontological difference in how the two disciplines view power. Policy studies views power as diffused and dispersed, one among many forces at work in the social field. Political economy sees it as congealed and structured, a central force in shaping the social field.[18]

18. Compare, for example, any of the numerous political economy analyses of media ownership and concentration with what little appears on this perspective in the public choice literature. Power, in its numerous manifestations, is central to the former, and virtually disappears from the latter (Demsetz and Lehn, 1985).

Cultural studies has certainly not ignored power and presents a variety of ways of seeing it, particularly emphasizing its personal, local, and inter-subjective dimensions. Nevertheless, there is a tendency for cultural studies to approach power in ways that put it in closer company with policy studies than with political economy. Culturalist perspectives do not place power at the center of their fundamental way of thinking about social relations. Moreover, their conception of power tends to be rooted in individual subjectivities, their identities, and collective action, rather than, as political economy would have it, structured in the institutions of society. Cultural studies tends to step back from conceptions of structure and, in extreme formulations (Laclau and Mouffe, 1985), tends to resist notions of society and social unity, even those presented with caution and contingency.

Political economy responds by reaffirming the value of theorizing the social totality not as the abstract and idealistic conception that systems theory defends, but rather as the concrete manifestation of mutual interests and structures of power. Acknowledging the value of thinking about the subjective dimensions of power, political economy, nevertheless, maintains that these are mutually constituted with objective conceptions of power that derive from the fundamental rules governing structures in society.

It is interesting to observe that policy studies and cultural studies, in effect, share a perspective on media content diversity. In their own particular ways, each conflates diversity with multiplicity and tends to discount the view that diversity is difficult to achieve or generally refuses to concede that it requires concerted political action. Among the many tendencies that constitute positions within policy studies, one of the central points of view is that content diversity can be equated with the sheer *number* of voices in the market or the community. This point of view opposes media concentration on the grounds that it restricts the flow of information and entertainment, but tends to be satisfied with remedies that expand the multiplicity of marketplace competitors. For example, the typical policy studies response to state monopoly control of broadcast channels in Europe is to license private carriers. Its standard response to private monopoly control of North American telecommunication is to support one or a few competitors. Its leading measures of concentration assess the number of producers and distributors in the marketplace to determine whether the market has enough voices to constitute sufficient competitive alternatives. Put simply, policy studies *equates diversity with multiplicity*. It is only on the outskirts of policy studies, where the discipline meets critical theories of the state and the political economy literature, that one begins to find a sustained effort to unhinge the link between what is viewed, in these heterodox formulations, as the fundamental difference between the sheer number of voices (multi-plicity) and the number of *different* voices (diversity). Orthodox policy studies argues that diversity tends to flow necessarily from the presence of competing units. From this vantage point, diversity is relatively easy to achieve – simply increase the number of units, of producers and distributors. There is little interest in addressing the thornier problem posed by the conclusion of the political economy literature: however numerous, producers offer and distributors deliver essentially the same messages – multiplicity does not necessarily lead to diversity. The introduction of Rupert Murdoch's Fox network in the United States promoted more voices into a marketplace led by the oligopoly of ABC, CBS, and NBC. But a political economic view questions whether the news and entertainment which it delivers differs in any fundamental way from standard network fare and consequently contends that there is no net gain, or little, in expanding the number of media voices without any guarantee of increased diversity.

In spite of differences in the general epistemological, theoretical, and substantive positions that cultural studies approaches to communication present in comparison with policy studies, they offer similar conclusions about the politics of media diversity.[19] Starting from the different vantage point of the audience, cultural studies approaches come to generally the same conclusion: media diversity is not a substantial problem because information and entertainment are *polysemic* or subject to multiple readings and interpretations that, in essence, create their own diversity, whatever the number of formal producers and distributors. The tendency in cultural studies is to see every recipient of a message as a producer, assigning a different meaning, partly a function of the receiver's particular 'subjectivity position' (to use Fiske's term) within the overlapping identities that make up social life. Media concentration does not restrict diversity because the interpretive range is not a function of who formally produces and distributes news, drama, comedy, etc. Rather, the wide range of subjective experiences that audiences bring to communication and information products produce textual diversity. This tendency in cultural studies responds to the twin problems of economism and productivism which, it maintains, confound political economy. In this context, and with notable exceptions, cultural studies sees economism as the tendency to read texts from the logic, structure, and dynamics of capital. A specific form of economism, *productivism*, reads the text from the circuit of capital that makes up the process of production.[20]

Political economy acknowledges with policy studies that additional providers can expand the number of messages, and political economists have intervened in the policy process to accomplish this. Moreover, it agrees with cultural studies that one cannot read a single audience response from a news

19. Wood (1989) argues that the similarities between public choice theory and post-structuralism are considerably greater than most commentators have adduced.

20. Hall's work reflects an exceptional ambivalence on this subject. In some of his work, he assigns powers to capital that defenders of cultural studies would have a hard time distinguishing from work they criticize as economistic. For example, he (1986: 11) has suggested that 'ownership and control' is sufficiently important that it 'gives the whole machinery of representation its fundamental orientation in the value-system of property and profit.' Capital, according to Hall, is so powerful that 'it prevents new kinds of grouping, new social purposes and new forms of control from entering, in a central way, into the production of culture.' In other work (1989a: 50), he is sharply critical, charging political economy with 'crudity and reductionism' and for having 'no conception of the struggle for meaning.'

or entertainment program. Nevertheless, political economy insists that a thorough understanding of how the process of commodification influences circuits of production, distribution, and consumption is vital to comprehending culture. Policy studies, from its various theoretical standpoints, recognizes this as well. Unfortunately, cultural studies has suffered because its comprehension of economics and of political economy is painfully limited. It has documented very little understanding of the depth, complexity, range of fault lines, and overall diversity of orthodox and heterodox economic and political economic arguments. As a result, rather than address them on their own terms, cultural studies has done little more than reject economic arguments on what amount to categorical grounds. Economic arguments are dismissed because they are economistic. The economic process of producing culture is set aside as productivist. This is particularly unfortunate because such a rejectionist position undermines insights that might otherwise contribute to the creation of useful zones of engagement with those starting from a political economic position. Consider this critique of productivism:

> The text-as-produced is a different object from the text-as-read. The problem with Adorno's analysis and perhaps productivist approaches in general is not only that they infer the text-as-read from the text-as-produced, but that also, in doing this, they ignore the elements of production in other moments, concentrating 'creativity' in producer or critic. Perhaps this is the deepest prejudice of all among the writers, the artists, the teachers, the educators, the communicators and the agitators within the intellectual divisions of labor! (Johnson, 1987: 58)

Political economy has no quarrel with the view that the text is different as produced and as read. Nor does it contend with the view that readers produce meaning. Furthermore, political economists have not retreated from examining contemporary media, from the traditional arts contained in museums and concert halls to the new media of the 'Information Society,' as fundamentally *cultural* forces (Babe, 1994; Schiller, 1989; Webster and Robins, 1989). Moreover, political economists have come to recognize the value of ethnographic methods that help to document the social experience of reading, listening, and viewing mass media (Pendakur, 1993). So far, so good. But to move from here to identify the ostensible conflation of writer with producer, as arguably the 'deepest prejudice' of a litany of knowledge workers, is a monumental overstatement.[21] *Audiences are not passive, but neither are producers dumb.* As Murdock (1989a: 439) has noted, this

21. To be fair, Johnson (1987: 67) also attacks the conception of the reader in most formalist cultural analyses:

> The absence of action by the reader is characteristic of formalist accounts. Even those theorists . . . who are concerned with productive, deconstructive or critical reading ascribe this capacity to types of text (e.g. 'writable' rather than 'readable' in Barthes' terminology) and not at all to a history of real readers. . . . At best particular acts of reading are understood as a replaying of primary human experiences.

Evans (1990: 152) expands on this point by noting that many of the social scientific approaches claiming an interpretive understanding of readers and audiences offer little more than warmed-over psychologism.

unfortunate leap from suggesting a grounds for debate to outright rejection-ism is all too prominent in some forms of cultural studies (Carey, 1994; Grossberg, 1991).[22] It neglects the interesting questions, such as, just how powerful are readers and audiences as producers of texts? To what degree can and do producers of texts act on the range of anticipated reader and audience responses? What is the relationship between control over the means of producing texts and the production of meaning? What is the relationship between location in social structure and location in the produc-tion of meaning?[23] What sorts of resources are required for opposition and alternatives to arise in the face of what Bakhtin referred to as the 'monologic discourse' of the cultural industry? These are areas that, once one stands back from rejectionist positions, offer grounds for useful exchange. However tempting, it is not enough to provide what amounts to 'a romantic celebra-tion of the individual's power to evaluate media content critically and consciously' (Evans, 1990: 152).[24] For example, the political economy approach accepts polysemy and the multiple production of texts, recognizes the need to analyze the full circuit of production, distribution, and consump-tion, and sees these as central moments in the realization of value and the construction of social life.[25] Nevertheless, political economy disagrees with the conclusion that diversity is the natural consequence of the multiplicity either of media units or of audiences. Many media units can nevertheless offer fundamentally the same media substance and form. Audience resist-ance, as Modleski (1986) maintains, is inscribed within limits established by the media industries. Moreover, one result of the focus on audience activity as the paramount social activity is to inflate what little social action is

22. With what Kellner (1995: 42) describes as degenerative consequences for cultural studies:

Neglecting political economy, celebrating the audience and the pleasures of the popular, neglecting social class and ideology, and failing to analyze or criticize the politics of cultural texts will make cultural studies merely another academic subdivision, harmless and ultimately of benefit primarily to the culture industries themselves.

23. Evans (1990: 150) puts this another way:

Except for the earlier-discussed hypodermic model, no tradition in mass communication research posits a passive audience. Thus, the real difference is not a question of active versus passive but rather the postulation of one kind of activity versus another kind.

24. Evans is certainly not alone in raising concerns about the romanticism and sentimentali-zation contained in weakly supported analyses of audience power and playfulness. See Schiller (1989) and Schudson (1987). It is also the case, as Murdock (1989a: 437) has noted, that even the first wave of cultural studies, including the work of Hoggart and Williams, 'was suffused with nostalgia for worlds that were rapidly disappearing' and 'was also tinged by a romantic evaluation of the "authenticity" of these vanishing ways of life . . . .'

25. As Evans (1990: 148) notes, cultural studies differentiates itself from traditional approaches, by criticizing 'hypodermic models' of media effects, which ostensibly warrant the view that media can be injected drug-like into an audience to produce desired impacts. But 'those guilty of employing hypodermic models are seldom named; in fact, some scholars suspect that the hypodermic model was never a serious tradition in the discipline and that this direct-effects model has been invoked largely as a polemical strawman against which other positions would easily seem more sophisticated.'

encountered beyond reasonable levels of significance. For example, viewer interpretations of television programs that do not conform to surface readings or heterodox uses of advertising material become significant acts of resistance, or evidence of an oppositional consciousness, even when, as Miller (1988) has noted, such acts are contained within the wider scope of marketing irony, i.e., using the viewer's sophisticated sense of the ploy as a means to create mutual identification. This tendency, marked most explicitly in the turn to post-structuralism, has encountered strong resistance from a wide range of critics (Ahmad, 1992; Norris, 1992; Palmer, 1990).

Moreover, the very term *audience* is not an analytical category, like class, gender or race, but a product of the media industry itself, which uses the term to identify markets and to define a commodity. References to audience activity give the term an analytical and experiential reality that has not been documented and which should therefore warrant greater care in use. At the very least, it is premature to assert that the demographic category 'audiences' *act* when we have not established the conceptual value of the term, particularly its relationship to social class, race, ethnicity, and gender, which are more than demographic groupings – they are lived experiences. People, organized as social actors in various class, gender, race and other social dimensions, carry out activities, including resistance to media presentations, the significance of which is an empirical question testable through a range of procedures. Media power, which gives those with control over markets the ability to fill channels with material embodying their interests, tends to structure the substance and form of polysemy, thereby limiting the diversity of interpretations to certain repeated central tendencies that stand out among the range of possibilities, including those marginalized few that diverge substantially from the norm. Far from rejecting oppositional readings categorically, as those who charge that economism and productivism are the contemporary version of the hypodermic model (see Grossberg, 1991 and footnote 25 above), political economy situates these readings within the specific power-geometry identified by the coordinates of commodification, spatialization, and structuration.[26]

Political economy also offers responses to the specific criticisms that arise individually from policy studies and cultural studies. In particular, it provides a corrective to instrumentalist, statist, and economistic tendencies within policy studies. Policy studies tends to instrumentalist explanations that address the process of policy formation by describing the actions of groups that pressure the state to act according to their interests. It maintains that policy is a function of who succeeds in using the state as an instrument to accomplish specific goals. According to this view, one might explain the trends to liberalization and deregulation of telecommunication as a result of the ability of large business users to capture the state policy apparatus and

26. Political economy prefers this to a position, prominent in much of cultural studies, conveying the sense of a free-floating opposition that, in Evans' (1990: 149) assessment, 'gives the impression that *non*hegemonic audience response is rather commonplace.'

make it an instrument to achieve their goals of creating low-cost, customized networks and services to meet their growing business needs. Similarly, an instrumentalist explains the growth in the power and profit of cable television firms as a consequence of the industry's ability to lobby and outmuscle broadcasters, consumer groups, and others to shape government policy in their interest.

Political economy acknowledges the value of such instrumentalist analyses, but aims to deeper levels of understanding that start from locating the communication industry within the wider totality of capitalist social relations. Specifically, this means situating the various components of the communication industry, the state regulatory and policy apparatus, and civil society groups within the domestic and international political economies that mutually constitute them. In order to understand the specific way in which the liberalization of telecommunication systems has been carried out, in various nations and regions, political economy calls for examining those forces in the domestic and international political economies that pressed large business users to develop both the understanding and organizational capacity to intervene on an unprecedented scale in the policy process; the forces at work within and around state systems that made them more receptive to change, including, for example, the development of activist elements within state agencies that broke with the traditional linkages between the state and monopoly telecommunication providers; the forces that opened divisions within civil society groups, with some pressing traditional concerns for public interest regulation and others joining the cause of large users by viewing competitive entry as the best vehicle to bring about industry change. In essence, political economy argues that understanding *how* requires more than comprehending *who* does *what* to *whom*. Moreover, *how* alone does not explain the process. This is accomplished by determining *why* actions take place, and this demands locating communication policy within the general political economy, including historical and contemporary tendencies. Finally, political economy moves beyond instrumentalism by calling for a critical understanding of the policy process, one that connects a structural and historical understanding to a set of values or a moral philosophical standpoint that assesses the process for its contribution to democracy, equality, participation, fairness, and justice. This valuational stance also helps to lift policy analysis out of its narrow, descriptive, and positivist tendencies by connecting the analysis of policy to the politics of changing it.

Political economy also affirms the need to balance tendencies in policy studies that give excessive emphasis to either the political or the economic dimensions. In the former, or *statist* approaches to policy studies, one proceeds on the assumption, varying with different degrees of emphasis, that ultimate decision-making authority resides with the state. This authority can be formal, denoting state legal control over the process of decision-making, and/or substantive, referring to the state's power over decision-making content. In the case of either or both, policy studies presumes that power resides with the state, so that even when it concludes that the state is 'captured' by some external (the industry) or internal (its own staff) group that makes the state its instrument, policy studies insists that it is the state which holds the power that one must capture in order to accomplish policy goals. The result is a tendency to focus almost entirely on the state, including its regulatory, legislative, executive, and juridical arms, to view it as the center of a decision-making universe that determines the structure of the industry, shapes its capabilities, including prices, services, and revenues, and sets the terms for consumer and public intervention. In essence, the standard statist approach to policy studies views the state as the power that determines the laws of motion of the policy-making process.

Partially in response to this, the public choice wing of policy studies tends to the opposite extreme, offering an economistic view of the policy process that replaces the institutional language of political structure and power with the economic language of markets, utilities, and preferences. Treating the policy arena as a marketplace that registers the wants of 'buyers' looking for favorable decisions and 'sellers' who can offer policy outputs, the public choice approach follows neoclassical economic models that aim to ascertain the equilibrium position where the preferences of policy actors presumably meet at the margins. One consequence of this position is a tendency to view the state simply as the repository of whatever is imperfect, inadequate, or simply wrong with the competitive market system. For Becker (1975), the burdens of administration and procedure leave the state with a tendency to mounting 'dead weight costs.' Peltzman (1975) argues that the growth of the state can be traced to the rise of special interest groups that feed on, what he perceives to be, the growing entitlement to egalitarianism in Western society. Finally, Stigler (1988) claims that even those state agencies, such as regulatory authorities, which ostensibly arise to correct market failures are really nothing more than inadequate instruments to redistribute income and accumulate power for regulators themselves.[27]

Political economy acknowledges the merit of both statist and economistic tendencies. It credits the former with identifying the independent significance of the state in the policy process against strands of political economy that simply 'read' policy decisions from the logic of capital. It also understands the public choice attempt to introduce the language of economics and thereby attenuate statism in policy studies. Nevertheless, political economy aims to rectify statist and economistic tendencies because they are partial, sacrificing critical elements of either the political or the economic, by starting from the mutual constitution of the political and the economic. Neither is the essential key to the policy process; both are required for a

27. In a confidence characteristic of public choice theorists, Stigler (1988: xiii) brushes aside the need to document this view of regulation:

This change in the fundamental role of regulation is so widely accepted, and so copiously documented, that it would be pedantic to cite the vast and growing host of supporting studies.

complete understanding. Concretely, this means resisting the temptation to view policy as essentially political because formal authority for the legal-regulatory regime resides with state agencies. Formal authority is only one form of power and is often relevant for little more than providing legitimacy for decisions arrived at outside the regulatory process. For example, different forces within business and the academic/intellectual community provided an enormous impetus for the adoption of measures that transformed electronic media and telecommunication through commercialization, privatization, liberalization, and internationalization. This pressure mounted to such an intensity that state adoption of these measures, though contested and significant, was, nevertheless, anticlimactic. Much of the policy research, assessment of alternatives, planning, and debate took place prior to, or parallel with, but generally *outside* the realm of formal legislative and regulatory consideration. Because of its tendency to concentrate on state-centered activities, much of the literature in policy studies tends to ignore or, at best, understate these developments. Political economy aims to correct the statist tendency by expanding the conception of the policy process to include those developments that take place outside the realm of formal state activity, including, for example, the activities of policy research and planning centers, the organization of corporate, trade unionist, consumer, and civil society groups to seize the policy agenda, including how and when policy issues will appear on the state's agenda and how policy decisions will be implemented. In sum, political economy responds to statist approaches by broadening the base of policy analysis, particularly by incorporating those social and economic actors and forces that mutually constitute the political process.

Similarly, political economy aims to correct the particular economistic tendency that public choice approaches bring to bear on policy studies. Specifically, though it acknowledges the value of introducing the economic, political economy rejects the tendency to incorporate the language and assumptions of neoclassical economics, which understates, or ignores entirely, the exercise of power, the influence of institutional actors, and the formation of social relations that structure individual choice. Moreover, political economy critiques the value of universalizing market models to analyze policy problems and impel solutions. Precisely questioning fundamental public choice assumptions, political economy raises a skeptical eye to the presumed existence of markets, the ability to create them, as well as their contestability. It furthermore questions the neutrality of markets, their responsiveness to incentives, and their presumed efficiency (Hula, 1988). Acknowledging the value of identifying the social costs of regulation, political economy reminds public choice theorists that there are social costs to competition that public choice analysts have either ignored or made little more than a half-hearted attempt to determine and evaluate. In essence, drawing on its general critique of neoclassical economics, political economy concludes that since the approach is fundamentally flawed, one can confidently expect to discern flaws in its application to policy studies. In the place of public choice economism, political economy brings to policy studies a broad-based analysis that centrally includes the processes of commodification, spatialization, and structuration which inform political economy in general. Specifically, it argues in favor of situating the policy process and its actors within the wider context shaped by the current state of commodification, the institutional map that constitutes the spatialization process, and the configuration of the social relations of class, gender, and race, as well as the social movements and processes of hegemony that make up structuration. Although markets, individual preference, and choice play a part in the economic dimension of policy studies, they do so only as dimensions of a wider economic process that political economy provides.

Political economy addresses several responses to the direct and implicit critiques served up by cultural studies. Though there are important political elements in some tendencies within cultural studies, particularly those emanating from Britain and Latin America, the approach has generally lacked a political focus, a sense of political projects and purposes which, over many years, however fiercely contested, have been a central driving force in political economy. There is no denying that political economy, including its application to communication studies, has been a contested terrain, with many different political tendencies aiming to gain the intellectual and political upper hand. But few within or, for that matter, outside the discipline, dating back to the time of its classical founders, would also decline to acknowledge that political economy is a distinctly political discipline, i.e., one that blurs, or eliminates entirely, the distinction between analysis and intervention. This is why praxis is identified among the vital components of a political economy approach.

In its entirety, cultural studies is less than clear about its commitment to political projects and purposes. The discipline is not without those who argue in favor of a political objective that, though different, is no less explicit than what political economy offers. Such thinking tends to shift the focus of political purpose away from social class, to gender, race, and other forms of identity, and to those new social movements that cross class lines to contend over such issues as the environment, feminism, and world peace. According to this view, by concentrating on those cultural practices and values that constitute social identities and divisions, cultural studies contributes to understanding the central features of the dominant hegemony, such as the authoritarian populism that brought so much of the working class into the Thatcher–Reagan fold, and also advances the formation of popular oppositional and alternative movements. But this view is not universally upheld within cultural studies. Some of its practitioners are considerably more ambiguous about its politics, arguing that cultural studies research contains less certain links to a specific political project, or that the primary, if not the only, political activity within cultural studies is the act of research itself. Reflecting on the political uncertainty within cultural studies, Jameson (1989: 43) wonders whether the approach is most comfortable identifying with 'an anarchist and populist spirit' that responds enthusiastically to what

Featherstone and others perceive to be 'a more democratic and culturally literate public everywhere in the world today.'[28] Finally, there are those, particularly identifying with post-structuralism, whose view of reality is limited to the construction of texts and discourse. These tend to dismiss any links between the process or substance of research and the political domain. However accurately this description conveys a sense of the range of views, the divisions within cultural studies are not this neatly compartmentalized. Suffice it to say, cultural studies is an enterprise that is entirely more uncertain about its political connections than is political economy.

Cultural studies is also considerably more uncertain about one of the central substantive goals of a political economy approach: understanding social totalities. Tetzlaff (1991: 10) argues that this tendency is rooted in a general tendency in cultural studies, most pronounced in post-structuralism and postmodernism, to equate unification with conceptions of social control and liberation with 'the fragmentation of this unity.'[29] Political economy tends to argue that the social totality exists not so much as a theoretical abstraction that can be necessarily read off the inherent characteristics of systems, but more specifically as the concrete manifestation of empirically observable social relations, specifically those operating within capitalism.[30] Capitalism is understood as a particular social whole constituted out of social processes whose starting points are commodification, spatialization, and structuration. These provide one means of comprehending capitalism as a concrete social totality, meaning a specific configuration of interrelated social processes. The nature of the configuration, and of the relationships among processes, is dynamic and therefore not absolutely specifiable, but it is the goal of political economy to describe, as adequately as its tools permit, both the state of the social totality and the direction in which its primary processes are taking it. Consequently, though political economy is open to a wide range of characterizations of the social whole and of the nature, form, and strength of the relationships that constitute the totality, the discipline maintains that understanding the social totality is unmistakably central to its substantive project.

Cultural studies is considerably less certain about the value of pursuing the social totality, because it doubts the empirical reality and theoretical usefulness of the concept. Preferring to concentrate on concepts like cultural

28. It is interesting to observe the support for anarchism from within both cultural studies and the economic wing of policy studies. Both appear to celebrate individual acts of what are interpreted to be resistance to power, particularly to the institutional power of national governments and corporate monopolists. It is also instructive to observe how Jameson distances himself from this position, acknowledging as accurate the criticism directed at his inability to celebrate the 'new anarchism' with sufficient enthusiasm.

29. This is in keeping with Lyotard's (1984) definition of the postmodern as 'incredulity toward metanarratives.'

30. Even a defender of formalism, including post-structuralism, must admit, with reference to Roland Barthes, that 'Barthes' "History" is suspiciously capitalized and emptied of content: unlike Marxism, semiology does not present us with a practice (unless it be Barthes' little essays) for reconstituting a complex whole from the different forms' (Johnson, 1987: 60).

difference, particular subjectivities, and local identities, it approaches with great caution efforts to suggest connections among categories, out of concern that connections can easily mount into systems and forms of objectification that submerge the particular, which has a privileged warrant in culturalist epistemology. Political economy recognizes that caution is warranted. It acknowledges, for example, that feminist research correctly concluded that efforts to establish a systemic class analysis diminished the recognition of powerful gender divisions within and across class categories. Mindful of the problems that attend to a pursuit of social totalities, political economy nevertheless recognizes the value in doing so. There is a danger that such a pursuit can result in rarefied systems thinking, what Laclau (1977: 12) has called 'the Platonic cave of class reductionism.' But there is also a danger that emphasis on difference, subjectivity, and the particular can end up with a multiplicity of individualisms whose connections, if any, are little more than chance occurrences that, in the extreme, amount to the general randomization (and therefore dismissal) of history, politics, and ideology (Wood, 1986) and a romanticism of difference that recognizes the mere fact of its achievement as an act of political defiance (Garnham, 1990).[31]

Such a view diminishes the significance of concentrated power, including class power, in the face of evidence suggesting that global class divisions are massively accelerating within and across nations. It also suggests that political resistance amounts to little more than putting together an appropriate package of symbols that provide a unique spin against orthodoxy. One consequence of this is a remarkable shift in focus that looks at material divisions, but sees little more than cultural difference. Consider this analysis of polysemy in a cultural studies text. Noting the limitations of the idea of polysemy, it is nevertheless suggested (During, 1993b: 7) that 'it did lead to more dynamic and complex theoretical concepts which help us describe how cultural products may be combined with new elements to produce different effects in different situations.' 'Hybridization' and 'negotiation' are cited as examples of different cultural processes which are embodied in the many uses of advertising images, such as that of the Marlboro man, whose visage can be:

> made into a shiny, hard-edged polythene sculpture à la Jeff Koons to achieve a postmodern effect in an expensive Manhattan apartment; ... cut out of the magazine and used to furnish a poor dwelling in Lagos ... ; or parodied on a CD/album cover.

31. Frederic Jameson's (1989: 33) work offers the unusual defense of the social totality from within a cultural studies framework. His near apologetic tone underscores the exceptional nature of his position:

> It has not escaped anyone's attention that my approach to post-modernism is a totalizing one. The interesting question today is then not why I adopt this perspective, but why so many people are scandalized (or have learned to be scandalized) by it. In the old days, abstraction was surely one of the strategic ways in which phenomena, particularly historical phenomena, could be estranged and defamiliarized; ....

Notwithstanding the accuracy of this description, it appears out of focus to a political economist because it takes the extremes of class division and seemingly looks right through them to the symbolic uses of cultural detritus that somehow distinguish both the Manhattan apartment dweller and the inhabitant of a Lagos slum, connecting them in symbolic community. The political economist looks at the wider social totality linking both people in a power relationship that holds differential consequences for their real lives. The analyst of cultural studies sees the achievement of identity in what amounts to different heterodox uses of cultural symbols. The latter may be accurate but arguably inconsequential in comparison to the canyon-like divide of power that separates their material and cultural lives.

Against this view, political economy maintains the intellectual and, necessarily linked to this, political significance of focusing on the social totality. It defends as a central intellectual concern the examination of those forces that link people in symmetrical and asymmetrical social relationships, ranging from power and dependency to equality and interdependence. Political economy also recognizes that the absence of an explicit relationship, demonstrated by some form of reciprocity, does not necessarily mean the lack of significant ties. As social network analysis has demonstrated, linkages are often very complex and some of the strongest ties among individuals and groups are those that connect them *through* others, rather than directly *to* one another (Burt, 1992).

Political economy also maintains the political significance of focusing attention on the social totality. Though political economists differ on precisely how to theorize capitalist structures, processes, and consequences, they tend to agree on the need to focus on capitalism as a social formation, a social whole whose parts form dynamic, but discernible, relationships. Admittedly, disagreement persists on how to characterize social relations of domination, hegemony, and resistance, but political economists tend to agree on the need to direct attention to the social or the collective nature of these relationships and to their patterned articulation. One of the primary reasons for upholding these positions is that they embody the nature of political struggles which are integral to the work of political economists, as intellectuals equally committed to explaining capitalism in order to transform it as they are committed to understanding social relations in order to advance their liberatory dimensions. For political economy, this requires engaging, however critically, with social totalities, such as the capitalist political economy, and with the social relations of class, gender, and race. For political economy, the focal movement is in the direction of unity and the social whole, with difference and particularity contained within these. The critics of political economy within cultural studies have pointed to the shortcomings of this approach, describing the problems of reading too much unity in capitalism and class power and of submerging important differences in social relations and culture. The political economy position and this critique mark one of the more significant boundaries between the approaches.

To conclude, political economists and other critics have concentrated on three principal points which tend to define the central dimensions of a political economy response to the extremes of cultural studies approaches. First, critics raise concerns about the shift from a realist to a nominalist epistemology that rejects the existence of knowable action outside of the text and which shifts from a view of research as an attempt to produce verifiable statements about action (a process which, in political economy, is connected to social praxis) to one of intervention in an ongoing conversation. Second, critics argue that this relativist approach to knowledge leads to a wider political relativism which loses a sense of politics as a definitive social project that incorporates the research act and rests almost entirely on politics as a struggle for individual identity. The self-contained nature of the research and the loss of concern for a wider political project foster intellectual insularity, so that the 'conversation' takes on an academic quality that is evidenced in a work whose language is inaccessible to all but those few who are intimately part of the conversational flow. According to the critics, such as Palmer (1990), who refers to this as the 'descent into discourse,' and Slater (1987), who questions 'the flight of use-value into the land of the sign,' the once widely accepted view insisting that good research is made accessible to wider social communities is all but lost.[32] Critics, including political economists, call on cultural studies to return to its roots, which maintained that culture is popular and that it reflects the needs and aspirations, including political ones, of widely placed social actors.

Conclusion: A Return to Class Power

It is appropriate to conclude the book with reference to class power because it has historically occupied a central place in political economic analysis and also marks an important boundary between political economy, cultural studies, and policy studies. This effort to rethink and renew the political economy of communication has been interested in broadening the epistemological, ontological, and substantive scope of the discipline by critically evaluating notions, such as essentialism and class power, which have long been central to debates about social theory. The result is a proposal to build a political economy of communication that

1   starts from a realist, inclusive (i.e., non-essentialist), and critical epistemology;
2   takes an ontological stance that warrants the ubiquity of social process and social change;

32. Slater (1987: 478–479) takes cultural studies to task for unnecessarily aiming to create an autonomous domain:

> What we take to be the autonomy of commodity aesthetics, the flight of use-value into the land of the sign, is really something rather less mystifying: the capture of use-value by an instrumental logic of market relations.

3   develops a substantive position built on the entry processes of commodi-
    fication, spatialization, and structuration.

These are the coordinates of social action within a political economic
framework. Social class is the starting point for examining the process of
structuration. Class power remains a central element in the political economy of communication, even if it gives up the essentialist view that would
make it the position to which all others can be reduced.

Because of its methodological and substantive individualism, and the
general tenor of capitalist triumphalism that inflects the work of its supporters, policy studies has little to say about social class. However, social class
and class power are not at all foreign to cultural studies. In fact, early work
in the field, including that of Hoggart (1957), Williams (1958), Thompson
(1963), Hall and Jefferson (1976), and Willis (1977), maintained a strong
commitment to an engaged class analysis, leading one to agree with
During's (1993b: 1–2) conclusion that 'early cultural studies did not flinch
from the fact that societies are structured unequally, that individuals are not
all born with the same access to education, money, health-care.' Over time,
particularly as it developed in the United States, cultural studies retreated
from class and from the general connection between material inequalities
and social power (Budd et al., 1990; Evans, 1990; Tetzlaff, 1991). One of
the reasons for this was the understandable interest to expand class analysis
to include gender, race, and ethnic divisions, as well as to account for the
apparent support for conservative politics within the working class, or at
least for the seeming indifference of working people in the face of declining
living standards, and for the rise of social movements that cut across class
divisions. But in addition to this arguably useful shift in attention, one
encounters a growing insularity, what amounts to a withdrawal into the text
which becomes a self-contained whole, accounting for itself and requiring
little or no reference to economic, political, social, or, in the extreme,
cultural practices. One of the more significant consequences of such an
approach is to eliminate almost entirely any interest in work and the labor
process in communication. Though the working class appears from time to
time in cultural studies research, it almost never shows up in the factory or
the office. There is extensive debate about whether audiences 'produce'
texts, but practically nothing on the material or symbolic nature of work
itself.[33] The political economist finds this puzzling and troubling. One can
comprehend a position that suggests rethinking the meaning and significance

33. It is particularly striking, for example, that a lengthy map of the cultural studies field,
by someone well versed in and sympathetic to Marxian theory, could include an analysis of the
rise and fall of the British automobile the Metro, containing numerous references to its design
and promotion, as well to its 'relations of power,' without saying a word about labor and the
labor process in the automotive industry and their relationship to circuits of culture (Johnson,
1987).

of class analysis, but it is difficult to understand the justification for bidding it farewell, in a world where the gap between rich and poor accelerates.[34]

Whatever the divisions between political economy and disciplines on its borders, the process of research should bring together, not separate, intellectuals and cultural producers. It ought to build a common understanding and common political purpose that can advance the democratization of culture and, through it, the democratization of social life. In making this call, critics, including political economists, remind themselves of their own wider purpose, which includes forging intellectual and political links across disciplinary boundaries. There is value in continuing the conversation, if not, as Williams (1981b: 54) wryly observed, so that we can be the 'guests, however occasionally untidy or unruly, of a decent pluralism,' then certainly insofar as our exchanges are connected to a sense that there is an understandable reality and that intellectual activity is organized to transform it for the wider benefit of all.

34. For the arguments in favor of leaving class behind see Gorz (1982). Jameson (1989: 44) offers a less radical stance:

> This is a transitional period between two stages of capitalism, in which the earlier forms of the economic are in the process of being restructured on a global scale, including the older forms of labour and its traditional organizational institutions and concepts. That a new international proletariat (taking forms we cannot yet imagine) will reemerge from this convulsive upheaval it needs no prophet to predict: we ourselves are still in the trough, however, and no one can say how long we will stay there.

References

Abler, Ron, Adam, John S., and Gould, Peter (1971) *Spatial Organization*. Englewood Cliffs, NJ: Prentice Hall.

Adorno, Theodor W. and Horkheimer, Max (1979) *Dialectic of Enlightenment*. Trans. by John Cumming, London: Verso (orig. 1944).

Aglietta, Michel (1979) *A Theory of Capitalist Regulation: The US Experience*. Trans. by David Fernbach, London: New Left Books.

Ahmad, Aijiz (1992) *In Theory: Classes, Nations, Literatures*. London: Verso.

Akhavan-Majid, Roya and Wolf, Gary (1991) 'American Mass Media and the Myth of Libertarianism: Toward an "Elite Power Group" Theory,' *Critical Studies in Mass Communication*, Vol. 8, No. 2, pp. 139–151.

Aksoy, Asu, and Robins, Kevin (1992) 'Hollywood for the 21st Century: Global Competition for Critical Mass in Image Markets,' *Cambridge Journal of Economics*, Vol. 16, No.1, pp. 1–22.

Alt, James E. and Shepsle, Kenneth A. (eds) (1990) *Perspectives on Positive Political Economy*. New York: Cambridge University Press.

Altman, Karen E. (1989) 'Television as Gendered Technology: Advertising the American Television Set,' *Journal of Popular Film and Television*, Vol. 17 (Summer), No. 2, pp. 46–56.

American Library Association (1988) *Less Access to Less Information by and about the US Government: A 1981–1987 Chronology*. Washington, DC: ALA.

Amin, Samir (1976) *Accumulation on a World Scale: A Critique of the Theory of Underdevelopment*. New York: Monthly Review Press.

Amott, Theresa and Matthaei, Julie (1991) *Race, Gender and Work: A Multicultural Economic History of Women in the United States*. Montreal: Black Rose Books.

Amsden, Alice (1992) 'Otiose Economics,' *Social Research*, Vol. 59 (Winter), No. 4, pp. 781–797.

Anderson, Gary, M. (1988) 'Mr. Smith and the Preachers: The Economics of Religion in the *Wealth of Nations*,' *Journal of Political Economy*, Vol. 96, No. 5, pp. 1066–1088.

Andrews, Edmund L. (1994) 'AT&T Will Cut 15,000 Jobs to Reduce Costs,' *The New York Times*, February 11, pp. D1, D14.

Ang, Ien (1990) 'Culture and Communication: Towards an Ethnographic Critique of Media Consumption in the Transnational Media System,' *European Journal of Communication*, Vol. 5, pp. 239–260.

Ang, Ien (1991) *Desparately Seeking the Audience*. London: Routledge.

Ansberry, Clare (1993) 'Hired Out: Workers are Forced to Take More Jobs with Fewer Benefits,' *Wall Street Journal*, March 11, pp. A1, A9.

Aronowitz, Stanley (1992) *The Politics of Identity: Class, Culture, and Social Movements*. New York: Routledge.

Attali, Jacques (1985) *Noise: The Political Economy of Music*. Trans. by Brian Massumi. Minneapolis: University of Minnesota Press.

Atwood, Rita and McAnany, Emile G. (eds) (1986) *Communication and Latin American Society*. Madison: University of Wisconsin Press.

Aufderheide, Patricia (1987) 'Universal Service: Telephone Policy in the Public Interest,' *Journal of Communication*, 37 (Winter), No. 1, pp. 1, 81–96.

Aufderheide, Patricia (1991) 'Public Television and the Public Sphere,' *Critical Studies in Mass Communication*, Vol. 8, No. 2, pp. 168–183.

Aufderheide, Patricia (1992) 'Cable Television and the Public Interest,' *Journal of Communication*, Vol. 42 (Winter), No. 1, pp. 52–65.

Aufderheide, Patricia (1994) 'The Media Monopolies Muscle In: Bell Atlantic–T.C.I. Merger,' *The Nation*, January 3/10, pp. 1, 18–21.

Babe, Robert E. (1990) *Telecommunications in Canada*. Toronto: University of Toronto Press.

Babe, Robert E. (1994) (ed.) *Information and Communication in Economics*. Boston: Kluwer.

Bagdikian, Ben H. (1992) *The Media Monopoly*. Boston: Beacon Press (4th rev. edn).

Bakhtin, Mikhail (1981) *The Dialogic Imagination*. Trans. by Caryl Emerson and Michael Holquist. Austin: University of Texas Press.

Balka, Ellen (1991) 'Womentalk Goes On-line: The Use of Computer Networks in the Context of Feminist Social Change.' Doctoral dissertation, Burnaby, British Columbia: Simon Fraser University.

Baran, Paul A. (1957) *The Political Economy of Growth*. New York: Monthly Review Press.

Baran, Paul A. and Sweezy, Paul M. (1965) 'Economics of Two Worlds,' in *On Political Economy and Econometrics*. Oxford: Pergamon, pp. 15–29.

Baran, Paul A. and Sweezy, Paul M. (1966) *Monopoly Capital: An Essay on the American Economic and Social Order*. New York: Monthly Review Press.

Barlow, William (1989) *'Looking up at Down': The Emergence of Blues Culture*. Philadelphia: Temple University Press.

Barrett, Michèle and McIntosh, Mary (1980) 'The Family Wage,' *Capital and Class*, No. 11 (Summer), pp. 51–72.

Bartlett, Donald L. and Steele, James B. (1992) *America: What Went Wrong?* Kansas City: Andrews and McMeel.

Baudrillard, Jean (1975) *The Mirror of Production*. Trans. by Mark Poster. St Louis: Telos Press.

Baudrillard, Jean (1981) *For a Critique of the Political Economy of the Sign*. Trans. by Charles Levin. St Louis: Telos Press.

Bauman, Zygmunt (1989) *Legislators and Interpreters*. Cambridge: Polity.

Becker, Gary S. (1975) *Human Capital*. New York: National Bureau of Economic Research.

Becker, Jörg (1988) 'Electronic Homework in West Germany,' in Mosco and Wasko (eds) (1988), pp. 247–273.

Becker, Jörg (ed.) (1989) *Telefonieren*. Marburg: Jonas.

Becker, Jörg (1990) *Fern-sprechen*. Stuttgart: Institute for Cultural Exchange.

Becker, Jörg, Hedebro, Goran, and Paldan, Leena (eds) (1986) *Communication and Domination: Essays to Honor Herbert I. Schiller*. Norwood, NJ: Ablex.

Bekken, Jon (1990) ' "This Paper is Owned by Many Thousands of Working Men and Women": Contradictions of a Socialist Daily,' Paper presented at the Annual Meeting of the Association for Education in Journalism and Mass Communication, Boston, August.

Bell, Daniel (1973) *The Coming of Postindustrial Society*. New York: Basic Books.

Bell, Daniel (1976) *The Cultural Contradictions of Capitalism*. New York: Basic Books.

Bell, Daniel (1981) 'Models and Reality in Economic Discourse,' in Daniel Bell and Irving Kristol (eds) *The Crisis in Economic Theory*. New York: Basic Books, pp. 46–80.

Bello, Walden and Rosenfeld, Stephanie (1992) *Dragons in Distress: Asia's Miracle Economies in Crisis*. New York: Penguin.

Beltrán, Luis R. (1976) 'Alien Premises, Objects, and Methods in Latin American Communication Research,' *Communication Research*, Vol. 3, No. 2, pp. 107–134.

Beltrán, Luis R. and Fox de Cardona, Elizabeth (1980) *Communicación Dominada: Estados Unidos en los Medios de América Latina*. Mexico City: Instituto Latinoamericano de Estudios Transnacionales/Nueva Imagen.

Beniger, James R. (1986) *The Control Revolution.* Cambridge, MA: Harvard University Press.

Bentham, Jeremy (1890) *Utilitarianism.* London.

Benton, Ted (1989) 'Marxism and Natural Limits: An Ecological Critique and Reconstruction,' *New Left Review*, No. 178 (Nov/Dec), pp. 51–86.

Berberoglu, Berch (ed.) (1993) *The Labor Process and Control of Labor: The Changing Nature of Work Relations in the Late Twentieth Century.* Westport, CT: Praeger.

Berland, Jody (1992) 'Angels Dancing: Cultural Technologies and the Production of Space,' in Grossberg et al. (1992), pp. 38–55.

Berman, Marshall (1988) *All That is Solid Melts into Air.* New York: Penguin (orig. 1982).

Bernstein, Richard (1989) 'Social Theory as Critique,' in David Held and John B. Thompson (eds), *Social Theory of Modern Societies: Anthony Giddens and His Critics.* New York: Cambridge University Press, pp. 19–33.

Bettig, Ronald V. (1992) 'Critical Perspectives on the History and Philosophy of Copyright,' *Critical Studies in Mass Communication*, Vol. 9 (June), No. 2, pp. 131–155.

Block, Fred (1990) *Postindustrial Possibilities: A Critique of Economic Discourse.* Berkeley: University of California Press.

Blumler, Jay G. and Nossiter, T.J. (eds) (1991) *Broadcasting Finance in Transition: A Comparative Handbook.* New York: Oxford University Press.

Boafo, S.T. Kwame (1991) 'Communication Technology and Dependent Development in Sub-Saharan Africa,' in Sussman and Lent (eds) (1991), pp. 103–124.

Boafo, S.T. Kwame and George, Nancy (eds) (1992) *Communication Research in Africa: Issues and Perspectives.* Nairobi: African Council on Communication Education.

Bohm, David and Hiley, B.J. (1993) *The Undivided Universe: An Ontological Interpretation of Quantum Theory.* London: Routledge.

Bowles, Samuel and Gintis, Herbert (1986) *Democracy and Capitalism: Property, Community, and the Contradictions of Modern Social Thought.* New York: Basic Books.

Bowles, Samuel, Gordon, David M., and Weisskopf, Thomas E. (1990) *After the Wasteland: A Democratic Economics for the Year 2000.* Armonk, NY: M.E. Sharpe.

Boyer, Robert (1986) *La Théorie de la Régulation: Une Analyse Critique.* Paris: La Découverte.

Braman, Sandra (1989) 'Defining Information: An Approach for Policymakers,' *Telecommunications Policy* (September), pp. 233–242.

Braudel, Fernand (1975) *Capitalism and Material Life: 1400–1800.* Trans. by Miriam Kochan. New York: Harper & Row.

Braverman, Harry (1974) *Labor and Monopoly Capital.* New York: Monthly Review Press.

Brennan, Geoffrey and Buchanan, James M. (1985) *The Reason of Rules: Constitutional Political Economy.* New York: Cambridge University Press.

Brennan, Timothy J. (1992) 'Integrating Communication Theory into Media Policy: An Economic Perspective,' *Telecommunications Policy* (August), pp. 460–474.

Bruck, Peter (1992) 'Discursive Movements and Social Movements: The Active Negotiation of Constraints,' in Wasko and Mosco (eds) (1992), pp. 138–158.

Brunn, Stanley D. and Leinbach, Thomas R. (eds) (1991) *Collapsing Space and Time: Geographic Aspects of Communication and Information.* London: HarperCollins Academic.

Buchanan, James (1986) *Liberty, Market and State: Political Economy in the 1980s.* Brighton: Wheatsheaf.

Buchanan, James and Tollison, Robert D. (eds) (1984) *The Theory of Public Choice – II.* Ann Arbor: University of Michigan Press.

Budd, Mike, Entman, Robert M., and Steinman, Clay (1990) 'The Affirmative Character of U.S. Cultural Studies,' *Critical Studies in Mass Communication*, Vol. 7, No. 2, pp. 169–184.

Buhle, Paul (ed.) (1987) *Popular Culture in America.* Minneapolis: University of Minnesota Press.

Burawoy, Michael (1979) *Manufacturing Consent.* Chicago: University of Chicago Press.

Burgess, Jacquelin (1990) 'The Production and Consumption of Environmental Meanings in the Mass Media: A Research Agenda for the 1990s,' *Transactions of the Institute of British Geographers*, Vol. 15, pp. 139–161.

Burke, Edmund (1910) *Reflections on the Revolution in France*. London: J.M. Dent & Sons, Ltd (orig. 1790).

Burke, Kenneth (1969a) *A Grammar of Motives*. Berkeley: University of California Press (orig. 1945).

Burke, Kenneth (1969b) *A Rhetoric of Motives*. Berkeley: University of California Press (orig. 1950).

Burt, Ronald S. (1992) *Structural Holes: The Social Structure of Competition*. Cambridge, MA: Harvard University Press.

Business Week (1994) 'The Information Revolution,' June 6, p. 26.

Buxton, William (1994) 'The Political Economy of Communications Research: The Rockefeller Foundation, the "Radio Wars" and the Princeton Radio Research Project,' in Babe (ed.) (1994), pp. 147–175.

Calabrese, Andrew and Jung, D. (1992) 'Broadband Telecommunications in Rural America: An Analysis of Emerging Infrastructures,' *Telecommunications Policy*, Vol. 16 (April), No. 3, pp. 225–236.

Canada, Statistics Canada (1993) *Selected Income Statistics*. Ottawa: Industry, Science, and Technology Canada, (1991 Census of Canada), Catalogue # 93–331.

Cardoso, F. H. (1993) 'Communication for a New World,' in José Marques de Melo (ed.) *Communication for a New World: Brazilian Perspectives*. São Paulo: University of São Paulo, pp. 9–19.

Cardoso, F.H. and Faletto, E. (1979) *Dependency and Development in Latin America*. Berkeley: University of California Press.

Carey, James W. (1979) 'Mass Communication Research and Cultural Studies: An American View,' in Curran et al. (eds) (1979), pp. 409–425.

Carey, James W. (1994) 'Communications and Economics,' in Babe (ed.) (1994), pp. 321–336.

Carlyle, Thomas (1984) *A Carlyle Reader*. Ed. by G.B. Tennyson. New York: Cambridge University Press.

Carragee, Kevin M. (1990) 'Interpretive Media Study and Interpretive Social Science,' *Critical Studies in Mass Communication*, Vol. 7, No. 2, pp. 81–96.

Castells, Manuel (1989) *The Informational City: Information Technology, Economic Restructuring, and the Urban-Regional Process*. Oxford: Blackwell.

Castells, Manuel and Henderson, Jeffrey (1987) 'Techno-Economic Restructuring, Socio-Political Processes and Spatial Transformation: A Global Perspective,' in Jeffrey Henderson and Manuel Castells (eds), *Global Restructuring and Territorial Development*. Beverly Hills: Sage.

CCCS Women's Studies Group (1978) *Women Take Issue*. London: Hutchinson.

Centre for Mass Communication Research, University of Leicester (1984) 'Background to the Establishment of the Centre,' Planning document submitted to the university.

Centre for Mass Communication Research, University of Leicester (1991) 'Research Programme, Postgraduate Studies, and Publications,' March.

Cesareo, Giovanni (1992) 'Privacy and Secrecy: Social Control and the Prospects for Democracy in the Information System,' In Wasko and Mosco (eds) (1992), pp. 87–97.

Chaffee, Steven H., Gomez-Palacio, Carlos, and Rogers, Everett M. (1990) 'Mass Communication Research in Latin America: Views from Here and There,' *Journalism Quarterly*, Vol. 67 (Winter), No. 4, pp. 1015–1024.

Challenger, Gray, and Christmas, (1994) *Harper's Magazine*, April, p. 17.

Chandler, Alfred D., Jr (1977) *The Visible Hand: The Managerial Revolution in American Business*. Cambridge, MA: Harvard University Press.

Chapman, Keith and Walker, David (1987) *Industrial Location*. Oxford: Blackwell.

Chase-Dunn, Christopher (1989) *Global Formation: Structures of the World-Economy*. Oxford: Blackwell.

Christopherson, Susan and Storper, Michael (1989) 'The Effects of Flexible Specialisation on Industrial Politics and the Labour Market: The Motion Picture Industry,' *Industrial and Labour Relations Review*, Vol. 42, No. 3, pp. 331–347.

Clark, Barry (1990) *Political Economy: A Comparative Approach*. New York: Praeger.

Clement, Andrew (1990) 'Computers and Organizations,' in Jacques Berleur, Andrew Clement, Richard Sizer, and Diane Whitehouse (eds), *The Information Society: Evolving Landscapes*. New York: Springer Verlag, pp. 305–326.

Clement, Andrew (1992) 'Electronic Workplace Surveillance: Sweatshops and Fishbowls,' *Canadian Journal of Information Science*, Vol. 17 (December), No. 4, pp. 18–45.

Clement, Wallace (1975) *The Canadian Corporate Elite: An Analysis of Economic Power*. Toronto: McClelland and Stewart.

Clement, Wallace (1977) *Continental Corporate Power: Economic Linkages Between Canada and the United States*. Toronto: McClelland and Stewart.

Clement, Wallace and Williams, Glen (1989) 'Introduction,' in Wallace Clement and Glen Williams (eds) *The New Canadian Political Economy*. Kingston and Montreal: McGill-Queen's University Press, pp. 3–15.

Coase, Ronald H. (1991) *The Nature of the Firm: Origins, Evolution, and Development*. New York: Oxford University Press.

Cohen, G.A. (1978) *Karl Marx's Theory of History: A Defense*. New York: Oxford University Press.

Cohen, G.A. (1991) 'The Future of a Disillusion,' *New Left Review*, No. 190, (Nov./Dec.), pp. 5–20.

Coletti, Lucio (1979) *Marxism and Hegel*. Trans. by Lawrence Garner. London: New Left Books (orig. 1973).

'Colloquy' (1995) *Critical Studies in Mass Communication*, Vol. 12, No. 1, pp. 60–100.

Comor, Edward A. (ed.) (1994) *The Global Political Economy of Communication: Hegemony, Telecommunication and the Information Economy*. New York: St Martin's Press.

Compaine, Benjamin M. (1986) 'Information Gaps: Myth or Reality?' *Telecommunications Policy* (March), pp. 5–12.

Compaine, Benjamin M. et al. (1982) *Who Owns the Media?: Concentration of Ownership in the Mass Communications Industry*. White Plains, NY: Knowledge Industry Publications (2nd rev. edn).

Connell, Rob (1987) *Power and Gender*. Stanford, CA: Stanford University Press.

Cooper, Kent (1942) *Barriers Down*. New York: Farrar.

Costello, Nicholas, Michie, Jonathan, and Milne, Seumas (1989) *Beyond the Casino Economy*. London: Verso.

Coulter, Bernard G. (1992) 'A New Social Contract for Canadian Telecommunication Policy'. Doctoral dissertation, Carleton University, Department of Sociology and Anthropology.

Cox, Meg (1993) ' "Madison County" Author Crosses Bridge to Music,' *The Wall Street Journal*, July 6, p. B1.

Cox, Meg (1994) 'Paramount Unit to Cut Number of Books Published Under the Macmillan Imprint,' *The Wall Street Journal*, January 24, p. B5.

Crandall, Robert W. (1991) *After the Breakup: U.S. Telecommunications in a More Competitive Era*. Washington, DC: Brookings Institution.

Crawford, Margaret (1992) 'The World in a Shopping Mall,' in Sorkin (ed.) (1992), pp. 3–30.

Creedon, Pamela J. (ed.) (1993) *Women in Mass Communication: Challenging Gender Values*. Newbury Park, CA: Sage (2nd edn).

Curran, James (1979) 'Capitalism and Control of the Press, 1800–1975,' in Curran et al. (1979), pp. 195–230.

Curran, James (1990) 'The New Revisionism in Mass Communication Research: A Reappraisal,' *European Journal of Communication*, Vol. 5, pp. 135–164.

Curran, James (1991) *Power without Responsibility*. London: Routledge (4th edn).

Curran, James and Gurevitch, Michael (1991) 'Introduction,' in James Curran and Michael Gurevitch (eds), *Mass Media and Society*. London: Edward Arnold, pp. 7–11.

Curran, James, Gurevitch, Michael, and Woollacott, Janet (eds) (1979) *Mass Communication and Society*. Beverly Hills: Sage.

Dahl, Robert A. (1982) *Dilemmas of Pluralist Democracy*. New Haven: Yale University Press.

Dahlgren, Peter and Sparks, Colin (eds) (1991) *Communication and Citizenship: Journalism and the Public Sphere in the New Media Age*. London: Routledge and Kegan Paul.

Danielian, N.R. (1939) *The AT&T*. New York: Vanguard.

Dates, Jannette L. and Barlow, William (eds) (1993) *Split Image: African Americans in the Mass Media*. Washington, DC: Howard University Press (2nd edn).

Davies, Paul (1993) 'The Holy Grail of Physics,' *The New York Times Book Review*, March 7, pp. 11–12.

Davis, John (1992) *Exchange*. Minneapolis: University of Minnesota Press.

Davis, Mike (1990) *City of Quartz*. New York: Verso.

Davis, Susan, G. (1986) *Parades and Power: Street Theater in Nineteenth-Century Philadelphia*. Philadelphia: Temple University Press.

de Haven-Smith, Lance (1988) *Philosophical Critiques of Policy Analysis: Lindblom, Habermas, and the Great Society*. Gainesville: University of Florida Press.

de la Haye, Yves (ed.) (1980) *Marx and Engels on the Means of Communication*. New York: International General.

De Witt, Karen (1993) 'The Nation's Library, for a Fee and a Modem,' *The New York Times*, February 28, p. E16.

Demsetz, Harold and Lehn, Kenneth (1985) 'The Structure of Corporate Ownership: Causes and Consequences,' *Journal of Political Economy*, Vol. 93, No. 6, pp. 1155–1177.

Denious, Robert D. (1986) 'The Subsidy Myth: Who Pays for the Local Loop?' *Telecommunications Policy* (September), pp. 259–267.

Derthick, Martha and Quirk, Paul J. (1985) *The Politics of Deregulation*. Washington, DC: Brookings Institution.

Dervin, Brenda (1987) 'The Potential Contribution of Feminist Scholarship to the Field of Communication,' *Journal of Communication*, Vol. 37 (Autumn), No. 4, pp. 107–120.

DeSimone, Mark (1992) 'Information is Value,' *The Globe and Mail*, March 3, p. B8.

Domhoff, G. William (1978) *The Powers That Be: Processes of Ruling Class Domination in America*. New York: Vintage.

Domhoff, G. William (1990) *The Power Elite and the State: How Policy is Made in America*. New York: A. de Gruyter.

Dorfman, Ariel and Mattelart, Armand (1975) *How to Read Donald Duck*. London: International General.

Dos Santos, T. (1970) 'The Structure of Dependency,' *American Economic Review* (May), pp. 231–236.

Douglas, Sarah (1986) *Labor's New Voice: Unions and the Mass Media*. Norwood, NJ: Ablex.

Douglas, Susan J. (1987) *Inventing American Broadcasting, 1899–1922*. Baltimore: Johns Hopkins University Press.

Downing, John D.H. (1984) *Radical Media*. Boston: South End Press.

Downing, John D.H. (1988) ' "The Cosby Show" and American Racial Discourse,' in Geneva Smitherman-Donaldson and Teun A. van Dijk (eds), *Discourse and Discrimination*. Detroit: Wayne State University Press, pp. 46–73.

Downing, John D.H. (1990) 'The Political Economy of U.S. Television,' *Monthly Review*, Vol. 42 (May), No. 1, pp. 30–41.

Dreier, Peter (1982) 'The Position of the Press in the US Power Structure,' *Social Problems*, Vol. 29, No. 3, pp. 293–310.

Drohan, Madelaine (1993) 'BBC Broadcasts Take Reality Out of the Studio,' *The Globe and Mail*, July 21, p. B17.

DuBoff, Richard (1984) 'The Rise of Communications Regulation: The Telegraph Industry, 1844–1880,' *Journal of Communication*, Vol. 34, No. 3, pp. 52–66.

DuBoff, Richard (1989) *Accumulation and Power: An Economic History of the United States.* Armonk, NY: M.E. Sharpe.

Dun's Marketing Services (1991) *Million Dollar Directory.* Parsippany, NJ: Dun and Bradstreet.

During, Simon (ed.) (1993a) *The Cultural Studies Reader.* London: Routledge.

During, Simon (1993b) 'Introduction,' in During (ed.) (1993a), pp. 1–25.

Dyson, Kenneth and Humphreys, Peter (1990) *The Political Economy of Communications: International and European Dimensions.* London: Routledge.

Eatwell, John, Milgate, Murray, and Newman, Peter (1987) *The New Palgrave: A Dictionary of Economics.* London: Macmillan.

Edwards, Richard (1979) *Contested Terrain: The Transformation of the Workplace in the Twentieth Century.* New York: Basic Books.

Ehrbar, Al (1993) 'Price of Progress: "Re-Engineering" Gives Firms New Efficiency, Workers the Pink Slip,' *The Wall Street Journal*, March 16, pp. A1, A11.

Eisenstein, Elizabeth (1979) *The Printing Press as an Agent of Change.* New York: Cambridge University Press.

Elliott, Philip and Golding, Peter (1972) 'Mass Communications and Social Change.' Paper given to the 1972 Conference of the British Sociological Association.

Elster, John (1985) *Making Sense of Marx.* Cambridge: Cambridge University Press.

Emmanuel, Arghiri (1972) *Unequal Exchange: A Study of the Imperialism of Trade.* Trans. by Brian Pearce. New York: Monthly Review Press.

Engels, Friedrich (1972) *The Origin of the Family, Private Property and the State.* London: Lawrence and Wishart (orig. 1889).

Enzensberger, Hans Magnus (1974) *The Consciousness Industry.* New York: Seabury Press.

Etzioni, Amitai (1988) *The Moral Dimension: Toward a New Economics.* New York: Free Press.

Evans, William A. (1990) 'The Interpretive Turn in Media Research: Innovation, Iteration, or Illusion,' *Critical Studies in Mass Communication*, Vol. 7, No. 2, pp. 147–168.

Ewen, Stuart (1976) *Captains of Consciousness.* New York: McGraw Hill.

Ewen, Stuart (1988) *All Consuming Images.* New York: Basic Books.

Fadul, Anamaria and Straubhaar, Joseph (1991) 'Communication, Culture, and Informatics in Brazil: The Current Challenges,' in Sussman and Lent (eds) (1991), pp. 214–233.

Fanon, Frantz (1965) *A Study in Dying Colonialism.* New York: Monthly Review Press (orig. 1959).

Featherstone, Mike (ed.) (1990) *Global Culture: Nationalism, Globalization, and Modernity.* Newbury Park, CA: Sage.

Fejes, Fred (1981) 'Media Imperialism: An Assessment,' *Media, Culture and Society*, Vol. 3, pp. 281–289.

Ferguson, Marjorie (1992) 'The Mythology About Globalization,' *European Journal of Communication*, Vol. 7, pp. 69–93.

Feyerabend, Paul K. (1988) *Against Method.* London: Verso (rev. edn).

Fishman, Mark (1980) *Manufacturing the News.* Austin: University of Texas Press.

Fiske, John (1989) *Understanding Popular Culture.* London: Unwin Hyman.

Flichy, Patrice (1991) *Une histoire de la communication moderne: Espace public et vie privée.* Paris: La Découverte.

Foster, John Bellamy (1988) 'The Fetish of Fordism,' *Monthly Review*, Vol. 39 (March), pp. 14–20.

Foucault, Michel (1982) *Power/Knowledge.* Trans. by Colin Gordon. New York: Pantheon.

Fox, Elizabeth (ed.) (1988) *Media and Politics in Latin America: The Struggle for Democracy.* Newbury Park, CA: Sage.

Fraser, Nancy (1993) 'Rethinking the Public Sphere: A Contribution to the Critique of Actually Existing Democracy,' in Robbins (ed.) (1993), pp. 1–32.

Freeman, Christopher (1984) *Long Waves in the World Economy.* London: Frances Pinter.

Freire, Paulo (1974) *Pedagogy of the Oppressed.* New York: Seabury Press.

Friedman, Benjamin M. (1988) *Day of Reckoning: The Consequences of American Economic Policy under Reagan and After*. New York: Random House.

Friesen, Valerie (1992) 'Trapped in Electronic Cages,' *Media, Culture and Society*, Vol. 14, pp. 31–49.

Fukuyama, Francis (1992) *The End of History and the Last Man*. New York: Free Press.

Galbraith, John Kenneth (1958) *The Affluent Society*. Boston: Houghton Mifflin (4th rev. edn).

Galbraith, John Kenneth (1967) *The New Industrial State*. Boston: Houghton Mifflin.

Galbraith, John Kenneth (1987) *Economics in Perspective: A Critical History*. Boston: Houghton Mifflin.

Galbraith, John Kenneth (1992) *The Culture of Contentment*. Boston: Houghton Mifflin.

Gallagher, Margaret (1980) *Unequal Opportunities: The Case of Women and the Media*. Paris: UNESCO.

Gallagher, Margaret (1984) *Employment and Positive Action for Women in the Television Organizations of the EEC Member States*. Brussels: Commission for European Communities.

Gallagher, Margaret (1985) *Unequal Opportunities: Update*. Paris: UNESCO.

Gallagher, Margaret (1992) 'Women and Men in the Media,' *Communication Research Trends*, special issue, Vol. 12, No. 1, pp. 1–36.

Gandy, Oscar, H. Jr (1992) 'The Political Economy Approach: A Critical Challenge,' *Journal of Media Economics* (Summer), pp. 23–42.

Gandy, Oscar H. Jr (1993) *The Panoptic Sort: The Political Economy of Personal Information*. Boulder, CO: Westview Press.

Gans, Herbert (1979) *Deciding What's News*. New York: Pantheon.

Garnham, Nicholas (1979) 'Contribution to a Political Economy of Mass Communication,' *Media, Culture and Society*, Vol. 1, 123–146.

Garnham, Nicholas (1981) 'Subjectivity, Ideology, Class and Historical Materialism,' *Screen*, Vol. 20, No. 1, pp. 121-133.

Garnham, Nicholas (1986) 'The Media and the Public Sphere,' in Golding et al. (eds) (1986), pp. 37–52.

Garnham, Nicholas (1988) 'In Appreciation: Raymond Williams, 1921–1988: A Cultural Analyst, A Distinctive Tradition,' *Journal of Communication*, Vol. 38 (Autumn), No. 4, pp. 123–131.

Garnham, Nicholas (1990) *Capitalism and Communication: Global Culture and the Economics of Information*. London: Sage.

Gates, Henry Louis, Jr (1989) 'Whose Canon Is It, Anyway?' *The New York Times Book Review*, February 26, pp. 1, 44–45.

Giddens, Anthony (1981) *A Contemporary Critique of Historical Materialism*. Berkeley: University of California Press.

Giddens, Anthony (1984) *The Constitution of Society: Outline of a Theory of Structuration*. Berkeley: University of California Press.

Giddens, Anthony (1990) *The Consequences of Modernity*. Stanford, CA: Stanford University Press.

Giddens, Anthony (1991) *Modernity and Self-Identity: Self and Society in the Late Modern Age*. Stanford, CA: Stanford University Press.

Giddens, Anthony and Held, David (eds) (1982) *Classes, Power, and Conflict: Classical and Contemporary Debates*. Berkeley: University of California Press.

Gill, Stephen and Law, David (1988) *The Global Political Economy*. Baltimore: Johns Hopkins University Press.

Gilman, Charlotte Perkins (1966) *Women and Economics: A Study of the Economic Relations between Men and Women as a Factor in Social Evolution*. New York: Harper and Row (orig. 1889).

Gilpin, Alan (1977) *Dictionary of Economic Terms*. London: Butterworths.

Gilpin, Robert (1987) *The Political Economy of International Relations*. Princeton: Princeton University Press.

Gitlin, Todd (1979) 'Media Sociology: The Dominant Paradigm,' *Theory and Society*, Vol. 6, No. 2, pp. 205–253.

Gitlin, Todd (1980) *The Whole World is Watching: Mass Media in the Making and the Unmaking of the New Left.* Berkeley: University of California Press.

Gitlin, Todd (1993) 'From Universality to Difference: Notes on the Fragmentation of the Idea of the Left,' *Contention: Debates in Society, Culture, and Science*, Vol. 2 (Winter), No. 2, pp. 15–40.

Gleick, James (1987) *Chaos: Making a New Science.* New York: Penguin.

Goldberg, Kim (1990) *The Barefoot Channel: Community Television as a Tool for Social Change.* Vancouver: New Star Books.

Golding, Peter and Middleton, Sue (1982) *Images of Welfare: Press and Public Attitudes to Poverty.* Oxford: Martin Robertson.

Golding, Peter and Murdock, Graham (1991) 'Culture, Communication, and Political Economy,' in James Curran and Michael Gurevitch (eds) *Mass Media and Society.* London: Edward Arnold, pp. 15–32.

Golding, Peter, Murdock, Graham, and Schlesinger, Philip (eds) (1986) *Communicating Politics: Mass Communication and the Political Process.* New York: Holmes and Meier.

Goldman, Robert and Rajagopal, Arvind (1991) *Mapping Hegemony: Television News Coverage of Industrial Conflict.* Norwood, NJ: Ablex.

Gomery, Douglas (1989) 'Media Economics: Terms of Analysis,' *Critical Studies in Mass Communication*, Vol. 6, No. 2, pp. 43–60.

Gorz, Andre (1982) *Farewell to the Working Class.* Trans. by Michael Soneenscher. London: Pluto.

Gramsci, Antonio (1971) *Selections from the Prison Notebooks.* Trans. by Geoffrey Nowell Smith. London: Lawrence and Wishart.

Gran, Peter (1990) 'Studies of Anglo-American Political Economy: Democracy, Orientalism, and the Left,' in Hisham Sharabi (ed.), *Theory, Politics and the Arab World: Critical Responses.* New York: Routledge, pp. 228–254.

Greenfeld, Liah (1992) *Nationalism: Five Roads to Modernity.* Cambridge, MA: Harvard University Press.

Grossberg, Lawrence (1991) 'Strategies of Marxist Cultural Interpretation,' in Robert K. Avery and David Eason (eds), *Critical Perspectives on Media and Society.* New York: Guilford Press, pp. 126–159.

Grossberg, Lawrence, Nelson, Cary, and Treichler, Paula (eds) (1992) *Cultural Studies.* New York: Routledge.

Guback, Thomas (1969) *The International Film Industry: Western Europe and America Since 1945.* Bloomington: Indiana University Press.

Guback, Thomas (1987) 'The Evolution of the Motion Picture Theater Business in the 1980s,' *Journal of Communication*, Vol. 37 (Spring), No. 2, pp. 60–77.

Guback, Thomas (1989) 'Should a Nation Have Its Own Film Industry?' *Directions*, Vol. 3, No. 1, pp. 489–492.

Guback, Thomas (1991) 'Capital, Labor Power, and the Identity of Film,' *Current Research in Film*, Vol. 5, pp. 126–134.

Guback, Thomas (ed.) (1993) *Counterclockwise: Perspectives on Communication – Dallas Smythe.* Boulder, CO: Westview Press.

Gunder Frank, André (1969) *Capitalism and Underdevelopment in Latin America.* New York: Monthly Review Press.

Gutiérrez, Félix (1990) 'Advertising and the Growth of Minority Markets and the Media,' *Journal of Communication Inquiry*, Vol. 14 (Winter), No. 1, pp. 6–16.

Habermas, Jürgen (1973) *Legitimation Crisis.* Trans. by Thomas McCarthy. Boston: Beacon Press.

Habermas, Jürgen (1989) *The Structural Transformation of the Public Sphere.* Trans. by Thomas Burger with Frederick Lawrence. Cambridge, MA: MIT Press (orig. 1962).

Hafner, Katie and Markoff, John (1991) *Cyberpunk: Outlaws and Hackers on the Computer Frontier.* New York: Simon and Schuster.

Hagerstrand, Torsten (1968) *Diffusion of Innovation*. Trans. by Allan Pred. Chicago: University of Chicago Press.

Haight, Timothy R., and Weinstein, Laurie R. (1981) 'Changing Ideology on Television by Changing Telecommunications Policy: Notes on a Contradictory Situation,' in Emile G. McAnany, Jorge Schnitman, and Noreene Janus (eds), *Communication and Social Structure*. New York: Praeger, pp. 110–144.

Hall, Peter and Preston, Paschal (1988) *The Carrier Wave: New Information Technology and the Geography of Innovation, 1846–2003*. London: Unwin and Hyman.

Hall, Stephen S. (1992) *Mapping the Next Millennium: Discovering the New Geographies*. New York: Random House.

Hall, Stuart (1973) 'A Reading of Marx's 1857 Introduction to the *Grundrisse*.' Stencilled Occasional Paper, Birmingham: Centre for Contemporary Cultural Studies.

Hall, Stuart (1980) 'Cultural Studies: Two Paradigms,' *Media, Culture and Society*, Vol. 2, pp. 57–72.

Hall, Stuart (1982) 'The Rediscovery of Ideology: Return of the Repressed in Media Studies,' in Michael Gurevitch, Tony Bennett, James Curran, and Jane Woollacott (eds), *Culture, Society, and the Media*. New York: Methuen, pp. 56–90.

Hall, Stuart (1986) 'Media Power and Class Power,' in James Curran (ed.), *Bending Reality: The State of the Media*. London: Pluto Press, pp. 5–14.

Hall, Stuart (1989a) 'Ideology and Communication Theory,' in Brenda Dervin, Lawrence Grossberg, Barbara J. O'Keefe, and Ellen Wartella (eds), *Rethinking Communication: Paradigm Issues*. Newbury Park, CA: Sage, pp. 40–52.

Hall, Stuart (1989b) 'Ethnicity: Identity and Difference,' *Radical America*, Vol. 23, No. 4, pp. 9–20.

Hall, Stuart (1993) 'Encoding, Decoding,' in During (ed.) (1993a), pp. 90–103.

Hall, Stuart and Jefferson, Tony (eds) (1976) *Resistance Through Rituals: Youth Subcultures in Post-War Britain*. London: Hutchinson.

Halloran, James (1963) *Control or Consent?: A Study of the Challenge of Mass Communication*. London: Sheed and Ward.

Halloran, James (1978) 'Further Development or Turning the Clock Back?: Social Research on Broadcasting,' *Journal of Communication*, Vol. 28 (Spring), No. 2, pp. 120–132.

Halloran, James (1981) 'The Context of Mass Communication Research,' In Emile McAnany, Jorge Schnitman, and Noreene Janus (eds), *Communication and Social Structure*. New York: Praeger, pp. 21–57.

Halloran, James (1983) 'Information and Communication: Information is the Answer but What is the Question?' *Journal of Information Science*, Vol. 7, pp. 158–167.

Hamelink, Cees (1983) *Finance and Information: A Study of Converging Interests*. Norwood, NJ: Ablex.

Hamelink, Cees and Linné, Olga (1992) *Mass Communication Research: In Honor of James D. Halloran*. Norwood, NJ: Ablex.

Hannigan, John (1991) 'Canadian Media Ownership and Control in an Age of Global Megamedia Empires,' in Benjamin Singer (ed.), *Communication and Canadian Society*. Scarborough, Ont.: Nelson, pp. 238–257.

Haraway, Donna J. (1991) *Simians, Cyborgs, and Women: The Reinvention of Nature*. New York: Routledge.

Harding, Sandra and Hintikka, Merrill B. (eds) (1983) *Discovering Reality: Feminist Perspectives on Epistemology, Metaphysics, Methodology, and Philosophy of Science*. Boston: D. Reidel.

Hardt, Hanno (1990) 'Newsworkers, Technology, and Journalism History,' *Critical Studies in Mass Communication*, Vol. 7, No. 4, pp. 346–365.

Hardt, Hanno (1992) *Critical Communication Studies: Communication, History and Theory in America*. London: Routledge.

Hartmann, Heidi I. (1979) 'The Unhappy Marriage of Marxism and Feminism: Towards a More Progressive Union,' *Capital and Class*, Vol. 8, pp. 1–33.

Harvey, David (1989) *The Condition of Postmodernity*. Oxford: Blackwell.

Haug, W.F. (1986) *Critique of Commodity Aesthetics*. Trans. by Robert Bock. Minneapolis: University of Minnesota Press.

Hawkesworth, M.E. (1988) *Theoretical Issues in Policy Analysis*. Albany: State University of New York Press.

Head, Sidney (1974) *Broadcasting in Africa*. Philadelphia: Temple University Press.

Heilbroner, Robert L. (1986) *The Worldly Philosophers*. New York: Simon and Schuster (6th rev. edn).

Heller, Walter W. (1967) *New Dimensions in Political Economy*. New York: W.W. Norton.

Hepworth, Mark (1989) *Geography of the Information Economy*. London: Belhaven Press.

Hepworth, Mark and Robins, Kevin (1988) 'Whose Information Society?: A View From the Periphery,' *Media, Culture and Society*, Vol. 10, pp. 323–343.

Herman, Edward S. and Chomsky, Noam (1988) *Manufacturing Consent: The Political Economy of the Mass Media*. New York: Pantheon.

Heyzer, Noeleen (1986) *Working Women in Southeast Asia: Development, Subordination, and Emancipation*. Philadelphia: Open University Press.

Hillard, Michael (1991) 'Domination and Technological Change: A Review and Appraisal of Braverman, Marglin, Noble,' *Rethinking Marxism*, Vol. 4 (Summer), No. 2, pp. 61–78.

Hills, Jill (1986) *Deregulating Telecoms: Competition and Control in the United States, Japan and Britain*. London: Frances Pinter.

Hills, Jill with Papathanassopoulos, Stylianos (1991) *The Democracy Gap: The Politics of Information and Communication Technologies in the United States and Europe*. New York: Greenwood.

Hirst, Paul and Zeitlin, Jonathan (1991) 'Flexible Specialization versus Post-Fordism: Theory, Evidence and Policy Implications,' *Economy and Society*, Vol. 20, No. 1 (February), pp. 1–56.

Hobsbawm, Eric (1973) 'Karl Marx's Contribution to Historiography,' in Robin Blackburn (ed.), *Ideology in the Social Sciences*. New York: Vintage.

Hobsbawm, Eric (1983) 'Introduction: Inventing Traditions,' in Eric Hobsbawm and Terrence Ranger (eds), *The Invention of Tradition*. Cambridge: Cambridge University Press, pp. 1–14.

Hoggart, Richard (1957) *The Uses of Literacy*. Harmondsworth: Penguin.

Honig, David (1984) 'The FCC and its Fluctuating Commitment to Minority Ownership of Broadcast Facilities,' *Howard Law Journal*, Vol. 27, No. 3, pp. 859–877.

Horkheimer, Max (1947) *The Eclipse of Reason*. New York: Oxford University Press.

Horton, Byrne J. (1948) *Dictionary of Modern Economics*. Washington DC: Public Affairs Press.

Horwitz, Robert (1989) *The Irony of Regulatory Reform*. New York: Oxford University Press.

Hula, Richard C. (1988) *Market-Based Public Policy*. New York: St Martin's Press.

Humphreys, Peter (1986) 'Legitimating the Communications Revolution: Governments, Parties and Trade Unions in Britain, France and West Germany,' in Kenneth Dyson and Peter Humphreys (eds), *The Politics of the Communications Revolution in Western Europe*. London: Frank Cass, pp. 163–194.

Hund, Wulf and Kirchoff-Hund, Barbel (1985) 'Problems of Political Economy,' trans. by Robert Peck, *Media, Culture and Society*, Vol. 5, pp. 83–88.

Ibrahim, S.M. (1981) *The Flow of News into Sudan, the Middle East and Africa*. Khartoum: El Sahafa Press.

IDATE (1992) *Industrial Analyses: The World Film and Television Market*, Vol. 1. Montpellier: IDATE.

Ingram, John Kells (1923) *A History of Political Economy*. London: A&C Black.

Innis, Harold (1972) *Empire and Communications*. Toronto: University of Toronto Press.

International Encyclopedia of Social Science (1968) New York: Macmillan and Free Press.

Ito, Youichi (1989) 'Major Concepts and Theories in Information Society Studies,' in *Proceedings: Asia's Experience in Informatization*. Taipei, Taiwan, May 10–12.

Jameson, Frederic (1989) 'Marxism and Postmodernism,' *New Left Review*, No. 176 (July/ August), pp. 31–45.

Jankowski, Nick, Prehn, Ole, and Stappers, James (1992) *The People's Voice: Local Radio and Television in Europe*. London: John Libbey.

Jansen, Sue Curry (1989) 'Gender and the Information Society: A Socially Structured Silence,' *Journal of Communication*, Vol. 39 (Summer), No. 3., pp. 196–215.

Janus, Noreene (1984) 'Advertising and the Creation of Global Markets: The Role of the New Communication Technologies,' in Mosco and Wasko (eds) (1984), pp. 57–70.

Janus, Noreene (1986) 'Transnational Advertising: Some Consideration on the Impact on Peripheral Societies,' in Atwood and McAnany (eds) (1986), pp. 127–142.

Jessop, Bob (1990) *State Theory: Putting Capitalist States in their Place*. University Park: Pennsylvania State University Press.

Jevons, William Stanley (1965) *The Theory of Political Economy*. New York: A.M. Kelley (orig. 1870).

Jhally, Sut (1990) *The Codes of Advertising: Fetishism and the Political Economy of Meaning in the Consumer Society*. New York: Routledge.

Jhally, Sut and Lewis, Justin (1992) *Enlightened Racism: The Cosby Show, Audiences, and the Myth of the American Dream*. Boulder, CO: Westview Press.

Johnson, Paul (1993) 'Colonialism's Back – and Not a Moment Too Soon,' *The New York Times Magazine*, April 18, pp. 22, 43.

Johnson, Richard (1987) 'What is Cultural Studies Anyway?' *Social Text*, Vol. 17 (Winter), pp. 38–80.

Jones, Alex S. (1991) 'Newspapers Try, Carefully, to Investigate Subscribers,' *The New York Times*, May 27, p. 22.

Jöuet, Josiane (1987) *L'Ecran apprivoisé: Télématique et informatique à domicile*. Paris: CNET.

Jussawalla, Meheroo (1986) *The Passing of Remoteness: The Information Revolution in the Asia-Pacific*. Singapore: Institute of Southeast Asian Studies.

Katz, Michael B., Doucet, Michael J., and Stern, Mark J. (1982) *The Social Organization of Early Industrial Capitalism*. Cambridge, MA: Harvard University Press.

Keane, John (1984) *Public Life and Late Capitalism: Toward a Socialist Theory of Democracy*. Cambridge: Cambridge University Press.

Keenan, Thomas (1993) 'Windows of Vulnerability,' in Robbins (ed.) (1993), pp. 121–141.

Kellner, Douglas (1989) *Jean Baudrillard: From Marxism to Postmodernism and Beyond*. Stanford, CA: Stanford University Press.

Kellner, Douglas (1990) *Television and the Crisis of Democracy*. Boulder, CO: Westview Press.

Kellner, Douglas (1995) *Media Culture*. New York: Routledge.

Keynes, John Maynard (1964) *The General Theory of Employment, Interest, and Money*. New York: Harcourt, Brace & World.

Kieve, Ronald A. (1986) 'From Necessary Illusion to Rational Choice? A Critique of Neo-Marxist Rational-Choice Theory,' *Theory and Society*, Vol. 15, No. 4, pp. 557–582.

Kilborn, Peter T. (1990) 'Workers Using Computers Find a Supervisor Inside,' *The New York Times*, December 23, pp. 1, 8.

King, Thomas R. (1993) ' "Jurassic Park" Offers a High-Stakes Test of Hollywood Synergy,' *The Wall Street Journal*, February 10, p. 1.

Kraft, Philip and Dubnoff, Steve (1986) 'Job Content, Fragmentation and Control in Computer Software Work,' *Industrial Relations*, Vol. 25, pp. 184–196.

Kramarae, Cheris (1989) 'Feminist Theories of Communication,' in *International Encyclopedia of Communication*. New York: Oxford University Press, pp. 157–160.

Krasnow, Erwin D., Longley, Lawrence D., and Terry, Herbert A. (1982) *The Politics of Broadcast Regulation*. New York: St Martin's Press (3rd edn).

Kristol, Irving (1983) *Reflections of a Neoconservative*. New York: Basic Books.

Kuhn, Thomas (1970) *The Structure of Scientific Revolutions*. Chicago: University of Chicago Press (2nd enlarged edn).

Kumar, Keval J. (1989) *Mass Communication in India*. Bombay: Jaico (2nd rev. edn).

Laclau, Ernesto (1977) *Politics and Ideology in Marxist Theory*. London: New Left Books.

Laclau, Ernesto and Mouffe, Chantal (1985) *Hegemony and Socialist Strategy: Toward a Radical Democratic Politics*. Trans. by Winston Moore and Paul Cammack. London: Verso.

Lakatos, Imre (1978) *The Methodology of Scientific Research Programmes*. Cambridge: Cambridge University Press. ✓

Lane, Robert E. (1991) *The Market Experience*. New York: Cambridge University Press.

Larson, Erik (1992) 'Watching Americans Watch TV,' *The Atlantic Monthly* (March), pp. 66–80.

Lash, Scott and Urry, John (1987) *The End of Organized Capitalism*. Madison: University of Wisconsin Press.

Latour, Bruno (1987) *Science in Action*. Cambridge, MA: Harvard University Press.

Lebowitz, Michael (1986) 'Too Many Blindspots on the Media,' *Studies in Political Economy*, No. 21 (August), pp. 165–173.

Lee, Jeong-Taik (1988) 'Dynamics of Labor Control and Labor Protest in the Process of Export-Oriented Industrialization in South Korea,' *Asian Perspectives*, Vol. 12 (Spring–Summer), No. 1., pp. 134–158.

Lefebvre, Henri (1979) 'Space: Social Product and Use Value,' in J.W. Freiberg (ed.), *Critical Sociology: European Perspectives*. New York: Irvington, pp. 285–295.

Lent, John A. (1985) *Women and Mass Media in Asia: An Annotated Bibliography*. Singapore: Asian Mass Communication Research and Information Centre.

Lent, John A. (ed.) (1990) *The Asian Film Industry*. London: Christopher Helm.

Lent, John A. (1991) *Women and Mass Communications: An International Annotated Bibliography*. New York: Greenwood Press.

Lerner, Daniel (1949) *Sykewar: Psychological Warfare against Germany, D-Day to V-E Day*. New York: Stewart.

Lerner, Daniel (1958) *The Passing of Traditional Society*. New York: Free Press.

Levins, Richard and Lewontin, Richard C. (1985) *The Dialectical Biologist*. Cambridge, MA: Harvard University Press.

Levy, Jonathan D. and Setzer, Florence O. (1984) 'Market Delineation, Measurement of Concentration, and F.C.C. Ownership Rules,' in Vincent Mosco (ed.), *Policy Research in Telecommunications*. Norwood, NJ: Ablex, pp. 201-212.

Lindblom, Charles E. (1977) *Politics and Markets*. New York: Basic Books.

Lindlof, Thomas R. (1991) 'Qualitative Study of Media Audiences,' *Journal of Broadcasting and Electronic Media*, Vol. 35 (Winter), No. 1, pp. 23–42.

Lipietz, Alain (1988) 'Reflections on a Tale: The Marxist Foundations of the Concepts of Regulation and Accumulation,' *Studies in Political Economy*, Vol. 26 (Summer), pp. 7–36.

Livant, William (1979) 'The Audience Commodity: On the "Blindspot" Debate,' *Canadian Journal of Political and Social Theory*, Vol. 3, No. 1, pp. 91–106.

Long, Elizabeth (1989) 'Feminism and Cultural Studies,' *Critical Studies in Mass Communication*, Vol. 6 (December), No. 4, pp. 427–435.

Lonidier, Fred (1992) 'Working with Unions II: A Photo Essay,' in Wasko and Mosco (eds) (1992), pp. 125–137.

Lovelock, J.E. (1987) *Gaia: A New Look at Life on Earth*. New York: Oxford University Press.

Lukács, Georg (1971) *History and Class Consciousness: Studies in Marxist Dialectics*. Trans. by Rodney Livingstone. Cambridge, MA: MIT Press.

Luke, Timothy (1989) *Screens of Power: Ideology, Domination, and Resistance in Informational Society*. Urbana and Chicago: University of Illinois Press.

Lunn, Eugene (1982) *Marxism and Modernism: An Historical Study of Lukács, Brecht, Benjamin and Adorno*. Berkeley: University of California Press.

Lux, Kenneth (1990) *Adam Smith's Mistake*. Boston: Shambhala.

Lyotard, Jean François (1984) *The Postmodern Condition: A Report on Knowledge.* Trans. by Geoff Bennington and Brian Massumi. Minneapolis: University of Minnesota Press.

McAnany, Emile G. (1986) 'Seminal Ideas in Latin American Critical Communication Research: An Agenda for the North,' in Atwood and McAnany (eds) (1986), pp. 28–47.

McChesney, Robert W. (1992a) 'Labor and the Marketplace of Ideas: WCFL and the Battle for Labor Radio Broadcasting, 1927–1934,' *Journalism Monographs*, No. 134 (August).

McChesney, Robert W. (1992b) 'Off Limits: An Inquiry into the Lack of Debate over the Ownership, Structure, and Control of the Mass Media in U.S. Political Life,' *Communication*, Vol. 13, pp. 1–19.

McChesney, Robert W. (1993) *Telecommunications, Mass Media and Democracy: The Battle for the Control of U.S. Broadcasting.* New York: Oxford University Press.

McCloskey, Donald N. (1985) *The Rhetoric of Economics.* Madison: University of Wisconsin Press.

MacDonald, J. Fred (1983) *Blacks and Whites: Afro-Americans in Television Since 1948.* Chicago: Nelson-Hall.

McIntyre, Richard (1992) 'Theories of Uneven Development and Social Change,' *Rethinking Marxism*, Vol. 5 (Fall), No. 3, pp. 75–105.

McKibben, Bill (1992) *The Age of Missing Information.* New York: Random House.

McLaughlin, John F. (1992) 'Unequal Access to Information Resources among Corporations: Causes and Implications.' Paper presented to the Ninth World Communications Forum, Tokyo, draft October 15.

McLaughlin, John F. with Antonoff, Anne Louise (1986) *Mapping the Information Business.* Publication P–86–9, Cambridge, MA: Harvard University, Program on Information Resources Policy.

McNally, David (1993) *Against the Market: Political Economy, Market Socialism and the Marxist Critique.* London: Verso.

McPhail, Thomas (1987) *Electronic Colonialism.* Beverly Hills, CA: Sage (rev. edn).

Magder, Ted (1989) 'Taking Culture Seriously: A Political Economy of Communications,' in Wallace Clement and Glen Williams (eds), *The New Canadian Political Economy.* Kingston and Montreal: McGill-Queen's University Press, pp. 278–296.

Mahon, Rianne (1980) 'Regulatory Agencies: Captive Agents or Hegemonic Apparatuses,' in J. Paul Grayson (ed.), *Class, State, Ideology, and Change.* Toronto: Holt, Rinehart, and Winston, pp. 154–168.

Mahoney, Eileen (1988) 'The Intergovernmental Bureau For Informatics: An International Organization Within the Changing World Political Economy,' in Mosco and Wasko (eds) (1988), pp. 297–315.

Malone, Thomas W. and Rockart, John F. (1991) 'Computers, Networks and the Corporation,' *Scientific American*, (September), pp. 128–136.

Mandel, Michael J. (1991) 'They're Not Eating Crow, But . . . : Radical Economists are Rewriting Their Critique of Capitalism,' *Business Week*, October 14, pp. 78, 81.

Mandel, Michael J. (1994) 'The Digital Juggernaut,' *Business Week*, June 6, pp. 22–37.

Manet, Enrique Gonzalez (1988) *The Hidden War of Information.* Trans. by Laurien Alexandre. Norwood, NJ: Ablex.

Mansell, Robin (1993) *The New Telecommunications: A Political Economy of Network Evolution.* Sage: London

Markovich, Denise E. and Pynn, Ronald E. (1988) *American Political Economy: Using Economics with Politics.* Pacific Grove, CA: Brooks/Cole.

Marques de Melo, José (ed.) (1991) *Communication and Democracy: Brazilian Perspectives.* São Paulo: ECA/USP.

Marshall, Alfred (1961) *Principles of Economics.* London: Macmillan (orig. 1890).

Martin, Michèle (1991) *'Hello, Central?': Gender, Technology, and Culture in the Formation of Telephone Systems.* Montreal and Kingston: McGill-Queen's University Press.

Marx, Karl (1973) *The Grundrisse: Foundations of the Critique of Political Economy.* Trans. by Martin Nicolaus. Harmondsworth: Penguin (orig. 1939).

Marx, Karl (1976a) *Capital: A Critique of Political Economy*, Vol. 1. Trans. by Ben Fowkes. London: Penguin (orig. 1867).

Marx, Karl (1976b) *Collected Works*, Vol. V. New York: International Publishers.

Massey, Doreen (1984) *Spatial Divisions of Labour*. London: Methuen.

Massey, Doreen (1992) 'Politics and Space/Time,' *New Left Review*, No. 196 (Nov./Dec.), pp. 65–84.

Masuda, Yoneji (1970) 'Social Impact of Computerization,' *Proceedings of the International Future Research Conference on Challenges from the Future*. Tokyo: Kodansha.

Masuda, Yoneji (1981) *The Information Society*. Washington, DC: World Future Society.

Mattelart, Armand (1983) 'Introduction: For a Class and Group Analysis of Popular Communication Practices,' in Mattelart and Siegelaub (eds) (1983), pp. 17–67.

Mattelart, Armand (ed.) (1986) *Communicating in Popular Nicaragua*. New York: International General.

Mattelart, Armand (1991) *Advertising International: The Privatisation of Public Space*. Trans. by Michael Chanan, London: Comedia and Routledge.

Mattelart, Armand and Mattelart, Michèle (1992) *Rethinking Media Theory: Signposts and New Directions*. Trans. by James A. Cohen and Marina Urquidi. Minneapolis: University of Minnesota Press (orig. 1986).

Mattelart, Armand and Siegelaub, Seth (eds) (1979) *Communication and Class Struggle. Vol. 1: Capitalism, Imperialism*. New York: International General.

Mattelart, Armand and Siegelaub, Seth (eds) (1983) *Communication and Class Struggle. Vol. 2: Liberation, Socialism*. New York: International General.

Mattelart, Armand, Delcourt, Xavier, and Mattelart, Michèle (1984) *International Image Markets: In Search of an Alternative Perspective*. London: Comedia (orig. 1983).

Mattelart, Michèle (1977) 'Création populaire et résistance au système des medias.' Paper presented at the International Conference on Cultural Imperialism, Algiers, October 11–15.

'The Media Charter of the African National Congress' (1992) *Media Development*, No. 2, p. 41.

Meehan, Eileen R. (1984) 'Ratings and the Institutional Approach: A Third Answer to the Commodity Question,' *Critical Studies in Mass Communication*, Vol. 1, No. 2, pp. 216–225.

Mehegan, David (1994) 'High Fliers and Bumpy Landings,' *Boston Sunday Globe*, January 2, p. 57.

Melody, William (1984) 'Direct Testimony to the Pennsylvania Public Utilities Commission,' Docket No. P–83045, August.

Melody, William (1990) 'The Information in I.T.: Where Lies the Public Interest,' *Intermedia*, Vol. 18 (June-July), No. 3, pp. 10–18.

Merton, Robert K. (1968) *Social Theory and Social Structure*. New York: Free Press.

Meyrowitz, Joshua (1985) *No Sense of Place*. New York: Oxford University Press.

Miège, Bernard (1987) 'The Logics at Work in the New Cultural Industries,' *Media, Culture and Society*, Vol. 9, pp. 273–289.

Miège, Bernard (1989) *The Capitalization of Cultural Production*. New York: International General.

Mignot-Lefèbvre, Yvonne (1993) 'Media Control and Freedom of Information in France.' Paper presented to the 1993 Meeting of the International Association for Mass Communication Research Conference on 'Europe in Turmoil,' Dublin, June.

Miliband, Ralph (1989) *Divided Societies: Class Struggle in Contemporary Capitalism*. London: Oxford University Press.

Mill, John Stuart (1848) *Principles of Political Economy*. Boston: C.C. Little and J.B. Brown.

Miller, David (1989) *Market, State, and Community*. New York: Oxford University Press.

Miller, Jeff (1994) 'Should Phone Companies Make Films?' *The New York Times*, January 2, p. F11.

Miller, John (1992) 'URPE and Radical Political Economy: Whence We Came,' *URPE Newsletter* (Fall), pp. 4–5.

Miller, Mark Crispin (1988) *Boxed In: The Culture of TV.* Evanston, IL: Northwestern University Press.

Mills, C. Wright (1956) *The Power Elite.* New York: Oxford University Press.

Mills, C. Wright (1959) *The Sociological Imagination.* New York: Oxford University Press.

Modleski, Tania (1986) 'Introduction,' in Tania Modleski (ed.), *Studies in Entertainment.* Bloomington: Indiana University Press, pp. xi–xix.

Modleski, Tania (1991) *Feminism without Women: Culture and Criticism in a 'Postfeminist' Age.* New York: Routledge.

Montgomery, Katherine C. (1989) *Target: Prime Time – Advocacy Groups and the Struggle over Entertainment Television.* New York: Oxford University Press.

Moody, Kim (1993) 'The Telecommunications Revolution: How Union Jobs are Being Lost in an Expanding Industry,' *Labor Notes,* December.

Morley, David (1986) *Family Television: Cultural Power and Domestic Leisure.* London: Comedia.

Morris-Suzuki, Tessa (1986) 'The Challenge of Computers,' *New Left Review,* No. 160 (Nov./Dec.), pp. 81–91.

Morris-Suzuki, Tessa (1988) *Beyond Computopia: Information, Automation, and Democracy in Japan.* London: Routledge.

Morris-Suzuki, Tessa (1989) *A History of Japanese Economic Thought.* New York: Routledge.

Morrison, David (1978) 'The Beginning of Modern Mass Communication Research,' *Archives of European Sociology,* Vol. XIX, No. 2, pp. 347–359.

Mosco, Vincent (1982) *Pushbutton Fantasies: Critical Perspectives on Videotex and Information Technology.* Norwood, NJ: Ablex.

Mosco, Vincent (1989a) *The Pay-per Society: Computers and Communication in the Information Age.* Toronto: Garamond; Norwood, NJ: Ablex.

Mosco, Vincent (1989b) 'Labour in Communication Industries: A Critical Sociological Perspective,' in Brenda Dervin, Lawrence Grossberg, Barbara O'Keefe, and Ellen Wartella (eds), *Rethinking Communication. Vol. II: Paradigm Exemplars.* Newbury Park, CA: Sage, pp. 213–225.

Mosco, Vincent (1990a) 'The Mythology of Telecommunications Deregulation,' *Journal of Communication,* Vol. 40 (Winter), No. 1, pp. 36–49.

Mosco, Vincent (1990b) 'Toward a Transnational World Information Order,' *Canadian Journal of Communication,* Vol. XV, No. 2, pp. 46–63.

Mosco, Vincent (1992) 'Une drôle de guerre,' *Media Studies Journal,* Vol. 6 (Spring), No. 2, pp. 47–60.

Mosco, Vincent (1993a) 'Communication and Information Technology for War and Peace,' in Roach (ed.) (1993a), pp. 41–70.

Mosco, Vincent (1993b) 'Transforming Telecommunications,' in Wasko, Mosco, and Pendakur (eds) (1993), pp. 132–151.

Mosco, Vincent (1995) 'Will Computer Communication End Geography?' Report P–95–4, Program on Information Resources Policy, Harvard University, September.

Mosco, Vincent and Herman, Andrew (1981) 'Critical Theory and Electronic Media,' *Theory and Society,* Vol. X, pp. 869–896.

Mosco, Vincent and Wasko, Janet (eds) (1983) *The Critical Communications Review. Vol. 1: Labor, the Working Class, and the Media.* Norwood, NJ: Ablex.

Mosco, Vincent and Wasko, Janet (eds) (1984) *The Critical Communications Review. Vol. 2: Changing Patterns of Communication Control.* Norwood, NJ: Ablex.

Mosco, Vincent and Wasko, Janet (eds) (1985) *The Critical Communications Review. Vol. 3: Popular Culture and Media Events.* Norwood, NJ: Ablex.

Mosco, Vincent and Wasko, Janet (eds) (1988) *The Political Economy of Information.* Madison: University of Wisconsin Press.

Mosco, Vincent and Zureik, Elia (1987) *Computers in the Workplace: Technological Change in the Telephone Industry*. Ottawa, Government of Canada, Department of Labour.

Mowlana, Hamid (1990) 'Civil Society, Information Society, and Islamic Society: A Comparative Society.' Paper presented to the Fourth International Colloquium on Communication and Culture. Bled, Yugoslavia, August 24–25.

Mowlana, Hamid (1993) 'The New Global Order and Cultural Ecology,' *Media, Culture and Society*, Vol. 15, pp. 9–27.

Mowlana, Hamid, Gerbner, George, and Schiller, Herbert I. (eds) (1992) *Triumph of the Image: The Media's War in the Persian Gulf – A Global Perspective*. Boulder, CO: Westview Press.

Moyal, Ann (1989) 'The Feminine Culture of the Telephone: People, Patterns and Policy,' *Prometheus*, Vol. 7 (June), No. 1, pp. 5–31.

Mulgan, G.J. (1991) *Communication and Control: Networks and the New Economics of Communication*. Cambridge: Polity Press.

Murdock, Graham (1978) 'Blindspots About Western Marxism: A Reply to Dallas Smythe,' *Canadian Journal of Political and Social Theory*, Vol. 2, No. 2, pp. 109–119.

Murdock, Graham (1989a) 'Cultural Studies: Missing Links,' *Critical Studies in Mass Communication*, Vol. 6, No. 4, pp. 436–440.

Murdock, Graham (1989b) 'Critical Inquiry and Audience Activity,' in Brenda Dervin, Lawrence Grossberg, Barbara O'Keefe, and Ellen Wartella (eds), *Rethinking Communication. Vol. II: Paradigm Exemplars*. Newbury Park, CA: Sage, pp. 226–249.

Murdock, Graham (1990a) 'Television and Citizenship: In Defense of Public Broadcasting,' in Alan Tomlinson (ed.), *Consumption, Identity and Style*. London: Routledge, pp. 77–101.

Murdock, Graham (1990b) 'Redrawing the Map of the Communication Industries,' in Marjorie Ferguson (ed.), *Public Communication: The New Imperatives*. Beverly Hills: Sage, pp. 1–15.

Murdock, Graham (1993) 'Communication and the Constitution of Modernity,' *Media, Culture and Society*, Vol. 15, pp. 521–539.

Murdock, Graham and Golding, Peter (1974) 'For a Political Economy of Mass Communications,' in Ralph Miliband and John Saville (eds), *Socialist Register*. London: Merlin Press, pp. 205–234.

Murdock, Graham and Golding, Peter (1979) 'Capitalism, Communication, and Class Relations,' in Curran et al. (eds) (1979), pp. 12–43.

Nagel, Ernest (1957) *Logic without Metaphysics and Other Essays in the Philosophy of Science*. Glencoe: Free Press.

Nasar, Sylvia (1992a) 'Employment in Service Industry, Engine for Boom of 80's, Falters,' *The New York Times*, January 2, pp. A1, D4.

Nasar, Sylvia (1992b) 'Puzzling Poverty of the 80's Boom,' *The New York Times*, February 14, p. D2.

Negrine, Ralph and Papathanassopoulos, Stylianos (1990) *The Internationalization of Television*. London: Frances Pinter.

Negt, Oskar and Kluge, Alexander (1972) *Öffentlichkeit und Erfahrung: Zur Organisationanalyse von bürgerlicher und proletarischer Öffentlichkeit*. Frankfurt: Suhrkamp.

Nesmith, Georgia (1991) 'Feminist Historiography and Journalism History: Time for Conceptual Change.' Paper presented to the Annual Conference of the Association for Education in Journalism, Boston, August.

Neuman, W. Russell (1991) *The Future of the Mass Audience*. New York: Cambridge University Press.

The New York Times (1991) 'As Libraries Face Cuts, Supporters Plan a Protest,' July 8, p. A1.

The New York Times (1992) 'Fed Gives New Evidence of 80's Gains by Richest,' April 21, p. A1.

The New York Times (1994) 'Tokyo's Magic Kingdom is a Winner,' March 7, p. D7.

Ng'wanakilala, Nkwabi (1981) *Mass Communication and Development of Socialism in Tanzania*. Dar-es-Salaam: Tanzania Publishing House.

Nielsen, Mike (1990) 'Labor's Stake in the Electronic Cinema Revolution,' *Jump Cut*, No. 35, pp. 78–84.

Nielsen, Richard P. (1976) 'Mass Media Public Policy Implications of the Political Economy of Rawls and Nozick,' *Mass Communication Review* (Spring), pp. 16–22.

Nisbet, Robert (1986) *Conservativism*. Minneapolis: University of Minnesota Press.

Noam, Eli. M. (1987) 'The Public Telecommunications Network: A Concept in Transition,' *Journal of Communication*, Vol. 37 (Winter), No. 1, pp. 30–48.

Nordenstreng, Kaarle (1968) 'Communication Research in the United States: A Critical Perspective,' *Gazette*, Vol. 14, pp. 207–216.

Nordenstreng, Kaarle (ed.) (1974) *Informational Mass Communication*. Helsinki: Tammi.

Nordenstreng, Kaarle (1984) *The Mass Media Declaration of UNESCO*. Norwood, NJ: Ablex.

Nordenstreng, Kaarle (1993) 'New Information Order and Communication Scholarship: Reflections on a Delicate Relationship,' in Wasko et al. (eds) (1993), pp. 251–273.

Nordenstreng, Kaarle and Schiller, Herbert (eds) (1979) *National Sovereignty and International Communication*. Norwood, NJ: Ablex.

Nordenstreng, Kaarle and Schiller, Herbert (eds) (1993) *Beyond National Sovereignty: International Communication in the 1990s*. Norwood, NJ: Ablex.

Nordenstreng, Kaarle and Varis, Tapio (1974) *Television Traffic: A One-Way Street?* Paris: UNESCO.

Norris, Christopher (1992) *Uncritical Theory: Postmodernism, Intellectuals, and the Gulf War*. London: Lawrence and Wishart.

Nove, Alec (1983) *The Economics of Feasible Socialism*. London: Allen and Unwin.

Oakeshott, Michael J. (1962) *Rationalism in Politics and Other Essays*. Indianapolis: Liberty Press (expanded edn).

Oakeshott, Michael J. (1975) *On Human Conduct*. Oxford: Clarendon.

O'Brien, Mary (1981) *The Politics of Reproduction*. London: Routledge and Kegan Paul.

O'Brien, Richard (1992) *Global Financial Integration and the End of Geography*. New York: Council on Foreign Relations Press.

O'Connor, Alan (1991) 'The Emergence of Cultural Studies in Latin America,' *Critical Studies in Mass Communication*, Vol. 8, No. 1, pp. 60–73.

O'Connor, James (1987) *The Meaning of Crisis: A Theoretical Introduction*. Oxford: Blackwell.

O'Connor, James (1991) 'Socialism and Ecology,' *Capitalism Nature Socialism*, Vol. 2, No. 3, pp. 1–12.

Oettinger, Anthony G. (1980) 'Information Resources: Knowledge and Power in the 21st Century,' *Science*, No. 209 (July 4), pp. 191–198.

Oettinger, Anthony G. (1988a) *The Formula is Everything: Costing and Pricing in the Telecommunications Industry*. Cambridge, MA: Harvard University Program on Information Resources Policy.

Oettinger, Anthony G. (1988b) 'Political, Scientific, and Other Truths in the Information World.' Samuel Lazerow Memorial Lecture, University of Pittsburgh, November 10.

Offe, Claus (1984) *Contradictions of the Welfare State*. Cambridge, MA: MIT Press.

Offe, Claus (1985) *Disorganized Capitalism*. Cambridge, MA: MIT Press.

Oliveira, Omar Souki (1991) 'Mass Media, Culture, and Dependency in Brazil: The Heritage of Dependency,' in Sussman and Lent (eds) (1991), pp. 200–213.

Oliveira, Omar Souki (1992) 'New Media and Information Technologies: For Freedom and Dependency.' Paper presented to the 1992 Conference of the International Association for Mass Communication Research, São Paulo, Brazil, August.

Olson, Mancur (1990) 'Toward a Unified View of Economics and the Other Social Sciences,' in Alt and Shepsle (eds) (1990), pp. 212–231.

Oppenheim, C. (1990) *Poverty: The Facts*. London: Child Poverty Action Group.

Ortega y Gasset, José (1957) *The Revolt of the Masses*. New York: Norton.

Outhwaite, William (1987) *New Philosophies of Social Science: Realism, Hermeneutics and Critical Theory*. Houndmills: Macmillan Education.

Owen, Bruce M. and Wildman, Steven S. (1992) *Video Economics*. Cambridge, MA: Harvard University Press.

Owen, Robert (1970) *The Book of the New Moral World*. New York: Kelley (orig. 1842).

Palgrave, Sir Robert Harry Inglis (1913) *Dictionary of Political Economy*, Vol. III. London: Macmillan and Co.

Palmer, Bryan D. (1990) *Descent into Discourse: The Reification of Language and the Writing of Social History*. Philadelphia: Temple University Press.

Papathanassopoulos, Stylianos (1990) 'The EC: "Television without Frontiers" but with Media Monopolies?' *Intermedia*, Vol. 18 (June–July), No. 3, pp. 27–30.

Parker, William (1986) *Economic History and the Modern Economist*. New York: Blackwell.

Parsons, Talcott (1966) *Societies*. Englewood Cliffs, NJ: Prentice Hall.

Parsons, Talcott and Shils, Edward (1951) *Toward a General Theory of Action*. Cambridge, MA: Harvard University Press.

Pasquali, Antonio (1967) *El Aparato Singular: Análisis de un Día de TV en Caracas*. Caracas: Universidad Central de Venezuela.

Passell, Peter (1992) 'George Bush's Sins of Omission,' *The New York Times*, August 20, p. D2.

Peiss, Kathy Lee (1986) *Cheap Amusements*. Philadelphia: Temple University Press.

Peiss, Kathy Lee (1991) 'Going Public: Women in Nineteenth Century Cultural History,' *American Literary History*, Vol. 3 (Winter), pp. 817–828.

Peltzman, Sam (1975) *Regulation of Automobile Safety*. Washington, DC: American Enterprise Institute.

Pendakur, Manjunath (1990a) *Canadian Dreams and American Control: The Political Economy of the Canadian Film Industry*. Detroit: Wayne State University Press.

Pendakur, Manjunath (1990b) 'India,' in Lent (ed.) (1990), pp. 229–252.

Pendakur, Manjunath (1991) 'A Political Economy of Television: State, Class and Corporate Confluence in India,' in Sussman and Lent (eds) (1991), pp. 234–262.

Pendakur, Manjunath (1993) 'Political Economy and Ethnography: Transformations in an Indian Village,' in Wasko et al. (eds) (1993), pp. 82–108.

Peters, Edgar E. (1991) *Chaos and Order in the Capital Markets: A New View of Cycles, Prices, and Market Volatility*. New York: Wiley.

Peters, John Durham (1993) 'Distrust of Representation: Habermas on the Public Sphere,' *Media, Culture and Society*, Vol. 15, pp. 541–571.

Phillips, Adam (1993) *On Kissing, Tickling, and Being Bored: Psychoanalytic Essays on the Unexamined Life*. Cambridge, MA: Harvard University Press.

Picard, Robert (1989) *Media Economics: Concepts and Issues*. Newbury Park, CA: Sage.

Piller, Charles and Weiman, Liza (1992) 'America's Computer Ghetto,' *The New York Times*, August 7, p. A27.

Piore, Michael and Sabel, Charles (1984) *The Second Industrial Divide*. New York: Basic Books.

Pizzigati, Sam and Solowey, Fred J. (eds) (1992) *The New Labor Press: Journalism for a Changing Union Movement*. Ithaca, NY: ILR Press.

Pogorel, Gerard (1991) 'New Information and Communication Technologies and the Structure of Firms: A European View,' *KEIO Communication Review*, Vol. 12 (March), pp. 91–109.

Porritt, Jonathon (1984) *Seeing Green: The Politics of Ecology Explained*. New York: Blackwell.

Posner, Richard A. (1992) *Sex and Reason*. Cambridge, MA: Harvard University Press.

Poster, Mark (1984) *Foucault, Marxism and History: Mode of Production versus Mode of Information*. Oxford: Blackwell.

Poulantzas, Nicos (1978) *State, Power, and Socialism*. London: New Left Books.

Pred, Alan (1966) *The Spatial Dynamics of U.S. Industrial Growth, 1800–1914: Interpretive and Theoretical Essays*. Cambridge, MA: Harvard University Press.

Press, Andrea Lee (1991) *Women Watching Television: Gender, Class and Generation in the American Television Experience.* Philadelphia: University of Pennsylvania Press.

Preston, William, Jr, Herman, Edward S., and Schiller, Herbert I. (1989) *Hope and Folly: The United States and UNESCO 1945–1985.* Minneapolis: University of Minnesota Press.

Prokop, Dieter (ed.) (1973) *Kritische Kommunikationsforschung: Aufsätze aus der 'Zeitschrift für Sozialforschung'.* Munich: Hanser.

Prokop, Dieter (1974) *Massenkultur und Spontaneität: Zur veranderten Warenform der Massenkommunikation in Spätkapitalismus (Aufsätze).* Frankfurt: Suhrkamp.

Prokop, Dieter (1983) 'Problems of Production and Consumption in the Mass Media,' *Media, Culture and Society,* Vol. 5, pp. 101–116.

Przeworski, Adam (1986) *Capitalism and Social Democracy.* Cambridge: Cambridge University Press.

Puette, William J. (1992) *Through Jaundiced Eyes: How the Media View Organized Labor.* Ithaca, NY: ILR Press.

Rabinach, Anson (1990) *The Human Motor: Energy, Fatigue, and the Origins of Modernity.* New York: Basic Books.

Raboy, Marc (1990) *Missed Opportunities.* Montreal and Kingston: McGill-Queen's Press.

Radway, Janice (1988) 'Reception Study: Ethnography and the Problems of Dispersed Audiences and Nomadic Subjects,' *Cultural Studies,* Vol. 2, No. 3, pp. 359–376.

Rakow, Lana F. (1988) 'Gendered Technology, Gendered Practice,' *Critical Studies in Mass Communication,* Vol. 5, No. 1, pp. 57–70.

Ramirez, Anthony (1991) 'Baby Bells are Accused of Overcharging,' *The New York Times,* December 18, p. D5.

Reeves, Geoffrey (1993) *Communications and the 'Third World'.* New York: Routledge.

Reich, Robert (1991) *The Work of Nations.* New York: Knopf.

Reid, Margaret G. (1934) *Economics of Household Production.* New York: Wiley.

Resnick, Stephen A. and Wolff, Richard D. (1987) *Knowledge and Class: A Marxian Critique of Political Economy.* Chicago: University of Chicago Press.

Reyes Matta, Fernando (1979) 'The Latin American Concept of News,' *Journal of Communication,* Vol. 29 (Spring), No. 2, pp. 164–171.

Reyes Matta, Fernando (1983) *Comunicación Alternativa y Búsquedas Democráticas.* Mexico City: ILET.

Rheingold, Howard (1993) *The Virtual Community: Homesteading on the Electronic Frontier.* Reading, MA: Addison-Wesley.

Ricardo, David (1819) *On the Principles of Political Economy and Taxation.* London.

Rideout, Vanda (1993) 'Telecommunication Policy for Whom?: An Analysis of Recent CRTC Decisions,' *Alternate Routes,* Vol. 10, pp. 27–56.

Ries, Al (1993) 'An Idea Whose Time Never Came,' *The New York Times,* November 21, p. F13.

Roach, Colleen (ed.) (1993a) *Communication and Culture in War and Peace.* Newbury Park, CA: Sage.

Roach, Colleen (1993b) 'Feminist Peace Researchers, Culture, and Communication,' in Roach (ed.) (1993a), pp. 175–191.

Robbins, Bruce (ed.) (1993) *The Phantom Public Sphere.* Minneapolis: University of Minnesota Press.

Robinson, Joan (1962) *Economic Philosophy.* Chicago: Aldine.

Roemer, John (1982) *A General Theory of Exploitation and Class.* Cambridge, MA: Harvard University Press.

Rogers, Everett (1976) 'Communication and Development: The Passing of the Dominant Paradigm,' *Communication Research,* Vol. 3, pp. 63–78.

Rogers, Everett with Shoemaker, F. Floyd (1971) *Communication of Innovations.* New York: Free Press.

Rogin, Leo (1956) *The Meaning and Validity of Economic Theory.* New York: Harper and Brothers.

Roll, Eric (1942) *A History of Economic Thought.* New York: Prentice Hall.

Roncagliolo, Rafael (1986) 'Transnational Communication and Culture,' in Atwood and McAnany (eds) (1986), pp. 79–88.

Rorty, Richard (1979) *Philosophy and the Mirror of Nature*. Princeton, NJ: Princeton University Press.

Ross, Andrew (1993) 'The Fine Art of Regulation,' in Robbins (ed.) (1993), pp. 257–268.

Ross, Steven J. (1991) 'Struggles for the Screen: Workers, Radicals, and the Political Uses of Silent Film,' *American Historical Review*, Vol. 96 (April), No. 2, pp. 333–367.

Rucinski, Diane (1991) 'The Centrality of Reciprocity to Communication and Democracy,' *Critical Studies in Mass Communication*, Vol. 8, No. 2, pp. 184–194.

Rusk, James (1991) ' "The Greatest Moral Challenge of Our Time",' *The Globe and Mail*, February 19, p. B8.

Russial, John T. (1989) 'Pagination and the Newsroom: Great Expectations.' Doctoral dissertation completed in the School of Communication, Temple University, Philadelphia, August.

Ryan, Charlotte (1991) *Prime Time Activism: Media Strategies for Grassroots Organizing*. Boston: South End Press.

Sahlins, Marshall (1976) *Culture and Practical Reason*. Chicago: University of Chicago Press.

Sainath, P. (1992a) *Patent Folly: Behind the Jargon on Intellectual Property Rights*. Bombay: Indian School for Social Science.

Sainath, P. (1992b) 'The New World *Odour*,' in Mowlana et al. (eds) (1992), pp. 67–74.

Sale, Kirkpatrick (1995) *Rebels Against the Future: The Luddites and their War on the Industrial Revolution*. Reading, MA: Addison-Wesley.

Salutin, Rick (1993) 'An Industrial Strategy for the Arts,' *The Globe and Mail*, June 4, p. C1.

Samarajiwa, Rohan (1985) 'Tainted Origins of Development Communication,' *Communicator* (April–July), pp. 5–9.

Samarajiwa, Rohan (1993) 'Down Dependency Road? The Canada–U.S. Free Trade Agreement and Canada's Copyright Amendments of 1988,' in Wasko et al. (eds) (1993), pp. 152–180.

Sassen, Saskia (1991) *The Global City: New York, London, Tokyo*. Princeton, NJ: Princeton University Press.

Saunders, Anthony (1989) 'New Communications Technologies, Banking, and Finance,' in Paula R. Newberg (ed.), *New Directions in Telecommunications Policy*. Durham, NC: Duke University Press, pp. 266–289.

Saxton, Alexander (1990) *The Rise and Fall of the White Republic: Class Politics and Mass Culture in Nineteenth-Century America*. New York: Verso.

Schiller, Dan (1981) *Objectivity and the News*. Philadelphia: University of Pennsylvania Press.

Schiller, Dan (1982) *Telematics and Government*. Norwood, NJ: Ablex.

Schiller, Dan (1985) 'The Emerging Global Grid: Planning for What?' *Media, Culture and Society*, Vol. 7, pp. 105–125.

Schiller, Dan (1986) 'Transformations of News in the US Information Market,' in Golding et al. (eds) (1986), pp. 19–36.

Schiller, Dan (1988) 'How to Think About Information,' in Mosco and Wasko (eds) (1988), pp. 27–43.

Schiller, Dan (1994) 'From Culture to Information and Back Again: Commoditization as a Route to Knowledge,' *Critical Studies in Mass Communication*, Vol. 11, No. 1, pp. 92–115.

Schiller, Herbert I. (1969/1992: 2nd updated edn) *Mass Communication and American Empire*. Boston: Beacon Press.

Schiller, Herbert I. (1973) *The Mind Managers*. Boston: Beacon Press.

Schiller, Herbert I. (1976) *Communication and Cultural Domination*. White Plains, NY: International Arts and Sciences Press.

Schiller, Herbert I. (1981) *Who Knows: Information in the Age of the Fortune 500.* Norwood, NJ: Ablex.

Schiller, Herbert I. (1984) *Information and the Crisis Economy.* Norwood, NJ: Ablex.

Schiller, Herbert I. (1989) *Culture, Inc.* New York: Oxford University Press.

Schiller, Herbert I. (1991) 'Public Information Goes Corporate,' *Library Journal*, October 1, pp. 42–45.

Schiller, Herbert I. (1993) 'Not Yet the Postimperialist Era,' in Roach (1993a), pp. 97–116.

Schlesinger, Philip (1991) *Media, State, and Nation: Political Violence and Collective Identities.* London: Sage.

Schor, Juliet B. (1992) *The Overworked American.* New York: Basic Books.

Schramm, Wilbur (1964) *Mass Media and National Development.* Stanford, CA: Stanford University Press.

Schudson, Michael (1984) *Advertising, The Uneasy Persuasion.* New York: Basic Books.

Schudson, Michael (1987) 'The New Validation of Popular Culture: Sense and Sentimentality in Academia,' *Critical Studies in Mass Communication*, Vol. 4, No. 1, pp. 51–68.

Schumpeter, Joseph (1942) *Capitalism, Socialism, and Democracy.* New York: Harper and Brothers.

Scott, John (1991) *Social Network Analysis: A Handbook.* Newbury Park, CA: Sage.

Seccombe, Wally (1974) 'The Housewife and Her Labour Under Capitalism,' *New Left Review*, No. 83 (Jan–Feb), pp. 3–24.

Sennett, Richard (1976) *The Fall of Public Man.* New York: Vintage.

Sherman, Howard J. (1987) *Foundations of Radical Political Economy.* Armonk, NY: M.E. Sharpe.

Shimony, Abner (1993) *Search for a Naturalistic World View. Vol. 1: Scientific Method and Epistemology.* New York: Cambridge University Press.

Sichterman, Barbara (1986) *Femininity: The Politics of the Personal.* Cambridge: Polity Press.

Siegelaub, Seth (1979) 'Preface: A Communication on Communication,' in Mattelart and Siegelaub (eds) (1979), pp. 11–21.

Siegelaub, Seth (1983) 'Working Notes on Social Relations in Communication and Culture,' in Mattelart and Siegelaub (eds) (1983), pp. 11–16.

Silk, Catherine and Silk, John (1990) *Racism and Anti-Racism in American Popular Culture: Portrayals of African-Americans in Fiction and Film.* Manchester: Manchester University Press.

Simon, Herbert (1957) *Models of Man.* New York: Wiley.

Simpson Grinberg, M. (1981) *Comunicacíon Alternativa y Cambio Social.* Mexico City: Universidad Nacional Autónoma de México.

Sivanandan, A. (1989) 'New Circuits of Imperialism,' *Race and Class*, Vol. 30 (April–June), No. 4, pp. 1–19.

Sivanandan, A. (1990) *Communities of Resistance: Writings on Black Struggles for Socialism.* London: Verso.

Slack, Jennifer D. (1984) *Communication Technologies and Society.* Norwood, NJ: Ablex.

Slater, Don (1987) 'On the Wings of the Sign: Commodity Culture and Social Practice,' *Media, Culture and Society*, Vol. 9, pp. 457–480.

Slaughter, Sheila A. (1984) *Serving Power: The Making of the Academic Social Science Expert.* Westport, CT: Greenwood.

Smith, Adam (1937) *An Inquiry into the Nature and Causes of The Wealth of Nations.* New York: Modern Library (orig. 1776).

Smith, Adam (1976) *The Theory of Moral Sentiments.* Indianapolis: Liberty Classics (orig. 1759).

Smith, Anthony (1989) 'The Public Interest,' *Intermedia*, Vol. 17 (June–July), No. 2, pp. 10–24.

Smith, Anthony (1991) *The Age of Behemoths.* New York: Priority Press.

Smythe, Dallas W. (1957) *The Structure and Policy of Electronic Communications.* Urbana: University of Illinois Press.

Smythe, Dallas W. (1977) 'Communications: Blindspot of Western Marxism,' *Canadian Journal of Political and Social Theory*, Vol. I, No. 3, pp. 1–27.

Smythe, Dallas W. (1978) 'Rejoinder to Graham Murdock,' *Canadian Journal of Political and Social Theory*, Vol. II, No. 2, pp. 120–127.

Smythe, Dallas W. (1981) *Dependency Road: Communication, Capitalism, Consciousness and Canada*. Norwood, NJ: Ablex.

Smythe, Dallas W. (1991) 'Theory About Communication and Information.' Draft paper originating in work at CIRCIT, Melbourne, Australia, May 1.

Smythe, Dallas W. and Melody, William H. (1985) *Factors Affecting the Canadian and U.S. Spectrum Management Processes: A Preliminary Evaluation*. Report prepared for the Federal Department of Communication, Ottawa, Canada, March.

Soja, Edward (1989) *Postmodern Geographies: The Reassertion of Space in Critical Social Theory*. New York: Verso.

Somavia, Juan (1979) *Democratización de las communicaciones: Una perspectiva latino-americana*. Mexico City: ILET.

Somavia, Juan (1981) 'The Democratization of Communications: From Minority Social Monopoly to Majority Social Representation,' *Development Dialogue*, Vol. 2, pp. 13–30.

Sorkin, Michael (ed.) (1992) *Variations on a Theme Park: The New American City and the End of Public Space*. New York: Hill and Wang.

Sparks, Colin (ed.) (1985) 'The Working-Class Press,' *Media, Culture and Society*, Vol. 7, No. 5.

Sparks, Colin and Dahlgren, Peter (eds) (1991) *Communication and Citizenship: Journalism and the Public Sphere in the New Media Age*. London: Routledge.

Spigel, Lynn (1989) 'The Domestic Economy of Television Viewing in Postwar America,' *Critical Studies in Mass Communication*, Vol. 6, No. 4, pp. 337–354.

Squires, James (1993) *Read All About It!: The Corporate Takeover of America's Newspapers*. New York: Random House.

Staniland, Martin (1985) *What is Political Economy?: A Study of Social Theory and Underdevelopment*. New Haven: Yale University Press.

Staples, Robert and Jones, Terry (1985) 'Culture, Ideology and Black Television Images,' *The Black Scholar*, Vol. 16 (May/June), pp. 10–20.

Steeves, H. Leslie (1987) 'Feminist Theories and Media Studies,' *Critical Studies in Mass Communication*, Vol. 4, No. 2, pp. 95–135.

Steeves, H. Leslie (1989) 'Gender and Mass Communication in a Global Context,' in Pamela J. Creedon (ed.), *Women in Mass Communication: Challenging Gender Values*. Newbury Park, CA: Sage, pp. 83–111.

Sterngold, James (1992) 'Fed Chief Says Economy is Resisting Remedies,' *The New York Times*, October 15, p. D2.

Steuart, James (1967) *An Inquiry in the Principles of Political Economy*. New York: Augustus M. Kelley (orig. 1761).

Stigler, George J. (1971) 'The Theory of Economic Regulation,' *Bell Journal of Economics & Management Science*, Vol. 2, No. 1 (Spring), pp. 3–21.

Stigler, George J. (ed.) (1988) *Chicago Studies in Political Economy*. Chicago: University of Chicago Press.

Stone, Alan (1991) *Public Service Liberalism: Telecommunications and Transitions in Public Policy*. Princeton, NJ: Princeton University Press.

Stone, Alan and Harpham, Edward J. (eds) (1982) *The Political Economy of Public Policy*. Beverly Hills: Sage.

Stouffer, Samuel Andrew (1949) *The American Soldier*. Princeton, NJ: Princeton University Press.

Strange, Susan (1988) *States and Markets*. London: Frances Pinter.

Strover, Sharon (1993) 'Trends in Coproductions: Demise of the National.' Paper presented at the Conference of the International Association for Mass Communication Research, Dublin, Ireland, June.

Sussman, Gerald (1984) 'Global Telecommunications in the Third World: Theoretical Considerations,' *Media, Culture and Society*, Vol. 6, pp. 289–300.

Sussman, Gerald and Lent, John A. (eds) (1991) *Transnational Communications: Wiring the Third World*. Newbury Park, CA: Sage.

Sutherland, John (1993) 'Where's the Lit. in Lit. Crit.?' *The New York Times Book Review*, February 7, p. 23.

Szecsko, Tamas (1986) 'The Political-Economic Approach to the Study of Mass Communication in Hungary,' *Massacommunicatie*, Vol. 14, No. 2–3, pp. 110–116.

Tabor, Mary (1991) 'Encouraging "Those Who Would Speak Out with Fresh Voice" Through FCC Minority Ownership Policies,' *Iowa Law Review*, Vol. 76 (March), pp. 609–639.

Tang, Wing Hung and Chan, Joseph Man (1990) 'The Political Economy of International News Coverage: A Study of Dependent Communication Development,' *Asian Journal of Communication*, Vol. 1, No. 1, pp. 53–80.

Tetzlaff, David (1991) 'Divide and Conquer: Popular Culture and Social Control in Late Capitalism,' *Media, Culture and Society*, Vol. 13, pp. 9–33.

Thomis, Malcolm I. (1972) *The Luddites: Machine-Breaking in Regency England*. New York: Schocken Books.

Thompson, E.P. (1963) *The Making of the English Working Class*. London: Victor Gollancz.

Thompson, John B. (1989) 'The Theory of Structuration,' in David Held and John B. Thompson (eds), *Social Theory of Modern Societies: Anthony Giddens and His Critics*. Cambridge: Cambridge University Press, pp. 56–76.

Thompson, John B. (1990) *Ideology and Modern Culture: Critical Social Theory in the Era of Mass Communication*. Stanford, CA: Stanford University Press.

Thrift, Nigel (1987) 'The Fixers: The Urban Geography of International Commercial Capital,' in Jeffrey Henderson and Manuel Castells (eds), *Global Restructuring and Territorial Development*, London: Sage, pp. 203–233.

Thrift, Nigel and Leyshon, Andrew (1988) ' "The Gambling Propensity": Banks, Developing Country Debt Exposures and the New International Financial System,' *Geoforum*, Vol. 19, No. 1, pp. 55–69.

Thurow, Lester (1992) *Head to Head: The Coming Economic Battle among Japan, Europe, and America*. New York: Warner Books.

Tierney, John (1993) 'Will They Sit by the Set, or Ride a Data Highway?' *The New York Times*, June 20, pp. 1, 24.

Time Warner Annual Report (1993).

Tinker, Tony (1985) *Paper Prophets: A Social Critique of Accounting*. New York: Praeger.

Tomlinson, John (1991) *Cultural Imperialism*. Baltimore: Johns Hopkins University Press.

Traber, Michael and Nordenstreng, Kaarle (eds) (1992) *Few Voices, Many Worlds: Towards a Media Reform Movement*. London: World Association for Christian Communication.

Tran van Dinh (1987) *Independence, Liberation, Revolution: An Approach to the Understanding of the Third World*. Norwood, NJ: Ablex.

Tuchman, Gaye (1978) *Making News*. New York: Free Press.

Tunstall, Jeremy (1977) *The Media are American*. New York: Columbia University Press.

Tunstall, Jeremy (1981) *Journalists at Work*. London: Constable.

Tunstall, Jeremy and Palmer, Michael (1991) *Media Moguls*. London: Routledge.

Turkel, Sherry (1984) *The Second Self*. New York: Simon and Schuster.

Turow, Joseph (1984) *Media Industries: The Production of News and Entertainment*. New York: Longman.

Uche, Luke Uke (1986) 'The Youth and Music Culture: A Nigerian Case Study,' *Gazette*, Vol. 37, Nos 1–2, pp. 63–78.

Ugboajah, F.O. (1986) 'Communication as Technology in African Rural Development,' *African Media Review*, Vol. 1, No. 1, pp. 1–19.

Umesao, Tadao (1963) 'Joho Sangyo Ron (On Information Industries),' *Chuokohron*, March.

UNESCO (1979) International Commission for the Study of Communication Problems, *Final Report*. Paris: UNESCO.

UNESCO (1983) *History in Black and White: An Analysis of South African School History Textbooks*. Paris: UNESCO.

UNESCO (1989) *World Communication Report*. Paris: UNESCO.

UNESCO (1990) *UNESCO Yearbook 1990*. Paris: UNESCO.

United Nations, International Telecommunications Union, Independent Commission for Worldwide Telecommunications Development (1985) *The Missing Link*. Geneva: ITU.

U.S., Congress, Office of Technology Assessment (1987) *The Electronic Supervisor: New Technologies/New Tensions*. OTA-CIT–333, Washington, DC: U.S. Government Printing Office.

U.S., Congress, Office of Technology Assessment (1990) *Critical Connections: Communications for the Future*. OTA-CIT–407. Washington, DC: U.S. Government Printing Office.

U.S., Congress, Office of Technology Assessment (1991) *Rural America at the Crossroads: Networking for the Future*. OTA-CIT–471. Washington, DC: U.S. Government Printing Office, April.

U.S. Congress, Senate, Committee on the Judiciary, Subcommittee on Technology and the Law (1991) *Motion Picture Anti-Piracy Act of 1991: Joint Hearing Before the Subcommittee on Technology and the Law and the Subcommittee on Patents, Copyrights, and Trademarks*. 102nd Cong., first sess., Washington, DC: Government Printing Office.

U.S., Congress, Senate, Subcommittee on Education, Arts and Humanities (1995) *Humanities Reauthorization: Testimony of Victor R. Swenson*, March 2.

U.S., Department of Commerce, Bureau of the Census (1990) *Statistical Abstract of the United States* (110th edn).

U.S., Department of Commerce, Bureau of the Census (1993) *Statistical Abstract of the United States* (113th edn).

U.S., FCC (1991) *Monitoring Report.*, CC Docket No. 87–339, prepared by the Staff of the Federal-State Joint Board in CC Docket No. 80–286, Washington, DC: U.S. Government Printing Office, January.

Useem, Michael (1984) *The Inner Circle: Large Corporations and the Rise of Business Political Power*. New York: Oxford University Press.

van Dijk, Teun A. (1991) *Racism and the Press*. London: Routledge.

van Zoonen, Liesbet (1991) 'Feminist Perspectives on the Media,' in James Curran and Michael Gurevitch (eds), *Mass Media and Society*. London: Edward Arnold, pp. 33–54.

van Zoonen, Liesbet (1992) 'Feminist Theory and Information Technology,' *Media, Culture and Society*, Vol. 14, pp. 9–29.

van Zoonen, Liesbet (1994) *Feminist Media Studies*. London: Sage.

Veblen, Thorstein (1932) *The Theory of the Business Enterprise*. New York: Scribner's (orig. 1904).

Veblen, Thorstein (1934) *The Theory of the Leisure Class*. New York: Modern Library (orig. 1899).

Vedel, Thierry and Luven, Ronan (1993) *La Télévision de demain: Cable, satellite et TVHD en France et dans le monde*. Paris: A. Colin.

Vernon, Raymond (1992) 'Transnational Corporations: Where are They Coming From, Where are They Headed?' *Transnational Corporations*, Vol. 1 (April), No. 2, pp. 7–35.

Veron, Eliseo (1987) *El Discurso Politico*. Buenos Aires: Hachette.

Vijayan, Jaikumar (1996) 'India,' *Computerworld*, February 26, p. 101.

Wall Street Journal (1993) 'Entertaining Numbers: A Statistical Look at the Global Entertainment Industry,' March 26, p. R16.

Wallerstein, Immanuel (1979) *The Capitalist World Economy*. New York: Cambridge University Press.

Wallerstein, Immanuel (1991) *Geopolitics and Geoculture: Essays on the Changing World-System*. New York: Cambridge University Press.

Ward, Dwayne (1977) *Toward a Critical Political Economics: A Critique of Liberal and Radical Economic Thought*. Santa Monica, CA: Goodyear Publishing.

Waring, Marilyn (1988) *If Women Counted: A New Feminist Economics*. New York: HarperCollins.

Wasko, Janet (1982) *Movies and Money: Financing the American Film Industry*. Norwood, NJ: Ablex.

Wasko, Janet (1983) 'Trade Unions and Broadcasting,' in Mosco and Wasko (eds) (1983), pp. 85–113.

Wasko, Janet (1984) 'New Methods in Analyzing Media Concentration,' in Vincent Mosco (ed.), *Policy Research in Telecommunications*. Norwood, NJ: Ablex, pp. 213–219.

Wasko, Janet (1989) 'What's So "New" About the "New" Technologies in Hollywood? An Example of the Study of Political Economy of Communications,' in Brenda Dervin, Lawrence Grossberg, Barbara O'Keefe, and Ellen Wartella (eds), *Rethinking Communication. Vol. II: Paradigm Exemplars*. Newbury Park, CA: Sage, pp. 474–485.

Wasko, Janet (1994) *Hollywood in the Information Age: Beyond the Silver Screen*. Cambridge: Polity Press.

Wasko, Janet and Mosco, Vincent (eds) (1992) *Democratic Communication in an Information Age*. Toronto: Garamond; and Norwood, NJ: Ablex.

Wasko, Janet and Philips, Mark (1993) 'Teal's the Deal in Sports Merchandise,' *Oregon Sports News* (Spring), pp. 48–51.

Wasko, Janet, Mosco, Vincent, and Pendakur, Manjunath (eds) (1993) *Illuminating the Blindspots: Essays in Honor of Dallas Smythe*. Norwood, NJ: Ablex.

Waterman, Peter (1990) 'Communicating Labor Internationalism: A Review of Relevant Literature and Resources,' *The European Journal of Communication*, Vol. 15, Nos 1/2, pp. 85–103.

Waterman, Peter (1992) 'The Transmission and Reception of International Labour Information in Peru,' in Wasko and Mosco (eds) (1992), pp. 224–241.

Weber, Max (1946) 'Science as a Vocation,' in *From Max Weber: Essays In Sociology*. Ed. by Hans Gerth and C. Wright Mills. New York: Oxford University Press.

Weber, Max (1978) *Economy and Society*. Trans. by Ephraim Fischoff. Berkeley: University of California Press.

Webster, Frank and Robins, Kevin (1986) *Information Technology: A Luddite Analysis*. Norwood, NJ: Ablex.

Webster, Frank and Robins, Kevin (1989) 'Plan and Control: Towards a Cultural History of the Information Society,' *Theory and Society*, Vol. 18, pp. 323–351.

Wedell, G. (ed.) (1986) *Making Broadcasting Useful: The African Experience*. Manchester: Manchester University Press.

Weinberg, Steven (1993) *Dreams of a Final Theory*. New York: Pantheon.

West, Edwin G. (1990) *Adam Smith and Modern Economics: From Market Behaviour to Public Choice*. Aldershot: Edward Elgar.

Williams, Raymond (1958) *Culture and Society: 1780–1950*. Harmondsworth: Penguin.

Williams, Raymond (1961) *The Long Revolution*. Harmondsworth: Penguin.

Williams, Raymond (1975) *Television, Technology and Cultural Form*. London: Fontana.

Williams, Raymond (1976) *Keywords: A Vocabulary of Culture and Society*. New York: Oxford University Press.

Williams, Raymond (1977) *Marxism and Literature*. New York: Oxford University Press.

Williams, Raymond (1980) *Problems in Materialism and Culture*. London: Verso.

Williams, Raymond (1981a) *Culture*. London: Fontana.

Williams, Raymond (1981b) 'Marxism, Structuralism, and Literary Analysis,' *New Left Review*, No. 129 (Sept./Oct.), pp. 51–66.

Williams, Raymond (1983) *Toward 2000*. London: Hogarth Press.

Willis, Paul (1977) *Learning to Labor: How Working Class Kids Get Working Class Jobs*. New York: Columbia University Press.

Wilson, Clint C., II and Gutiérrez, Félix (1985) *Minorities and the Media: Diversity and the End of Mass Communication*. Beverly Hills: Sage.

Wilson, Edward O. (1992) *The Diversity of Life*. Cambridge, MA: Harvard University Press.

Wilson, James Q. (ed.) (1980) *The Politics of Regulation.* New York: Basic Books.

Wilson, Kevin (1992) 'Deregulating Telecommunications and the Problem of Natural Monopoly: A Critique of Economics in Telecommunications Policy,' *Media, Culture and Society*, Vol. 14, pp. 343–368.

Winseck, Dwayne (1993) 'A Study of Regulatory Change and the Deregulatory Process in Canadian Telecommunications With Particular Emphasis on Telecommunications Labor Unions.' Doctoral dissertation, University of Oregon, School of Journalism and Communication.

Winston, Brian (1986) *Misunderstanding Media.* Cambridge, MA: Harvard University Press.

Wood, Ellen Meiksins (1981) 'The Separation of the Economic and the Political in Capitalism,' *New Left Review*, No. 127 (May–June), pp. 66–95.

Wood, Ellen Meiksins (1986) *The Retreat from Class: A New 'True' Socialism.* London: Verso.

Wood, Ellen Meiksins (1989) 'Rational Choice Marxism: Is the Game Worth the Candle?' *New Left Review*, No. 177, pp. 41–88.

Wood, Ellen Meiksins (1990) 'The Uses and Abuses of "Civil Society",' in Ralph Miliband and Leo Panitch (eds), *Socialist Register, 1990: The Retreat of the Intellectuals.* London: Merlin Press, pp. 61–84.

Wright, Karen (1990) 'The Road to the Global Village,' *Scientific American*, March, pp. 83–94.

Yates, JoAnne (1989) *Control through Communication: The Rise of System in American Management.* Baltimore: Johns Hopkins University Press.

Zachary, G. Pascal and Ortega, Bob (1993) 'Age of Angst: Workplace Revolution Boosts Productivity at Cost of Job Security,' *The Wall Street Journal*, March 19, pp. A1, A6.

Zimbalist, Andrew (1979) 'Technology and the Labor Process in the Printing Industry,' in Andrew Zimbalist (ed.), *Case Studies in the Labor Process.* New York: Monthly Review Press, pp. 103–126.

Zuboff, Shoshana (1988) *In the Age of the Smart Machine.* New York: Basic Books.

Index